Lord Lytton

Falkland; The Pilgrims of the Rhine; Pausanias, the Spartan

Lord Lytton

Falkland; The Pilgrims of the Rhine; Pausanias, the Spartan

ISBN/EAN: 9783337176549

Printed in Europe, USA, Canada, Australia, Japan

Cover: Foto ©ninafisch / pixelio.de

More available books at **www.hansebooks.com**

FRONTISPIECE.

Falkland
The Pilgrims of the Rhine
Pausanias, the Spartan

BY
THE RIGHT HON. LORD LYTTON

LONDON
GEORGE ROUTLEDGE AND SONS
BROADWAY, LUDGATE HILL
GLASGOW AND NEW YORK
—
1888

PREFATORY NOTE TO THE KNEBWORTH EDITION.

"FALKLAND" is the earliest of Lord Lytton's prose fictions. Published before "Pelham," it was written in the boyhood of its illustrious author. In the maturity of his manhood and the fulness of his literary popularity he withdrew it from print. This is the first English edition of his collected works in which the tale reappears. It is because the morality of it was condemned by his experienced judgment, that the author of "Falkland" deliberately omitted it from each of the numerous reprints of his novels and romances which were published in England during his lifetime.

Messrs. Routledge therefore desire to state the motives which have induced them, with the consent of the author's son, to include "Falkland" in the present edition of his collected works.

In the first place, this work has been for many years, and still is, accessible to English readers in every country except England. The continental edition of it, published by Baron Tauchnitz, has a wide circulation; and, since for this reason the book cannot practically be withheld from the public, it is thought desirable that the publication of it should at least be accompanied by some record of the above-mentioned fact.

In the next place, the considerations which would naturally guide an author of established reputation in the selection of early compositions for subsequent republication, are obviously inapplicable to the preparation of a posthumous standard edition of his collected works. Those who read the tale of "Falkland" eight-and-forty years ago[1] have long survived the age when character is influenced by the literature of sentiment. The readers to whom it is now presented are not Lord Lytton's contemporaries; they are his posterity. To them his works have already become classical. It is only upon the minds of the young that the works of sentiment have any appreciable moral influence. But the sentiment of each

[1] It was published in 1827.

age is peculiar to itself; and the purely moral influence of sentimental fiction seldom survives the age to which it was first addressed. The youngest and most impressionable reader of such works as the "Nouvelle Helöise," "Werthe," "The Robbers," "Corinne," or "René," is not now likely to be morally influenced, for good or ill, by the perusal of those masterpieces of genius. Had Byron attained the age at which great authors most realize the responsibilities of fame and genius, he might possibly have regretted, and endeavoured to suppress, the publication of "Don Juan"; but the possession of that immortal poem is an unmixed benefit to posterity, and the loss of it would have been an irreparable misfortune.

"Falkland," although the earliest, is one of the most carefully finished of its author's compositions. All that was once turbid, heating, unwholesome in the current of sentiment which flows through this history of a guilty passion, "Death's immortalizing winter" has chilled and purified. The book is now a harmless, and it may be hoped, a not uninteresting, evidence of the precocity of its author's genius. As such, it is here reprinted.

FALKLAND.

BOOK I.

FROM ERASMUS FALKLAND, ESQ., TO THE HON.
FREDERICK MONKTON.

L——, *May*—, 1822.

YOU are mistaken, my dear Monkton! Your description of the gaiety of "the season" gives me no emotion. You speak of pleasure; I remember no labour so wearisome: you enlarge upon its changes; no sameness appears to me so monotonous. Keep, then, your pity for those who require it. From the height of my philosophy I compassionate *you*. No one is so vain as a recluse; and your jests at my hermitship and hermitage cannot penetrate the folds of a self-conceit, which does not envy you in your suppers at D—— House, nor even in your waltzes with Eleanor ——.

It is a ruin rather than a house which I inhabit. I have not been at L—— since my return from abroad, and during those years the place has gone rapidly to decay; perhaps, for that reason, it suits me better, *tel maître telle maison*.

Of all my possessions this is the least valuable in itself, and derives the least interest from the associations of childhood, for it was not at L—— that any part of that period was spent. I have, however, chosen it for my present retreat, because here only I am personally unknown, and therefore little likely to be disturbed. I do not, indeed, wish for the interruptions designed as civilities; I rather gather around myself, link after link, the chains that connected me with the world; I find among my own thoughts that variety and occupation which you only experience in your intercourse with others; and I make, like the Chinese, my map of the universe consist of a circle in a square—the circle is my own empire of thought *and self;* and it is to the scanty corners which it leaves without, that I banish whatever belongs to the remainder of mankind.

About a mile from L—— is Mr. Mandeville's beautiful villa of E——, in the midst of grounds which form a delightful contrast to the savage and wild scenery by which they are surrounded. As the house is at present quite deserted, I have obtained, through the gardener, a free admittance into his domains, and I pass there whole hours, indulging, like the hero of the *Lutrin*, "*une sainte oisiveté*," listening to a little noisy brook, and letting my thoughts be almost as vague and idle as the birds which wander among the trees that surround me. I could wish, indeed, that this simile were in all things correct—that those thoughts, if as free, were also as happy as the objects of my comparison; and could, like them, after the rovings of the day, turn at evening to a resting-place, and be still. We are the dupes and the victims of our senses: while we use them to gather from external things the hoards that we store within, we cannot foresee the punishments we prepare for ourselves; the remembrance which stings, and the hope which deceives, the passions which promise us rapture, which reward us with despair, and the thoughts which if they constitute the healthful action, make also the feverish excitement of our minds. What sick man has not dreamt in his delirium everything that our philosophers have said?[1] But I am growing into my old habit of gloomy reflection, and it is time that I should conclude. I meant to have written you a letter as light as your own; if I have failed, it is no wonder.—"Notre cœur est un instrument incomplet—une lyre où il manque des cordes, et où nous sommes forcés de rendre les accens de la joie, sur le ton consacré aux soupirs."

FROM THE SAME TO THE SAME.

You ask me to give you some sketch of my life, and of that *bel mondo* which wearied me so soon. Men seldom reject an opportunity to talk of themselves; and I am not unwilling to re-examine the past, to re-connect it with the present, and to gather from a consideration of each what hopes and expectations are still left to me for the future.

But my detail must be rather of thought than of action: most of those whose fate has been connected with mine are now living, and I would not, even to you, break that tacit confidence which much of my history would require. After all, you will have no loss. The actions of another may interest—but, for the most part, it is only his

[1] Quid aegrotus unquam somniavit quod philosophorum aliquis non dixerit?
—LACTANTIUS.

reflections which come home to us; for few have acted, nearly all of us have thought.

My own vanity too would be unwilling to enter upon incidents which had their origin either in folly or in error. It is true that those follies and errors have ceased, but their effects remain. With years our *faults* diminish, but our *vices* increase.

You know that my mother was Spanish, and that my father was one of that old race of which so few scions remain, who, living in a distant country, have been little influenced by the changes of fashion, and, priding themselves on the antiquity of their names, have looked with contempt upon the modern distinctions and the mushroom nobles which have sprung up to discountenance and eclipse the plainness of more venerable and solid respectability. In his youth my father had served in the army. He had known much of men and more of books; but his knowledge, instead of rooting out, had rather been engrafted on his prejudices. He was one of that class (and I say it with a private reverence, though a public regret), who, with the best intentions, have made the worst citizens, and who think it a duty to perpetuate whatever is pernicious by having learnt to consider it as sacred. He was a great country gentleman, a great sportsman, and a great Tory; perhaps the three worst enemies which a country can have. Though beneficent to the poor, he gave but a cold reception to the rich; for he was too refined to associate with his inferiors, and too proud to like the competition of his equals. One ball and two dinners a-year constituted all the aristocratic portion of our hospitality, and at the age of twelve, the noblest and youngest companions that I possessed, were a large Danish dog and a wild mountain pony, as unbroken and as lawless as myself. It is only in later years that we can perceive the immeasurable importance of the early scenes and circumstances which surrounded us. It was in the loneliness of my unchecked wanderings that my early affection for my own thoughts was conceived. In the seclusion of Nature—in whatever court she presided—the education of my mind was begun; and, even at that early age, I rejoiced (like the wild hart the Grecian poet[1] had described) in the stillness of the great woods, and the solitudes unbroken by human footstep.

The first change in my life was under melancholy auspices; my father fell suddenly ill, and died; and my mother, whose very existence seemed only held in his presence, followed him in three months. I remember that, a few hours before her death, she called me to her: she reminded me that, through her, I was of Spanish extraction; that in her country I received my birth, and that, not the less

[1] Eurip. Bacchae, 1. 874.

for its degradation and distress, I might hereafter find in the relations which I held to it a remembrance to value, or even a duty to fulfil. On her tenderness to me at that hour, on the impression it made upon my mind, and on the keen and enduring sorrow which I felt for months after her death, it would be useless to dwell.

My uncle became my guardian. He is, you know, a member of parliament of some reputation; very sensible and very dull; very much respected by men, very much disliked by women; and inspiring all children, of either sex, with the same unmitigated aversion which he feels for them himself.

I did not remain long under his immediate care. I was soon sent to school—that preparatory world, where the great primal principles of human nature, in the aggression of the strong and the meanness of the weak, constitute the earliest lesson of importance that we are taught; and where the forced *primitiæ* of that less universal knowledge which is useless to the many who, in after life, neglect, and bitter to the few who improve it, are the first motives for which our minds are to be broken to terror, and our hearts initiated into tears.

Bold and resolute by temper, I soon carved myself a sort of career among my associates. A hatred to all oppression, and a haughty and unyielding character, made me at once the fear and aversion of the greater powers and principalities of the school; while my agility at all boyish games, and my ready assistance or protection to every one who required it, made me proportionally popular with, and courted by, the humbler multitude of the subordinate classes. I was constantly surrounded by the most lawless and mischievous followers whom the school could afford; all eager for my commands, and all pledged to their execution.

In good truth, I was a worthy Rowland of such a gang: though I excelled in, I cared little for, the ordinary amusements of the school: I was fonder of engaging in marauding expeditions contrary to our legislative restrictions, and I valued myself equally upon my boldness in planning our exploits, and my dexterity in eluding their discovery. But exactly in proportion as our school terms connected me with those of my own years, did our vacations unfit me for any intimate companionship but that which I already began to discover in myself.

Twice in the year, when I went home, it was to that wild and romantic part of the country where my former childhood had been spent. There, alone and unchecked, I was thrown utterly upon my own resources. I wandered by day over the rude scenes which surrounded us; and at evening I pored, with an unwearied delight, over the ancient legends which made those scenes sacred to my imagination. I grew by degrees of a more thoughtful and visionary nature. My temper imbibed the romance of my studies; and whether, in winter, basking by the large hearth of our old hall, or stretched, in the indolent voluptuousness of summer, by the rushing streams which formed the chief characteristic of the country around us, my hours were equally wasted in those dim and luxurious dreams, which constituted, perhaps, the essence of that poetry I had not the genius to embody. It was then, by that alternate restlessness of action and idleness of reflection, into which my young years were divided, that the impress of my character was stamped: that fitfulness of temper, that affection for extremes has accompanied me through life. Hence, not only all intermediums of emotion appear to me as tame, but even the most overwrought excitation can bring neither novelty nor zest. I have, as it were, feasted upon the passions; I have made that my daily food, which, in its strength and excess, would have been poison to others; I have rendered my mind unable to enjoy the ordinary aliments of nature; and I have wasted, by a premature indulgence, my resources and my powers, till I have left my heart, without a remedy or a hope, to whatever disorders its own intemperance has engendered.

FROM THE SAME TO THE SAME.

When I left Dr. ——'s, I was sent to a private tutor in D——e. Here I continued for about two years. It was during that time that— but what *then* befel me is for no living ear! The characters of that history are engraven on my heart in letters of fire; but it is a language that none but myself have the authority to read. It is enough for the purpose of my confessions that the events of that period were connected with the first awakening of the most powerful of human passions, and that, whatever their commencement, their end was despair! and *she*—the object of that love—the only being in the world who ever possessed the secret and the spell of my nature—*her* life was the bitterness and the fever of a troubled heart,—her rest is the grave—

> Non la conobbe il mondo mentre l'ebbe
> Con ibill 'io, ch 'a pianger qui rimasi.

That attachment was not so much a single event, as the first link in a long chain which was coiled around my heart. It were a tedious and bitter history, even were it permitted, to tell you of all the sins and misfortunes to which in after-life that passion was connected. I will only speak of the more hidden but general effect it had upon my mind; though, indeed, naturally inclined to a morbid and melancholy philosophy, it is more than probable, but for that occurrence, that it would never have found matter for excitement. Thrown early among mankind, I should early have imbibed their feelings, and grown like them by the influence of custom. I should not have carried within me one unceasing remembrance, which was to teach **me,** like Faustus, to find nothing in knowledge but its inutility, or in hope but its deceit ; and to bear like him, through the blessings of youth and the allurements of pleasure, the curse and the presence of a fiend.

FROM THE SAME TO THE SAME.

It was after the first violent grief produced by that train of circumstances to which I must necessarily so darkly allude, that I began **to** apply with earnestness to books. Night and day I devoted myself unceasingly to study, and from this fit I was only recovered by the long and dangerous illness it produced. **Alas**! there is no fool like him who wishes for knowledge! It is only through woe that we are taught to reflect, and we gather the honey of worldly wisdom, not from flowers, but thorns.

" Une grande passion malheureuse est un grand moyen de sagesse." **From the** moment in which the buoyancy of my spirit was first **broken by real** anguish, the losses of the *heart* were repaired **by the** experience of the *mind*. I passed at once, like Melmoth, from youth to age. What were any longer to me the ordinary avocations of my contemporaries ? I had exhausted years in moments—I had wasted, like the Eastern Queen, my richest jewel in a draught. I ceased to hope, to feel, to act, to burn ; such are the impulses of the young ! I learned to doubt, to reason, to analyze : such are the habits of the old ! From that time, if I have not avoided the pleasures of life, I have not enjoyed them. Women, wine, the society of the gay, the commune of the wise, the lonely pursuit of knowledge, the daring visions of ambition, all have occupied me in turn, and all alike have deceived me ; but, like the Widow in the story of Voltaire, I have built at last a temple to " Time, the Comforter: " I have grown calm and unrepining with years ; and, if I am now shrinking from men, I have derived at least this advantage from the loneliness first made habitual **by** regret ;—that while I feel increased benevolence to others, I have learned to look for happiness only in myself.

They alone are independent of Fortune who have made themselves **a** separate existence from the world.

FROM THE SAME TO THE SAME.

I went to the University **with** a great fund of general reading, and habits of constant application. My uncle, who having no children of his own, began to be ambitious for me, formed great expectations of my career at Oxford. I stayed there three years, and did nothing! I did not gain a single prize, nor did I attempt anything above the ordinary degree. The fact is, that nothing seemed to me worth the labour of success. I conversed with those who had obtained the highest academical reputation, and I smiled with a consciousness of superiority at the boundlessness of their vanity, and the narrowness of their views. The limits of the distinction they had gained seemed to them as wide as the most extended renown; and the little knowledge their youth had acquired only appeared to them an excuse for the ignorance and the indolence of maturer years. Was it to equal these that I was to labour? I felt that I already surpassed them! Was it to gain *their* good opinion, or, still worse, that of their admirers? Alas! I had too long learned to live for myself to find any happiness in the respect of the idlers I despised.

I left Oxford at the age of twenty-one. I succeeded to the large estates of my inheritance, and for the first time I felt the vanity so natural to youth when I went up to London to enjoy the resources of the Capital, and to display the powers I possessed to revel in whatever those resources could yield. I found society like the Jewish temple: any one is admitted into its threshold; none but the chiefs of the institution into its recesses.

Young, rich, of an ancient and honourable name, pursuing pleasure rather as a necessary excitement than an occasional occupation, and agreeable to the associates I drew around me because my profusion contributed to their enjoyment, and my temper to their amusement—I found myself courted by many, and avoided by none. I soon discovered that all civility is but the mask of design. I smiled at the kindness of the fathers who, hearing that I was talented, and knowing that I was rich, looked to my support in whatever political side they had espoused. I saw in the notes of the mothers their anxiety for the establishment of their daughters, and their respect for my acres; and in the cordiality of the sons who had horses to sell and rouge-et-noir debts to pay, I detected all that veneration for my money which implied such contempt for its possessor. By nature observant, and by misfortune sarcastic, I looked upon the various colourings of society with a searching and philosophic eye: I unravelled the intricacies which knit servility with arrogance, and meanness with ostentation; and I traced to its sources that universal vulgarity of inward sentiment and external manner, which, in all classes, appears to me to constitute the only unvarying characteristic of our countrymen. In proportion as I increased my knowledge of others, I shrunk with a deeper disappointment and dejection into my own resources. The first moment of real happiness which I experienced for a whole year was when I found myself about to seek, beneath the influence of other skies, that more extended acquaintance with my species which might either draw me to them with a closer connection, or at least reconcile me to the ties which already existed.

I will not dwell upon my adventures abroad: there is little to interest others in a recital which awakens no interest in one's self. I sought for wisdom, and I acquired but knowledge. I thirsted for the truth, the tenderness of love, and I found but its fever and its falsehood. Like the two Florimels of Spenser, I mistook, in my delirium, the delusive fabrication of the senses for the divine reality of the heart; and I only awoke from my deceit when the phantom I had worshipped melted into snow. Whatever I pursued partook of the energy, yet fitfulness of my nature; mingling to-day in the tumults of the city, and to-morrow alone with my own heart in the solitude of unpeopled nature; now revelling in the wildest excesses, and now tracing, with a painful and unwearied search, the intricacies of science; alternately governing others, and subdued by the tyranny which my own passions imposed—I passed through the ordeal unshrinking yet unscathed. "The education of life," says De Staël, "perfects the thinking mind, but depraves the frivolous." I do not inquire, Monkton, to which of these classes I belong; but I feel too well, that though my mind has not been depraved, it has found no perfection but in misfortune; and that whatever be the acquirements of later years, they have nothing which can compensate for the losses of our youth.

FROM THE SAME TO THE SAME.

I returned to England. I entered again upon the theatre of its world; but I mixed now more in its greater than its lesser pursuits. I looked rather at the mass than the leaven of mankind; and while I felt aversion for the few whom I knew, I glowed with philanthropy for the crowd which I know not.

It is in contemplating men at a distance that we become benevolent. When we mix with them, we suffer by the contact, and grow, if not malicious from the injury, at least selfish from the circumspection which our safety imposes: but when, while we feel our relationship, we are not galled by the tie; when neither jealousy, nor envy, nor resentment are excited, we have nothing to interfere with those more complacent and kindliest sentiments which our earliest impressions have rendered natural to our hearts. We may fly men in hatred because they have galled us, but the feeling ceases with the cause: none will willingly feed long upon bitter thoughts. It is thus that, while in the narrow circle in which we move we suffer daily from those who approach us, we can, in spite of our resentment to *them*, glow with a general benevolence to the wider relations from which we are remote; that while smarting beneath the treachery of friendship, the sting of ingratitude, the faithlessness of love, we would almost sacrifice our lives to realize some idolized theory of legislation; and that, distrustful, calculating, selfish in private, there are thousands who would, with a credulous fanaticism, fling themselves as victims before that unrecompensing Moloch which they term the Public.

Living, then, much by myself, but reflecting much upon the world, I learned to love mankind. Philanthropy brought ambition; for I was ambitious, not for my own aggrandizement, but for the service of others—for the poor—the toiling—the degraded; these constituted that part of my fellow beings which I the most loved, for these were bound to me by the most engaging of all human ties—misfortune! I began to enter into the intrigues of the state; I extended my observation and inquiry from individuals to nations; I examined into the mysteries of the science which has arisen in these later days to give the lie to the wisdom of the past, to reduce into the simplicity of problems the intricacies of political knowledge, to teach us the fallacy of the system which had governed by restriction, and imagined that the happiness of nations depended upon the perpetual interference of its rulers, and to prove to us that the only unerring policy of art is to leave a free and unobstructed progress to the hidden energies and providence of Nature. But it was not only the *theoretical* investigation of the state which employed me. I mixed, though in secret, with the agents of its springs. While I seemed only intent upon pleasure, I locked in my heart the consciousness and vanity of power. In the levity of the lip I disguised the workings and the knowledge of the brain; and I looked, as with a gifted eye, upon the mysteries of the hidden depths, while I seemed to float an idler, with the herd, only on the surface of the stream.

Why was I disgusted, when I had but to put forth my hand and grasp whatever object my ambition might desire? Alas! there was in my heart always something too soft for the aims and cravings of my mind. I felt that I was wasting the young years of my life in a barren and wearisome pursuit. What to me, who had outlived vanity, would have been the admiration of the crowd! I sighed for the sympathy of *the one!* and I shrunk in sadness from the prospect of renown to ask my heart for the reality of love! For what purpose, too, had I devoted myself to the service of men? As I grew more sensible of the labour of pursuing, I saw more of the inutility of accomplishing, individual measures. There is one great and moving order of events which we may retard, but we cannot arrest, and to which, if we endeavour to hasten them, we only give a dangerous and unnatural impetus. Often, when in the fever of the midnight, I have paused from my unshared and unsoftened studies, to listen to the deadly pulsation of my heart,[1] when I have felt in its painful and tumultuous beating the very life waning and wasting within me, I have sickened to my inmost soul to remember that, amongst all those whom I was exhausting the health and enjoyment of youth to benefit, there was not one for whom my life had an interest, or by whom my death would be honoured by a tear. There is a beautiful passage in Chalmers on the want of sympathy we experience in the world. From my earliest childhood I had one deep, engrossing, yearning desire,—and that was to love and to be loved. I found, too young, the realization of that dream—it passed! and I have never known it again. The experience of long and bitter years teaches me to look with suspicion on that far recollection of the past, and to doubt if this earth could indeed produce a living form to satisfy the visions of one who has dwelt among the boyish creations of fancy—who has shaped out in his heart an imaginary idol, arrayed it in whatever is most beautiful in nature, and breathed into the image the pure but burning spirit of that innate love from which it sprung! It is true that my manhood has been the undeceiver of my youth, and that the meditation upon facts has disenthralled me from the visionary broodings over fiction; but what remuneration have I found in reality? If the line of the satirist be not true,

"Souvent de tous nos maux la raison est le pire,"[2]

at least, like the madman of whom he speaks, I owe but little gratitude to the act which, "in drawing me from my error, has robbed me also of a paradise."

I am approaching the conclusion of my confessions. Men who have no ties in the world, and who have been accustomed to solitude, find, with every disappointment in the former, a greater yearning for the enjoyments which the latter can afford. Day by day I relapsed more into myself; "man delighted me not, nor woman either." In my ambition, it was not in the means, but the end, that I was disappointed. In my friends, I complained not of treachery, but insipidity; and it was not because I was deserted,

[1] Falkland suffered much, from very early youth, from a complaint in his heart.
[2] Boileau.

but wearied by more tender connections, that I ceased to find either excitement in seeking, or triumph in obtaining, their love. It was not, then, in a momentary disgust, but rather in the calm of satiety, that I formed that resolution of retirement which I have adopted now.

Shrinking from my kind, but too young to live wholly for myself, I have made a new tie with nature; I have come to cement it here. I am like a bird which has wandered afar, but has returned home to its nest at last. But there is one feeling which had its origin in the world, and which accompanies me still; which consecrates my recollections of the past; which contributes to take its gloom from the solitude of the present:—Do you ask me its nature, Monkton? It is my friendship for you.

FROM THE SAME TO THE SAME.

I wish that I could convey to you, dear Monkton, the faintest idea of the pleasures of indolence. You belong to that class which is of all the most busy, though the least active. Men of pleasure never have time for anything. No lawyer, no statesman, no bustling, hurrying, restless underling of the counter or the Exchange, is so eternally occupied as a lounger "about town." He is linked to labour by a series of undefinable nothings. His independence and idleness only serve to fetter and engross him, and his leisure seems held upon the condition of never having a moment to himself. Would that you could see me at this instant in the luxury of my summer retreat, surrounded by the trees, the waters, the wild birds, and the hum, the glow, the exultation which teem visibly and audibly through creation in the noon of a summer's day! I am undisturbed by a single intruder. I am unoccupied by a single pursuit. I suffer one moment to glide into another, without the remembrance that the next must be filled up by some laborious pleasure, or some wearisome enjoyment. It is here that I feel all the powers, and gather together all the resources of my mind. I recall my recollections of men; and, unbiassed by the passions and prejudices which we do not experience *alone*, because their very existence depends upon others, I endeavour to perfect my knowledge of the human heart. He who would acquire that better science must arrange and analyze in private the experience he has collected in the crowd. Alas, Monkton, when you have expressed surprise at the gloom which is so habitual to my temper, did it never occur to you that my acquaintance with the world would alone be sufficient to account for it?—that knowledge is neither for the good nor the happy. Who can touch pitch, and not be defiled? Who can look upon the workings of grief and rejoice, or associate with guilt and be pure?

It has been by mingling with men, not only in their *haunts* but their *emotions*, that I have learned to know them. I have descended into the receptacles of vice; I have taken lessons from the brothel and the hell; I have watched feeling in its unguarded sallies, and drawn from the impulse of the moment conclusions which gave the lie to the previous conduct of years. But all knowledge brings us disappointment, and *this* knowledge the most—the satiety of good, the suspicion of evil, the decay of our young dreams, the premature iciness of age, the reckless, aimless, joyless indifference which follows an overwrought and feverish excitation—*These* constitute the lot of men who have renounced *hope* in the acquisition of *thought*, and who, in learning the motives of human actions, learn only to despise the persons and the things which enchanted them like divinities before.

FROM THE SAME TO THE SAME.

I told you, dear Monkton, in my first letter, of my favourite retreat in Mr. Mandeville's grounds. I have grown so attached to it, that I spend the greater part of the day there. I am not one of those persons who always perambulate with a book in their hands, as if neither nature nor their own reflections could afford them any rational amusement. I go there more frequently *en paresseux* than *en savant*; a small brooklet which runs through the grounds broadens at last into a deep, clear, transparent lake. Here fir and elm and oak fling their branches over the margin; and beneath their shade I pass all the hours of noon-day in the luxuries of a dreamer's reverie. It is true, however, that I am never less idle than when I appear the most so. I am like Prospero in his desert island, and surround myself with spirits. A spell trembles upon the leaves; every wave comes fraught to me with its peculiar music: and an Ariel seems to whisper the secrets of every breeze, which comes to my forehead laden with the perfumes of the West. But do not think, Monkton, that it is only good spirits which haunt the recesses of my solitude. To push the metaphor to exaggeration—Memory is my Sycorax, and Gloom is the Caliban she conceives. But let me digress from myself to my less idle occupations;—I have of late diverted my thoughts in some measure by a recurrence to a study to which I once was particularly devoted—history. Have you ever remarked, that people who live the most by themselves reflect the most upon others; and that he who lives surrounded by the million never thinks of any but the one individual—himself? Philosophers—moralists—historians, whose thoughts, labours, lives, have been devoted to the consideration of mankind, or the analysis of public events, have usually been remarkably attached to solitude and seclusion. We are indeed so linked to our fellow-beings, that, where we are not chained to them by action, we are carried to and connected with them by thought.

I have just quitted the observations of my favourite Bolingbroke upon history. I cannot agree with him as to its utility. The more I consider, the more I am convinced that its study has been upon the whole pernicious to mankind. It is by those details, which are always as unfair in their inference as they must evidently be doubtful in their facts, that party animosity and general prejudice are supported and sustained. There is not one abuse—one intolerance—one remnant of ancient barbarity and ignorance existing at the present day, which is not advocated, and actually confirmed by some vague deduction from the bigotry of an illiterate chronicler, or the obscurity of an uncertain legend. It is through the constant appeal to our ancestors that we transmit wretchedness and wrong to our posterity: we should require, to corroborate an evil originating in the present day, the clearest and most satisfactory proof; but the minutest defence is sufficient for an evil handed down to us by the barbarism of antiquity. We reason from what even in old times was dubious, as if we were adducing what was certain in those in which we live. And thus we have made no sanction to abuses so powerful as history, and no enemy to the present like the past.

FROM THE LADY EMILY MANDEVILLE TO MRS. ST. JOHN.

At last, my dear Julia, I am settled in my beautiful retreat. Mrs. Dalton and Lady Margaret Leslie are all whom I could prevail upon to accompany me. Mr. Mandeville is full of the corn-laws. He is chosen chairman to a select committee in the House. He is murmuring agricultural distresses in his sleep; and when I asked him occasionally to come down here to see me, he started from a reverie, and exclaimed—"Never, Mr. Speaker, as a landed proprietor; never will I consent to my own ruin."

My boy, my own, my beautiful companion, is with me. I wish you could see how fast he can run, and how sensibly he can talk. "What a fine figure he has for his age!" said I to Mr. Mandeville the other day. "Figure! age!" said his father; "in the House of Commons he shall make a figure to every age." I know that in writing to you, you will not be contented if I do not say a great deal about myself. I shall therefore proceed to tell you, that I feel already much better from the air and exercise of the journey, from the conversation of my two guests, and, above all, from the constant society of my dear boy. He was three last birthday. I think that at the age of twenty-one, I am the least childish of the two. Pray remember me to all in town who have not quite forgotten me. Beg Lady —— to send Elizabeth a subscription ticket for Almack's, and —oh, talking of Almack's, I think my boy's eyes are even more blue and beautiful than Lady C——'s.

Adieu, my dear Julia,

Ever, &c.,

E. M.

Lady Emily Mandeville was the daughter of the Duke of Lindvale. She married, at the age of sixteen, a man of large fortune, and some parliamentary reputation. Neither in person nor in character was he much beneath or above the ordinary standard of men. He was one of Nature's Macadamized achievements. His great fault was his equality; and you longed for a hill though it were to climb, or a stone though it were in your way. Love attaches itself to something prominent, even if that something be what others would hate. One can scarcely feel extremes for mediocrity. The few years Lady Emily had been married had but little altered her character. Quick in feeling, though regulated in temper; gay, less from levity, than from that first *spring-tide* of a heart which has never yet known occasion to be sad; beautiful and pure, as an enthusiast's dream of heaven, yet bearing within the latent and powerful passion and tenderness of earth: she mixed with all a simplicity and innocence which the extreme earliness of her marriage, and the ascetic temper of her husband, had tended less to diminish than increase. She had much of what is termed genius—its warmth of emotion—its vividness of conception—its admiration for the grand —its affection for the good, and that dangerous contempt for whatever is mean and worthless, the very indulgence of which is an offence against the habits of the world. Her tastes were, however, too feminine and chaste ever to render her eccentric: they were rather calculated to conceal than to publish the deeper recesses of her nature; and it was beneath that polished surface of manner common to those with whom she mixed, that she hid the treasures of a mine which no human eye had beheld.

Her health, naturally delicate, had lately suffered much from the dissipation of London, and it was by the advice of her physicians that she had now come to spend the summer at E——. Lady

Margaret Leslie, who was old enough to be tired with the caprices of society, and Mrs. Dalton, who having just lost her husband, was forbidden at present to partake of its amusements, had agreed to accompany her to her retreat. Neither of them was perhaps much suited to Emily's temper, but youth and spirits make almost any one congenial to us: it is from the years which confirm our habits, and the reflections which refine our taste, that it becomes easy to revolt us, and difficult to please.

On the third day after Emily's arrival at E——, she was sitting after breakfast with Lady Margaret and Mrs. Dalton. "Pray," said the former, "did you ever meet my relation, Mr. Falkland? he is in your immediate neighbourhood." "Never; though I have a great curiosity: that fine old ruin beyond the village belongs to him, I believe." "It does. You ought to know him: you would like him so!" "Like him!" repeated Mrs. Dalton, who was one of those persons of *ton* who, though everything collectively, are nothing individually: "Like him? impossible!" "Why?" said Lady Margaret, indignantly—"he has every requisite to please—youth, talent, fascination of manner, and great knowledge of the world." "Well," said Mrs. Dalton, "I cannot say I discovered his perfections. He seemed to me conceited and satirical, and—and—in short, very disagreeable; *but then, to be sure, I have only seen him once.*" "I have heard many accounts of him," said Emily, "all differing from each other: I think, however, that the generality of people rather incline to Mrs. Dalton's opinion than to yours, Lady Margaret." "I can easily believe it. It is very seldom that he takes the trouble to please; but when he does, he is irresistible. Very little, however, is generally known respecting him. Since he came of age, he has been much abroad; and when in England, he never entered with eagerness into society. He is supposed to possess very extraordinary powers, which, added to his large fortune and ancient name, have procured him a consideration and rank rarely enjoyed by one so young. He had refused repeated offers to enter into public life; but he is very intimate with one of the ministers, who, it is said, has had the address to profit much by his abilities. All other particulars concerning him are extremely uncertain. Of his person and manners you had better judge yourself; for I am sure, Emily, that my petition for inviting him here is already granted." "By all means," said Emily: "you cannot be more anxious to see him than I am." And so the conversation dropped. Lady Margaret went to the library; Mrs. Dalton seated herself on the ottoman, dividing her attention between the last novel and her Italian greyhound; and Emily left the room in order to revisit her former and favourite haunts. Her young son was her companion, and she was not sorry that he was her only one. To be the instructress of an infant, a mother should be its playmate; and Emily was, perhaps, wiser than she imagined, when she ran with a laughing eye and a light foot over the grass, occupying herself almost with the same earnestness as her child in the same infantine amusements. As they passed the wood which led to the lake at the bottom of the grounds, the boy, who was before Emily, suddenly stopped. She came hastily up to him; and scarcely two paces before, though half hid by the steep bank of the lake beneath which he reclined, she saw a man apparently asleep. A volume of Shakespeare lay beside him: the child had seized it. As she took it from him in order to replace it, her eye rested upon the passage the boy had accidentally opened. How often in after days was that passage recalled as an omen! It was the following:—

> Ah me! for aught that ever I could read,
> Could ever hear by tale or history—
> The course of true love never did run smooth!
> *Midsummer Night's Dream.*

As she laid the book gently down she caught a glimpse of the countenance of the sleeper: never did she forget the expression which it wore,—stern, proud, mournful even in repose!

She did not wait for him to awake. She hurried home through the trees. All that day she was silent and abstracted; the face haunted her like a dream. Strange as it may seem, she spoke neither to Lady Margaret nor to Mrs. Dalton of her adventure. *Why?* Is there in our hearts any prescience of their misfortunes?

On the next day, Falkland, who had received and accepted Lady Margaret's invitation, was expected to dinner. Emily felt a strong yet excusable curiosity to see one of whom she had heard so many and such contradictory reports. She was alone in the saloon when he entered. At the first glance she recognized the person she had met by the lake on the day before, and she blushed deeply as she replied to his salutation. To her great relief Lady Margaret and Mrs. Dalton entered in a few minutes, and the conversation grew general.

Falkland had but little of what is called animation in manner; but his wit, though it rarely led to mirth, was sarcastic, yet refined, and the vividness of his imagination threw a brilliancy and originality over remarks which in others might have been commonplace and tame.

The conversation turned chiefly upon society; and though Lady Margaret had told her he had entered but little into its ordinary routine, Emily was struck alike by his accurate acquaintance with men, and the justice of his reflections upon manners. There also mingled with his satire an occasional melancholy of feeling, which appeared to Emily the more touching because it was always unexpected and unassumed. It was after one of these remarks, that for the first time she ventured to examine into the charm and peculiarity of the countenance of the speaker. There was spread over it that expression of mingled energy and languor, which betokens that much, whether of thought, sorrow, passion, or action, has been undergone, but resisted: has wearied, but not subdued. In the broad and noble brow, in the chiselled lip, and the melancholy depths of the calm and thoughtful eye, there sat a resolution and a power, which, though mournful, were not without their pride; which, if they had borne the worst, had also defied it. Notwithstanding his mother's country, his complexion was fair and pale; and his hair, of a light chestnut, fell in large *antique* curls over his forehead. That forehead, indeed, constituted the principal feature of his countenance. It was neither in its height nor expansion alone that its remarkable beauty consisted; but if ever thought to conceive and courage to execute high designs were embodied and visible, they were imprinted *there.*

Falkland did not stay long after dinner; but to Lady Margaret he promised all that she required of future length and frequency in his visits. When he left the room, Lady Emily went instinctively to the window to watch him depart; and all that night his low soft voice rung in her ear, like the music of an indistinct and half-remembered dream.

FROM MR. MANDEVILLE TO LADY EMILY.

DEAR EMILY,—Business of great importance to the country has prevented my writing to you before. I hope you have continued well since I heard from you last, and that you do all you can to preserve that retrenchment of unnecessary expenses, and observe that attention to a prudent economy, which is no less incumbent upon individuals than nations.

Thinking that you must be dull at E——, and ever anxious both to entertain and to improve you, I send you an excellent publication by Mr. Tooke,[1] together with my own two last speeches, corrected by myself.

Trusting to hear from you soon, I am, with best love to Henry,
Very affectionately yours,
JOHN MANDEVILLE.

[1] The Political Economist.

FROM ERASMUS FALKLAND, ESQ., TO THE HON.
FREDERICK MONKTON.[1]

Well, Monkton, I have been to E——; that important event in my monastic life has been concluded. Lady Margaret was as talkative as usual; and a Mrs. Dalton, who, I find, is an acquaintance of yours, asked very tenderly after your poodle and yourself. But Lady Emily! Ay, Monkton, I know not well how to describe her to you. Her beauty interests not less than it dazzles. There is that deep and eloquent softness in her every word and action, which, of all charms, is the most dangerous. Yet she is rather of a playful than of the melancholy and pensive nature which generally accompanies such gentleness of manner; but there is no levity in her character; nor is that playfulness of spirit ever carried into the exhilaration of what we call "mirth." She seems, if I may use the antithesis, at once too feeling to be gay, and too innocent to be sad. I remember having frequently met her husband. Cold and pompous, without anything to interest the imagination, or engage the affections, I am not able to conceive a person less congenial to his beautiful and romantic wife. But she must have been exceedingly young when she married him; and she, probably, knows not yet that she is to be pitied, because she has not yet learned that she can love.

> Le veggio in fronte amor come in suo seggio
> Sul crin, negli occhi—su le labra amore
> Sol d'intorno al suo cuore amor non veggio.

I have been twice to her house since my first admission there. I love to listen to that soft and enchanting voice, and to escape from the gloom of my own reflections to the brightness, yet simplicity, of hers. In my earlier days this comfort would have been attended with danger; but we grow callous from the excess of feeling. We cannot re-illumine ashes! I can gaze upon her dream-like beauty, and not experience a single desire which can sully the purity of my worship. I listen to her voice when it melts in endearment over her birds, her flowers, or, in a deeper devotion, over her child; but my heart does not thrill at the tenderness of the sound. I touch her hand, and the pulses of my own are as calm as before. Satiety of the past is our best safeguard from the temptations of the future; and the perils of youth are over when it has acquired that dulness and apathy of affection which should belong only to the insensibility of age.

[1] A letter from Falkland, mentioning Lady Margaret's invitation, has been omitted.

Such were Falkland's opinions at the time he wrote. Ah! what is so delusive as our affections? Our security is our danger—our defiance our defeat! Day after day he went to E——. He passed the mornings in making excursions with Emily over that wild and romantic country by which they were surrounded; and in the dangerous but delicious stillness of the summer twilights, they listened to the first whispers of their hearts.

In his relationship to Lady Margaret, Falkland found his excuse for the frequency of his visits; and even Mrs. Dalton was so charmed with the fascination of his manner, that (in spite of her previous dislike) she forgot to inquire how far his intimacy at E—— was at variance with the proprieties of the world she worshipped, or in what proportion it was connected with herself.

It is needless for me to trace through all its windings the formation of that affection, the subsequent records of which I am about to relate. What is so unearthly, so beautiful, as the first birth of a woman's love? The air of heaven is not purer in its wanderings—its sunshine not more holy in its warmth. Oh! why should it deteriorate in its nature, even while it increases in its degree? Why should the step which *prints*, *sully* also the snow? How often, when Falkland met that guiltless yet thrilling eye, which revealed to him those internal secrets that Emily was yet awhile too happy to discover; when, like a fountain among flowers, the goodness of her heart flowed over the softness of her manner to those around her, and the benevolence of her actions to those beneath; how often he turned away with a veneration too deep for the selfishness of human passion, and a tenderness too sacred for its desires! It was in this temper (the earliest and the most fruitless prognostic of real love) that the following letter was written:—

FROM ERASMUS FALKLAND, ESQ., TO THE HON. FREDERICK MONKTON.

I have had two or three admonitory letters from my uncle. "The summer (he says) is advancing, yet you remain stationary in your indolence. There is still a great part of Europe which you have not seen; and since you will neither enter society for a wife, nor the House of Commons for fame, spend your life, at least while it is yet free and unshackled, in those active pursuits which will render idleness hereafter more sweet; or in that observation and enjoyment among others, which will increase your resources in yourself." All this sounds well; but I have already acquired more knowledge than will be of use either to others or myself, and I am not willing to lose *tranquillity* here for the chance of obtaining *pleasure* elsewhere. Pleasure is indeed a holiday sensation which does not occur in ordinary life. We lose the peace of years when we hunt after the rapture of moments.

I do not know if you ever felt that existence was ebbing away without being put to its full value: as for me, I am never conscious of life without being also conscious that it is not enjoyed to the utmost. This is a bitter feeling, and its worst bitterness is our ignorance how to remove it. My indolence I neither seek nor wish to defend, yet it is rather from necessity than choice: it seems to me that there is nothing in the world to arouse me. I only ask for action, but I can find no motive sufficient to excite it: let me then, in my indolence, not, like the world, be idle, yet dependent on others; but at least dignify the failing by some appearance of that freedom which retirement only can bestow.

My seclusion is no longer solitude; yet I do not value it the less. I spend a great portion of my time at E——. Loneliness is attractive to men of reflection, not so much because they like their own thoughts, as because they dislike the thoughts of others. Solitude ceases to charm the moment we can find a single being whose ideas are more agreeable to us than our own. I have not, I think, yet described to you the person of Lady Emily. She is tall, and slightly, yet beautifully, formed. The ill health which obliged her to leave London for E——, in the height of the season, has given her cheek a more delicate hue than I should think it naturally wore. Her eyes are light, but their lashes are long and dark; her hair is black and luxuriant, and worn in a fashion peculiar to herself; but her manners, Monkton! how can I convey to you their fascination? so simple, and therefore so faultless—so modest, and yet so tender—she seems, in acquiring the intelligence of the woman, to have only perfected the purity of the child; and now, after all that I have said, I am only more deeply sensible of the truth of Bacon's observation, that "the best part of beauty is that which no picture can express." I am loth to finish this description, because it seems to me scarcely begun; I am unwilling to continue it, because every word seems to show me more clearly those recesses of my heart, which I would have hidden even from myself. I do not *yet* love, it is true, for the time is past when I was lightly moved to passion; but I will not incur that danger, the probability of which I am seer enough to foresee. Never shall that pure and innocent heart be sullied by one who would die to shield it from the lightest misfortune. I find in myself a powerful seconder to my uncle's wishes. I shall be in London next week; till then, farewell.   E. F.

When the proverb said, that "Jove laughs at lovers' vows," it meant not (as in the ordinary construction) a sarcasm on their insincerity, but *inconsistency*. We deceive others far less than we deceive ourselves. What to Falkland were resolutions which a word, a glance, could overthrow? In the world he might have dissipated his thoughts: in loneliness he concentred them; for the passions are like the sounds of Nature, only heard in her solitude! He lulled his soul to the reproaches of his conscience; he surrendered himself to the intoxication of so golden a dream; and amidst those beautiful scenes there arose, as an offering to the summer heaven, the incense of two hearts which had, through those very fires so guilty in themselves, purified and ennobled every other emotion they had conceived.

God made the country, and man made the town,

says the hackneyed quotation; and the feelings awakened in each, differ with the genius of the place. Who can compare the frittered and divided affections formed in cities with that which crowds cannot distract by opposing temptations, or dissipation infect with its frivolities?

I have often thought that had the execution of Atala equalled its design, no human work could have surpassed it in its grandeur. What picture is more simple, though more sublime, than the vast solitude of an unpeopled wilderness, the woods, the mountains, the face of nature, cast in the fresh yet giant mould of a new and unpolluted world; and, amidst those most silent and mighty temples of THE GREAT GOD, the lone spirit of Love reigning and brightening over all?

BOOK II.

IT is dangerous for women, however wise it be for men, "to commune with their own hearts, and to be still!" Continuing to pursue the follies of the world had been to Emily more prudent than to fly them; to pause, to separate herself from the herd, was to discover, to feel, to murmur at the vacuum of her being; and to occupy it with the feelings which it craved, could in her be but the hoarding a provision for despair.

Married, before she had begun the bitter knowledge of *herself*, to a man whom it was impossible to love, yet deriving from nature a tenderness of soul, which shed itself over every thing around, her only escape from misery had been in the dormancy of feeling. The birth of her son had opened to her a new field of sensations, and she drew the best charm of her own existence from the life she had given to another. Had she not met Falkland, all the deeper sources of affection would have flowed into one only and legitimate channel; but those whom *he* wished to fascinate had never resisted his power, and the attachment he inspired was in proportion to the strength and ardour of his own nature.

It was not for Emily Mandeville to love such as Falkland without feeling that from that moment a separate and selfish existence had ceased *to be*. Our senses may captivate us with beauty; but in absence we forget, or by reason we can conquer, so superficial an impression. Our vanity may enamour us with rank; but the affections of vanity are traced in sand; but who can love *Genius*, and not feel that the sentiments it excites partake of its own intenseness and its own immortality? It arouses, concentrates, engrosses all our emotions, even to the most subtle and concealed. Love what is common, and ordinary objects can replace or destroy a sentiment which an ordinary object has awakened. Love what we shall not meet again amidst the littleness and insipidity which surround us, and where can we turn for a new object to replace that which has no parallel upon earth? The recovery from such a delirium is like return from a fairy land; and still fresh in the recollections of a bright and immortal clime, how can we endure the dulness of that human existence to which for the future we are condemned?

It was some weeks since Emily had written to Mrs. St. John; and her last letter, in mentioning Falkland, had spoken of him with a reserve which rather alarmed than deceived her friend. Mrs. St. John had indeed a strong and secret reason for fear. Falkland had been the object of her own and her earliest attachment, and she knew well the singular and mysterious power which he exercised at will over the mind. He had, it is true, never returned, nor even known of, her feelings towards him; and during the years which had elapsed since she last saw him, and in the new scenes which her marriage with Mr. St. John had opened, she had almost forgotten her early attachment, when Lady Emily's letter renewed its remembrance. She wrote in answer an impassioned and affectionate caution to her friend. She spoke much (after complaining of Emily's late silence) in condemnation of the character of Falkland, and in warning of its fascinations; and she attempted to arouse alike the virtue and the pride which so often triumph in alliance, when separately they would so easily fail. In this Mrs. St. John probably imagined she was actuated solely by friendship; but in the best actions there is always some latent evil in the motive; and the selfishness of a jealousy, though hopeless not conquered, perhaps predominated over the less interested feelings which were all that she acknowledged to herself.

In this work it has been my object to portray the progress of the passions; to chronicle a history rather by thoughts and feelings than by incidents and events; and to lay open those minuter and more subtle mazes and secrets of the human heart, which in modern writings have been so sparingly exposed. It is with this view that I have from time to time broken the thread of narration, in order to bring forward more vividly the characters it contains; and in laying no claim to the ordinary ambition of tale-writers, I have deemed myself at liberty to deviate from the ordinary courses they pursue. Hence the motive and the excuse for the insertion of the following extracts, and of occasional letters. They portray the interior struggle when Narration would look only to the external event, and trace the lightning "home to its cloud," when History would only mark the spot where it scorched or destroyed.

EXTRACTS FROM THE JOURNAL OF LADY EMILY MANDEVILLE.

Tuesday.—More than seven years have passed since I began this journal! I have just been looking over it from the commencement. Many and various are the feelings which it attempts to describe—anger, pique, joy, sorrow, hope, pleasure, weariness, ennui; but never, never once, humiliation or remorse!—these were not doomed to be my portion in the bright years of my earliest youth. How shall I describe them now? I have received—I have read, as well as my tears would let me, a long letter from Julia. It is true that I have not dared to write to her: when shall I answer this? She has shown me the state of my heart; I more than suspected it before. Could I have dreamed two months—six weeks since—that I should have a single feeling of which I could be ashamed? *He* has just been here—*He*—the only one in the world, for all the world seems concentred in him. He observed my distress, for I looked on him; and my lips quivered and my eyes were full of tears. He came to me—he sat next to me—he whispered his interest, his anxiety—and was this all? Have I loved before I even knew that I was beloved? No, no; the tongue was silent, but the eye, the cheek, the manner —alas! *these* have been but too eloquent!

Wednesday.—It was so sweet to listen to his low and tender voice; to watch the expression of his countenance—even to breathe the air that he inhaled. But now that I know its cause, I feel that this pleasure is a crime, and I am miserable even when he is with me. He has not been here to-day. It is past three. Will he come? I rise from my seat—I go to the window for breath—I am restless, agitated, disturbed. Lady Margaret speaks to me—I scarcely answer her. My boy—yes, my dear, dear Henry comes, and I feel that I am again a mother. Never will I betray that duty, though I have forgotten one as sacred, though less dear! Never shall my son have cause to blush for his parent! I will fly hence—I will see *him* no more!

FROM ERASMUS FALKLAND, ESQ., TO THE HON.
FREDERICK MONKTON.

Write to me, Monkton—exhort me, admonish me, or forsake me for ever. I am happy, yet wretched: I wander in the delirium of a fatal fever, in which I see dreams of a brighter life, but every one of them only brings me nearer to death. Day after day I have lingered here, until weeks have flown—and for what? Emily is not like the women of the world—virtue, honour, faith, are not to her the mere *convenances* of society. "There is no crime," said Lady A., "where there is concealment." Such can never be the creed of Emily Mandeville. She will not disguise guilt either in the levity of the world, or in the affectations of sentiment. She will be wretched, and for ever. *I* hold the destinies of her future life, and yet I am base enough to hesitate whether to save or destroy her. Oh, how fearful, how selfish, how degrading, is unlawful love!

You know my theoretical benevolence for everything that lives; you have often smiled at its vanity. I see now that you were right; for it seems to me almost superhuman virtue not to destroy the person who is dearest to me on earth.

I remember writing to you some weeks since that I would come to London. Little did I know of the weakness of my own mind. I told her that I intended to depart. She turned pale—she trembled—but she did not speak. Those signs which should have hastened my departure have taken away the strength even to think of it.

I am here still! I go to E—— every day. Sometimes we sit in silence; I dare not trust myself to speak. How dangerous are such moments! *Ammutiscon lingue parlen l'alme.*

Yesterday they left us alone. We had been conversing with Lady Margaret on indifferent subjects. There was a pause for some minutes. I looked up; Lady Margaret had left the room. The blood rushed into my cheek—my eyes met Emily's; I would have given worlds to have repeated with my lips what those eyes expressed. I could not even speak—I felt choked with contending emotions. There was not a breath stirring; I heard my very heart beat. A thunderbolt would have been a relief. Oh God! if there be a curse, it is to burn, swell, madden with feelings which you are doomed to conceal! This is, indeed, to be "a cannibal of one's own heart." [1]

It was sunset. Emily was alone upon the lawn which sloped towards the lake, and the blue still waters beneath broke, at bright intervals, through the scattered and illuminated trees. She stood watching the sun sink with wistful and tearful eyes. Her soul was sad within her. The ivy which love first wreathes around his work had already faded away, and she now only saw the desolation of the ruin it concealed. Never more for her was that freshness of unwakened feeling which invests all things with a perpetual daybreak of sunshine, and incense, and dew. The heart may survive the decay or rupture of an innocent and lawful affection—"la marque reste, mais la blessure guérit"—but the love of darkness and guilt is branded in a character ineffaceable—eternal! The one is, like lightning, more likely to dazzle than to destroy, and, divine even in its danger, it *makes holy what it sears;* [2] but the other is like that sure and deadly fire which fell upon the cities of old, graving in the barrenness of the desert it had wrought the record and perpetuation of a curse. A low and thrilling voice stole upon Emily's ear. She turned—Falkland stood beside her. "I felt restless and

---

[1] Bacon.
[2] According to the ancient superstition.

unhappy," he said, "and I came to seek you. If (writes one of the fathers) a guilty and wretched man could behold, though only for a few minutes, the countenance of an angel, the calm and glory which it wears would so sink into his heart, that he would pass at once over the gulf of gone years into his first unsullied state of purity and hope; perhaps I thought of that sentence when I came to you." "I know not," said Emily, with a deep blush at this address, which formed her only answer to the compliment it conveyed; "I know not why it is, but to me there is always something melancholy in this hour—something mournful in seeing the beautiful day die with all its pomp and music, its sunshine, and songs of birds."

"And yet," replied Falkland, "if I remember the time when my feelings were more in unison with yours (for at present external objects have lost for me much of their influence and attraction), the melancholy you perceive has in it a vague and ineffable sweetness not to be exchanged for more exhilarated spirits. The melancholy which arises from no cause within ourselves is like music—it enchants us in proportion to its effect upon our feelings. Perhaps its chief charm (though this it requires the contamination of after years before we can fathom and define) is in the purity of the sources it springs from. Our feelings can be but little sullied and worn while they can yet respond to the passionless and primal sympathies of nature; and the sadness you speak of is so void of bitterness, so allied to the best and most delicious sensations we enjoy, that I should imagine the *very happiness of Heaven partook rather of melancholy than mirth.*"

There was a pause of some moments. It was rarely that Falkland alluded even so slightly to the futurity of another world; and when he did, it was never in a careless and commonplace manner, but in a tone which sank deep into Emily's heart. "Look," she said, at length, "at that beautiful star! the first and brightest! I have often thought it was like the promise of life beyond the tomb—a pledge to us that, even in the depths of midnight, the earth shall have a light, unquenched and unquenchable, from Heaven!"

Emily turned to Falkland as she said this, and her countenance sparkled with the enthusiasm she felt. But *his* face was deadly pale. There went over it, like a cloud, an expression of changeful and unutterable thought; and then, passing suddenly away, it left his features calm and bright in all their noble and intellectual beauty. Her soul yearned to him, as she looked, with the tenderness of a sister.

They walked slowly towards the house. "I have frequently," said Emily, with some hesitation, "been surprised at the little enthusiasm you appear to possess even upon subjects where your conviction must be strong." "*I have thought enthusiasm away!*" replied Falkland; "it was the loss of hope which brought me reflection, and in reflection I forgot to feel. Would that I had not found it so easy to recall what I thought I had lost for ever!"

Falkland's cheek changed as he said this, and Emily sighed faintly, for she felt his meaning. In him that allusion to his love had aroused a whole train of dangerous recollections; for Passion is the avalanche of the human heart—*a single breath can dissolve it from its repose.*

They remained silent; for Falkland would not trust himself to speak, till, when they reached the house, he faltered out his excuses for not entering, and departed. He turned towards his solitary home. The grounds at E—— had been laid out in a classical and costly manner, which contrasted forcibly with the wild and simple nature of the surrounding scenery. Even the short distance between Mr. Mandeville's house and L—— wrought as distinct a change in the character of the country as any length of space could have effected. Falkland's ancient and ruinous abode, with its shattered arches and moss-grown parapets, was situated on a gentle declivity, and surrounded by dark elm and larch trees. It still retained some traces both of its former consequence, and of the perils to which that consequence had exposed it. A broad ditch, overgrown with weeds, indicated the remains of what once had been a moat; and huge rough stones, scattered around it, spoke of the outworks the fortification had anciently possessed, and the stout resistance they had made in "the Parliament Wars" to the sturdy followers of Ireton and Fairfax. The moon, that flatterer of decay, shed its rich and softening beauty over a spot which else had, indeed, been desolate and cheerless, and kissed into light the long and unwaving herbage which rose at intervals from the ruins, like the false parasites of fallen greatness. But for Falkland the scene had no interest or charm, and he turned with a careless and unheeding eye to his customary apartment. It was the only one in the house furnished with luxury, or even comfort. Large book-cases, inlaid with curious carvings in ivory; busts of the few public characters the world had ever produced worthy, in Falkland's estimation, of the homage of posterity; elaborately wrought hangings from Flemish looms; and French fauteuils and sofas of rich damask, and massy gilding (relics of the magnificent days of Louis Quatorze) bespoke a costliness of design suited rather to Falkland's wealth than to the ordinary simplicity of his tastes.

A large writing-table was overspread with books in various languages, and upon the most opposite subjects. Letters and papers were scattered amongst them; Falkland turned carelessly over the latter. One of the epistolary communications was from Lord ——, the ——. He smiled bitterly, as he read the exaggerated compliments it contained, and saw to the bottom of the shallow artifice they were meant to conceal. He tossed the letter from him, and opened the scattered volumes, one after another, with that languid and sated feeling common to all men who have read deeply enough to feel how much they have learned, and how little they know. "We pass our lives," thought he, "in sowing what we are never to reap! We endeavour to erect a tower which shall reach the heavens, in order to escape *one* curse, and lo! we are smitten by *another!* We would soar from a common evil, and from that moment *we are divided by a separate language from our race!* Learning, science, philosophy, the world of men and of imagination, I ransacked—and for what? I centred my happiness in wisdom. I looked upon the aims of others with a scornful and loathing eye. I held commune with those who have gone before me; I dwelt among the monuments of their minds, and made their records familiar to me as friends: I penetrated the womb of nature, and went with the secret elements to their home: I arraigned the stars before me, and learned the method and the mystery of their courses: I asked the tempest its bourn, and questioned the winds of their path. This was not sufficient to satisfy my thirst for knowledge, and I searched in this lower world for new sources to content it. Unseen and unsuspected, I saw and agitated the springs of the automaton that we call "the Mind." I found a clue for the labyrinth of human motives, and I surveyed the hearts of those around me as through a glass. Vanity of vanities! What have I acquired? I have separated myself from my kind, but not from those worst enemies, my passions! I have made a solitude of my soul, but I have not mocked it with the appellation of Peace.[1] In flying the herd, I have not escaped from myself; like the wounded deer, the barb was within me, and *that* I could not fly!" With these thoughts he turned from his reverie, and once more endeavoured to charm his own reflections by those which ought to speak to us of quiet, for they are graven on the pages of the dead; but his attempts were as idle as before. His thoughts were still wandering and confused, and could neither be quieted nor collected; he read, but he scarcely distinguished one page from another: he wrote—the ideas refused to flow at his call; and the only effort at connecting his feelings which even partially succeeded, was in the verses which I am about to place before the reader. It is a common

---

[1] "Solitudinem faciunt, pacem appellant."—TACITUS.
"They make a solitude, and call it peace."—BYRON.

property of poetry, however imperfectly the gift be possessed, to speak to the hearts of others in proportion as the sentiments it would express are felt in our own; and I subjoin the lines which bear the date of that evening, in the hope that, more than many pages, they will show the morbid yet original character of the writer, and the particular sources of feeling from which they took the bitterness that pervades them:—

KNOWLEDGE.

*Ergo hominum genus incassum frustraque laborat
Semper, et in curis consumit inanibus aevum.*—LUCRET.

'Tis midnight! Round the lamp which o'er
  My chamber sheds its lonely beam,
Is wisely spread the varied lore
  Which feeds in youth our feverish dream—

The dream—the thirst—the wild desire,
  Delirious yet divine—to *know;*
Around to roam—above aspire—
  And drink the breath of Heaven below!

From Ocean—Earth—the Stars—the Sky
  To lift mysterious Nature's pall;
And bare before the kindling eye
  In MAN the darkest mist of all!

Alas! what boots the midnight oil?
  The madness of the struggling mind?
Oh, vague the hope, and vain the toil,
  Which only leave us doubly blind!

What learn we from the Past?—the same
  Dull course of glory, guilt, and gloom:
I ask'd the Future, and there came
  No voice from its unfathom'd womb.

The Sun was silent, and the wave;
  The air but answer'd with its breath;
But Earth was kind; and from the grave
  Arose the eternal answer—*Death!*

And *this* was all! We need no sage
  To teach us Nature's only truth!
O fools! o'er Wisdom's idle page
  To waste the hours of golden youth!

In Science wildly do we seek
  What only withering years should bring—
The languid pulse—the feverish cheek—
  The spirits drooping on their wing!

To think—is but to learn to groan—
  To scorn what all beside adore—
To feel amid the world alone,
  An alien on a desert shore;—

> To lose the only ties which seem
> To idler gaze in mercy given!—
> To find love, faith, and hope, a dream,
> And turn to dark despair from heaven!

* * * * *

I pass on to a wilder period of my history. The passion, as yet only revealed by the eye, was now to be recorded by the lip; and the scene which witnessed the first confession of the lovers was worthy of the last conclusion of their loves!

E—— was about twelve miles from a celebrated cliff on the seashore, and Lady Margaret had long proposed an excursion to a spot, curious alike for its natural scenery and the legends attached to it. A day was at length fixed for accomplishing this plan. Falkland was of the party. In searching for something in the pockets of the carriage, his hand met Emily's, and involuntarily pressed it. She withdrew it hastily, but he felt it tremble. He did not dare to look up: that single contact had given him a new life: intoxicated with the most delicious sensations, he leaned back in silence. A fever had entered his veins—the thrill of the touch had gone like fire into his system—all his frame seemed one nerve.

Lady Margaret talked of the weather and the prospect, wondered how far they had got, and animadverted on the roads, till at last, like a child, she talked herself to rest. Mrs. Dalton read "Guy Mannering;" but neither Emily nor her lover had any occupation or thought in common with their companions: silent and absorbed, they were only alive to the vivid existence of the present. Constantly engaged, as we are, in looking behind us or before, if there be one hour in which we feel only the time being—in which we feel sensibly that we live, and that those moments of the present are full of the enjoyment, the rapture of existence—it is when we are with the *one* person whose life and spirits have become the great part and principle of our own. They reached their destination—a small inn close by the shore. They rested there a short time, and then strolled along the sands towards the cliff. Since Falkland had known Emily, her character was much altered. Six weeks before the time I write of, and in playfulness and lightness of spirits she was almost a child: now those indications of an unawakened heart had mellowed into a tenderness full of that melancholy so touching and holy, even amid the voluptuous softness which it breathes and inspires. But this day, whether from that coquetry so common to all women, or from some cause more natural to *her*, she seemed gayer than Falkland ever remembered to have seen her. She ran over the sands, picking up shells, and tempting the waves with her small and fairy feet, not daring to look at him, and yet speaking to him at times with a quick tone of levity which hurt and offended him, even though he knew the depth of those feelings she could not disguise either from him or from herself. By degrees his answers and remarks grew cold and sarcastic. Emily affected pique ; and when it was discovered that the cliff was still nearly two miles off, she refused to proceed any farther. Lady Margaret talked her at last into consent, and they walked on as sullenly as an English party of pleasure possibly could do, till they were within three quarters of a mile of the place, when Emily declared she was so tired that she really could not go on. Falkland looked at her, perhaps, with no very amiable expression of countenance, when he perceived that she seemed really pale and fatigued ; and when she caught his eyes, tears rushed into her own.

"Indeed, indeed, Mr. Falkland," said she, eagerly, "this is *not* affectation. I am very tired ; but rather than prevent your amusement, I will endeavour to go on." "Nonsense, child," said Lady Margaret, "you *do* seem tired. Mrs. Dalton and Falkland shall go to the rock, and I will stay here with you." This proposition, however, Lady Emily (who knew Lady Margaret's wish to see the rock) would not hear of; she insisted upon staying by herself. "Nobody will run away with me ; and I can very easily amuse myself with picking up shells till you come back." After a long remonstrance, which produced no effect, this plan was at last acceded to. With great reluctance Falkland set off with his two companions; but after the first step, he turned to look back. He caught her eye, and felt from that moment that their reconciliation was sealed. They arrived, at last, at the cliff. Its height, its excavations, the romantic interest which the traditions respecting it had inspired, fully repaid the two women for the fatigue of their walk. As for Falkland, he was unconscious of everything around him ; he was full of "sweet and bitter thoughts." In vain the man whom they found loitering there, in order to serve as a guide, kept dinning in his ear stories of the marvellous, and exclamations of the sublime. The first words which aroused him were these—"It's lucky, please your Honour, that you have just saved the tide. It is but last week that three poor people were drowned in attempting to come here ; as it is, you will have to go home round the cliff. Falkland started : he felt his heart stand still. "Good God !" cried Lady Margaret, "what will become of Emily ?"

They were at that instant in one of the caverns, where they had already been loitering too long. Falkland rushed out to the sands. The tide was hurrying in with a deep sound, which came on his soul like a knell. He looked back towards the way they had come : not one hundred yards distant, and the waters had already covered the path! An eternity would scarcely atone for the horror of that moment! One great characteristic of Falkland was his presence of mind. He turned to the man who stood beside him—he gave him a cool and exact description of the spot where he had left Emily. He told him to repair with all possible speed to his home—to launch his boat—to row it to the place he had described. "Be quick," he added, "and you *must* be in time: if you are, you shall never know poverty again." The next moment he was already several yards from the spot. He ran or rather flew, till he was stopped by the waters. He rushed in; they were over a hollow between two rocks —they were already up to his chest. "There is yet hope," thought he, when he had passed the spot, and saw the smooth sand before him. For some minutes he was scarcely sensible of existence; and then he found himself breathless at *her* feet. Beyond, towards T—— (the small inn I spoke of), the waves had already reached the foot of the rocks, and precluded all hope of return. Their only chance was the possibility that the waters had not yet rendered impassable the hollow through which Falkland had just waded. He scarcely spoke; at least he was totally unconscious of what he said. He hurried her on breathless and trembling, with the sound of the booming waters ringing in his ear, and their billows advancing to his very feet. They arrived at the hollow: a single glance sufficed to show him that their solitary hope was past! The waters, before up to his chest, had swelled considerably: he could not swim. He saw in that instant that they were girt with a hastening and terrible death. Can it be believed that with that certainty ceased his fear? He looked in the pale but calm countenance of her who clung to him, and a strange tranquillity, even mingled with joy, possessed him. Her breath was on his cheek—her form was reclining on his own— his hand clasped hers; if they were to die, it was thus. What could life afford to him more dear? "It is in this moment," said he, and he knelt as he spoke, "that I dare tell you what otherwise my lips never should have revealed. I love—I adore you! Turn not away from me thus. In life our persons were severed; if our hearts are united in death, then death will be sweet." She turned—*her cheek was no longer pale!* He rose—he clasped her to his bosom: his lips pressed hers. Oh! that long, deep, burning pressure!—youth, love, life, soul, all concentrated in that one kiss! Yet the same cause which occasioned the avowal hallowed also the madness of his heart. What had the passion, declared only at the approach of death, with the more earthly desires of life? They looked to heaven —it was calm and unclouded: the evening lay there in its balm and perfume, and the air was less agitated than their sighs. They turned towards the beautiful sea which was to be their grave: the wild birds flew over it exultingly: the far vessels seemed "rejoicing to run their course." All was full of the breath, the glory, the life of nature; and in how many minutes was all to be as *nothing!* Their existence would resemble the ships that have gone down at sea in the very smile of the element that destroyed them. They looked into each other's eyes, and they drew still nearer together. Their hearts, in safety apart, mingled in peril and became one. Minutes rolled on, and the great waves came dashing round them. They stood on the loftiest eminence they could reach. The spray broke over their feet; the billows rose—rose—they were speechless. He thought he heard her heart beat, but her lip trembled not. A speck—a boat! "Look up, Emily! look up! See how it cuts the waters. Nearer —nearer! but a little longer, and we are safe. It is but a few yards off—it approaches—it touches the rock!" Ah! what to them henceforth was the value of life, when the moment of discovering its charm became also the date of its misfortunes, and when the death they had escaped was the only method of cementing their union without consummating their guilt?

FROM ERASMUS FALKLAND, ESQ., TO THE HON. FREDERICK MONKTON.

I will write to you at length to-morrow. Events have occurred to alter, perhaps, the whole complexion of the future. I am now going to Emily to propose to her to fly. We are not *les gens du monde*, who are ruined by the loss of public opinion. She has felt that I can be to her far more than the world; and as for me, what would I not forfeit for one touch of her hand?

EXTRACTS FROM THE JOURNAL OF LADY EMILY MANDEVILLE.

Friday.—Since I wrote yesterday in these pages the narrative of our escape, I have done nothing but think over those moments, too dangerous because too dear; but at last I have steeled my heart—I have yielded to my own weakness too long—I shudder at the abyss from which I have escaped. I can yet fly. He will come here to-day—he shall receive my farewell.

Saturday morning, four o'clock.—I have sat in this room alone since eleven o'clock. I cannot give vent to my feelings; they seem as if crushed by some load from which it is impossible to rise. "*He is gone, and for ever!*" I sit repeating those words to myself, scarcely

c

conscious of their meaning. Alas! when to-morrow comes, and the next day, and the next, and yet I see him not, I shall awaken, indeed, to all the agony of my loss! He came here—he saw me alone—he implored me to fly. I did not dare to meet his eyes; I hardened my heart against his voice. I knew the part I was to take—I have adopted it; but what struggles, what misery, has it not occasioned me! Who could have thought it had been so hard to be virtuous! His eloquence drove me from one defence to another, and then I had none but *his* mercy. I opened my heart—I showed him its weakness —I implored his forbearance. My tears, my anguish, convinced him of my sincerity. We have parted in bitterness, but, thank Heaven, not in guilt! He has entreated permission to write to me. How could I refuse him? Yet I may not—cannot—write to him again! How *could* I, indeed, suffer my heart to pour forth one of its feeelings in reply? for would there be one word of regret, or one term of endearment, which my inmost soul would not echo?

Sunday.—Yes, *that day*—but I must not think of this; my very religion I dare not indulge. Oh God! how wretched I am! His visit was always the great æra in the day; it employed all my hopes till he came, and all *my memory* when he was gone. I sit now and look at the place he used to fill, till I feel the tears rolling silently down my cheek: they come without an effort—they depart without relief.

Monday.—Henry asked me where Mr. Falkland was gone; I stooped down to hide my confusion. When shall I hear from him? To-morrow? Oh that it were come! I have placed the clock before me, and I actually count the minutes. He left a book here; it is a volume of "Melmoth." I have read over every word of it, and whenever I have come to a pencil-mark by him, I have paused to dream over that varying and eloquent countenance, the low soft tone of that tender voice, till the book has fallen from my hands, and I have started to find the utterness of my desolation!

FROM ERASMUS FALKLAND, ESQ., TO LADY EMILY MANDEVILLE.

— Hotel, London.

For the first time in my life I write to you! How my hand trembles—how my cheek flushes! a thousand, thousand thoughts rush upon me, and almost suffocate me with the variety and confusion of the emotions they awaken! I am agitated alike with the rapture of writing to you, and with the impossibility of expressing the feelings which I cannot distinctly unravel even to myself. You love me, Emily, and yet I have fled from you, and at your command;

but the thought that, though absent, I am not forgotten, supports me through all.

It was with a feverish sense of weariness and pain that I found myself entering this vast reservoir of human vices. I became at once sensible of the sterility of that polluted soil so incapable of nurturing affection, and I clasped your image the closer to my heart. It is you, who, when I was most weary of existence, gifted me with a new life. You breathed into me a part of your own spirit; my soul feels that influence, and becomes more sacred. I have shut myself from the idlers who would molest me: I have built a temple in my heart: I have set within it a divinity; and the vanities of the world shall not profane the spot which has been consecrated to *you*. Our parting, Emily,—do you recall it? Your hand clasped in mine; your cheek resting, though but for an instant, on my bosom; and the tears which love called forth, but which virtue purified even at their source. Never were hearts so near, yet so divided; never was there an hour so tender yet so unaccompanied with danger. Passion, grief, madness, all sank beneath your voice, and lay hushed like a deep sea within my soul! "Tu abbia veduto il leone ammansarsi alla sola tua voce." [1]

I tore myself from you; I hurried through the wood; I stood by the lake, on whose banks I had so often wandered with you: I bared my breast to the winds; I bathed my temples with the waters. Fool that I was! the fever, the fever was within! But it is not thus, my adored and beautiful friend, that I should console and support you. Even as I write, passion melts into tenderness, and pours itself in softness over your remembrance. The virtue so gentle, yet so strong; the feelings so kind, yet so holy, the tears which wept over the decision your lips proclaimed—these are the recollections which come over me like dew. Let your own heart, my Emily, be your reward; and know that your lover only forgets that he *adores*, to remember that he *respects* you!

FROM THE SAME TO THE SAME.

— Park.

I could not bear the tumult and noise of London. I sighed for solitude, that I might muse over your remembrance undisturbed. I came here yesterday. It is the home of my childhood. I am surrounded on all sides by the scenes and images consecrated by the fresh recollections of my unsullied years. *They* are not changed. The seasons which come and depart renew in them the havoc which

---

[1] Ultime lettere di Jacopo Ortis.

they make. If the December destroys, the April revives; but man has but one spring, and the desolation of the heart but one winter! In this very room have I sat and brooded over dreams and hopes which—but no matter—those dreams could never show me a vision to equal you, or those hopes hold out to me a blessing so precious as your love.

Do you remember, or rather can you ever forget, that moment in which the great depths of our souls were revealed? Ah! not in the scene in which such vows should have been whispered to your ear, and your tenderness have blushed its reply. The passion concealed in darkness was revealed in danger; and the love, which in life was forbidden, was our comfort amidst the terrors of death! And that long and holy kiss, the first, the only moment in which our lips shared the union of our souls!—do not tell me that it is wrong to recall it!—do not tell me that I sin, when I own to you the hours I sit alone, and nurse the delirium of that voluptuous remembrance. The feelings you have excited may render me wretched, but not guilty; for the love of *you* can only *hallow* the heart—it is a fire which consecrates the altar on which it burns. I feel, even from the hour that I loved, that my soul has become more pure. I could not have believed that *I* was capable of so unearthly an affection, or that the love of woman could possess that divinity of virtue which I worship in yours. The world is no fosterer of our young visions of purity and passion: embarked in its pursuits, and acquainted with its pleasures, while the latter sated me with what is evil, the former made me incredulous to what is pure. I considered your sex as a problem which my experience had already solved. Like the French philosophers, who lose truth by endeavouring to condense it, and who forfeit the *moral* from their regard to the *maxim*, I concentrated my knowledge of women into aphorisms and antitheses; and I did not dream of the exceptions, if I did not find myself deceived in the general conclusion. I confess that I erred; I renounce from this moment the colder reflections of my manhood,—the fruits of a bitter experience,—the wisdom of an inquiring yet agitated life. I return with transport to my earliest visions of beauty and love; and I dedicate them upon the altar of my soul to you, who have embodied, and concentrated, and breathed them into life!

EXTRACTS FROM THE JOURNAL OF LADY EMILY MANDEVILLE.

Monday.—This is the most joyless day in the whole week; for it can bring me no letter from him. I rise listlessly, and read over again and again the last letter I received from him—useless task! it is graven on my heart! I long only for the day to be over, because to-morrow I may, perhaps, hear from him again. When I wake at night from my disturbed and broken sleep, I look if the morning is near; not because it gives light and life, but because it may bring tidings of him. When his letter is brought to me, I keep it for minutes unopened—I feed my eyes on the handwriting—I examine the seal—I press it with my kisses, before I indulge myself in the luxury of reading it. I then place it in my bosom, and take it thence only to read it again and again,—to moisten it with my tears of gratitude and love, and, alas! of penitence and remorse! What can be the end of this affection? I dare neither to hope that it may continue or that it may cease; in either case I am wretched for ever!

Monday night, twelve o'clock.—They observe my paleness; the tears which tremble in my eyes; the listlessness and dejection of my manner. I think Mrs. Dalton guesses the cause. Humbled and debased in my own mind, I fly, Falkland, for refuge to you! Your affection cannot raise me to my former state, but it can reconcile—no—not reconcile, but support me in my present. This dear letter, I kiss it again—oh! that to-morrow were come!

Tuesday.—Another letter, so kind, so tender, so encouraging: would that I deserved his praises! alas! I sin even in reading them. I know that I ought to struggle more against my feelings—*once* I attempted it; I prayed to Heaven to support me; I put away from me everything that could recall him to my mind—for three days I would not open his letters. I could then resist no longer; and my weakness became the more confirmed from the feebleness of the struggle. I remember one day that he told us of a beautiful passage in one of the ancients, in which the bitterest curse against the wicked is, that they may see virtue, but not be able to obtain it;[1]—*that* punishment is mine!

Wednesday.—My boy has been with me: I see him now from the windows gathering the field-flowers, and running after every butterfly which comes across him. Formerly he made all my delight and occupation; now he is even dearer to me than ever; but he no longer engrosses all my thoughts. I turn over the leaves of this journal; once it noted down the little occurrences of the day; it marks nothing now but the monotony of sadness. *He* is not here—*he* cannot come. What event then *could* I notice?

[1] Persius.

FROM ERASMUS FALKLAND, ESQ., TO LADY EMILY MANDEVILLE.[1]

— Park.

If you knew how I long, how I thirst, for one word from you—one word to say you are well, and have not forgotten me!—but I will not distress you. You will guess my feelings, and do justice to the restraint I impose on them, when I make no effort to alter your resolution not to write. I know that it is just, and I bow to my sentence; but can you blame me if I am restless, and if I repine? It is past twelve; I always write to you at night. It is then, my own love, that my imagination can the more readily transport me to you: it is then that my spirit holds with you a more tender and undivided commune. In the day the world can force itself upon my thoughts, and its trifles usurp the place which "I love to keep for only thee and Heaven;" but in the night all things recall you the more vividly: the stillness of the gentle skies,—the blandness of the unbroken air,—the stars, so holy in their loveliness, all speak and breathe to me of you. I think your hand is clasped in mine; and I again drink the low music of your voice, and imbibe again in the air the breath which has been perfumed by your lips. You seem to stand in my lonely chamber in the light and stillness of a spirit, who has wandered on earth to teach us the love which is felt in Heaven.

I cannot, believe me, I cannot endure this separation long; it must be more or less. You must be mine for ever, or our parting must be without a mitigation, which is rather a cruelty than a relief. If you will not accompany me, I will leave this country alone. I must not wean myself from your image by degrees, but break from the enchantment at once. And when, Emily, I am once more upon the world, when no tidings of my fate shall reach your ear, and all its power of alienation be left to the progress of time—then, when you will at last have forgotten me, when your peace of mind will be restored, and, having no struggles of conscience to undergo, you will have no remorse to endure; then, Emily, when we are indeed divided, let the scene which has witnessed our passion, the letters which have recorded my vow, the evil we have suffered, and the temptation we have overcome; let these in our old age be remembered, and in declaring to Heaven that we were innocent, add also—*that we loved*.

[1] Most of the letters from Falkland to Lady E. Mandeville I have thought it expedient to suppress.

FROM DON ALPHONSO D'AGUILA TO DON ——.

London.

Our cause gains ground daily. The great, indeed the only ostensible object of my mission is nearly fulfilled; but I have another charge and attraction which I am now about to explain to you. You know that my acquaintance with the English language and country arose from my sister's marriage with Mr. Falkland. After the birth of their only child I accompanied them to England: I remained with them for three years, and I still consider those days among the whitest in my restless and agitated career. I returned to Spain; I became engaged in the troubles and dissensions which distracted my unhappy country. Years rolled on, *how* I need not mention to *you*. One night they put a letter into my hands; it was from my sister; it was written on her death-bed. Her husband had died suddenly. She loved him as a Spanish woman loves, and she could not survive his loss. Her letter to me spoke of her country and her son. Amid the new ties she had formed in England, she had never forgotten the land of her fathers. "I have already," she said, "taught my boy to remember that he has two countries; that the one, prosperous and free, may afford him his pleasures; that the other, struggling and debased, demands from him his duties. If, when he has attained the age in which you can judge of his character, he is respectable only from his rank, and valuable only from his wealth; if neither his head nor his heart will make him useful to *our* cause, suffer him to remain undisturbed in his prosperity *here:* but if, as I presage, he becomes worthy of the blood which he bears in his veins, then I conjure you, my brother, to remind him that he has been sworn by me on my death-bed to the most sacred of earthly altars."

Some months since, when I arrived in England, before I ventured to find him out in person, I resolved to inquire into his character. Had he been as the young and the rich generally are—had dissipation become habitual to him, and frivolity grown around him as a second nature, then I should have acquiesced in the former injunction of my sister much more willingly than I shall now obey the latter. I find that he is perfectly acquainted with our language, that he has placed a large sum in our funds, and that from the general liberality of his sentiments he is as likely to espouse, as (in that case) he would be certain, from his high reputation for talent, to serve, our cause. I am, therefore, upon the eve of seeking him out. I understand that he is living in perfect retirement in the county of ——, in the immediate neighbourhood of Mr. Mandeville, an Englishman of considerable fortune, and warmly attached to our cause.

Mr. Mandeville has invited me to accompany him down to his estate for some days, and I am too anxious to see my nephew not to accept eagerly of the invitation. If I can persuade Falkland to aid us, it will be by the influence of his name, his talents, and his wealth. It is not of him that we can ask the stern and laborious devotion to which we have consecrated ourselves. The perfidy of friends, the vigilance of foes, the rashness of the bold, the cowardice of the wavering; strife in the closet, treachery in the senate, death in the field; *these* constitute the fate we have pledged ourselves to bear. Little can any, who do not endure it, imagine of the life to which those who share the contests of an agitated and distracted country are doomed; but if they know not our griefs, neither can they dream of our consolation. We move like the delineation of Faith, over a barren and desert soil: the rock, and the thorn, and the stings of the adder, are round our feet; but we clasp a crucifix to our hearts for our comfort, and we fix our eyes upon the heavens for our hope!

EXTRACTS FROM THE JOURNAL OF LADY EMILY MANDEVILLE.

Wednesday.—His letters have taken a different tone: instead of soothing, they add to my distress; but I deserve all—all that can be inflicted upon me. I have had a letter from Mr. Mandeville. He is coming down here for a few days, and intends bringing some friends with him: he mentions particularly a Spaniard—*the uncle of Mr. Falkland, whom he asks if I have seen.* The Spaniard is particularly anxious to meet his nephew—he does not then know that Falkland is gone. It will be some relief to see Mr. Mandeville alone; but even then how shall I meet him? What shall I say when he observes my paleness and alteration? I feel bowed to the very dust.

Thursday evening.—Mr. Mandeville has arrived: fortunately, it was late in the evening before he came, and the darkness prevented his observing my confusion and alteration. He was kinder than usual. Oh! how bitterly my heart avenged him! He brought with him the Spaniard, Don Alphonso d'Aguila; I think there is a faint family likeness between him and Falkland. Mr. Mandeville brought also a letter from Julia. She will be here the day after to-morrow. The letter is short, but kind: she does not allude to *him;* it is some days since I heard from him.

FROM ERASMUS FALKLAND, ESQ., TO THE HON.
FREDERICK MONKTON.

I have resolved, Monkton, to go to her again! I am sure that it will be better for both of us to meet once more; perhaps, to unite for ever! None who have once loved me can easily forget me. I do not say this from vanity, because I owe it not to my being *superior* to, but *different* from, others. I am sure that the remorse and affliction she feels now are far greater than she would experience, even were she more guilty, and with me. *Then*, at least, she would have some one to soothe and sympathize in whatever she might endure. To one so pure as Emily, the full crime is already incurred. It is not the innocent who insist upon that nice line of morality between the thought and the action: such distinctions require reflection, experience, deliberation, prudence of head, or coldness of heart; these are the traits, not of the guileless, but of the worldly. It is the *affections*, not the *person*, of a virtuous woman, which it is difficult to obtain: that difficulty is the safeguard to her chastity; that difficulty I have, in this instance, overcome. I have endeavoured to live without Emily, but in vain. Every moment of absence only taught me the impossibility. In twenty-four hours I shall see her again. I feel my pulse rise into fever at the very thought.

Farewell, Monkton. My next letter, I hope, will record my triumph.

BOOK III.

EXTRACTS FROM THE JOURNAL OF LADY EMILY MANDEVILLE.

RIDAY.—Julia is here, and so kind! She has not mentioned *his* name, but she sighed so deeply when she saw my pale and sunken countenance, that I threw myself into her arms and cried like a child. We had no need of other explanation: those tears spoke at once my confession and my repentance. No letter from him for several days! Surely he is not ill! how miserable that thought makes me!

Saturday.—A note has just been brought me from him. He is come back—*here!* Good heavens! how very imprudent! I am so agitated that I can write no more.

Sunday.—I have seen him! Let me repeat that sentence—*I have seen him.* Oh that moment! did it not atone for all that I have suffered? I dare not write everything he said, but he wished me to fly with him——*him*—what happiness, yet what guilt, in the very thought! Oh! this foolish heart—would that it might break! I feel too well the sophistry of his arguments, and yet I cannot resist them. He seems to have thrown a spell over me, which precludes even the effort to escape.

Monday.—Mr. Mandeville has asked several people in the country to dine here to-morrow, and there is to be a ball in the evening. Falkland is of course invited. We shall meet then, and *how?* I have been so little accustomed to disguise my feelings, that I quite tremble to meet him with so many witnesses around. Mr. Mandeville has been so harsh to me to-day; if Falkland ever looked at me so, or ever said one such word, my heart would indeed break. What is it Alfieri says about the two demons to whom he is for ever a prey? "*La mente e il cor in perp.tua lite.*" Alas! at times I start from my reveries with such a keen sense of agony and shame! How, how am I fallen!

Tuesday.—He is to come here to-day, and I shall see him!

Wednesday morning.—The night is over, thank Heaven! Falkland came late to dinner: every one else was assembled. How gracefully he entered! how superior he seemed to all the crowd that stood around him! He appeared as if he were resolved to exert powers which he had disdained before. He entered into the conversation, not only with such brilliancy, but with such a blandness and courtesy of manner! There was no scorn on his lip, no haughtiness on his forehead—nothing which showed him for a moment conscious of his immeasurable superiority over every one present. After dinner, as we retired, I caught his eyes. What volumes they told!—and then I had to listen to his praises, *and say nothing*. I felt angry even in my pleasure. Who but I had a right to speak of him so well!

The ball came on: I felt languid and dispirited. Falkland did not dance. He sat himself by me—he urged me to—O God! O God! would that I were dead!

FROM ERASMUS FALKLAND, ESQ., TO LADY EMILY MANDEVILLE.

How are you this morning, my adored friend? You seemed pale and ill when we parted last night, and I shall be *so* unhappy till I hear something of you. Oh Emily, when you listened to me with those tearful and downcast looks: when I saw your bosom heave at every word which I whispered in your ear; when, as I accidentally touched your hand, I felt it tremble beneath my own; oh! was there nothing in those moments at your heart which pleaded for me more eloquently than words? Pure and holy as you are, you know not, it is true, the feelings which burn and madden in me. When you are beside me, your hand, if it trembles, is not on fire: your voice, if it is more subdued, does not falter with the emotions it dares not express: your heart is not, like mine, devoured by a parching and wasting flame: your sleep is not turned by restless and turbulent dreams from the healthful renewal, into the very consumer, of life. No, Emily! God forbid that you *should* feel the guilt, the agony which preys upon me; but, at least, in the fond and gentle tenderness of your heart, there must be a voice you find it difficult to silence. Amidst all the fictitious ties and fascinations of art, you cannot dismiss from your bosom the unconquerable impulses of nature. What is it you fear?—you will answer, *disgrace!* But *can* you feel it, Emily, when you share it with me? Believe me that the love which is nursed through shame and sorrow is of a deeper and holier nature than that which is reared in pride, and fostered in joy. But, if not shame, it is guilt, perhaps, which you dread? Are you then so innocent *now?* The adultery of the heart is no less a crime than that of the deed ; and—yet **I will** not deceive you —it *is* guilt to which I tempt you !—*it is* a **fall** from the proud eminence you hold **now.** I grant this, and I offer **you** nothing in recompense but my love. If you loved like me, you **would** feel that it was something of pride—of triumph—to dare all **things,** even crime, **for** the one **to** whom all things are as nought ! **As for me, I** know that if **a voice from** Heaven told me to desert you, **I would** only **clasp you** the **closer to** my heart !

I **tell** you, my own love, that when your hand is in mine, when **your** head rests upon my bosom, when those soft and thrilling eyes **shall be** fixed upon my own, when every sigh shall be mingled with my breath, and every tear be kissed away at the very instant it rises from its source—I tell you that then you shall only feel that every pang of the past, and every fear for the future, shall be but a new link to bind us the firmer to each other. Emily, my life, my love, you cannot, if you would, desert me. Who can separate **the** waters, which are once united, or divide the hearts which have met and mingled into one ?

Since **they had once** more met, it will be perceived that Falkland had **adopted a new tone in** expressing his passion to Emily. **In** the **book of** guilt another page, branded in a deeper and more burning character, had been turned. He lost no opportunity of summoning the earthlier emotions to the support of his cause. He wooed her fancy with the golden language of poetry, and strove to arouse the latent feelings of her sex by the soft magic of his voice, and the passionate meaning it conveyed. But at times there came over him a deep and keen sentiment of remorse ; and even, as his experienced and practised eye saw the moment of his triumph approach, he felt that the success he was hazarding his own soul and hers to obtain, might bring him a momentary transport, but not a permanent happiness. There is always this difference in the love of women and of men ; that in the former, when once admitted, it engrosses all the sources of thought, and excludes every object but itself ; but in the latter, it is shared with all the former reflections and feelings which the past yet bequeaths us, and can neither (however powerful **be** its nature) constitute *the whole* of our happiness or woe. The **love** of **man** in his maturer years is not indeed so much a new emotion, **as a** revival and concentration of all his departed affections to others ; and the deep and intense nature of Falkland's passion for Emily was linked with the recollections of whatever he had formerly cherished as tender or dear ; it touched— it awoke a long chain of young and enthusiastic feelings, which arose, perhaps, the fresher from their slumber. Who, when he turns to recall his first and fondest associations; when he throws off, one by one, the layers of earth and stone which have grown and hardened over the records of the past: who has not been surprised to discover how fresh and unimpaired those buried treasures rise again upon his heart? They have been laid up in the store-house of Time; they have not perished; their very concealment has preserved them! *We remove the lava, and the world of a gone day is before us!*

The evening of the day on which Falkland had written the above letter was rude and stormy. The various streams with which the country abounded were swelled by late rains into an unwonted rapidity and breadth; and their voices blended with the rushing sound of the winds, and the distant roll of the thunder, which began at last sullenly to subside. The whole of the scene around L—— was of that savage yet sublime character, which suited well with the wrath of the aroused elements. Dark woods, large tracts of unenclosed heath, abrupt variations of hill and vale, and a dim and broken outline beyond of uninterrupted mountains, formed the great features of that romantic country.

It was filled with the recollections of his youth, and of the wild delight which he took then in the convulsions and varieties of nature, that Falkland roamed abroad that evening. The dim shadows of years, crowded with concealed events and corroding reflections, all gathered around his mind, and the gloom and tempest of the night came over him like the sympathy of a friend.

He passed a group of terrified peasants; they were cowering under a tree. The oldest hid his head and shuddered; but the youngest looked steadily at the lightning which played at fitful intervals over the mountain stream that rushed rapidly by their feet. Falkland stood beside them unnoticed and silent, with folded arms and a scornful lip. To him, nature, heaven, earth, had nothing for fear, and everything for reflection. In youth, thought he (as he contrasted the fear felt at one period of life with the indifference at another), there are so many objects to divide and distract life, that we are scarcely sensible of the collected conviction that we live. We lose the sense of what *is* by thinking rather of what is *to be*. But the old, who have no future to expect, are more vividly alive to the present, and they feel death more, because they have a more settled and perfect impression of existence.

He left the group, and went on alone by the margin of the winding and swelling stream. "It is (said a certain philosopher) in the conflicts of Nature that man most feels his littleness." Like all general maxims, this is only partially true. The mind, which takes its first ideas from perception, must take also its tone from the character of the objects perceived. In mingling our spirits with the great elements, we partake of their sublimity; we awaken thought from the secret depths where it had lain concealed; our feelings are too excited to remain riveted to ourselves; they blend with the mighty powers which are abroad; and, as in the agitations of men, the individual arouses from himself to become a part of the crowd, so in the convulsions of nature we are equally awakened from the littleness of self, to be lost in the grandeur of the conflict by which we are surrounded.

Falkland still continued to track the stream: it wound its way through Mandeville's grounds, and broadened at last into the lake which was so consecrated to his recollections. He paused at that spot for some moments, looking carelessly over the wide expanse of waters, now dark as night, and now flashing into one mighty plain of fire beneath the coruscations of the lightning. The clouds swept on in massy columns, dark and aspiring—veiling, while they rolled up to, the great heavens, like the shadows of human doubt. Oh! weak, weak was that dogma of the philosopher! There is a *pride* in the storm which, according to his doctrine, would debase us; a stirring music in its roar; even a savage joy in its destruction: for we can exult in a defiance of its power, even while we share in its triumphs, in a consciousness of a superior spirit within us to that which is around. We can mock at the fury of the elements, for they are less terrible than the passions of the heart; at the devastations of the awful skies, for they are less desolating than the wrath of man; at the convulsions of that surrounding nature which has no peril, no terror to the soul, which is more indestructible and eternal than itself. Falkland turned towards the house which contained *his* world; and as the lightning revealed at intervals the white columns of the porch, and wrapped in sheets of fire, like a spectral throng, the tall and waving trees by which it was encircled, and then as suddenly ceased, and "the jaws of darkness" devoured up the scene; he compared, with that bitter alchymy of feeling which resolves all into one crucible of thought, those alternations of light and shadow to the history of his own guilty love—that passion whose birth was the womb of Night: shrouded in darkness, surrounded by storms, and receiving only from the angry heavens a momentary brilliance, more terrible than its customary gloom.

As he entered the saloon, Lady Margaret advanced towards him. "My dear Falkland," said she, "how good it is in you to come in such a night. We have been watching the skies till Emily grew terrified at the lightning ; *formerly* it did not alarm her." And Lady Margaret turned, utterly unconscious of the reproach she had conveyed, towards Emily.

Did not Falkland's look turn also to that spot? Lady Emily was sitting by the harp which Mrs. St. John appeared to be most seriously employed in tuning : her countenance was bent downwards, and burning beneath the blushes called forth by the gaze which she *felt* was upon her.

There was in Falkland's character a peculiar dislike to all outward display of less worldly emotions. He had none of the vanity most men have in conquest ; he would not have had any human being know that he was loved. He was right ! No altar should be so unseen and inviolable as the human heart ! He saw at once and relieved the embarrassment he had caused. With the remarkable fascination and grace of manner so peculiarly his own, he made his excuses to Lady Margaret for his disordered dress ; he charmed his uncle, Don Alphonso, with a quotation from Lopez de Vega ; he inquired tenderly of Mrs. Dalton touching the health of her Italian greyhound ; and then—nor till then—he ventured to approach Emily, and speak to her in that soft tone, which, like a fairy language, is understood only by the person it addresses. Mrs. St. John rose and left the harp ; Falkland took her seat. He bent down to whisper to Emily. His long hair touched her cheek ! it was still wet with the night dew. She looked up as she felt it, and met his gaze : better had it been to have lost earth than to have drunk the soul's poison from that eye when it tempted to sin.

Mrs. St. John stood at some distance : Don Alphonso was speaking to her of his nephew, and of his hopes of ultimately gaining him to the cause of his mother's country. "See you not," said Mrs. St. John, and her colour went and came, "that while he has such attractions to detain him, your hopes are in vain?" "What mean you?" replied the Spaniard ; but his eye had followed the direction she had given it, and the question came only from his lips. Mrs. St. John drew him to a still remoter corner of the room, and it was in the conversation that then ensued between them, that they agreed to unite for the purpose of separating Emily from her lover—"I to save my friend," said Mrs. St. John, "and you your kinsman." Thus it is with human virtue :—the fair show and the good deed without—the one eternal motive of selfishness within. During the Spaniard's visit at E——, he had seen enough of Falkland to perceive the great consequence he might, from his perfect knowledge of the Spanish language, from his singular powers, and, above all, from his command of wealth, be to the cause of that party he himself had adopted. His aim, therefore, was now no longer confined to procuring Falkland's good will and aim at home: he hoped to secure his personal assistance in Spain; and he willingly coincided with Mrs. St. John in detaching his nephew from a tie so likely to detain him from that service to which Alphonso wished he should be pledged.

Mandeville had left E—— that morning: he suspected nothing of Emily's attachment. This, on his part, was less confidence than indifference. He was one of those persons who have no existence separate from their own: his senses all turned inwards; they reproduced selfishness. Even the House of Commons was only an object of interest because he imagined it *a part of him, not he of it.* He said, with the insect on the wheel, "Admire *our* rapidity." But did the defects of his character remove Lady Emily's guilt? No! and this, at times, was her bitterest conviction. Whoever turns to these pages for an apology for sin will be mistaken. They contain the burning records of its sufferings, its repentance, and its doom. If there be one crime in the history of woman worse than another, it is adultery. It is, in fact, the only crime to which, in ordinary life, she is exposed. Man has a thousand temptations to sin—woman has but one; if she cannot resist it, she has no claim upon our mercy. The heavens are just! her own guilt is her punishment! Should these pages, at this moment, meet the eyes of one who has become the centre of a circle of disgrace—the contaminator of her house—the dishonour of her children,—no matter what the excuse for her crime —no matter what the exchange of her station—in the very arms of her lover, in the very cincture of the new ties which she has chosen— I call upon her to answer me if the fondest moments of rapture are free from humiliation, though they have forgotten remorse; and if the passion itself of her lover has not become no less the penalty than the recompense of her guilt? But at that hour of which I now write, there was neither in Emily's heart, nor in that of her seducer, any recollection of their sin. Those hearts were too full for thought— they had forgotten everything but each other. Their love was their creation: beyond, all was night—chaos—nothing!

Lady Margaret approached them. "You will sing to us, Emily, to-night? it is *so* long since we have heard you!" It was in vain that Emily tried—her voice failed. She looked at Falkland, and could scarcely restrain her tears. She had not yet learned the latest art which sin teaches us—*its concealment!* "I will supply Lady Emily's place," said Falkland. *His* voice was calm, and *his* brow serene: the world had left nothing for him to learn. "Will you play the air," he said to Mrs. St. John, "that you gave us some nights ago?

I will furnish the words." Mrs. St. John's hand trembled as she obeyed.

SONG.

1.

Ah, let us love while yet we may,
   Our summer is decaying ;
And woe to hearts which, in their gray
   December, go a-maying.

2.

Ah, let us love, while of the fire
   Time hath not yet bereft us :
With years our warmer thoughts expire,
   Till only ice is left us !

3.

We'll fly the bleak world's bitter air—
   A brighter home shall win us ;
And if our hearts grow weary there,
   We'll find a world within us.

4.

They preach that passion fades each hour,
   That nought will pall like pleasure ;
My bee, if Love's so frail a flower,
   Oh, haste to hive its treasure.

5.

Wait not the hour, when all the mind
   Shall to the crowd be given :
For links, which to the *million* bind,
   Shall from the *one* be riven.

6.

But let us love while yet we may :
   Our summer is decaying ;
And woe to hearts which, in their gray
   December, go a-maying.

The next day Emily rose ill and feverish. In the absence of Falkland, her mind always awoke to the full sense of the guilt she had incurred. She had been brought up in the strictest, even the most fastidious, principles ; and her nature was so pure, that merely to err appeared like a change in existence—like an entrance into some new and unknown world, from which she shrank back, in terror, to herself.

Judge, then, if she easily habituated her mind to its present degradation. She sat, that morning, pale and listless ; her book lay unopened before her ; her eyes were fixed upon the ground, heavy with suppressed tears. Mrs. St. John entered : no one else was in the room. She sat by her, and took her hand. Her countenance was scarcely less colourless than Emily's, but its expression was more calm and composed. "It is not too late, Emily," she said; "you have done much that you should repent—nothing to render repentance unavailing. Forgive me, if I speak to you on this subject. It is time—in a few days your fate will be decided. I have looked on, though hitherto I have been silent: I have witnessed that eye when it dwelt upon you; I have heard that voice when it spoke to your heart. None ever resisted their influence long: do you imagine that you are the first who have found the power? Pardon me, pardon me, I beseech you, my dearest friend, if I pain you. I have known you from your childhood, and I only wish to preserve you spotless to your old age."

Emily wept, without replying. Mrs. St. John continued to argue and expostulate. What is so wavering as passion? When, at last, Mrs. St. John ceased, and Emily shed upon her bosom the hot tears of her anguish and repentance, she imagined that her resolution was taken, and that she could almost have vowed an eternal separation from her lover; Falkland came that evening, and she loved him more madly than before.

Mrs. St. John was not in the saloon when Falkland entered. Lady Margaret was reading the well-known story of Lady T—— and the Duchess of M——, in which an agreement had been made and kept, that the one who died first should return once more to the survivor. As Lady Margaret spoke laughingly of the anecdote, Emily, who was watching Falkland's countenance, was struck with the dark and sudden shade which fell over it. He moved in silence towards the window where Emily was sitting. "Do you believe," she said, with a faint smile, "in the possibility of such an event?" "I believe—though I reject—nothing!" replied Falkland, "but I would give worlds for such a proof that death does not destroy." "Surely," said Emily, "you do not deny that evidence of our immortality which we gather from the Scriptures?—are they not all that a voice from the dead could be?" Falkland was silent for a few moments: he did not seem to hear the question; his eyes dwelt upon vacancy; and when he at last spoke, it was rather in commune with himself than in answer to her. "I have watched," said he, in a low internal tone, "over the tomb: I have called, in the agony of my heart, unto her who slept beneath; I would have *dissolved my very soul* into a spell, could it have summoned before me for one, one moment, the being who had once been the spirit of my life! I have been, as it were, *entranced* with the intensity of my own adjuration; I have gazed upon the empty air, and worked upon my mind to fill it with imaginings; I have called aloud unto the winds, and tasked my soul to waken their silence to reply. All was a waste—a stillness—an infinity—without a wanderer or a voice! The dead answered me not, when I invoked them; and in the vigils of the still night I looked from the rank grass and the mouldering stones to the Eternal Heavens, as man looks from decay to immortality! Oh! that awful magnificence of repose—that living sleep—that breathing yet unrevealing divinity, spread over those still worlds! To *them* also I poured my thoughts—*but in a whisper.* I did not dare to breathe *aloud* the unhallowed anguish of my mind to the majesty of the unsympathizing stars! In the vast order of creation —in the midst of the stupendous system of universal life, my doubt and inquiry were murmured forth—*a voice crying in the wilderness, and returning without an echo, unanswered unto myself!*"

The deep light of the summer moon shone over Falkland's countenance, which Emily gazed on, as she listened, almost tremblingly, to his words. His brow was knit and hueless, and the large drops gathered slowly over it, as if wrung from the strained yet impotent tension of the thoughts within. Emily drew nearer to him—she laid her hand upon his own. "Listen to me," she said: "if a herald from the grave could satisfy your doubt, *I would gladly die that I might return to you!*" "Beware," said Falkland, with an agitated but solemn voice; "the *words, now so lightly spoken, may be registered on high.*" "*Be it so!*" replied Emily firmly, and she felt what she said. *Her* love penetrated beyond the tomb, and she would have forfeited all here for their union hereafter.

"In my earliest youth," said Falkland, more calmly than he had yet spoken, "I found in the present and the past of this world enough to direct my attention to the futurity of another: if I did not credit all with the enthusiast, I had no sympathies with the scorner: I sat myself down to examine and reflect: I pored alike over the pages of the philosopher and the theologian; I was neither baffled by the subtleties, nor deterred by the contradictions of either. As men first ascertained the geography of the earth by observing the signs of the heavens, I did homage to the Unknown God, and sought from that worship to inquire into the reasonings of mankind. I did not confine myself to books—all things breathing or inanimate constituted my study. From death itself I endeavoured to extract its secret; and whole nights I have sat in the crowded asylums of the dying, watching the last spark flutter and decay. Men die away as in sleep, without effort, or struggle, or emotion. I have looked on their countenances a moment before death, and the serenity of repose was upon them, waxing only more deep as it approached that slumber *which is never broken:* the breath grew gentler and gentler, till the lips it came from fell from each other, and all was hushed; the light had departed from the cloud, but the cloud itself, gray, cold, altered as it seemed, was as before. *They died and made no sign.* They had left the labyrinth without bequeathing us its clew. It is in vain that I have sent my spirit into the land of shadows—it has borne back no witness of its inquiry. As Newton said of himself, 'I picked up a few shells by the sea-shore, but the great ocean of truth lay undiscovered before me.'"

There was a long pause. Lady Margaret had sat down to chess with the Spaniard. No look was upon the lovers: their eyes met, and with that one glance the whole current of their thoughts was changed. The blood, which a moment before had left Falkland's cheek so colourless, rushed back to it again. The love which had so penetrated and pervaded his whole system, and which abstruser and colder reflection had just calmed, thrilled through his frame with redoubled power. As if by an involuntary and mutual impulse, their lips met: he threw his arm round her; he strained her to his bosom. "Dark as my thoughts are," he whispered, "evil as has been my life, will you not yet soothe the one, and guide the other? My Emily! my love! the *Heaven to the tumultuous ocean of my heart—* will you not be mine—mine only—wholly—and for ever?" She did not answer—she did not turn from his embrace. Her cheek flushed as his breath stole over it, and her bosom heaved beneath the arm which encircled that empire so devoted to him. "Speak one word, only one word," he continued to whisper: "will you not be mine? Are you not mine at heart even at this moment?" Her head sank upon his bosom. Those deep and eloquent eyes looked up to his through their dark lashes. "I *will* be yours," she murmured: "I am at your mercy; I have no longer any existence but in you. My only fear is, that I shall cease to be worthy of your love!"

Falkland pressed his lips once more to her own: it was his only answer, and the last seal to their compact. As they stood before the open lattice, the still and unconscious moon looked down upon that record of guilt. There was not a cloud in the heavens to dim her purity: the very winds of night had hushed themselves to do her homage; all was silent but *their* hearts. They stood beneath the calm and holy skies, a guilty and devoted pair—a fearful contrast of the sin and turbulence of this unquiet earth to the passionless serenity of the eternal heaven. The same stars, that for thousands of unfathomed years had looked upon the changes of this nether world, gleamed pale, and pure, and steadfast upon their burning but transitory vow. In a few years what of the condemnation or the recorders of that vow would remain? From other lips, on that spot, other oaths might be plighted; new pledges of unchangeable fidelity exchanged: and, year after year, in each succession of scene and time, the same stars will look from the mystery of their untracked and impenetrable home, to mock, as now, with their immutability, the variations and shadows of mankind!

FROM ERASMUS FALKLAND, ESQ., TO LADY EMILY MANDEVILLE.

At length, then, you are to be mine—you have consented to fly with me. In three days we shall leave this country, and have no home—no world but in each other. We will go, my Emily, to those golden lands where Nature, the only companion we will suffer, woos us, like a mother, to find our asylum in her breast; where the breezes are languid beneath the passion of the voluptuous skies; and where the purple light that invests all things with its glory is only less tender and consecrating than the spirit which we bring. Is there not, my Emily, in the external nature which reigns over creation, and that human nature centred in ourselves, some secret and undefinable intelligence and attraction? Are not the impressions of the former as spells over the passions of the latter? and in gazing upon the loveliness around us, do we not gather, as it were, and store within our hearts, an increase of the yearning and desire of love? What can we demand from earth but its solitudes—what from heaven but its unpolluted air? All that others would ask from either, we can find in ourselves. Wealth—honour—happiness—every object of ambition or desire, exist not for us without the circle of our arms! But the bower that surrounds us shall not be unworthy of your beauty or our love. Amidst the myrtle and the vine, and the valleys where the summer sleeps, and the rivers that murmur the memories and the legends of old; amidst the hills and the glossy glades, and the silver fountains, still as beautiful as if the Nymph and Spirit yet held and decorated an earthly home;—amidst these we will make the couch of our bridals, and the moon of Italian skies shall keep watch on our repose.

Emily!—Emily!—how I love to repeat and to linger over that beautiful name! If to see, to address, and, more than all, to touch you, has been a rapture, what word can I find in the vocabulary of happiness to express the realization of that hope which now burns within me—to mingle our youth together into one stream, wheresoever it flows; to respire the same breath; to be almost blent in the same existence; to grow, as it were, on one stem, and knit into a *single* life the feelings, the wishes, the *being* of both!

To-night I shall see you again : let one day more intervene, and—
I cannot conclude the sentence ! As I have written, the tumultuous
happiness of hope has come over me to confuse and overwhelm everything else. At this moment my pulse riots with fever ; the room
swims before my eyes ; everything is indistinct and jarring—a chaos
of emotions. Oh ! that happiness should ever have such excess !

When Emily received and laid this letter to her heart, she felt
nothing in common with the spirit which it breathed. With that quick
transition and inconstancy of feeling common in women, and which
is as frequently their safety as their peril, her mind had already
repented of the weakness of the last evening, and relapsed into the
irresolution and bitterness of her former remorse. Never had there
been in the human breast a stronger contest between conscience
and passion ;—if, indeed, the extreme softness (notwithstanding its
power) of Emily's attachment could be called passion : it was rather
a love that had refined by the increase of its own strength ; it
contained nothing but the primary guilt of conceiving it, which that
order of angels, *whose nature is love*, would have sought to purify
away. To see him, to live with him, to count the variations of his
countenance and voice, to touch his hand at moments when waking,
and watch over his slumbers when he slept—this was the essence of
her wishes, and constituted the limit to her desires. Against the
temptations of the present was opposed the whole history of the past.
Her mind wandered from each to each, wavering and wretched, as
the impulse of the moment impelled it. Hers was not, indeed, a
strong character ; her education and habits had weakened, while
they rendered more feminine and delicate a nature originally too soft.
Every recollection of former purity called to her with the loud voice
of duty, as a warning from the great guilt she was about to incur ;
and whenever she thought of her child—that centre of fond and
sinless sensations, where once she had so wholly garnered up her
heart—her feelings melted at once from the object which had so
wildly held them riveted as by a spell, to dissolve and lose themselves in the great and sacred fountain of a mother's love.

When Falkland came that evening, she was sitting at a corner of
the saloon, apparently occupied in reading, but her eyes were fixed
upon her boy, whom Mrs. St. John was endeavouring at the opposite
end of the room to amuse. The child, who was fond of Falkland,
came up to him as he entered ; Falkland stooped to kiss him ; and
Mrs. St. John said, in a low voice which just reached his ear,
" Judas, too, kissed before he betrayed." Falkland's colour changed :
he felt the sting the words were intended to convey. On that child,

now so innocently caressing him, he was indeed about to inflict a disgrace and injury the most sensible and irremediable in his power. But who ever indulges reflection in passion? He banished the remorse from his mind as instantaneously as it arose ; and, seating himself by Emily, endeavoured to inspire her with a portion of the joy and hope which animated himself. Mrs. St. John watched them with a jealous and anxious eye: she had already seen how useless had been her former attempt to arm Emily's conscience effectually against her lover ; but she resolved at least to renew the impression she had then made. The danger was imminent, and any remedy must be prompt ; and it was something to protract, even if she could not finally break off, an union against which were arrayed all the angry feelings of jealousy, as well as the better affections of the friend. Emily's eye was already brightening beneath the words that Falkland whispered in her ear, when Mrs. St. John approached her. She placed herself on a chair beside them, and unmindful of Falkland's bent and angry brow, attempted to create a general and commonplace conversation. Lady Margaret had invited two or three people in the neighbourhood ; and when these came in, music and cards were resorted to immediately, with that English *politesse,* which takes the earliest opportunity to show that the conversation of our friends is the last thing for which we have invited them. But Mrs. St. John never left the lovers ; and at last, when Falkland, in despair at her obstinacy, arose to join the card-table, she said, " Pray Mr. Falkland, were you not intimate at one time with * * * * , who eloped with Lady * * * *?" "I knew him but slightly," said Falkland ; and then added, with a sneer, "the only times I ever met him were at your house." Mrs. St. John, without noticing the sarcasm, continued :—" What an unfortunate affair that proved ! They were very much attached to one another in early life—the *only* excuse, perhaps, for a woman's breaking her subsequent vows. They eloped. The remainder of their history is briefly told : it is that of all who forfeit everything for passion, and forget that of everything it is the briefest in duration. He who had sacrificed his honour for her, sacrificed her also as lightly for another. She could not bear his infidelity ; and how could she reproach him ? In the very act of yielding to, she had become unworthy of, his love. She *did not* reproach him—she died of a broken heart ! I saw her just before her death, for I was distantly related to her, and I could not forsake her utterly even in her sin. She then spoke to me only of the child by her former marriage, whom she had left in the years when it most needed her care : she questioned me of its health—its education—its very growth : the minutest thing was not beneath her inquiry. His tidings were all that brought back to her mind 'the redolence of joy and spring.' I brought that child to her one day: *he* at least had never forgotten her. How bitterly both wept when they were separated! and she—poor, poor Ellen—an hour after their separation was no more!" There was a pause for a few minutes. Emily was deeply affected. Mrs. St. John had anticipated the effect she had produced, and concerted the method to increase it. "It is singular," she resumed, "that, the evening before her elopement, some verses were sent to her anonymously—I do not think, Emily, that you have ever seen them. Shall I sing them to you now?" and, without waiting for a reply, she placed herself at the piano; and with a low but sweet voice, greatly aided in effect by the extreme feeling of her manner, she sang the following verses:—

TO * * *

1.

And wilt thou leave that happy home,
  Where once it was so sweet to live?
Ah! think, before thou seek'st to roam,
  What safer shelter Guilt can give!

2.

The Bird may rove, and still regain
  With spotless wings her wonted rest;
But home, once lost, is ne'er again
  Restored to Woman's erring breast!

3.

If wandering o'er a world of flowers,
  The heart at times would ask repose;
But *thou* wouldst lose the only bowers
  Of rest amid a world of woes.

4.

Recall thy youth's unsullied vow—
  The past which on thee smiled so fair;
Then turn from thence to picture now
  The frowns thy future fate must wear!

5.

No hour, no hope, can bring relief
  To her who hides a blighted name;
For hearts unbow'd by stormiest *grief*
  Will break beneath one breeze of *shame!*

6.

And when thy child's deserted years
  Amid life's early woes are thrown,
Shall menial bosoms soothe the tears
  That should be shed on thine alone?

7.

When on thy name his lips shall call,
  (That tender name, the earliest taught !)
Thou wouldst not Shame and Sin were all
  The memories link'd around its thought !

8.

If Sickness haunt his infant bed,
  Ah ! what could then replace thy care ?
Could hireling steps as gently tread
  As if a Mother's soul was there ?

9.

Enough ! 'tis not too late to shun
  The bitter draught thyself wouldst fill ;
The latest link is not undone—
  Thy bark is in the haven still.

10.

If doom'd to grief through life thou art,
  'Tis thine at least unstain'd to die !
Oh'! better break at once thy heart
  Than rend it from its holiest tie !

It were vain to attempt describing Emily's feelings when the song ceased. The scene floated before her eyes indistinct and dark. The violence of the emotions she attempted to conceal pressed upon her almost to choking. She rose, looked at Falkland with one look of such anguish and despair that it froze his very heart, and left the room without uttering a word. A moment more—they heard a noise—a fall. They rushed out—Emily was stretched on the ground, apparently lifeless. *She had broken a blood-vessel !*

BOOK IV.

FROM MRS. ST. JOHN TO ERASMUS FALKLAND, ESQ.

AT last I can give a more favourable answer to your letters. Emily is now *quite* out of danger. Since the day you forced yourself, with such a disinterested regard for her health and reputation, into her room, she grew (no thanks to your forbearance) gradually better. I trust that she will be able to see you in a few days. I hope this the more, because she now feels and decides that it will be for the last time. You have, it is true, injured her happiness for life: her virtue, thank Heaven, is yet spared; and though you have made her wretched, you will never, I trust, succeed in making her despised.

You ask me, with some menacing and more complaint, why I am so bitter against you. I will tell you. I not only know Emily, and feel confident, from that knowledge, that nothing can recompense her for the reproaches of conscience, but I know *you*, and am convinced that you are the last man to render her happy. I set aside, for the moment, all rules of religion and morality in general, and speak to you (to use the cant and abused phrase) "without prejudice" as to the particular instance. Emily's nature is soft and susceptible, yours fickle and wayward in the extreme. The smallest change or caprice in you, which would not be noticed by a mind less delicate, would wound *her* to the heart. You know that the very softness of her character arises from its want of strength. Consider, for a moment, if she could bear the humiliation and disgrace which visit so heavily the offences of an English wife? She has been brought up in the strictest notions of morality; and, in a mind not naturally strong, nothing can efface the first impressions of education. She is not—indeed she is not—fit for a life of sorrow or degradation. In another character, another line of conduct might be desirable; but with regard to *her*, pause, Falkland, I beseech you, before you attempt again to destroy her for ever. I have said all. Farewell.

Your, and above all, Emily's friend.

FROM ERASMUS FALKLAND, ESQ., TO LADY EMILY MANDEVILLE.

You will see me, Emily, now that you are recovered sufficiently to do so without danger. I do not ask this as a favour. If my love has deserved anything from yours, if past recollections give me any claim over you, if my nature has not forfeited the spell which it formerly possessed upon your own, I demand it as a right.

The bearer waits for your answer.

FROM LADY EMILY MANDEVILLE TO ERASMUS FALKLAND, ESQ.

See you, Falkland! Can you doubt it? Can you think for a moment that your commands can ever cease to become a law to me? Come here whenever you please. If, during my illness, they have prevented it, it was without my knowledge. I await you; but I own that this interview will be the last, if I can claim anything from your mercy.

FROM ERASMUS FALKLAND, ESQ., TO LADY EMILY MANDEVILLE.

I have seen you, Emily, and for the last time! My eyes are dry —my hand does not tremble. I live, move, breathe, as before—and yet I have seen you for the last time! You told me—even while you leaned on my bosom, even while your lip pressed mine—you told me (and I saw your sincerity) to spare you, and to see you no more. You told me you had no longer any will, any fate of your own; that you would, if I still continued to desire it, leave friends, home, honour, for me; but you did not disguise from me that you would, in so doing, leave happiness also. You did not conceal from me that I was not sufficient to constitute all your world: you threw yourself, as you had done once before, upon what you called my generosity: you did not deceive yourself then; you have not deceived yourself now. In two weeks I shall leave England, probably for ever. I have another country still more dear to me, from its afflictions and humiliation. Public ties differ but little in their nature from private; and this confession of preference of what is debased to what is exalted, will be an answer to Mrs. St. John's assertion, that we cannot love in disgrace as we can in honour. Enough of this. In the choice, my poor Emily, that you have made, I cannot reproach you. You have done wisely, rightly, virtuously. You said that this separation must rest rather with me than with yourself; that you would be mine the moment I demanded it. I will not now or ever accept this promise. No one, much less one whom I love so intensely, so truly as I do you, shall ever receive disgrace at my hands, unless she can feel that that disgrace would be dearer to her **than glory** elsewhere; that the **simple fate** of **being mine was not so much a** recompense as a reward; **and** that, in spite of worldly **depreciation** and shame, it would constitute and concentrate all her **visions** of happiness and pride. I am now going to bid you farewell. May you—I say this disinterestedly, and from my very heart—may you soon forget how much you have loved and yet love **me**! **For** this purpose, you cannot have a better companion **than Mrs. St. John.** Her opinion of me is loudly expressed, and **probably true;** at all events, you will do wisely to believe it. You **will hear me** attacked and reproached by many. I do not deny the charges; you know best what I have deserved from *you*. God bless you, Emily. Wherever I go, I shall never cease to love you as I do now. May you be happy in your child and in your conscience! Once more, God bless you, and farewell!

FROM **LADY EMILY MANDEVILLE TO ERASMUS FALKLAND, ESQ.**

O Falkland! **you** have conquered!—I am yours—*yours only—Wholly and for **ever.*** . When your letter came, my hand trembled so, that I could **not** open it for several minutes; and when I did, I felt **as if the** very earth had passed from my feet. You were going from **your** country; you were about **to be lost to me** for ever. I could restrain myself **no** longer; all my **virtue**, my pride, forsook me **at once.** Yes, yes, you are indeed **my** world. I will fly with you **anywhere**—everywhere. Nothing **can be** dreadful, but not seeing **you**; I would be **a** servant—a **slave**—a dog, as long as I could **be with** you; hear **one tone** of **your** voice, catch one glance of **your eye. I** scarcely see **the paper before** me, my thoughts are **so** straggling and confused. **Write to me one** word, Falkland; one **word,** and I will lay it **to my heart, and be** happy.

FROM **ERASMUS FALKLAND TO LADY** EMILY MANDEVILLE.

—— **Hotel**, London.

I hasten to **you**, Emily—my own and only love. Your letter has restored me to **life.** To-morrow we shall meet.

It was with mingled feelings, alloyed and embittered, in spite of the burning hope which predominated over all, that Falkland returned to E——. He knew that he was near the completion of his most ardent wishes; that he was within the grasp of a prize which included all the thousand objects of ambition, into which, among other men, the desires are divided : the only dreams he had ventured to form for years were about to kindle into life. He had every reason to be happy ;—such is the inconsistency of human nature, that he was almost wretched. The morbid melancholy, habitual to him, threw its colourings over every emotion and idea. He knew the character of the woman whose affections he had seduced ; and he trembled to think of the doom to which he was about to condemn her. With this, there came over his mind a long train of dark and remorseful recollections. Emily was not the only one whose destruction he had prepared. All who had loved him, he had repaid with ruin ; and *one*—the first—the fairest—and the most loved, with death.

That last remembrance, more bitterly than all, possessed him. It will be recollected that Falkland, in the letters which begin this work, speaking of the ties he had formed after the loss of his first love, says, that it was the senses, not the affections, that were engaged. Never, indeed, since her death, till he met Emily, had his *heart* been unfaithful to her memory. Alas ! none but those who have cherished in their souls an image of the death ; who have watched over it for long and bitter years in secrecy and gloom ; who have felt that it was to them as a holy and fairy spot which no eye but theirs could profane ; who have filled all things with *recollections* as with a spell, and made the universe one wide mausoleum of the lost ;—none but those can understand the mysteries of that regret which is shed over every after passion, though it be more burning and intense ;—that sense of sacrilege with which we fill up the haunted recesses of the spirit with a new and living idol, and perpetrate the last act of infidelity to that buried love, which the heavens that now receive her, the earth where we beheld her, tell us, with the unnumbered voices of Nature, to worship with the incense of our faith.

His carriage stopped at the lodge. The woman who opened the gates gave him the following note :—

"Mr. Mandeville is returned ; I almost fear that he suspects our attachment. Julia says, that if you come again to E——, she will inform him. I dare not, dearest Falkland, see you here. What is to be done ? I am very ill and feverish : my brain burns so, that I can think, feel, remember nothing, but the one thought, feeling, and remembrance—that through shame, and despite of guilt, in life, and till death, I am yours.

"E. M."

As Falkland read this note, his extreme and engrossing love for Emily doubled with each word: an instant before, and the certainty of seeing her had suffered his mind to be divided into a thousand objects; now, doubt united them once more into one.

He altered his route to L——, and despatched from thence a short note to Emily, imploring her to meet him that evening by the lake, in order to arrange their ultimate flight. Her answer was brief, and blotted with her tears; but it was assent.

During the whole of that day, at least from the moment she received Falkland's letter, Emily was scarcely sensible of a single idea: she sat still and motionless, gazing on vacancy, and seeing nothing within her mind, or in the objects which surrounded her, but one dreary blank. Sense, thought, feeling, even remorse, were congealed and frozen; and the tides of emotion were still, *but they were ice!*

As Falkland's servant had waited without to deliver the note to Emily, Mrs. St. John had observed him: her alarm and surprise only served to quicken her presence of mind. She intercepted Emily's answer under pretence of giving it herself to Falkland's servant. She read it, and her resolution was formed. After carefully resealing and delivering it to the servant, she went at once to Mr. Mandeville, and revealed Lady Emily's attachment to Falkland. In this act of treachery, she was solely instigated by her passions; and when Mandeville, roused from his wonted apathy to a paroxysm of indignation, thanked her again and again for the generosity of friendship which he imagined was all that actuated her communication, he dreamed not of the fierce and ungovernable jealousy which envied the very disgrace that her confession was intended to award. Well said the French enthusiast, "that the heart, the most serene to appearance, resembles that calm and glassy fountain which cherishes the monster of the Nile in the bosom of its waters." Whatever reward Mrs. St. John proposed to herself in this action, verily she has had the recompense that was her due. Those consequences of her treachery, which I hasten to relate, have ceased to others—to *her* they remain. Amidst the pleasures of dissipation, one reflection has rankled at her mind; one dark cloud has rested between the sunshine and her soul: like the murderer in Shakspeare, the revel where she fled for forgetfulness has teemed to her with the spectres of remembrance. O thou untameable conscience! thou that never flatterest—thou that watchest over the human heart never to slumber or to sleep—it is thou that takest from us the present, barrest to us the future, and knittest the eternal chain that binds us to the rock and the vulture of the past!

The evening came on still and dark; a breathless and heavy apprehension seemed gathered over the air: the full large clouds lay without motion in the dull sky, from between which, at long and scattered intervals, the wan stars looked out; a double shadow seemed to invest the grouped and gloomy trees that stood unwaving in the melancholy horizon. The waters of the lake lay heavy and unagitated, as the sleep of death; and the broken reflections of the abrupt and winding banks rested upon their bosoms, like the dream-like remembrance of a former existence.

The hour of the appointment was arrived: Falkland stood by the spot, gazing upon the lake before him; his cheek was flushed, his hand was parched and dry with the consuming fire within him. His pulse beat thick and rapidly; the demon of evil passions was upon his soul. He stood so lost in his own reflections, that he did not for some moments perceive the fond and tearful eye which was fixed upon him: on that brow and lip, thought seemed always so beautiful, so divine, that to disturb its repose was like a profanation of something holy; and though Emily came towards him with a light and hurried step, she paused involuntarily to gaze upon that noble countenance which realized her earliest visions of the beauty and majesty of love. He turned slowly, and perceived her; he came to her with his own peculiar smile; he drew her to his bosom in silence; he pressed his lips to her forehead: she leaned upon his bosom, and forgot all but him. Oh! if there be one feeling which makes Love, even guilty Love, a god, it is the knowledge that in the midst of this breathing world he reigns aloof and alone; and that those who are occupied with his worship know nothing of the pettiness, the strife, the bustle, which pollute and agitate the ordinary inhabitants of earth! What was now to them, as they stood alone in the deep stillness of nature, everything that had engrossed them before they had met and loved? Even in her, the recollections of guilt and grief subsided: she was only sensible of one thought—the presence of the being who stood beside her,

That ocean to the rivers of her soul.

They sat down beneath an oak: Falkland stooped to kiss the cold and pale cheek that still rested upon his breast. His kisses were like lava: the turbulent and stormy elements of sin and desire were aroused even to madness within him. He clasped her still nearer to his bosom: her lips answered to his own: they caught perhaps something of the spirit which they received: her eyes were half-closed; the bosom heaved wildly that was pressed to his beating and burning heart. The skies grew darker and darker, as the night stole over them : one low roll of thunder broke upon the curtained and heavy air—*they* did not hear it ; and yet it was the knell of peace —virtue—hope—lost, lost for ever to their souls !

*   *   *   *   *   *
*   *   *   *   *   *
*   *   *   *   *   *

They separated as they had never done before. In Emily's bosom there was a dreary void—a vast blank—over which there went a low deep voice like a Spirit's—a sound indistinct and strange, that spoke a language she knew not ; but felt that it told of woe—guilt —doom. Her senses were stunned : the vitality of her feelings was numbed and torpid : the first herald of despair is insensibility. "To-morrow, then," said Falkland—and his voice for the first time seemed strange and harsh to her—" we will fly hence for ever: meet me at daybreak—the carriage shall be in attendance—we cannot now unite too soon—would that at this very moment we were prepared !"—"To-morrow!" repeated Emily, "at day-break ! " and as she clung to him, he felt her shudder : "to-morrow—ay— to-morrow!—" one kiss—one embrace—one word—*farewell*—and they parted.

Falkland returned to L——: a gloomy, foreboding rested upon his mind : that dim and indescribable fear, which no earthly or human cause can explain—that shrinking within self—that vague terror of the future—that grappling, as it were, with some unknown shade—that wandering of the spirit—whither ?—that cold, cold creeping dread—of what ? As he entered the house, he met his confidential servant. He gave him orders respecting the flight of the morrow, and then retired into the chamber where he slept. It was an antique and large room : the wainscot was of oak ; and one broad and high window looked over the expanse of country which stretched beneath. He sat himself by the casement in silence—he opened it : the dull air came over his forehead, not with a sense of freshness, but, like the parching atmosphere of the east, charged with a weight and fever that sank heavy into his soul. He turned :— he threw himself upon the bed, and placed his hands over his face. His thoughts were scattered into a thousand indistinct forms, but over all, there was one rapturous remembrance ; and that was, that the morrow was to unite him for ever to her whose possession had only rendered her more dear. Meanwhile, the hours rolled on ; and as he lay thus silent and still, the clock of the distant church struck with a distinct and solemn sound upon his ear. It was the half-hour after midnight. At that moment an icy thrill ran, slow and curd- ling, through his veins. His heart, as if with a presentiment of what was to follow, beat violently, and then stopped; life itself seemed ebbing away; cold drops stood upon his forehead; his eyelids trembled, and the balls reeled and glazed, like those of a dying man; a deadly fear gathered over him, so that his flesh quivered, and every hair in his head seemed instinct with a separate life, the very marrow of his bones crept, and his blood waxed thick and thick, as if stagnating into an ebbless and frozen substance. He started in a wild and unutterable terror. There stood, at the far end of the room, a dim and thin shape like moonlight, without outline or form; still, and indistinct, and shadowy. He gazed on, speechless and motionless; his faculties and senses seemed locked in an unnatural trance. By degrees the shape became clearer and clearer to his fixed and dilating eye. He saw, as through a floating and mist-like veil, the features of Emily; but how changed!—sunken, and hueless, and set in death. The dropping lip, from which there seemed to trickle a deep red stain like blood; the lead-like and lifeless eye; the calm, awful, mysterious repose which broods over the aspect of the dead;—all grew, as it were, from the hazy cloud that encircled them for one, one brief, agonizing moment, and then as suddenly faded away. The spell passed from his senses. He sprang from the bed with a loud cry. All was quiet. There was not a trace of what he had witnessed. The feeble light of the skies rested upon the spot where the apparition had stood; upon that spot he stood also. He stamped upon the floor—it was firm beneath his footing. He passed his hands over his body—he was awake—he was unchanged: earth, air, heaven, were around him as before. What had thus gone over his soul to awe and overcome it to such weakness? To these questions his reason could return no answer. Bold by nature, and sceptical by philosophy, his mind gradually recovered its original tone: he did not give way to conjecture: he endeavoured to discard it: he sought by natural causes to account for the apparition he had seen or imagined; and, as he felt the blood again circulating in its accustomed courses, and the night air coming chill over his feverish frame, he smiled with a stern and scornful bitterness at the terror which had so shaken, and the fancy which had so deluded, his mind.

Are there not "more things in heaven and earth than are dreamed of in our philosophy?" A Spirit may hover in the air that we breathe: the depth of our most secret solitudes may be peopled by the invisible: our uprisings and our downsittings may be marked by a witness from the grave. In our walks the dead may be behind us; in our banquets they may sit at the board; and the chill breath of the night wind that stirs the curtains of our bed may bear a message

D

our senses receive **not, from** lips that once **have** pressed kisses on our own! Why is it **that at** moments there creeps over us an awe, a terror, overpowering, but undefined? Why is **it** that we shudder without **a** cause, and **feel** the warm life-blood **stand** still in its courses? *Are the dead too near ?* Do unearthly wings **touch** us as they flit around? **Has** our soul **any** intercourse which **the** body shares **not,** though it feels, with the supernatural world—mysterious revealings—unimaginable communion—a language of dread and power, shaking to its centre the fleshly barrier that divides the spirit from its race?

How fearful is the very **life which we** hold! We have our being beneath a cloud, and are a marvel even to ourselves. There is not a single thought which has its affixed limits. Like circles in the **water, our** researches weaken as they extend, and vanish at last into **the** immeasurable and unfathomable space of **the vast** unkown. We are like children in the dark; we tremble in a shadowy and terrible void, peopled with our fancies! Life is our real night, and the first gleam of the morning, which brings us certainty, *is death.*

Falkland sat **the** remainder of that night by the window, watching the clouds become **gray as** the dawn rose, and its earliest breeze awoke. He heard **the** trampling of the horses beneath: he drew his **cloak** round him, and descended. It was on a turning **of** the road beyond the lodge that he directed the carriage to wait, and he then proceeded **to** the place appointed. Emily was not yet there. He walked to and fro with an agitated and hurried step. The impression of the night had in a great measure been effaced from his mind, and he gave himself up without reserve to the warm and sanguine hopes which he had so much reason to conceive. He thought too, at moments, of those bright climates beneath which he designed their asylum, where the very air is music, and the light is **like** the colourings of love; and he associated the sighs of a mutual **rapture** with the fragrance of myrtles, and the breath of a Tuscan **heaven.** Time glided on. The hour was long past, yet Emily came not! The sun rose, and Falkland turned in dark and angry discontent from its beams. With every moment his impatience increased, and at last he could restrain himself no longer. He proceeded towards the house. He stood for some time at a distance; but as all seemed still hushed in repose, he drew nearer and nearer till he reached the door: to his astonishment it was open. He saw forms passing rapidly through the hall. He heard a confused and indistinct murmur. At length he caught a glimpse of Mrs. St. John. He could command himself no more. He sprang forwards —entered the door—the hall—and caught her by a part of her dress.

He could not speak, but his countenance said all which his lips refused. Mrs. St. John burst into tears when she saw him. "Good God!" she said, "why are you here? Is it possible you have yet learned——" Her voice failed her. Falkland had by this time recovered himself. He turned to the servants who gathered around him. "Speak," he said calmly. "What has occurred?" "My lady—my lady!" burst at once from several tongues. "What of her?" said Falkland, with a blanched cheek, but unchanging voice. There was a pause. At that instant a man, whom Falkland recognized as the physician of the neighbourhood, passed at the opposite end of the hall. A light, a scorching and intolerable light, broke upon him. "She is dying—she is dead, perhaps," he said, in a low sepulchral tone, turning his eye around till it had rested upon every one present. *Not one answered.* He paused a moment, as if stunned by a sudden shock, and then sprang up the stairs. He passed the boudoir, and entered the room where Emily slept. The shutters were only partially closed: a faint light broke through, and rested on the bed; beside it bent two women. Them he neither heeded nor saw. He drew aside the curtains. He beheld—the same as he had seen it in his vision of the night before—the changed and lifeless countenance of Emily Mandeville! That face, still so tenderly beautiful, was partially turned towards him. Some dark stains upon the lip and neck told how she had died—the blood-vessel she had broken before had burst again. The bland and soft eyes, which for him never had but *one* expression, were closed; and the long and dishevelled tresses half hid, while they contrasted that bosom, which had but the night before first learned to thrill beneath his own. Happier in her fate than she deserved, she passed from this bitter life ere the punishment of her guilt had begun. She was not doomed to wither beneath the blight of shame, nor the coldness of estranged affection. From him whom she had so worshipped, she was not condemned to bear wrong nor change. She died while his passion was yet in its spring—before a blossom, a leaf, had faded; and she sank to repose while his kiss was yet warm upon her lip, and her last breath almost mingled with his sigh. For the woman who has erred, life has no exchange for such a death. Falkland stood mute and motionless: not one word of grief or horror escaped his lips. At length he bent down. He took the hand which lay outside the bed; he pressed it; it replied not to the pressure, but fell cold and heavy from his own. He put his cheek to her lips; not the faintest breath came from them; and then for the first time a change passed over his countenance: he pressed upon those lips one long and last kiss, and, without word, or sign, or tear, he turned from the chamber. Two hours afterwards he was found senseless upon the ground : it was upon the spot where he had met Emily the night before.

For weeks he knew nothing of this earth—he was encompassed with the spectres of a terrible dream. All was confusion, darkness, horror—a series and a change of torture ! At one time he was hurried through the heavens in the womb of a fiery star, girt above and below and around with unextinguishable but unconsuming flames. Wherever he trod, as he wandered through his vast and blazing prison, the molten fire was his footing, and the breath of fire was his air. Flowers, and trees, and hills were in that world as in ours, but wrought from one lurid and intolerable light ; and, scattered around, rose gigantic palaces and domes of the living flame, like the mansions of the city of Hell. With every moment there passed to and fro shadowy forms, on whose countenances was engraven unutterable anguish ; but not a shriek, not a groan, rung through the red air ; *for the doomed, who fed and inhabited the flames, were forbidden the consolation of voice.* Above there sat, fixed and black, a solid and impenetrable cloud—*Night frozen into substance ;* and from the midst there hung a banner of a pale and sickly flame, on which was written "For Ever." A river rushed rapidly beside him. He stooped to slake the agony of his thirst—the waves *were waves of fire;* and, as he started from the burning draught, he longed to shriek aloud, *and could not.* Then he cast his despairing eyes above for mercy ; and saw on the livid and motionless banner "For Ever."

A change came o'er the spirit of his dream :

·He was suddenly borne upon the winds and storms to the oceans of an eternal winter. He fell stunned and unstruggling upon the ebbless and sluggish waves. Slowly and heavily they rose over him as he sank : then came the lengthened and suffocating torture of that drowning death—the impotent and convulsive contest with the closing waters—the gurgle, the choking, the bursting of the pent breath,—the flutter of the heart, its agony, *and its stillness.* He recovered. He was a thousand fathoms beneath the sea, chained to a rock round which the heavy waters rose as a wall. He felt his own flesh rot and decay, perishing from his limbs piece by piece ; and he saw the coral banks, which it requires a thousand ages to form, rise slowly from their slimy bed : and spread atom by atom, till they became a shelter for the leviathan : *their growth was his only record of eternity;* and ever and ever, around and above him, came vast and misshapen things—the wonders of the secret deeps ;

and the sea serpent, the huge chimæra of the north, made its resting-place by his side, glaring upon him with a livid and death-like eye, wan, yet burning *as an expiring sun*. But over all, in every change, in every moment of that immortality, there was present one pale and motionless countenance, never turning from his own. The fiends of hell, the monsters of the hidden ocean, had no horror so awful *as the human face of the dead whom he had loved*.

The word of his sentence was gone forth. Alike through that delirium and its more fearful awakening, through the past, through the future, through the vigils of the joyless day, and the broken dreams of night, there was a charm upon his soul—a hell within himself; and the curse of his sentence was—*never to forget!*

When Lady Emily returned home on that guilty and eventful night, she stole at once to her room : she dismissed her servant, and threw herself upon the ground in that deep despair which on this earth can never again know hope. She lay there without the power to weep, or the courage to pray — how long, she knew not. Like the period before creation, her mind was a chaos of jarring elements, and knew neither the method of reflection, nor the division of time.

As she rose, she heard a slight knock at the door, and her husband entered. Her heart misgave her ; and when she saw him close the door carefully before he approached her, she felt as if she could have sunk into the earth, alike from her internal shame, and her fear of its detection.

Mr. Mandeville was a weak, commonplace character; indifferent in ordinary matters, but, like most imbecile minds, violent and furious when aroused. "Is this, Madam, addressed to you?" he cried, in a voice of thunder, as he placed a letter before her (it was one of Falkland's) ; "and this, and this, Madam?" said he, in a still louder tone, as he flung them out one after another from her own escritoire, which he had broken open.

Emily sank back, and gasped for breath. Mandeville rose, and, laughing fiercely, seized her by the arm. He grasped it with all his force. She uttered a faint scream of terror : he did not heed it ; he flung her from him, and, as she fell upon the ground, the blood gushed in torrents from her lips. In the sudden change of feeling which alarm created, he raised her in his arms. *She was a corpse!* At that instant the clock struck upon his ear with a startling and solemn sound : *it was the half-hour after midnight!*

The grave is now closed upon that soft and erring heart, with its guiltiest secret unrevealed. She went to that last home with a blest and unblighted name; for her guilt was unknown, and her virtues are yet recorded in the memories of the Poor.

* * * * *
* * * * *

They laid her in the stately vaults of her ancient line, and her bier was honoured with tears from hearts not less stricken, because their sorrow, if violent, was brief. For the dead there are many mourners, but only one monument—the bosom which loved them *best*. The spot where the hearse rested, the green turf beneath, the surrounding trees, the gray tower of the village church, and the proud halls rising beyond,—all had witnessed the childhood, the youth, the bridal-day of the being whose last rites and solemnities they were to witness now. The very bell which rang for her birth had rung also for the marriage peal; it *now* tolled for her death. But a little while, and she had gone forth from that home of her young and unclouded years, amidst the acclamations and blessings of all, a bride with the insignia of bridal pomp—in the first bloom of her girlish beauty—in the first innocence of her unawakened heart, weeping, not for the future she was entering, but for the past she was about to leave, and smiling through her tears, as if innocence had no business with grief. On the same spot, where he had then waved his farewell, stood the father now. On the grass which they had then covered, flocked the peasants whose wants her childhood had relieved; by the same priest who had blessed her bridals, bent the bridegroom who had plighted his vow. There was not a tree, not a blade of grass withered. The day itself was bright and glorious; such was it when it smiled upon her nuptials. And *she—she—*but four little years, and all youth's innocence darkened, and earth's beauty come to dust! Alas! not for her, but the mourner whom she left! In death even love is forgotten; but in life there is no bitterness so utter as to feel everything is unchanged, except the One Being who was the soul of all—to know *the world* is the same, but that *its sunshine* is departed.

* * * * *
* * * * *
* * * * *

The noon was still and sultry. Along the narrow street of the small village of Lodar poured the wearied but yet unconquered band, which embodied in that district of Spain the last hope and energy of freedom. The countenances of the soldiers were haggard and dejected; they displayed even less of the vanity, than their accoutrements exhibited of the pomp and circumstances of war. Yet their garments were such as even the peasants had disdained:

covered with blood and dust, and tattered into a thousand rags, they betokened nothing of chivalry but its endurance of hardship; even the rent and sullied banners drooped sullenly along their staves, as if the winds themselves had become the minions of fortune, and disdained to swell the insignia of those whom she had deserted. The glorious music of battle was still. An air of dispirited and defeated enterprise hung over the whole array. "Thank Heaven," said the chief, who closed the last file as it marched on to its scanty refreshment and brief repose; "thank Heaven, we are at least out of the reach of pursuit; and the mountains, those last retreats of liberty, are before us!" "True, Don Rafael," replied the youngest of two officers who rode by the side of the commander; "and if we can cut our passage to Mina, we may yet plant the standard of the Constitution in Madrid." "Ay," added the elder officer, "and sing Riego's hymn in the place of the Escurial!" "Our sons may!" said the chief, who was indeed Riego himself, "but for us—all hope is over! Were we united, we could scarcely make head against the armies of France; and divided as we are, the wonder is that we have escaped so long. Hemmed in by invasion, our great enemy has been ourselves. Such has been the hostility faction has created between Spaniard and Spaniard, that we seem to have none left to waste upon Frenchmen. We cannot establish freedom if men are willing to be slaves. We have no hope, Don Alphonso—no hope—but that of death!" As Riego concluded this desponding answer, so contrary to his general enthusiasm, the younger officer rode on among the soldiers, cheering them with words of congratulation and comfort; ordering their several divisions; cautioning them to be prepared at a moment's notice; and impressing on their remembrance those small but essential points of discipline, which a Spanish troop might well be supposed to disregard. When Riego and his companion entered the small and miserable hovel which constituted the head-quarters of the place, this man still remained without; and it was not till he had slackened the girths of his Andalusian horse, and placed before it the undainty provender which the *écurie* afforded, that he thought of rebinding more firmly the bandages wound around a deep and painful sabre cut in the left arm, which for several hours had been wholly neglected. The officer, whom Riego had addressed by the name of Alphonso, came out of the hut just as his comrade was vainly endeavouring, with his teeth and one hand, to replace the ligature. As he assisted him, he said, "You know not, my dear Falkland, how bitterly I reproach myself for having ever persuaded you to a cause where contest seems to have no hope, and danger no glory." Falkland smiled bitterly. "Do not deceive yourself, my dear uncle," said he; "your persuasions would have been unavailing but for the suggestions of my own wishes. I am not one of those enthusiasts who entered on your cause with high hopes and chivalrous designs: I asked but forgetfulness and excitement—I have found them! I would not exchange a single pain I have endured for what would have constituted the pleasures of other men:—but enough of this. What time, think you, have we for repose?" "Till the evening," answered Alphonso; "our route will then most probably be directed to the Sierra Morena. The General is extremely weak and exhausted, and needs a longer rest than we shall gain. It is singular that with such weak health he should endure so great an excess of hardship and fatigue." During this conversation they entered the hut. Riego was already asleep. As they seated themselves to the wretched provision of the place, a distant and indistinct noise was heard. It came first on their ears like the birth of the mountain wind—low, and hoarse, and deep: gradually it grew loud and louder, and mingled with other sounds which they defined too well—the hum, the murmur, the trampling of steeds, the ringing echoes of the rapid march of armed men! They heard and knew the foe was upon them!—a moment more, and the drum beat to arms. "By St. Pelagio," cried Riego, who had sprung from his light sleep at the first sound of the approaching danger, unwilling to believe his fears, "it cannot be: the French are far behind:" and then, as the drum beat, his voice suddenly changed,—"the enemy! the enemy! D'Aguilar, to horse!" and with those words he rushed out of the hut. The soldiers, who had scarcely begun to disperse, were soon re-collected. In the mean while the French commander, D'Argout, taking advantage of the surprise he had occasioned, poured on his troops, which consisted solely of cavalry, undaunted and undelayed by the fire of the posts. On, on they drove like a swift cloud charged with thunder, and gathering wrath as it hurried by, before it burst in tempest on the beholders. They did not pause till they reached the farther extremity of the village: there the Spanish infantry were already formed into two squares. "Halt!" cried the French commander: the troop suddenly stopped, confronting the nearer square. There was one brief pause—the moment before the storm. "Charge!" said D'Argout, and the word rang throughout the line up to the clear and placid sky. Up flashed the steel like lightning; on went the troop like the dash of a thousand waves when the sun is upon them; and before the breath of the riders was thrice drawn, came the crash—the shock—the slaughter of battle. The Spaniards made but a faint resistance to the impetuosity of the onset: they broke on every side

beneath the force of the charge, like the weak barriers of a rapid
and swollen stream; and the French troops after a brief but bloody
victory (joined by a second squadron from the rear), advanced
immediately upon the Spanish cavalry. Falkland was by the side
of Riego. As the troop advanced, it would have been curious to
notice the contrast of expression in the face of each; the Spaniard's
features lighted up with the daring enthusiasm of his nature; every
trace of their usual languor and exhaustion vanished beneath the
unconquerable soul that blazed out the brighter for the debility of
the frame; the brow knit; the eye flashing; the lip quivering:—
and close beside, the calm, stern, passionless repose that brooded
over the severe yet noble beauty of Falkland's countenance. To
him danger brought scorn, not enthusiasm: he rather despised than
defied it. "The dastards! they waver," said Riego, in an accent
of despair, as his troop faltered beneath the charge of the French:
and so saying, he spurred his steed on to the foremost line. The
contest was longer, but not less decisive, than the one just concluded. The Spaniards, thrown into confusion by the first shock,
never recovered themselves. Falkland, who, in his anxiety to
rally and inspirit the soldiers, had advanced with two other officers
beyond the ranks, was soon surrounded by a detachment of dragoons:
the wound in his left arm scarcely suffered him to guide his horse:
he was in the most imminent danger. At that moment D'Aguilar,
at the head of his own immediate followers, cut his way into the
circle, and covered Falkland's retreat; another detachment of the
enemy came up, and they were a second time surrounded. In the
mean while, the main body of the Spanish cavalry were flying in all
directions, and Riego's deep voice was heard at intervals, through
the columns of smoke and dust, calling and exhorting them in vain.
D'Aguilar and his scanty troop, after a desperate skirmish, broke
again through the enemy's line drawn up against their retreat. The
rank closed after them, like waters when the object that pierced
them has sunk: Falkland and his two companions were again envi-
roned: he saw his comrades cut to the earth before him. He pulled
up his horse for one moment, clove down with one desperate blow
the dragoon with whom he was engaged, and then setting his spurs
to the very rowels into his horse, dashed at once through the circle
of his foes. His remarkable presence of mind, and the strength and
sagacity of his horse, befriended him. Three sabres flashed before
him, and glanced harmless from his raised sword, like lightning on
the water. The circle was passed! As he galloped towards Riego,
his horse started from a dead body that lay across his path. He
reined up for one instant, for the countenance, which looked upwards,

D 2

struck him as familiar. What was his horror, when in that livid and distorted face, he recognized his uncle! The thin grizzled hairs were besprent with gore and brains, and the blood yet oozed from the spot where the ball had passed through his temple. Falkland had but a brief interval for grief; the pursuers were close behind: he heard the snort of the foremost horse before he again put spurs into his own. Riego was holding a hasty consultation with his principal officers. As Falkland rode breathless up to them, they had decided on the conduct expedient to adopt. They led the remaining square of infantry towards the chain of mountains against which the village, as it were, leaned; and there the men dispersed in all directions. "For us," said Riego to the followers on horseback who gathered around him, "for us the mountains still promise a shelter. We must ride, gentlemen, for our lives—Spain will want *them* yet."

Wearied and exhausted as they were, that small and devoted troop fled on into the recesses of the mountains for the remainder of that day—twenty men out of the two thousand who had halted at Lodar. As the evening stole over them, they entered into a narrow defile: the tall hills rose on every side, covered with the glory of the setting son, as if Nature rejoiced to grant her bulwarks as a protection to liberty. A small clear stream ran through the valley, sparkling with the last smile of the departing day; and ever and anon, from the scattered shrubs and the fragrant herbage, came the vesper music of the birds, and the hum of the wild bee.

Parched with thirst, and drooping with fatigue, the wanderers sprung forward with one simultaneous cry of joy to the glassy and refreshing wave which burst so unexpectedly upon them: and it was resolved that they should remain for some hours in a spot where all things invited them to the repose they so imperiously required. They flung themselves at once upon the grass; and such was their exhaustion, that rest was almost synonymous with sleep. Falkland alone could not immediately forget himself in repose: the face of his uncle, ghastly and disfigured, glared upon his eyes whenever he closed them. Just, however, as he was sinking into an unquiet and fitful doze, he heard steps approaching: he started up, and perceived two men, one a peasant, the other in the dress of a hermit. They were the first human beings the wanderers had met; and when Falkland gave the alarm to Riego, who slept beside him, it was immediately proposed to detain them as guides to the town of Carolina, where Riego had hopes of finding effectual assistance, or the means of ultimate escape. The hermit and his companion refused, with much vehemence, the office imposed upon them; but

Riego ordered them to be forcibly detained. He had afterwards reason bitterly to regret this compulsion.

Midnight came on in all the gorgeous beauty of a southern heaven, and beneath its stars they renewed their march.

As Falkland rode by the side of Riego, the latter said to him in a low voice, "There is yet escape for you and my followers; none for me: they have set a price on my head, and the moment I leave these mountains, I enter upon my own destruction." "No, Rafael!" replied Falkland; "you can yet fly to England, that asylum of the free, though ally of the despotic; the abettor of tyranny, but the shelter of its victims!" Riego answered, with the same faint and dejected tone, "I care not now what becomes of me! I have lived solely for Freedom; I have made her my mistress, my hope, my dream: I have no existence but in her. With the last effort of my country let me perish also! I have lived to view liberty not only defeated, but derided: I have seen its efforts not aided, but mocked. In my own country, those only, who wore it, have been respected who used it as a covering to ambition. In other nations, the free stood aloof when the charter of their own rights was violated in the invasion of ours. I cannot forget that the senate of that England, where you promise me a home, rang with insulting plaudits when her statesman breathed his ridicule on our weakness, not his sympathy for our cause; and I—*I*—fanatic—dreamer—enthusiast, as I may be called, whose whole life has been one unremitting struggle for the opinion I have adopted, am at least not so blinded by my infatuation, but I can see the mockery it incurs. If I die on the scaffold to-morrow, I shall have nothing of martyrdom but its doom; not the triumph—the incense—the immortality of popular applause: I should have no hope to support me at such a moment, gleaned from the glories of the future—nothing but one stern and prophetic conviction of the vanity of that tyranny by which my sentence will be pronounced." Riego paused for a moment before he resumed, and his pale and death-like countenance received an awful and unnatural light from the intensity of the feeling that swelled and burned within him. His figure was drawn up to its full height, and his voice rang through the lonely hills with a deep and hollow sound, that had in it a tone of prophecy, as he resumed: "It is in vain that they oppose OPINION; anything else they may subdue. They may conquer wind, water, nature itself; but to the progress of that secret, subtle, pervading spirit, their imagination can devise, their strength can accomplish, no bar: *its votaries* they may seize, they may destroy; *itself* they cannot touch. If they check it in one place, it invades them in another. They cannot build a wall across the whole earth;

and, even if they could, it would pass over its summit! Chains cannot bind it, for it is immaterial—dungeons enclose it, for it is universal. Over the faggot and the scaffold—over the bleeding bodies of its defenders which they pile against its path, it sweeps on with a noiseless but unceasing march. Do they levy armies against it, it presents to them no palpable object to oppose. *Its camp is the universe; its asylum is the bosoms of their own soldiers.* Let them depopulate, destroy as they please, to each extremity of the earth; but as long as they have a single supporter themselves—as long as they leave a single individual into whom that spirit can enter—so long they will have the same labours to encounter, and the same enemy to subdue."

As Riego's voice ceased, Falkland gazed upon him with a mingled pity and admiration. Sour and ascetic as was the mind of that hopeless and disappointed man, he felt somewhat of a kindred glow at the pervading and holy enthusiasm of the patriot to whom he had listened; and though it was the character of his own philosophy to question the purity of human motives, and to smile at the more vivid emotions he had ceased to feel, he bowed his soul in homage to those principles whose sanctity he acknowledged, and to that devotion of zeal and fervour with which their defender cherished and enforced them. Falkland had joined the constitutionalists with respect, but not ardour, for their cause. He demanded excitation; he cared little where he found it. He stood in this world a being who mixed in all its changes, performed all its offices, took, as if by the force of superior mechanical power, a leading share in its events; but whose thoughts and soul were as offsprings of another planet, imprisoned in a human form, and *longing for their home!*

As they rode on, Riego continued to converse with that imprudent unreserve which the openness and warmth of his nature made natural to him: not one word escaped the hermit and the peasant (whose name was Lopez Lara) as they rode on two mules behind Falkland and Riego. "Remember," whispered the hermit to his comrade, "the reward!" "I do," muttered the peasant.

Throughout the whole of that long and dreary night, the wanderers rode on incessantly, and found themselves at daybreak near a farmhouse: this was Lara's own home. They made the peasant Lara knock; his own brother opened the door. Fearful as they were of the detection to which so numerous a party might conduce, only Riego, another officer (Don Luis de Sylva), and Falkland entered the house. The latter, whom nothing ever seemed to render weary or forgetful, fixed his cold stern eye upon the two brothers, and, seeing some signs pass between them, locked the door, and so prevented their escape. For a few hours they reposed in the stables with their horses, their drawn swords by their sides. On waking, Riego found it absolutely necessary that his horse should be shod. Lopez started up, and offered to lead it to Arguillas for that purpose. "No," said Riego, who, though naturally imprudent, partook in this instance of Falkland's habitual caution: "your brother shall go and bring hither the farrier." Accordingly the brother went: he soon returned. "The farrier," he said, "was already on the road." Riego and his companions, who were absolutely fainting with hunger, sat down to breakfast; but Falkland, who had finished first, and who had eyed the man since his return with the most scrutinizing attention, withdrew towards the window, looking out from time to time with a telescope which they had carried about them, and urging them impatiently to finish. "Why?" said Riego, "famished men are good for nothing, either to fight or fly—and we *must* wait for the farrier." "True," said Falkland, "but——" he stopped abruptly. Sylva had his eyes on his face at that moment. Falkland's colour suddenly changed: he turned round with a loud cry. "Up! up! Riego! Sylva! We are undone—the soldiers are upon us!" "Arm!" cried Riego, starting up. At that moment Lopez and his brother seized their own carbines, and levelled them at the betrayed constitutionalists. "The first who moves," cried the former, "is a dead man!" "Fools!" said Falkland, with a calm bitterness, advancing deliberately towards them. He moved only three steps—Lopez fired. Falkland staggered a few paces, recovered himself, sprang towards Lara, clove him at one blow from the skull to the jaw, and fell, with his victim, lifeless upon the floor. "Enough!" said Riego to the remaining peasant; "we are your prisoners; bind us!" In two minutes more the soldiers entered, and they were conducted to Carolina. Fortunately Falkland was known, when at Paris, to a French officer of high rank then at Carolina. He was removed to the Frenchman's quarters. Medical aid was instantly procured. The first examination of his wound was decisive; recovery was hopeless!

* * * * *
* * * * *
* * * * *

Night came on again, with her pomp of light and shade—the night that for Falkland had no morrow. One solitary lamp burned in the chamber where he lay alone with God and his own heart. He had desired his couch to be placed by the window, and requested his attendants to withdraw. The gentle and balmy air stole over him, as free and bland as if it were to breathe for him for ever; and the silver moonlight came gleaming through the lattice, and played upon his wan brow, like the tenderness of a bride that sought to kiss him to repose. "In a few hours," thought he, as he lay gazing on the high stars which seemed such silent witnesses of an eternal and unfathomed mystery, "in a few hours either this feverish and wayward spirit will be at rest for ever, or it will have commenced a new career in an untried and unimaginable existence! In a very few hours I may be amongst the very heavens that I survey—a part of their own glory—a new link in a new order of beings—breathing amidst the elements of a more gorgeous world—arrayed myself in the attributes of a purer and diviner nature—a wanderer among the planets—an associate of angels—the beholder of the arcana of the great God—redeemed, regenerate, immortal, or—*dust!*

"There is no Œdipus to solve the enigma of life. We are—whence came we? We are *not*—whither do we go? All things *in* our existence have their object; existence has none. We live, move, beget our species, perish—and *for what!* We ask the past its moral; we question the gone years of the reason of our being, and from the clouds of a thousand ages there goes forth no answer. Is it merely to pant beneath this weary load; to sicken of the sun; to grow old; to drop like leaves into the grave; and to bequeath to our heirs the worn garments of toil and labour that we leave behind? Is it to sail for ever on the same sea, ploughing the ocean of time with new furrows, and feeding its billows with new wrecks, or ——" and his thoughts paused, blinded and bewildered.

No man, in whom the mind has not been broken by the decay of the body, has approached death in full consciousness, as Falkland did that moment, and not thought intensely on the change he was about to undergo; and yet what new discoveries upon that subject has any one bequeathed us? There the wildest imaginations are driven from originality into triteness: there all minds, the frivolous and the strong, the busy and the idle, are compelled into the same path and limit of reflection. Upon that unknown and voiceless gulf of inquiry broods an eternal and impenetrable gloom; no wind breathes over it—no wave agitates its stillness: over the dead and solemn calm there is no change propitious to adventure—there goes forth no vessel of research, which is not driven, baffled and broken, again upon the shore.

The moon waxed high in her career. Midnight was gathering slowly over the earth: the beautiful, the mystic hour, blent with a thousand memories, hallowed by a thousand dreams, made tender to remembrance by the vows our youth breathed beneath its star, and solemn by the old legends which are linked to its majesty and peace—*the hour in which men should die ;* the isthmus between two worlds; the climax of the past day; the verge of that which is to come; wrapping us in sleep after a weary travail, and promising us a morrow *which since the first birth of Creation has never failed.* As the minutes glided on, Falkland felt himself grow gradually weaker and weaker. The pain of his wound had ceased, but a deadly sickness gathered over his heart: the room reeled before his eyes, and the damp chill mounted from his feet up—up to the breast in which the life-blood waxed dull and thick.

As the hand of the clock pointed *to the half-hour after midnight,* the attendants who waited in the adjoining room heard a faint cry. They rushed hastily into Falkland's chamber; they found him stretched half out of the bed. His hand was raised towards the opposite wall; it dropped gradually as they approached him; and his brow, which was at first stern and bent, softened shade by shade, into his usual serenity. But the dim film gathered fast over his eye, and the last coldness upon his limbs. He strove to raise himself as if to speak; the effort failed, and he fell motionless on his face. They stood by the bed for some moments in silence: at length they raised him. Placed against his heart was an open locket of dark hair, which one hand still pressed convulsively. They looked upon his countenance—(a single glance was sufficient)—it was hushed—proud—passionless—the seal of Death was upon it!

THE PILGRIMS OF THE RHINE.

TO

HENRY LYTTON BULWER.

ALLOW me, my dear Brother, to dedicate this Work to you. The greater part of it (viz., the tales which vary and relieve the voyages of Gertrude and Trevylyan) was written in the pleasant excursion we made together some years ago. Among the associations—some sad, and some pleasing—connected with the general design, none are so agreeable to me as those that remind me of the friendship subsisting between us, and which, unlike that of near relations in general, has grown stronger and more intimate as our footsteps have receded farther from the fields where we played together in our childhood. I dedicate this Work to you with the more pleasure, not only when I remember that it has always been a favourite with yourself, but when I think that it is one of my writings most liked in foreign countries; and I may possibly, therefore, have found a record destined to endure the affectionate esteem which this Dedication is intended to convey.

Yours, &c.

E. L. B.

LONDON, *April* 23, 1840.

ADVERTISEMENT TO THE FIRST EDITION.

Could I prescribe to the critic and to the public, I would wish that this work might be tried by the rules rather of poetry than prose, for according to those rules have been both its conception and its execution;—and I feel that something of sympathy with the author's design is requisite to win indulgence for the superstitions he has incorporated with his tale; for the floridity of his style and the redundance of his descriptions. Perhaps, indeed, it would be impossible, in attempting to paint the scenery and embody some of the Legends of the Rhine, not to give (it may be, too loosely) the reins to the imagination, or to escape the influence of that wild German spirit which I have sought to transfer to a colder tongue.

I have made the experiment of selecting for the main interest of my work the simplest materials, and weaving upon them the ornaments given chiefly to subjects of a more fanciful nature. I know not how far I have succeeded, but various reasons have conspired to make this work, above all others that I have written, which has given me the most delight (though not unmixed with melancholy) in producing, and in which my mind, for the time, has been the most completely absorbed. But the ardour of composition is often disproportioned to the merit of the work; and the public sometimes, nor unjustly, avenges itself for that forgetfulness of its existence, which makes the chief charm of an author's solitude—and the happiest, if not the wisest, inspiration of his dreams.

PREFACE

TO

PILGRIMS OF THE RHINE.

WITH the younger class of my readers, this work has had the good fortune to find especial favour; perhaps because it is in itself a collection of the thoughts and sentiments that constitute the Romance of youth. It has little to do with the positive truths of our actual life, and does not pretend to deal with the larger passions and more stirring interests of our kind. It is but an episode out of the graven epic of human destinies. It requires no explanation of its purpose, and no analysis of its story; the one is evident, the other simple:—the first seeks but to illustrate visible nature through the poetry of the affections; the other is but the narrative of the most real of mortal sorrows which the Author attempts to take out of the region of pain, by various accessories from the Ideal. The connecting tale itself is but the string that binds into a garland the wild flowers cast upon a grave.

The descriptions of the Rhine have been considered by Germans sufficiently faithful to render this tribute to their land and their legends one of the popular guide-books along the course it illustrates —especially to such tourists as wish not only to take in with the eye the inventory of the river, but to seize the peculiar spirit which invests the wave and the bank with a beauty that can only be made visible by reflexion. He little comprehends the true charm of the Rhine, who gazes on the vines on the hill-tops without a thought of the imaginary world with which their recesses have been peopled by the graceful credulity of old; who surveys the steep ruins that overshadow the water, untouched by one lesson from the pensive morality of Time. Everywhere around us is the evidence of perished opinions and departed races—everywhere around us, also, the rejoicing fertility of unconquerable Nature, and the calm progress of Man himself through the infinite cycles of decay. He who would judge adequately of a landscape, must regard it not only with the painter's eye, but with the poet's. The feelings which the sight of any scene in nature conveys to the mind—more especially of any scene on which history or fiction has left its trace—must depend upon our sympathy with those associations which make up what may be called the spiritual character of the spot. If indifferent to those associations, we should see only hedge-rows and ploughed land in the battle-field of Bannockburn; and the traveller would but look on a dreary waste, whether he stood amidst the piles of the Druid on Salisbury plain, or trod his bewildered way over the broad expanse on which the Chaldean first learned to number the stars.

To the former editions of this tale was prefixed a poem on "The Ideal," which had all the worst faults of the author's earliest compositions in verse. The present poem (with the exception of a very few lines) has been entirely re-written, and has at least the comparative merit of being less vague in the thought, and less unpolished in the diction, than that which it replaces.

EMS, 1840.

THE IDEAL WORLD.

I.

THE IDEAL WORLD—ITS REALM IS EVERYWHERE AROUND US—ITS INHABITANTS ARE THE IMMORTAL PERSONIFICATIONS OF ALL BEAUTIFUL THOUGHTS—TO THAT WORLD WE ATTAIN BY THE REPOSE OF THE SENSES.

AROUND " this visible diurnal sphere,"
   There floats a World that girds us like the space;
On wandering clouds and gliding beams career
   Its ever-moving, murmurous Populace.
There, all the lovelier thoughts conceived below,
   Ascending live, and in celestial shapes.
To that bright World, O Mortal, wouldst thou go?—
   Bind but thy senses, and thy soul escapes:
To care, to sin, to passion close thine eyes;
Sleep in the flesh, and see the Dreamland rise!
Hark, to the gush of golden waterfalls,
Or knightly tromps at Archimagian Walls!
In the green hush of Dorian Valleys mark
   The River Maid her amber tresses knitting:—
When glow-worms twinkle under coverts dark,
   And silver clouds o'er summer stars are flitting,
With jocund elves invade "the Moone's sphere,
"Or hang a pearl in every cowslip's ear;"[1]
Or, list! what time the roseate urns of dawn
   Scatter fresh dews, and the first skylark weaves
Joy into song—the blithe Arcadian Faun
   Piping to wood-nymphs under Bromian leaves,
While slowly gleaming through the purple glade
Come Evian's panther car, and the pale Naxian Maid.

Such, O Ideal World, thy habitants!
   All the fair children of creative creeds—

[1] Midsummer Night's Dream.

All the lost tribes of Phantasy are thine—
From antique Saturn in Dodonian haunts,
  Or Pan's first music waked from shepherd reeds,
To the last sprite when Heaven's pale lamps decline,
 Heard wailing soft along the solemn Rhine.

II.

OUR DREAMS BELONG TO THE IDEAL—THE DIVINER LOVE FOR WHICH YOUTH SIGHS, NOT ATTAINABLE IN LIFE—BUT THE PURSUIT OF THAT LOVE, BEYOND THE WORLD OF THE SENSES, PURIFIES THE SOUL, AND AWAKES THE GENIUS—PETRARCH—DANTE.

Thine are the Dreams that pass the Ivory Gates,
  With prophet shadows haunting poet eyes!
Thine the beloved illusions youth creates
  From the dim haze of its own happy skies.
In vain we pine—we yearn on earth to win
  The being of the heart, our boyhood's dream.
The Psyche and the Eros ne'er have been,
  Save in Olympus, wedded!—As a stream
Glasses a star, so life the ideal love;
Restless the stream below—serene the orb above!
Ever the soul the senses shall deceive;
Here custom chill, their kinder fate bereave:
For mortal lips unmeet eternal vows!
And Eden's flowers for Adam's mournful brows!
We seek to make the moment's angel guest
  The household dweller at a human hearth;
We chase the bird of Paradise whose nest
  Was never found amid the bowers of earth.[1]
Yet loftier joys the vain pursuit may bring,
  Than sate the senses with the boons of time;
The bird of Heaven hath still an upward wing,
  The steps it lures are still the steps that climb,
And in the ascent, altho' the soil be bare,
More clear the daylight and more pure the air.
Let Petrarch's heart the human mistress lose,
He mourns the Laura, but to win the Muse.

---

[1] According to a belief in the East, which is associated with one of the loveliest and most familiar of Oriental superstitions, the bird of Paradise is never seen to rest upon the earth—and its nest is never to be found.

Could all the charms which Georgian maids combine
Delight the soul of the dark Florentine,
Like one chaste dream of childlike Beatrice
Awaiting Hell's dark pilgrim in the skies,
Snatch'd from below to be the guide above,
And clothe Religion in the form of Love ?[1]

III.

GENIUS, **LIFTING ITS** LIFE TO THE IDEAL, BECOMES ITSELF **A PURE** IDEA—IT MUST COMPREHEND ALL EXISTENCE : ALL **HUMAN** SINS AND SUFFERINGS—BUT IN COMPREHENDING, IT TRANSMUTES **THEM—THE POET IN HIS** TWO-FOLD BEING —THE ACTUAL AND THE IDEAL—THE **INFLUENCE** OF GENIUS OVER THE **STERNEST REALITIES OF EARTH**—OVER OUR PASSIONS — **WARS AND SUPERSTITIONS** — ITS **IDENTITY IS** WITH HUMAN PROGRESS—ITS AGENCY, EVEN WHERE UN-ACKNOWLEDGED, **IS UNIVERSAL.**

O, thou true Iris ! sporting on thy bow
  Of tears and smiles—Jove's herald, Poetry,
Thou reflex image of all joy and woe—
  Both fused in light by thy dear phantasy !
Lo ! from the clay how Genius lifts its life,
  And grows one pure Idea—one calm soul !
True, its own clearness must reflect our strife ;
  True, its completeness must comprise our whole :
But as the sun transmutes the sullen hues
  Of marsh-grown vapours into vermeil dyes,
And melts them later into twilight dews,
  Shedding on flowers the baptism of the skies ;
So glows the Ideal in the air we breathe—
  So from the fumes of sorrow and of sin,
Doth its warm light in rosy colours wreathe
  Its playful cloudland, storing balms within.

Survey the Poet in his mortal mould,
  Man, amongst men, descended from his throne !
The moth that chased the star now frets the fold,
  Our cares, our faults, our follies are his own.

---

[1] It is supposed by many of the commentators on Dante, that in the form of his lost Beatrice, who guides him in his Vision of Heaven, he allegorizes Religious Faith.

Passions as idle, and desires as vain,
Vex the wild heart, and dupe the erring brain.
From Freedom's field the recreant Horace flies
To kiss the hand by which his country dies;
From Mary's grave the mighty Peasant turns,
And hoarse with orgies rings the laugh of Burns.
While Rousseau's lips a lackey's vices own,—
Lips that could draw the thunder on a throne!
But when from Life the Actual GENIUS springs,
    When, self-transform'd by its own magic rod,
It snaps the fetters and expands the wings,
    And drops the fleshly garb that veil'd the god,
How the mists vanish as the form ascends!—
How in its aureole every sunbeam blends!
By the Arch-Brightener of Creation seen,
    How dim the crowns on perishable brows!
The snows of Atlas melt beneath the sheen,
    Thro' Thebaid caves the rushing splendour flows.
Cimmerian glooms with Asian beams are bright,
And Earth reposes in a belt of light.
Now stern as Vengeance shines the awful form,
Arm'd with the bolt and glowing thro' the storm;
Sets the great deeps of human passion free,
And whelms the bulwarks that would breast the sea.
Roused by its voice the ghastly Wars arise,
Mars reddens earth, the Valkyrs pale the skies;
Dim Superstition from her hell escapes,
With all her shadowy brood of monster shapes;
Here life itself the scowl of Typhon[1] takes;
There Conscience shudders at Alecto's snakes;
From Gothic graves at midnight yawning wide,
In gory cerements gibbering spectres glide;
And where o'er blasted heaths the lightnings flame,
Black secret hags "do deeds without a name!"
Yet thro' its direst agencies of awe,
Light marks its presence and pervades its law,
And, like Orion when the storms are loud,
It links creation while it gilds a cloud.
By ruthless Thor, free Thought, frank Honour stand,
Fame's grand desire, and zeal for Fatherland.

[1] The gloomy Typhon of Egypt assumes many of the mystic attributes of the Principle of Life which, in the Grecian Apotheosis of the Indian Bacchus, is represented in so genial a character of exuberant joy and everlasting youth.

The Ideal World.

The grim Religion of Barbarian Fear,
With some Hereafter still connects the Here,
Lifts the gross sense to some spiritual source,
And thrones some Jove above the Titan Force,
Till, love completing what in awe began,
From the rude savage dawns the thoughtful man.

Then, O behold the glorious Comforter!
   Still bright'ning worlds, but gladd'ning now the hearth,
Or like the lustre of our nearest star,
   Fused in the common atmosphere of earth.
It sports like hope upon the captive's chain;
Descends in dreams upon the couch of pain;
To wonder's realm allures the earnest child;
To the chaste love refines the instinct wild;
And as in waters the reflected beam,
Still where we turn, glides with us up the stream;
And while in truth the whole expanse is bright,
Yields to each eye its own fond path of light,
So over life the rays of Genius fall,
Give each his track because illuming all.

IV.

FORGIVENESS TO THE ERRORS OF OUR BENEFACTORS.

Hence is that secret pardon we bestow
   In the true instinct of the grateful heart,
Upon the Sons of Song. The good they do
   In the clear world of their Uranian art
Endures for ever; while the evil done
   In the poor drama of their mortal scene,
Is but a passing cloud before the sun;
   Space hath no record where the mist hath been.
Boots it to us, if Shakespeare err'd like man?
   Why idly question that most mystic life?
Eno' the giver in his gifts to scan;
   To bless the sheaves with which thy fields are rife,
Nor, blundering, guess thro' what obstructive clay
The glorious corn-seed struggled up to day.

V.

THE IDEAL IS NOT CONFINED TO POETS—ALGERNON SIDNEY RECOGNIZES HIS IDEAL IN LIBERTY, AND BELIEVES IN ITS TRIUMPH WHERE THE MERE PRACTICAL MAN COULD BEHOLD BUT ITS RUINS—YET LIBERTY IN THIS WORLD MUST EVER BE AN IDEAL, AND THE LAND THAT IT PROMISES CAN BE FOUND BUT IN DEATH.

But not to you alone, O Sons of Song,
The wings that float the loftier airs along.
Whoever lifts us from the dust we are,
   Beyond the sensual to spiritual goals;
Who from the MOMENT and the SELF afar
   By deathless deeds allures reluctant souls,
Gives the warm life to what the Limner draws,
Plato but thought what godlike Cato was.[1]
Recall the wars of England's giant-born,
   Is Elyot's voice—is Hampden's death in vain?
Have all the meteors of the vernal morn
   But wasted light upon a frozen main?
Where is that child of Carnage, Freedom, flown?
The Sybarite lolls upon the Martyr's throne.
Lewd, ribald jests succeed to solemn zeal;
And things of silk to Cromwell's men of steel.
Cold are the hosts the tromps of Ireton thrill'd
And hush'd the senates Vane's large presence fill'd.
In what strong heart doth the old manhood dwell?
Where art thou, Freedom?—Look—in Sidney's cell!
There still as stately stands the living Truth,
Smiling on age as it had smiled on youth.
Her forts dismantled, and her shrines o'erthrown,
The headsman's block her last dread altar-stone,
No sanction left to Reason's vulgar hope—
Far from the wrecks expands her prophet's scope.
Millennial morns the tombs of Kedron gild,
The hands of saints the glorious walls rebuild,—
Till each foundation garnish'd with its gem,
High o'er Gehenna flames Jerusalem!
O thou blood-stained Ideal of the free,
Whose breath is heard in clarions—Liberty!

[1] "What Plato thought, and godlike Cato was."—POPE.

Sublimer for thy grand illusions past,
Thou spring'st to Heaven—Religion at the last.
Alike below, or commonwealths, or thrones,
Where'er men gather some crush'd victim groans;
Only in death thy real form we see,
All life is bondage—souls alone are free.
Thus through the waste the wandering Hebrews went,
Fire on the march, but cloud upon the tent.
At last on Pisgah see the prophet stand,
Before his vision spreads the PROMISED LAND;
But where reveal'd the Canaan to his eye?—
Upon the mountain he ascends to die.

VI.

YET ALL HAVE TWO ESCAPES INTO THE IDEAL WORLD—
VIZ., MEMORY AND HOPE—EXAMPLE OF HOPE IN YOUTH,
HOWEVER EXCLUDED FROM ACTION AND DESIRE—
NAPOLEON'S SON.

Yet whatsoever be our bondage here,
All have two portals to the Phantom sphere,—
Who hath not glided through those gates that ope
Beyond the Hour, to MEMORY or to HOPE!
Give Youth the Garden,—still it soars above—
Seeks some far glory—some diviner love.
Place Age amidst the Golgotha—its eyes
Still quit the graves, to rest upon the skies;
And while the dust, unheeded, moulders there,
Track some lost angel through cerulean air.

Lo! where the Austrian binds, with formal chain,
The crownless son of earth's last Charlemain—
Him, at whose birth laugh'd all the violet vales
  (While yet unfallen stood thy sovereign star,
O Lucifer of Nations)—hark, the gales
  Swell with the shout from all the hosts, whose war
Rended the Alps, and crimson'd Memphian Nile—
  "Way for the coming of the Conqueror's Son:
Woe to the Merchant-Carthage of the Isle!
  Woe to the Scythian Ice-world of the Don!
O Thunder Lord, thy Lemnian bolts prepare,
The Eagle's eyrie hath its eagle heir!"

Hark, at that shout from north to south, gray Power
　Quails on its weak, hereditary thrones;
And widowed mothers prophesy the hour
　Of future carnage to their cradled sons.
What! shall our race to blood be thus consign'd,
And Até claim an heirloom in mankind?
Are these red lots unshaken in the urn?
Years pass—approach, pale Questioner—and learn.
Chain'd to his rock, with brows that vainly frown,
The fallen Titan sinks in darkness down!
And sadly gazing through his gilded grate,
Behold the child whose birth was as a fate!
Far from the land in which his life began;
Wall'd from the healthful air of hardy man;
Rear'd by cold hearts, and watch'd by jealous eyes,
His guardians gaolers, and his comrades spies.
Each trite convention courtly fears inspire
To stint experience and to dwarf desire;
Narrows the action to a puppet stage,
And trains the eaglet to the starling's cage.
On the dejected brow and smileless cheek,
What weary thought the languid lines bespeak:
Till drop by drop, from jaded day to day,
The sickly life-streams ooze themselves away.
　Yet oft in Hope a boundless realm was thine,
　That vaguest Infinite—the Dream of Fame;
　　Son of the sword that first made kings divine,
　　Heir to man's grandest royalty—a Name!
- Then didst thou burst upon the startled world,
　And keep the glorious promise of thy birth;
Then were the wings that bear the bolt unfurl'd,
　A monarch's voice cried, "Place upon the Earth"
A new Philippi gain'd a second Rome,
And the Son's sword avenged the greater Cæsar's doom.

II.

EXAMPLE OF MEMORY AS LEADING TO THE IDEAL—AMIDST LIFE HOWEVER HUMBLE, AND IN A MIND HOWEVER IGNORANT—THE VILLAGE WIDOW.

But turn the eye to life's sequester'd vale,
   And lowly roofs remote in hamlets green,
Oft in my boyhood where the moss-grown pale
   Fenced quiet graves, a female form was seen;
Each eve she sought the melancholy ground,
And lingering paused, and wistful look'd around
If yet some footstep rustled thro' the grass,
Timorous she shrunk, and watch'd the shadow pass.
Then, when the spot lay lone amidst the gloom,
Crept to one grave too humble for a tomb,
There silent bowed her face above the dead,
For, if in prayer, the prayer was inly said;
Still as the moonbeam, paused her quiet shade,
Still as the moonbeam, thro' the yews to fade.
Whose dust thus hallowed by so fond a care?
What the grave saith not—let the heart declare.
   On yonder green two orphan children play'd;
By yonder rill two plighted lovers stray'd.
In yonder shrine two lives were blent in one,
And joy-bells chimed beneath a summer sun.
Poor was their lot—their bread in labour found;
No parent bless'd them, and no kindred own'd;
They smiled to hear the wise their choice condemn;
They loved—they loved—and love was wealth to them!
Hark—one short week—again the holy bell!
Still shone the sun; but dirge-like boom'd the knell
The icy hand had severed breast from breast;
Left life to toil, and summon'd Death to rest.
Full fifty years since then have pass'd away,
Her cheek is furrow'd, and her hair is gray.
Yet, when she speaks of *him*, (the times are rare,)
Hear in her voice how youth still trembles there.
The very name of that young life that died,
Still heaves the bosom, and recalls the bride.
Lone o'er the widow's hearth those years have fled,
The daily toil still wins the daily bread;

THE IDEAL WORLD.

No books deck sorrow with fantastic dyes :
Her fond romance her woman heart supplies ;
And, haply in the few still moments given,
(Day's taskwork done)—to memory, death, and heaven,
To that unutter'd poem may belong
Thoughts of such pathos as had beggar'd song.

VIII.

HENCE IN HOPE, MEMORY, AND PRAYER, ALL OF US ARE POETS.

Yes, while thou hopest, music fills the air,
   While thou rememberest, life reclothes the clod ;
While thou canst feel the electric chain of prayer,
   Breathe but a thought, and be a soul with God !
Let not these forms of matter bound thine eye,
   He who the vanishing point of Human things
Lifts from the landscape—lost amidst the sky,
   Has found the Ideal which the poet sings—
Has pierced the pall around the senses thrown,
And is himself a poet—tho' unknown.

IX.

APPLICATION OF THE POEM TO THE TALE TO WHICH IT IS PREFIXED—THE RHINE—ITS IDEAL CHARACTER IN ITS HISTORICAL AND LEGENDARY ASSOCIATIONS.

Eno' !—my song is closing, and to thee,
   Land of the North, I dedicate its lay ;
As I have done the simple tale to be
   The drama of this prelude !—
                     Far away
Rolls the swift Rhine beneath the starry ray ;
But to my ear its haunted waters sigh ;
Its moonlit mountains glimmer on my eye ;
On wave, on marge, as on a wizard's glass,
Imperial ghosts in dim procession pass ;
Lords of the wild—the first great Father-men,
Their fane the hill-top—and their home the glen ;
Frowning they fade—a bridge of steel appears
With frank-eyed Cæsar smiling thro' the spears ;
The march moves onwards, and the mirror brings
The Gothic crowns of Carlovingian kings :

Vanish'd alike! The Hermit rears his Cross,
And barbs neigh shrill, and plumes in tumult toss,
While (knighthood's sole sweet conquest from the Moor)
Sings to Arabian lutes the Troubadour.
　Not yet, not yet—still glide some lingering shades—
Still breathe some murmurs as the starlight fades—
Still from her rock I hear the Siren call,
And see the tender ghost in Roland's mouldering hall!

X.

APPLICATION OF THE POEM CONTINUED—THE IDEAL LENDS ITS AID TO THE MOST FAMILIAR AND THE MOST ACTUAL SORROW OF LIFE — FICTION COMPARED TO SLEEP — IT STRENGTHENS WHILE IT SOOTHES.

TRITE were the tale I tell of love and doom,
(Whose life hath loved not, whose not mourn'd a tomb?)
But fiction draws a poetry from grief,
As art its healing from the wither'd leaf.
Play thou, sweet Fancy, round the sombre truth,
　Crown the sad Genius ere it lower the torch!
When death the altar, and the victim youth,
　Flutes fill the air, and garlands deck the porch.
As down the river drifts the Pilgrim sail,
Clothe the rude hill-tops, lull the Northern gale;
With child-like lore the fatal course beguile,
And brighten death with Love's untiring smile,
Along the banks let fairy forms be seen
"By fountain clear, or spangled starlight sheen."[1]
Let sound and shape to which the sense is dull,
Haunt the soul opening on the Beautiful.
And when at length, the symbol voyage done,—
Surviving Grief shrinks lonely from the sun,
By tender types show Grief what memories bloom
From lost delight—what fairies guard the tomb.
Scorn not the dream, O world-worn,—pause awhile,
New strength shall nerve thee as the dreams beguile,
Strung by the rest—less far shall seem the goal!
As sleep to life, so fiction to the soul.

[1] Midsummer Night's Dream.

THE PILGRIMS OF THE RHINE.

CHAPTER I.

IN WHICH THE READER IS INTRODUCED TO QUEEN NYMPHALIN.

IN one of those green woods which belong so peculiarly to our island (for the Continent has its forests, but England its woods), there lived, a short time ago, a charming little fairy called Nymphalin. I believe she is descended from a younger branch of the house of Mab, but perhaps that may only be a genealogical fable, for your fairies are very susceptible to the pride of ancestry, and it is impossible to deny that they fall somewhat reluctantly into the liberal opinions so much in vogue at the present day.

However that may be, it is quite certain that all the courtiers in Nymphalin's domain (for she was a queen fairy) made a point of asserting her right to this illustrious descent; and, accordingly, she quartered the Mab arms with her own—three acorns vert, with a grasshopper rampant. It was as merry a little court as could possibly be conceived, and on a fine midsummer night it would have been worth while attending the queen's balls—that is to say, if you could have got a ticket; a favour not obtained without great interest.

But, unhappily, until both men and fairies adopt Mr. Owen's proposition, and live in parallelograms, they will always be the victims of *ennui*. And Nymphalin, who had been disappointed in love, and was still unmarried, had for the last five or six months been exceedingly tired even of giving balls. She yawned very frequently, and consequently yawning became a fashion.

"But why don't we have some new dances, my Pipalee?" said Nymphalin to her favourite maid of honour; "these waltzes are very old-fashioned."

"Very old-fashioned," said Pipalee.

The queen gaped, and Pipalee did the same.

It was a gala night; the court was held in a lone and beautiful hollow, with the wild brake closing round it on every side, so that no human step could easily gain the spot. Wherever the shadows fell upon the brake, a glow-worm made a point of exhibiting itself, and the bright August-moon sailed slowly above, pleased to look down upon so charming a scene of merriment; for they wrong the moon who assert that she has an objection to mirth;—with the mirth of fairies she has all possible sympathy. Here and there in the thicket the scarce honeysuckles—in August, honeysuckles are somewhat out of season—hung their rich festoons, and at that moment they were crowded with the elderly fairies, who had given up dancing and taken to scandal. Besides the honeysuckle you might see the hawkweed and the white convolvulus, varying the soft verdure of the thicket; and mushrooms in abundance had sprung up in the circle, glittering in the silver moonlight, and acceptable beyond measure to the dancers: every one knows how agreeable a thing tents are in a *fête champêtre!* I was mistaken in saying that the brake closed the circle *entirely* round; for there was one gap, scarcely apparent to mortals, through which a fairy at least might catch a view of a brook that was close at hand, rippling in the stars, and chequered at intervals by the rich weeds floating on the surface, interspersed with the delicate arrowhead and the silver water-lily. Then the trees themselves, in their prodigal variety of hues; the blue, the purple, the yellowing tint—the tender and silvery verdure, and the deep mass of shade frowning into black; the willow, the elm, the ash, the fir, the lime, "and, best of all, Old England's haunted oak:" these hues were broken again into a thousand minor and subtler shades, as the twinkling stars pierced the foliage, or the moon slept with a richer light upon some favoured glade.

It was a gala night; the elderly fairies, as I said before, were chatting among the honeysuckles; the young were flirting, and dancing, and making love; the middle-aged talked politics under the mushrooms; and the queen herself, and half-a-dozen of her favourites, were yawning their pleasure from a little mound, covered with the thickest moss.

"It has been very dull, madam, ever since Prince Fayzenheim left us," said the fairy Nip.

The queen sighed.

"How handsome the prince is!" said Pipalee.

The queen blushed.

"He wore the prettiest dress in the world; and what a moustache!" cried Pipalee, fanning herself with her left wing.

"He was a coxcomb," said the lord treasurer, sourly. The lord treasurer was the honestest and most disagreeable fairy at court; he was an admirable husband, brother, son, cousin, uncle, and godfather; it was these virtues that had made him a lord treasurer. Unfortunately they had not made him a sensible fairy. He was like Charles the Second in one respect, for he never did a wise thing; but he was not like him in another—for he very often said a foolish one.

The queen frowned.

"A young prince is not the worse for that," retorted Pipalee. "Heigho! does your majesty think his highness likely to return?"

"Don't tease me," said Nymphalin, pettishly.

The lord treasurer, by way of giving the conversation an agreeable turn, reminded her majesty that there was a prodigious accumulation of business to see to, especially that difficult affair about the emmet-wasp loan. Her Majesty rose, and leaning on Pipalee's arm, walked down to the supper-tent.

"Pray," said the fairy Trip to the fairy Nip, "what is all this talk about Prince Fayzenheim? Excuse my ignorance; I am only just out, you know."

"Why," answered Nip, a young courtier, not a marrying fairy, but very seductive, "the story runs thus: Last summer a foreigner visited us, calling himself Prince Fayzenheim: one of your German fairies, I fancy; no great things, but an excellent waltzer. He wore long spurs, made out of the stings of the horse-flies in the Black Forest; his cap sat on one side, and his mustachios curled like the lip of the dragon-flower. He was on his travels, and amused himself by making love to the queen. You can't fancy, dear Trip, how fond she was of hearing him tell stories about the strange creatures of Germany—about wild huntsmen, water-sprites, and a pack of such stuff," added Nip, contemptuously, for Nip was a free thinker.

"In short?" said Trip.

"In short, she loved," cried Nip, with a theatrical air.

"And the prince?"

"Packed up his clothes, and sent on his travelling-carriage, in order that he might go at his ease on the top of a stage-pigeon; in short—as you say—in short, he deserted the queen, and ever since she has set the fashion of yawning."

"It was very naughty in him," said the gentle Trip.

"Ah, my dear creature," cried Nip, "if it had been *you* to whom he had paid his addresses!"

Trip simpered, and the old fairies from their seats in the honeysuckles observed she was "sadly conducted;" but the Trips had never been *too* respectable.

Meanwhile the queen, leaning on Pipalee, said, after a short pause, "Do you know I have formed a plan!"

"How delightful!" cried Pipalee. "Another gala!"

"Pooh, surely even you must be tired with such levities: the spirit of the age is no longer frivolous; and I dare say as the march of gravity proceeds, we shall get rid of galas altogether." The queen said this with an air of inconceivable wisdom, for the "Society for the Diffusion of General Stupefaction" had been recently established among the fairies, and its tracts had driven all the light reading out of the market. "The Penny Proser" had contributed greatly to the increase of knowledge and yawning, so visibly progressive among the courtiers.

"No," continued Nymphalin; "I have thought of something better than galas.—Let us travel!"

Pipalee clasped her hands in ecstasy.

"Where shall we travel?"

"Let us go up the Rhine," said the queen, turning away her head. "We shall be amazingly welcomed; there are fairies without number, all the way by its banks; and various distant connections of ours, whose nature and properties will afford interest and instruction to a philosophical mind."

"Number Nip, for instance," cried the gay Pipalee.

"The Red Man!" said the graver Nymphalin.

"Oh, my queen, what an excellent scheme!" and Pipalee was so lively during the rest of the night, that the old fairies in the honeysuckle insinuated that the lady of honour had drunk a buttercup too much of the Maydew.

CHAPTER II.

THE LOVERS.

WISH only for such readers as give themselves heart and soul up to me—if they begin to cavil I have done with them; their fancy should put itself entirely under my management; and, after all, ought they not to be too glad to get out of this hackneyed and melancholy world, to be run away with by an author who promises them something new?

From the heights of Bruges, a Mortal and his betrothed gazed upon the scene below. They saw the sun set slowly amongst purple masses of cloud, and the lover turned to his mistress and sighed deeply ; for her cheek was delicate in its blended roses, beyond the beauty that belongs to the hues of health ; and when he saw the sun sinking from the world, the thought came upon him, that *she* was his sun, and the glory that she shed over his life might soon pass away into the bosom of the "everduring Dark." But against the clouds rose one of the many spires that characterize the town of Bruges ; and on that spire, tapering into heaven, rested the eyes of Gertrude Vane. The different objects that caught the gaze of each was emblematic both of the different channel of their thoughts, and the different elements of their nature: he thought of the sorrow, she of the consolation : his heart prophesied of the passing away from earth—hers of the ascension into heaven. The lower part of the landscape was wrapped in shade ; but, just where the bank curved round in a mimic bay, the waters caught the sun's parting smile, and rippled against the herbage that clothed the shore, with a scarcely noticeable wave. There were two of the numerous mills which are so picturesque a feature of that country, standing at a distance from each other on the rising banks, their sails perfectly still in the cool silence of the evening, and adding to the rustic tranquillity which breathed around. For to me there is something in the stilled sails of one of those inventions of man's industry peculiarly eloquent of repose : the rest seems typical of the repose of our own passions— short and uncertain, contrary to their natural ordination ; and doubly impressive from the feeling which admonishes us how precarious is the stillness—how utterly dependent on every wind rising at any moment and from any quarter of the heavens ! They saw before them no living forms, save of one or two peasants yet lingering by the water-side.

Trevylyan drew closer to his Gertrude ; for his love was inexpressibly tender, and his vigilant anxiety for her made his stern frame feel the first coolness of the evening, even before she felt it herself.

"Dearest, let me draw your mantle closer round you."

Gertrude smiled her thanks.

"I feel better than I have done for weeks," said she ; "and when once we get into the Rhine, you will see me grow so strong as to shock all your interest for me."

"Ah, would to Heaven my interest for you may be put to such an ordeal !" said Trevylyan ; and they turned slowly to the inn, where Gertrude's father already awaited them.

Trevylyan was of a wild, a resolute, and an active nature. Thrown on the world at the age of sixteen, he had passed his youth in alternate pleasure, travel, **and solitary study.** At the age in which manhood is least susceptible **to caprice, and** most perhaps to passion, he fell in **love with** the loveliest **person that ever** dawned upon a poet's vision. I **say this** without exaggeration, for Gertrude Vane's was indeed **the** beauty, but the perishable beauty, of a dream. It happened most singularly to Trevylyan, (but he was a singular man,) that being naturally one whose affections it was very difficult to excite, **he** should have fallen in love at first sight with a person whose **disease,** already declared, would have deterred any other heart from risking its treasures on a bark so utterly unfitted for the voyage of life. Consumption, but consumption in its most beautiful shape, **had** set its seal upon Gertrude Vane, when Trevylyan first saw her, and at once loved.—He knew the danger of the disease; he did not, except **at** intervals, deceive himself; he wrestled against the new passion: but, stern as his nature was, he could not conquer it. He loved, he confessed his love, and Gertrude returned it.

In a love like this, there is something **ineffably** beautiful—it is essentially the poetry of passion. Desire grows hallowed by fear, and, scarce permitted to indulge its vent in the common channel of the senses, breaks forth into those vague yearnings—those lofty aspirations, which **pine** for the Bright, the Far, the Unattained. It is **" the desire of** the moth for the star "—it is the love of the soul!

Gertrude was advised by the Faculty to try a southern climate; but Gertrude was the daughter of a German mother, and her young fancy had been nursed in all the wild legends and the alluring visions that belong to the children of the Rhine. Her imagination, more romantic than classic, yearned for the vine-clad hills and haunted forests, which are so fertile in their spells to those who have once drunk, even sparingly, of the Literature of the North. Her desire strongly expressed her declared conviction, that if any change of scene could yet **arrest** the progress of her malady, it would be the shores of the **river** she had so longed to visit, prevailed with her physicians and **her father,** and they consented to that pilgrimage along the Rhine on which Gertrude, her father, and her lover were now bound.

It was **by** the green curve of the banks which the lovers saw from the heights of Bruges, that our fairy travellers met. They were reclining on the water-side, playing at dominoes with eyes bright and the black specks **of the** trefoil;—viz., Pipalee, Nip, Trip, and the lord treasurer, (for **that** was all the party selected by the queen for her travelling *cortège*,) and waiting for her majesty, who, being a curious little elf, had gone round the town to reconnoitre.

" Bless me!" said the lord treasurer; "what a mad freak is this!

Crossing that immense pond of water! And was there ever such bad grass as this?—one may see that the fairies thrive ill here."

"You are always discontented, my lord," said Pipalee; "but then you are somewhat too old to travel—at least unless you go in your nutshell and four."

The lord treasurer did not like this remark, so he muttered a peevish pshaw, and took a pinch of honeysuckle dust to console himself for being forced to put up with so much frivolity.

At this moment, ere the moon was yet at her middest height, Nymphalin joined her subjects.

"I have just returned," said she, with a melancholy expression on her countenance, "from a scene that has almost renewed in me that sympathy with human beings which of late years our race has well-nigh relinquished.

"I hurried through the town without noticing much food for adventure. I paused for a moment on a fat citizen's pillow, and bade him dream of love. He woke in a fright, and ran down to see that his cheeses were safe. I swept with a light wing over a politician's eyes, and straightway he dreamed of theatres and music. I caught an undertaker in his first nap, and I have left him whirled into a waltz. For what would be sleep if it did not contrast life? Then I came to a solitary chamber, in which a girl, in her tenderest youth, knelt by the bed-side in prayer, and I saw that the death-spirit had passed over her, and the blight was on the leaves of the rose. The room was still and hushed—the angel of Purity kept watch there. Her heart was full of love, and yet of holy thoughts, and I bade her dream of the long life denied to her—of a happy home—of the kisses of her young lover—of eternal faith, and unwaning tenderness. Let her at least enjoy in dreams what Fate has refused to Truth!—And, passing from the room, I found her lover stretched in his cloak beside the door; for he reads with a feverish and desperate prophecy the doom that waits her; and so loves he the very air she breathes, the very ground she treads, that when she has left his sight he creeps, silently and unknown to her, to the nearest spot hallowed by her presence, anxious that while yet she is on earth not an hour, not a moment, should be wasted upon other thoughts than those that belong to her; and feeling a security, a fearful joy, in lessening the distance that *now* only momentarily divides them. And that love seemed to me not as the love of the common world, and I stayed my wings and looked upon it as a thing that centuries might pass and bring no parallel to, in its beauty and its melancholy truth. But I kept away the sleep from the lover's eyes, for well I knew that sleep was a tyrant, that shortened the brief time of waking tenderness for

E 2

the living, yet spared him; and one sad, anxious thought of her was sweeter, in spite of its sorrow, than the brightest of fairy dreams. So I left him awake, and watching there through the long night, and felt that the children of earth have still something that unites them to the spirits of a finer race, so long as they retain amongst them the presence of real love!"

And oh! Is there not a truth also in our fictions of the Unseen World. Are there not yet bright lingerers by the forest and the stream? Do the moon and the soft stars look out on no delicate and winged forms bathing in their light? Are the fairies, and the invisible hosts, but the children of our dreams; and not their inspiration? Is that all a delusion which speaks from the golden page? And is the world only given to harsh and anxious travellers, that walk to and fro in pursuit of no gentle shadows? Are the chimeras of the passions the sole spirits of the universe? No! while my remembrance treasures in its deepest cell the image of one no more—one who was "not of the earth, earthy"—one in whom love was the essence of thoughts divine—one whose shape and mould, whose heart and genius, would, have Poesy never before have dreamed it, have called forth the first notion of spirits resembling mortals, but not of them;—no, Gertrude! while I remember you, the faith, the trust in brighter shapes and fairer natures than the world knows of, comes clinging to my heart; and still will I think that Fairies might have watched over your sleep, and Spirits have ministered to your dreams.

CHAPTER III.

FEELINGS.

GERTRUDE and her companions proceeded by slow, and, to her, delightful stages, to Rotterdam. Trevylyan sat by her side, and her hand was ever in his; and when her delicate frame became sensible of fatigue, her head drooped on his shoulder as its natural resting-place. Her father was a man who had lived long enough to have encountered many reverses of fortune, and they had left him, as I am apt to believe long adversity usually *does* leave its prey, somewhat chilled and somewhat hardened to affection; passive and quiet of hope, resigned to the worst as to the common order of events, and expecting little from the best, as an unlooked-for incident in the regularity of human afflictions. He was insensible of his daughter's danger, for he was not one whom the fear of love endows with prophetic vision; and he lived tranquilly in the present, without asking what new misfortune awaited him in the future. Yet he loved his child, his only child, with whatever of affection was left him by the many shocks his heart had received; and in her approaching connection with one rich and noble as Trevylyan, he felt even something bordering upon pleasure. Lapped in the apathetic indifference of his nature, he leaned back in the carriage, enjoying the bright weather that attended their journey, and sensible—for he was one of fine and cultivated taste—of whatever beauties of nature or remains of art varied their course. A companion of this sort was the most agreeable that two persons never needing a third could desire; he left them undisturbed to the intoxication of their mutual presence; he marked not the interchange of glances; he listened not to the whisper, the low delicious whisper, with which the heart speaks its sympathy to heart. He broke not that charmed silence which falls over us when the thoughts are full, and words leave nothing to explain; that repose of feeling; that certainty that we are understood without the effort of words, which makes the real luxury of intercourse and the true enchantment of travel. What a memory hours like these bequeath, after we have settled down into the calm occupations of common life!—how beautiful, through the vista of years, seems that brief moonlight track upon the waters of our youth!

And Trevylyan's nature, which, as I have said before, was naturally hard and stern, which was hot, irritable, ambitious, and prematurely tinctured with the policy and lessons of the world, seemed utterly changed by the peculiarities of his love; every hour, every moment was full of incident to him; every look of Gertrude's was entered in the tablets of his heart, so that his love knew no languor, it required no change: he was absorbed in it—*it was himself!* And he was soft and watchful as the step of a mother by the couch of her sick child; the lion within him was tamed by indomitable love; the sadness, the presentiment that was mixed with all his passion for Gertrude, filled him too with that poetry of feeling which is the result of thoughts weighing upon us, and not to be expressed by ordinary language. In this part of their journey, as I find by the date, were the following lines written; they are to be judged as the lines of one in whom emotion and truth were the only inspiration:—

I.

"As leaves left darkling in the flush of day,
  When glints the glad sun chequering o'er the tree,
 I see the green earth brightening in the ray,
  Which only casts a shadow upon me!

II.

What are the beams, the flowers, the glory, all
  Life's glow and gloss—the music and the bloom,
When every sun but speeds the Eternal Pall,
  And Time is Death that dallies with the Tomb?

III.

And yet—oh yet, so young, so pure!—the while
  Fresh laugh the rose-hues round youth's morning sky,
That voice,—those eyes,—the deep love of that smile.
  Are they not soul—*all* soul—and *can* they die?

IV.

Are there the words 'No **More**' for thoughts like ours?
  Must the bark sink upon so soft a **wave**?
Hath the short summer of thy life no flowers
  But those which bloom above thine early grave?

V.

O God! and what is life, that I should live?
  '**Hath not** the world enow of common clay?'
And she—the Rose—whose life a soul could give
  To the void desert, sigh its sweets away?

VI.

And I that love thee thus, to whom the air,
  Blest by thy breath, makes heaven where'er it be,
Watch thy cheek wane, and smile away despair—
  Lest it should dim one hour yet left to Thee.

VII.

Still let me conquer **self,—oh, still conceal**
  By the smooth brow **the snake that coils below**;
Break, break my heart, it comforts yet to feel
  That *she* dreams **on, unwaken'd by my wo**!

VIII.

Hush'd, where the Star's soft angel loves to keep
  Watch o'er their tide, the mourning waters roll:
So glides my spirit—darkness in the deep,
  But o'er the wave the presence of thy soul!"

Gertrude had not as yet the presentiments that filled the soul of Trevylyan. She thought too little of herself to know her danger, and those hours to her were hours of unmingled sweetness. Sometimes, indeed, the exhaustion of her disease tinged her spirits with a vague sadness, an abstraction came over her, and a languor she vainly struggled against. These fits of dejection and gloom touched Trevylyan to the quick; his eye never ceased to watch them, nor his heart to soothe. Often when he marked them, he sought to attract her attention from what he fancied, though erringly, a sympathy with his own forebodings, and to lead her young and romantic imagination through the temporary beguilements of fiction; for Gertrude was yet in the first bloom of youth, and all the dews of beautiful childhood sparkled freshly from the virgin blossoms of her mind. And Trevylyan, who had passed some of his early years among the students of Leipsic, and was deeply versed in the various world of legendary lore, ransacked his memory for such tales as seemed to him most likely to win her interest; and often with false smiles entered into the playful tale, or oftener, with more faithful interest, into the graver legend of trials that warned of yet beguiled them from their own. Of such tales I have selected but a few; I know not that they are the least unworthy of repetition; they are those which many recollections induce me to repeat the most willingly. Gertrude loved these stories, for she had not yet lost, by the coldness of the world, one leaf from that soft and wild romance which belonged to her beautiful mind. And, more than all, she loved the sounds of a voice which every day became more and more musical to her ear. "Shall I tell you," said Trevylyan, one morning, as he observed her gloomier mood stealing over the face of Gertrude, "shall I tell you, ere yet we pass into the dull land of Holland, a story of Malines, whose spires we shall shortly see?" Gertrude's face brightened at once, and, as she leaned back in the carriage as it whirled rapidly along, and fixed her deep blue eyes on Trevylyan, he began the following tale.

CHAPTER IV.

THE MAID OF MALINES.

IT was noonday in the town of Malines, or Mechlin, as the English usually term it; the Sabbath bell had summoned the inhabitants to divine worship; and the crowd that had loitered round the Church of St. Rembauld had gradually emptied itself within the spacious aisles of the sacred edifice.

A young man was standing in the street, with his eyes bent on the ground, and apparently listening for some sound; for, without raising his looks from the rude pavement, he turned to every corner of it with an intent and anxious expression of countenance; he held in one hand a staff, in the other a long slender cord, the end of which trailed on the ground; every now and then he called, with a plaintive voice, "Fido, Fido, come back! Why hast thou deserted me?"—Fido returned not; the dog, wearied of confinement, had slipped from the string, and was at play with his kind in a distant quarter of the town, leaving the blind man to seek his way as he might to his solitary inn.

By-and-by a light step passed through the street, and the young stranger's face brightened.

"Pardon me," said he, turning to the spot where his quick ear had caught the sound, "and direct me, if you are not much pressed for a few moments' time, to the hotel *Mortier d'Or*."

It was a young woman, whose dress betokened that she belonged to the middling class of life, whom he thus addressed:—"It is some distance hence, sir," said she; "but if you continue your way straight on for about a hundred yards, and then take the second turn to your right hand——"

"Alas!" interrupted the stranger, with a melancholy smile, "your direction will avail me little; my dog has deserted me, and I am blind!"

There was something in these words, and in the stranger's voice, which went irresistibly to the heart of the young woman.—"Pray forgive me," she said, almost with tears in her eyes, "I did not perceive your—" misfortune, she was about to say, but she checked herself with an instinctive delicacy.—"Lean upon me, I will conduct you to the door; nay, sir," observing that he hesitated, "I have time enough to spare, I assure you."

The stranger placed his hand on the young woman's arm, and though Lucille was naturally so bashful that even her mother would laughingly reproach her for the excess of a maiden virtue, she felt not the least pang of shame, as she found herself thus suddenly walking through the streets of Malines alone with a young stranger, whose dress and air betokened him of rank superior to her own.

"Your voice is very gentle," said he, after a pause; "and that," he added, with a slight sigh, "is the only criterion by which I know the young and the beautiful!" Lucille now blushed, and with a slight mixture of pain in the blush, for she knew well that to beauty she had no pretension. "Are you a native of this town?" continued he.

"Yes, sir; my father holds a small office in the customs, and my mother and I eke out his salary by making lace. We are called poor, but we do not feel it, sir."

"You are fortunate! there is no wealth like the heart's wealth—content," answered the blind man, mournfully.

"And, monsieur," said Lucille, feeling angry with herself that she had awakened a natural envy in the stranger's mind, and anxious to change the subject—"and, monsieur, has he been long at Malines?"

"But yesterday. I am passing through the Low Countries on a tour; perhaps you smile at the tour of a blind man—but it is wearisome even to the blind to rest always in the same place. I thought during church-time, when the streets were empty, that I might, by the help of my dog, enjoy safely at least the air, if not the sight of the town: but there are some persons, methinks, who cannot have even a dog for a friend!"

The blind man spoke bitterly—the desertion of his dog had touched him to the core. Lucille wiped her eyes. "And does monsieur travel then alone?" said she; and looking at his face more attentively than she had yet ventured to do, she saw that he was scarcely above two-and-twenty. "His father, his *mother*," she added, with an emphasis on the last word, "are they not with him?"

"I am an orphan!" answered the stranger; "and I have neither brother nor sister."

The desolate condition of the blind man quite melted Lucille; never had she been so strongly affected. She felt a strange flutter at the heart—a secret and earnest sympathy, that attracted her at once towards him. She wished that Heaven had suffered her to be his sister.

The contrast between the youth and the form of the stranger, and the affliction which took hope from the one, and activity from the other, increased the compassion he excited. His features were remarkably regular, and had a certain nobleness in their outline; and his frame was gracefully and firmly knit, though he moved cautiously, and with no cheerful step.

They had now passed into a narrow street leading towards the hotel, when they heard behind them the clatter of hoofs; and Lucille, looking hastily back, saw that a troop of the Belgian horse was passing through the town.

She drew her charge close by the wall, and trembling with fear for him, she stationed herself by his side. The troop passed at a full trot through the street; and at the sound of their clanging arms, and the ringing hoofs of their heavy chargers, Lucille might have seen, had she looked at the blind man's face, that its sad features kindled with enthusiasm, and his head was raised proudly from its wonted and melancholy bend. "Thank Heaven!" she said, as the troop had nearly passed them, "the danger is over!" Not so. One of the last two soldiers who rode abreast, was unfortunately mounted on a young and unmanageable horse. The rider's oaths and digging spur only increased the fire and impatience of the charger: it plunged from side to side of the narrow street.

"Look to yourselves!" cried the horseman, as he was borne on to the place where Lucille and the stranger stood against the wall. "Are ye mad?—why do you not run?"

"For Heaven's sake—for mercy's sake, he is blind!" cried Lucille, clinging to the stranger's side.

"Save yourself, my kind guide!" said the stranger. But Lucille dreamed not of such desertion. The trooper wrested the horse's head from the spot where they stood; with a snort, as it felt the spur, the enraged animal lashed out with its hind-legs; and Lucille, unable to save *both*, threw herself before the blind man, and received the shock directed against him; her slight and delicate arm fell broken by her side—the horseman was borne onward. "Thank God, *you* are saved!" was poor Lucille's exclamation; and she fell, overcome with pain and terror, into the arms which the stranger mechanically opened to receive her.

"My guide! my friend!" cried he, "you are hurt, you——"

"No, sir," interrupted Lucille, faintly, "I am better—I am well. *This* arm, if you please—we are not far from your hotel now."

But the stranger's ear, tutored to every inflection of voice, told him at once of the pain she suffered; he drew from her by degrees the confession of the injury she had sustained; but the generous girl did not tell him it had been incurred solely in his protection. He now insisted on reversing their duties, and accompanying *her* to her home; and Lucille, almost fainting with pain, and hardly able to move, was forced to consent. But a few steps down the next turning stood the humble mansion of her father—they reached it—and Lucille scarcely crossed the threshold, before she sank down, and for some minutes was insensible to pain. It was left to the stranger to explain, and to beseech them immediately to send for a surgeon, "the most skilful—the most practised in the town," said he. "See, I am rich, and this is the least I can do to atone to your generous daughter, for not forsaking even a stranger in peril."

He held out his purse as he spoke, but the father refused the offer; and it saved the blind man some shame, that he could not see the blush of honest resentment, with which so poor a species of remuneration was put aside.

The young man stayed till the surgeon arrived, till the arm was set; nor did he depart until he had obtained a promise from the mother that he should learn the next morning how the sufferer had passed the night.

The next morning, indeed, he had intended to quit a town that offers but little temptation to the traveller; but he tarried day after day, until Lucille herself accompanied her mother, to assure him of her recovery.

You know, or at least I do, dearest Gertrude, that there *is* such a thing as love at the first meeting—a secret, an unaccountable affinity between persons, (strangers before,) which draws them irresistibly together. As if there were truth in Plato's beautiful phantasy, that our souls were a portion of the stars, and that spirits, thus attracted to each other, have drawn their original light from the same orb; and yearn for a renewal of their former union. Yet without recurring to such fanciful solutions of a daily mystery, it was but natural that one in the forlorn and desolate condition of Eugene St. Amand, should have felt a certain tenderness for a person who had so generously suffered for his sake.

The darkness to which he was condemned did not shut from his mind's eye the haunting images of ideal beauty; rather, on the contrary, in his perpetual and unoccupied solitude, he fed the reveries of an imagination naturally warm, and a heart eager for sympathy and commune.

He had said rightly that his only test of beauty was in the melody of voice; and never had a softer or a more thrilling tone than that of the young maiden touched upon his ear. Her exclamation, so beautifully denying self, so devoted in its charity, "Thank God, *you* are saved!" uttered too in the moment of her own suffering, rang constantly upon his soul, and he yielded, without precisely defining their nature, to vague and delicious sentiments, that his youth had never awakened to till then. And Lucille,—the very accident that had happened to her on his behalf, only deepened the interest she had already conceived for one who, in the first flush of youth, was thus cut off from the glad objects of life, and left to a night of years desolate and alone. There is, to your beautiful and kindly sex, a natural inclination to *protect*. This makes them the angels of sickness, the comforters of age, the fosterers of childhood; and this feeling, in Lucille peculiarly developed, had already inexpressibly linked her compassionate nature to the lot of the unfortunate traveller. With ardent affections, and with thoughts beyond her station and her years, she was not without that modest vanity which made her painfully susceptible to her own deficiencies in beauty. Instinctively conscious of how deeply she herself could love, she believed it impossible that she could ever be so loved in return. This stranger, so superior in her eyes to all she had yet seen, was the first who had ever addressed her in that voice which by tones, not words, speaks that admiration most dear to a woman's heart. To *him* she was beautiful, and her lovely mind spoke out undimmed by the imperfections of her face. Not, indeed, that Lucille was wholly without personal attraction; her light step and graceful form were elastic with the freshness of youth, and her mouth and smile had so gentle and tender an expression, that there were moments when it would not have been the blind only who would have mistaken her to be beautiful. Her early childhood had indeed given the promise of attractions, which the smallpox, that then fearful malady, had inexorably marred. It had not only seared the smooth skin and the brilliant hues, but utterly changed even the character of the features. It so happened that Lucille's family were celebrated for beauty, and vain of that celebrity; and so bitterly had her parents deplored the effects of the cruel malady, that poor Lucille had been early taught to consider them far more grievous than they really were, and to exaggerate the advantages of that beauty, the loss of which was considered by her parents so heavy a misfortune. Lucille too had a cousin named Julie, who was the wonder of all Malines for her personal perfections; and as the cousins were much together, the contrast was too striking not to occasion frequent mortification to Lucille. But every misfortune has something of a counterpoise; and the consciousness of personal inferiority had meekened, without souring, her temper, had given gentleness to a spirit that otherwise might have been too high, and humility to a mind that was naturally strong, impassioned, and energetic.

And yet Lucille had long conquered the one disadvantage she most dreaded in the want of beauty. Lucille was never known but to be loved. Wherever came her presence, her bright and soft mind diffused a certain inexpressible charm; and where she was not, a something was absent from the scene which not even Julie's beauty could replace.

"I propose," said St. Amand to Madame le Tisseur, Lucille's mother, as he sat in her little salon,—for he had already contracted that acquaintance with the family which permitted him to be led to their house, to return the visits Madame le Tisseur had made him, and his dog, once more returned a penitent to his master, always conducted his steps to the humble abode, and stopped instinctively at the door,—"I propose," said St. Amand, after a pause, and with some embarrassment, "to stay a little while longer at Malines; the air agrees with me, and I like the quiet of the place! but you are aware, madame, that at a hotel among strangers, I feel my situation somewhat cheerless. I have been thinking"—St. Amand paused again—"I have been thinking that if I could persuade some agreeable family to receive me as a lodger,—I would fix myself here for some weeks. I am easily pleased."

"Doubtless there are many in Malines who would be too happy to receive such a lodger."

"Will you receive me?" asked St. Amand, abruptly. "It was of *your* family I thought."

"Of us? Monsieur is too flattering. But we have scarcely a room good enough for you."

"What difference between one room and another can there be to me? That is the best apartment to my choice in which the human voice sounds most kindly."

The arrangement was made, and St. Amand came now to reside beneath the same roof as Lucille. And was she not happy that *he* wanted so constant an attendance? was she not happy that she was ever of use? St Amand was passionately fond of music; he played himself with a skill that was only surpassed by the exquisite melody of his voice; and was not Lucille happy when she sat mute and listening to such sounds as in Malines were never heard before? Was she not happy in gazing on a face to whose melancholy aspect her voice instantly summoned the smile? Was she not happy when the music ceased, and St. Amand called "Lucille?" Did not her own name uttered by that voice seem to her even sweeter than the music? Was she not happy when they walked out in the still evenings of summer, and her arm thrilled beneath the light touch of one to whom she was so necessary? Was she not proud in her happiness, and was there not something like worship in the gratitude she felt to him, for raising her humble spirit to the luxury of feeling herself beloved?

St. Amand's parents were French. They had resided in the neighbourhood of Amiens, where they had inherited a competent property, to which he had succeeded about two years previous to the date of my story.

He had been blind from the age of three years. "I know not," said he, as he related these particulars to Lucille one evening when they were alone; "I know not what the earth may be like, or the heaven, or the rivers whose voice at least I can hear, for I have no recollection beyond that of a confused, but delicious blending of a thousand glorious colours—a bright and quick sense of joy—A VISIBLE MUSIC. But it is only since my childhood closed that I have mourned, as I now unceasingly mourn, for the light of day. My boyhood passed in a quiet cheerfulness; the least trifle then could please and occupy the vacancies of my mind; but it was as I took delight in being read to,—as I listened to the vivid descriptions of

Poetry, as I glowed at the recital of great deeds, as I was made acquainted by books with the energy, the action, the heat, the fervour, the pomp, the enthusiasm of life, that I gradually opened to the sense of all I was for ever denied. I felt that I existed, not lived; and that, in the midst of the Universal Liberty, I was sentenced to a prison, from whose blank walls there was no escape. Still, however, while my parents lived, I had something of consolation; at least I was not alone. They died, and a sudden and dread solitude, a vast and empty dreariness, settled upon my dungeon. One old servant only, who had attended me from my childhood, who had known me in my short privilege of light, by whose recollections my mind could grope back its way through the dark and narrow passages of memory to faint glimpses of the sun, was all that remained to me of human sympathies. It did not suffice, however, to content me with a home where my father and my mother's kind voice were *not*. A restless impatience, an anxiety to move possessed me, and I set out from my home, journeying whither I cared not, so that at least I could change an air that weighed upon me like a palpable burthen. I took only this old attendant as my companion; he too died three months since at Bruxelles, worn out with years. Alas! I had forgotten that he was old, for I saw not his progress to decay; and now, save my faithless dog, I was utterly alone, till I came hither and found *thee*."

Lucille stooped down to caress the dog; she blessed the desertion that had led him to a friend who never could desert.

But however much, and however gratefully, St. Amand loved Lucille, her power availed not to chase the melancholy from his brow, and to reconcile him to his forlorn condition.

"Ah! would that I could see thee! Would that I could look upon a face that my heart vainly endeavours to delineate!"

"If thou couldst," sighed Lucille, "thou wouldst cease to love me."

"Impossible!" cried St. Amand, passionately. "However the world may find thee, *thou* wouldst become my standard of beauty; and I should judge not of thee by others, but of others by thee."

He loved to hear Lucille read to him, and mostly he loved the descriptions of war, of travel, of wild adventure, and yet they occasioned him the most pain. Often she paused from the page as she heard him sigh, and felt that she would even have renounced the bliss of being loved by him, if she could have restored to him that blessing, the desire for which haunted him as a spectre.

Lucille's family were Catholic, and, like most in their station, they possessed the superstitions, as well as the devotion of the faith.

Sometimes they amused themselves of an evening by the various legends and imaginary miracles of their calendar : and once, as they were thus conversing with two or three of their neighbours, "The Tomb of the Three Kings of Cologne" became the main topic of their wondering recitals. However strong was the sense of Lucille, she was, as you will readily conceive, naturally influenced by the belief of those with whom she had been brought up from her cradle, and she listened to tale after tale of the miracles wrought at the consecrated tomb, as earnestly and undoubtingly as the rest.

And the Kings of the East were no ordinary saints; to the relics of the Three Magi, who followed the Star of Bethlehem, and were the first potentates of the earth who adored its Saviour, well might the pious Catholic suppose that a peculiar power, and a healing sanctity, would belong. Each of the circle (St. Amand, who had been more than usually silent, and even gloomy during the day, had retired to his own apartment, for there were some moments when, in the sadness of his thoughts, he sought that solitude which he so impatiently fled from at others)—each of the circle had some story to relate equally veracious and indisputable, of an infirmity cured, or a prayer accorded, or a sin atoned for at the foot of the holy tomb. One story peculiarly affected Lucille ; the narrator, a venerable old man with gray locks, solemnly declared himself a witness of its truth.

A woman at Anvers had given birth to a son, the offspring of an illicit connection, who came into the world deaf and dumb. The unfortunate mother believed the calamity a punishment for her own sin. " Ah ! would," said she, "that the affliction had fallen only upon me ! Wretch that I am, my innocent child is punished for my offence !" This idea haunted her night and day : she pined and could not be comforted. As the child grew up, and wound himself more and more round her heart, his caresses added new pangs to her remorse ; and at length (continued the narrator) hearing perpetually of the holy fame of the Tomb of Cologne, she resolved upon a pilgrimage barefoot to the shrine. "God is merciful," said she, "and he who called Magdalene his sister, may take the mother's curse from the child." She then went to Cologne ; she poured her tears, her penitence, and her prayers, at the sacred tomb. When she returned to her native town, what was her dismay as she approached her cottage to behold it a heap of ruins !—its blackened rafters and yawning casements betokened the ravages of fire. The poor woman sunk upon the ground utterly overpowered. Had her son perished ? At that moment she heard the cry of a child's voice, and, lo ! her child rushed to her arms, and called her "mother !"

He had been saved from the fire, which had broken out seven days before; but in the terror he had suffered, the string that tied his tongue had been loosened; he had uttered articulate sounds of distress; the curse was removed, and one word at least the kind neighbours had already taught him, to welcome his mother's return. What cared she now that her substance was gone, that her roof was ashes?—she bowed in grateful submission to so mild a stroke; her prayer had been heard, and the sin of the mother was visited no longer on the child.

I have said, dear Gertrude, that this story made a deep impression upon Lucille. A misfortune so nearly akin to that of St. Amand, removed by the prayer of another, filled her with devoted thoughts, and a beautiful hope. "Is not the tomb still standing?" thought she. "Is not God still in heaven?—He who heard the guilty, may He not hear the guiltless? Is He not the God of love? Are not the affections the offerings that please Him best? and what though the child's mediator was his mother, can even a mother love her child more tenderly than I love Eugene? But if, Lucille, thy prayer be granted, if he recover his sight, *thy* charm is gone, he will love thee no longer. No matter! be it so—I shall at least have made him happy!"

Such were the thoughts that filled the mind of Lucille; she cherished them till they settled into resolution, and she secretly vowed to perform her pilgrimage of love. She told neither St. Amand nor her parents of her intention; she knew the obstacles such an announcement would create. Fortunately she had an aunt settled at Bruxelles, to whom she had been accustomed, once in every year, to pay a month's visit, and at that time she generally took with her the work of a twelvemonth's industry, which found a readier sale at Bruxelles than at Malines. Lucille and St. Amand were already betrothed; their wedding was shortly to take place; and the custom of the country leading parents, however poor, to nourish the honourable ambition of giving some dowry with their daughters, Lucille found it easy to hide the object of her departure, under the pretence of taking the lace to Bruxelles, which had been the year's labour of her mother and herself—it would sell for sufficient, at least, to defray the preparations for the wedding.

"Thou art ever right, child," said Madame le Tisseur; "the richer St. Amand is, why the less oughtest thou to go a beggar to his house."

In fact, the honest ambition of the good people was excited; their pride had been hurt by the envy of the town and the current congratulations on so advantageous a marriage; and they employed themselves in counting up the fortune they should be able to give to their only child, and flattering their pardonable vanity with the notion that there would be no such great disproportion in the connection after all. They were right, but not in their own view of the estimate; the wealth that Lucille brought was what fate could not lessen,—reverse could not reach,—the ungracious seasons could not blight its sweet harvest,—imprudence could not dissipate, fraud could not steal, one grain from its abundant coffers! Like the purse in the Fairy Tale, its use was hourly, its treasure inexhaustible.

St. Amand alone was not to be won to her departure; he chafed at the notion of a dowry; he was not appeased even by Lucille's representation, that it was only to gratify and not to impoverish her parents. "And *thou*, too, canst leave me!" he said, in that plaintive voice which had made his first charm to Lucille's heart. "It is a double blindness!"

"But for a few days; a fortnight at most, dearest Eugene."

"A fortnight! you do not reckon time as the blind do," said St. Amand, bitterly.

"But listen, listen, dear Eugene," said Lucille, weeping.

The sound of her sobs restored him to a sense of his ingratitude. Alas, he knew not how much he had to be grateful for. He held out his arms to her: "Forgive me," said he. "Those who can see nature know not how terrible it is to be alone."

"But my mother will not leave you."

"She is not you!"

"And Julie," said Lucille, hesitatingly.

"What is Julie to me?"

"Ah, you are the only one, save my parents, who could think of me in her presence."

"And why, Lucille?"

"Why! She is more beautiful than a dream."

"Say not so. Would I could see, that I might prove to the world how much more beautiful thou art. There is no music in *her* voice."

The evening before Lucille departed, she sat up late with St. Amand and her mother. They conversed on the future; they made plans; in the wide sterility of the world they laid out the garden of household love, and filled it with flowers, forgetful of the wind that scatters and the frost that kills. And when, leaning on Lucille's arm, St. Amand sought his chamber, and they parted at his door, which closed upon her; she fell down on her knees at the threshold, and poured out the fulness of her heart in a prayer for his safety, and the fulfilment of her timid hope.

At daybreak she was consigned to the conveyance that performed the short journey from Malines to Bruxelles. When she entered the town, instead of seeking her aunt, she rested at an auberge in the suburbs, and confiding her little basket of lace to the care of its hostess, she set out alone, and on foot, upon the errand of her heart's lovely superstition. And erring though it was, her faith redeemed its weakness—her affection made it even sacred. And well may we believe, that the Eye which reads all secrets, scarce looked reprovingly on that fanaticism whose only infirmity was love.

So fearful was she, lest, by rendering the task too easy, she might impair the effect, that she scarcely allowed herself rest or food. Sometimes, in the heat of noon, she wandered a little from the roadside, and under the spreading lime trees surrendered her mind to its sweet and bitter thoughts; but ever the restlessness of her enterprise urged her on, and faint, weary, and with bleeding feet, she started up and continued her way. At length she reached the ancient city, where a holier age has scarce worn from the habits and aspects of men the Roman trace. She prostrated herself at the tomb of the Magi; she proffered her ardent but humble prayer to Him before whose Son those fleshless heads (yet to faith at least preserved) had, eighteen centuries ago, bowed in adoration. Twice every day, for a whole week, she sought the same spot, and poured forth the same prayer. The last day an old priest, who, hovering in the church, had observed her constantly at devotion, with that fatherly interest which the better ministers of the Catholic sect (that sect which has covered the earth with the mansions of charity) feel for the unhappy, approached her as she was retiring with moist and downcast eyes, and saluting her, assumed the privilege of his order, to inquire if there was ought in which his advice or aid could serve. There was something in the venerable air of the old man which encouraged Lucille; she opened her heart to him; she told him all. The good priest was much moved by her simplicity and earnestness. He questioned her minutely as to the peculiar species of blindness with which St. Amand was afflicted; and after musing a little while, he said, "Daughter, God is great and merciful; we must trust in his power, but we must not forget that he mostly works by mortal agents. As you pass through Louvain in your way home, fail not to see there a certain physician, named Le Kain. He is celebrated through Flanders for the cures he has wrought among the blind, and his advice is sought by all classes from far and near. He lives hard by the Hôtel de Ville, but any one will inform you of his residence. Stay, my child, you shall take him a note from me; he is a benevolent and kindly man, and you shall tell him exactly the same story (and with the same voice) you have told to me."

So saying the priest made Lucille accompany him to his home, and forcing her to refresh herself less sparingly than she had yet done since she had left Malines, he gave her his blessing, and a letter to Le Kain, which he rightly judged would ensure her a patient hearing from the physician. Well known among all men of science was the name of the priest, and a word of recommendation from him went farther, where virtue and wisdom were honoured, than the longest letter from the haughtiest sieur in Flanders.

With a patient and hopeful spirit, the young pilgrim turned her back on the Roman Cologne; and now about to rejoin St. Amand, she felt neither the heat of the sun nor the weariness of the road. It was one day at noon that she again passed through Louvain, and she soon found herself by the noble edifice of the Hôtel de Ville. Proud rose its spires against the sky, and the sun shone bright on its rich tracery and Gothic casements; the broad open street was crowded with persons of all classes, and it was with some modest alarm that Lucille lowered her veil and mingled with the throng. It was easy, as the priest had said, to find the house of Le Kain; she bade the servant take the priest's letter to his master, and she was not long kept waiting before she was admitted to the physician's presence. He was a spare, tall man, with a bald front, and a calm and friendly countenance. He was not less touched than the priest had been, by the manner in which she narrated her story, described the affliction of her betrothed, and the hope that had inspired the pilgrimage she had just made.

"Well," he said, encouragingly, "we must see our patient. You can bring him hither to me."

"Ah, sir, I had hoped——" Lucille stopped suddenly.

"What, my young friend?"

"That I might have had the triumph of bringing you to Malines. I know, sir, what you are about to say; and I know, sir, your time must be very valuable; but I am not so poor as I seem, and Eugene, that is, Monsieur St. Amand, is very rich, and—and I have at Bruxelles, what I am sure is a large sum; it was to have provided for the wedding, but it is most heartily at your service, sir."

Le Kain smiled; he was one of those men who love to read the human heart when its leaves are fair and undefiled; and, in the benevolence of science, he would have gone a longer journey than from Louvain to Malines to give sight to the blind, even had St. Amand been a beggar.

"Well, well," said he; "but you forget that Monsieur St.

'Amand is not the only one in the world who wants me. I must look at my note-book, and see if I can be spared for a day or two."

So saying, he glanced at his memoranda; everything smiled on Lucille; he had no engagements that his partner could not fulfil, for some days; he consented to accompany Lucille to Malines.

Meanwhile, cheerless and dull had passed the time to St. Amand, he was perpetually asking Madame le Tisseur what hour it was; it was almost his only question. There seemed to him no sun in the heavens, no freshness in the air, and he even forbore his favourite music; the instrument had lost its sweetness since Lucille was not by to listen.

It was natural that the gossips of Malines should feel some envy at the marriage Lucille was about to make with one, whose competence report had exaggerated into prodigal wealth, whose birth had been elevated from the respectable to the noble, and whose handsome person was clothed, by the interest excited by his misfortune, with the beauty of Antinous. Even that misfortune, which ought to have levelled all distinctions, was not sufficient to check the general envy; perhaps to some of the damsels of Malines, blindness in a husband would not have seemed an unwelcome infirmity! But there was one in whom this envy rankled with a peculiar sting; it was the beautiful, the all-conquering Julie. That the humble, the neglected Lucille should be preferred to her; that Lucille, whose existence was well-nigh forgot beside Julie's, should become thus suddenly of importance; that there should be one person in the world, and that person young, rich, handsome, to whom she was less than nothing, when weighed in the balance with Lucille, mortified to the quick a vanity that had never till then received a wound. "It is well," she would say with a bitter jest, "that Lucille's lover is blind. To be the one it is necessary to be the other!"

During Lucille's absence she had been constantly in Madame le Tisseur's house; indeed, Lucille had prayed her to be so. She had sought, with an industry that astonished herself, to supply Lucille's place, and among the strange contradictions of human nature, she had learned during her efforts to please, to love the object of those efforts,—as much at least as she was capable of loving.

She conceived a positive hatred to Lucille; she persisted in imagining that nothing but the accident of first acquaintance had deprived her of a conquest with which she persuaded herself her happiness had become connected. Had St. Amand never loved Lucille and proposed to Julie, his misfortune would have made her reject him, despite his wealth and his youth; but to be Lucille's lover, and a conquest to be won from Lucille, raised him instantly to an importance not his own. Safe, however, in his affliction, the arts and beauty of Julie fell harmless on the fidelity of St. Amand. Nay, he liked her less than ever, for it seemed an impertinence in any one to counterfeit the anxiety and watchfulness of Lucille.

"It is time, surely it is time, Madame le Tisseur, that Lucille should return! She might have sold all the lace in Malines by this time," said St. Amand one day peevishly.

"Patience, my dear friend, patience; perhaps she may return to-morrow."

"To-morrow! let me see, it is only six o'clock—only six, you are sure?"

"Just five, dear Eugene; shall I read to you? this is a new book from Paris; it has made a great noise," said Julie.

"You are very kind, but I will not trouble you."

"It is anything but trouble."

"In a word, then, I would rather not."

"Oh! that he could see," thought Julie; "would I not punish him for this!"

"I hear carriage wheels; who can be passing this way? Surely it is the voiturier from Bruxelles," said St. Amand, starting up; "it is his day—his hour, too. No, no, it is a lighter vehicle," and he sank down listlessly on his seat.

Nearer and nearer rolled the wheels; they turned the corner; they stopped at the lowly door; and, overcome, overjoyed, Lucille was clasped to the bosom of St. Amand.

"Stay," said she, blushing, as she recovered her self-possession, and turned to Le Kain; "pray pardon me, sir. Dear Eugene, I have brought with me one who, by God's blessing, may yet restore you to sight."

"We must not be sanguine, my child," said Le Kain; "anything is better than disappointment."

To close this part of my story, dear Gertrude, Le Kain examined St. Amand, and the result of the examination was a confident belief in the probability of a cure. St. Amand gladly consented to the experiment of an operation; it succeeded—the blind man saw! Oh! what were Lucille's feelings, what her emotion, what her joy, when she found the object of her pilgrimage,—of her prayers—fulfilled! That joy was so intense, that in the eternal alternations of human life she might have foretold from its excess how bitter the sorrows fated to ensue.

As soon as by degrees the patient's new sense became reconciled to the light, his first, his only demand, was for Lucille. "No, let me not see her alone, let me see her in the midst of you all, that I may convince you that the heart never is mistaken in its instincts." With a fearful, a sinking presentiment, Lucille yielded to the request, to which the impetuous St. Amand would hear indeed no denial. The father, the mother, Julie, Lucille, Julie's younger sisters, assembled in the little parlour; the door opened, and St. Amand stood hesitating on the threshold. One look around sufficed to him; his face brightened, he uttered a cry of joy. "Lucille! Lucille!" he exclaimed, "it is you, I know it, *you* only!" He sprang forward *and fell at the feet of Julie!*

Flushed, elated, triumphant, Julie bent upon him 'her sparkling eyes; *she* did not undeceive him.

"You are wrong, you mistake," said Madame le Tisseur, in confusion; "that is her cousin Julie—this is your Lucille."

St. Amand rose, turned, saw Lucille, and at that moment she wished herself in her grave. Surprise, mortification, disappointment, almost dismay, were depicted in his gaze. He had been haunting his prison-house with dreams, and, now set free, he felt how unlike they were to the truth. Too new to observation to read the woe, the despair, the lapse and shrinking of the whole frame, that his look occasioned Lucille, he yet felt, when the first shock of his surprise was over, that it was not thus he should thank her who had restored him to sight. He hastened to redeem his error;—ah! how could it be redeemed?

From that hour all Lucille's happiness was at an end; her fairy palace was shattered in the dust; the magician's wand was broken up; the Ariel was given to the winds; and the bright enchantment no longer distinguished the land she lived in from the rest of the barren world. It was true that St. Amand's words were kind; it is true that he remembered with the deepest gratitude all she had done in his behalf; it is true that he forced himself again and again to say, "She is my betrothed—my benefactress!" and he cursed himself to think that the feelings he had entertained for her were fled. Where was the passion of his words? where the ardour of his tone? where that play and light of countenance which her step, *her* voice, could formerly call forth? When they were alone he was embarrassed and constrained, and almost cold; his hand no longer sought hers; his soul no longer missed her if she was absent a moment from his side. When in their household circle he seemed visibly more at ease; but did his eyes fasten upon her who had opened them to the day? did they not wander at every interval with a too eloquent admiration to the blushing and radiant face of the exulting Julie? This was not, you will believe, suddenly perceptible in one day or one week, but every day it was perceptible more and more. Yet still—bewitched, ensnared, as St. Amand was—he never perhaps would have been guilty of an infidelity that he strove with the keenest remorse to wrestle against, had it not been for the fatal contrast, at the first moment of his gushing enthusiasm, which Julie had presented to Lucille; but for that he would have formed no previous idea of real and living beauty to aid the disappointment of his imaginings and his dreams. He would have seen Lucille young and graceful, and with eyes beaming affection, contrasted only by the wrinkled countenance and bended frame of her parents, and she would have completed her conquest over him before he had discovered that she was less beautiful than others; nay, more—that infidelity never could have lasted above the first few days, if the vain and heartless object of it had not exerted every art, all the power and witchery of her beauty, to cement and continue it. The unfortunate Lucille—so susceptible to the slightest change in those she loved, so diffident of herself, so proud too in that diffidence—no longer necessary, no longer missed, no longer loved—could not bear to endure the galling comparison between the past and the present. She fled uncomplainingly to her chamber to indulge her tears, and thus, unhappily, absent as her father generally was during the day, and busied as her mother was either at work or in household matters, she left Julie a thousand opportunities to complete the power she had begun to wield over—no, not the heart!—the *senses* of St. Amand! Yet, still not suspecting, in the open generosity of her mind, the whole extent of her affliction, poor Lucille buoyed herself at times with the hope that when once married, when, once in that intimacy of friendship, the unspeakable love she felt for him could disclose itself with less restraint than at present,—she should perhaps regain a heart which had been so devotedly hers, that she could not think that without a fault it was irrevocably gone: on that hope she anchored all the little happiness that remained to her. And still St. Amand pressed their marriage, but in what different tones! In fact, he wished to preclude from himself the possibility of a deeper ingratitude than that which he had incurred already. He vainly thought that the broken reed of love might be bound up and strengthened by the ties of duty; and at least he was anxious that his hand, his fortune, his esteem, his gratitude, should give to Lucille the only recompense it was now in his power to bestow. Meanwhile left alone so often with Julie, and Julie bent on achieving the last triumph over his heart, St. Amand was gradually preparing a far different reward, a far different return for her to whom he owed so incalculable a debt.

There was a garden, behind the house, in which there was a small arbour, where often in the summer evenings, Eugene and Lucille had sat together—hours never to return! One day she heard from her own chamber, where she sat mourning, the sound of St. Amand's flute swelling gently from that beloved and consecrated bower. She wept as she heard it, and the memories that the music bore, softening and endearing his image, she began to reproach herself that she had yielded so often to the impulse of her wounded feelings; that chilled by *his* coldness, she had left him so often to himself, and had not sufficiently dared to tell him of that affection which, in her modest self-depreciation, constituted her only pretension to his love. "Perhaps he is alone now," she thought; "the air too is one which he knows that I love:" and with her heart in her step, she stole from the house and sought the arbour. She had scarce turned from her chamber when the flute ceased; as she neared the arbour she heard voices—Julie's voice in grief, St. Amand's in consolation. A dread foreboding seized her; her feet clung rooted to the earth.

"Yes, marry her—forget me," said Julie; "in a few days you will be another's, and I, I—forgive me, Eugene, forgive me that I have disturbed your happiness. I am punished sufficiently—my heart will break, but it will break in loving you:" sobs choked Julie's voice.

"Oh, speak not thus," said St. Amand. "I, *I* only am to blame; I, false to both, to both ungrateful. Oh, from the hour that these eyes opened upon you I drank in a new life; the sun itself to me was less wonderful than your beauty. But—but—let me forget that hour. What do I not owe to Lucille? I shall be wretched— I shall deserve to be so; for shall I not think, Julie, that I have embittered your life with our ill-fated love? But all that I can give —my hand—my home—my plighted faith—must be hers. Nay, Julie, nay—why that look? could I act otherwise? can I dream otherwise? Whatever the sacrifice, *must* I not render it? Ah, what do I owe to Lucille, were it only for the thought that but for her I might never have seen thee!"

Lucille stayed to hear no more; with the same soft step as that which had borne her within hearing of these fatal words, she turned back once more to her desolate chamber.

That evening, as St. Amand was sitting alone in his apartment, he heard a gentle knock at the door. "Come in," he said, and Lucille entered. He started in some confusion, and would have taken her hand, but she gently repulsed him. She took a seat opposite to him, and looking down, thus addressed him :—

"My dear Eugene, that is, Monsieur St. Amand, I have something on my mind that I think it better to speak at once; and if I do not exactly express what I would wish to say, you must not be offended with Lucille: it is not an easy matter to put into words what one feels deeply." Colouring, and suspecting something of the truth, St. Amand would have broken in upon her here; but she with a gentle impatience, motioned him to be silent, and continued :—

"You know that when you once loved me, I used to tell you that you would cease to do so, could you see how undeserving I was of your attachment? I did not deceive myself, Eugene; I always felt assured that such would be the case, that your love for me necessarily rested on your affliction: but for all that, I never at least had a dream, or a desire, but for your happiness; and God knows, that if again, by walking bare-footed, not to Cologne, but to Rome—to the end of the world, I could save you from a much less misfortune than that of blindness, I would cheerfully do it; yes, even though I might foretell all the while that, on my return, you would speak to me coldly, think of me lightly, and that the penalty to me would—would be—what it has been!" Here Lucille wiped a few natural tears from her eyes; St. Amand, struck to the heart, covered his face with his hands without the courage to interrupt her. Lucille continued :—

"That which I foresaw has come to pass; I am no longer to you what I once was, when you could clothe this poor form and this homely face, with a beauty they did not possess; you would wed me still, it is true; but I am proud, Eugene, and cannot stoop to gratitude where I once had love. I am not so unjust as to blame you; the change was natural, was inevitable. I should have steeled myself more against it; but I am now resigned: we must part; you love Julie—that too is natural—and *she* loves you; ah! what also more in the probable course of events? Julie loves you, not yet, perhaps, so much as I did, but then she has not known you as I have, and she whose whole life has been triumph, cannot feel the gratitude I felt at fancying myself loved; but this will come—God grant it! Farewell, then, for ever, dear Eugene; I leave you when you no longer want me; you are now independent of Lucille; wherever you go, a thousand hereafter can supply my place;—farewell!"

She rose, as she said this, to leave the room; but St. Amand seizing her hand, which she in vain endeavoured to withdraw from his clasp, poured forth incoherently, passionately, his reproaches on himself, his eloquent persuasions against her resolution.

"I confess," said he, "that I have been allured for a moment; I confess that Julie's beauty made me less sensible to your stronger, your holier, oh! far, far holier title to my love! But forgive me, dearest Lucille; already I return to you, to all I once felt for you; make me not curse the blessing of sight that I owe to you. You must not leave me; never can we two part; try me, only try me, and if ever, hereafter, my heart wander from you, *then*, Lucille, leave me to my remorse!"

Even at that moment Lucille did not yield; she felt that his prayer was but the enthusiasm of the hour; she felt that there was a virtue in her pride; that to leave him was a duty to herself. In vain he pleaded; in vain were his embraces, his prayers; in vain he reminded her of their plighted troth, of her aged parents, whose happiness had become wrapped in her union with him: "How,— even were it as you wrongly believe,—how, in honour to them, can I desert you, can I wed another!"

"Trust that, trust all, to me," answered Lucille; "your honour shall be my care, none shall blame *you*; only do not let your marriage with Julie be celebrated here before their eyes: that is all I ask, all they can expect. God bless you! do not fancy I shall be unhappy, for whatever happiness the world gives you, shall I not have contributed to bestow it?—and with that thought, I am above compassion."

She glided from his arms, and left him to a solitude more bitter even than that of blindness; that very night Lucille sought her mother; to her she confided all. I pass over the reasons she urged, the arguments she overcame; she conquered rather than convinced, and leaving to Madame le Tisseur the painful task of breaking to her father her unaltered resolution, she quitted Malines the next morning, and with a heart too honest to be utterly without comfort, paid that visit to her aunt which had been so long deferred.

The pride of Lucille's parents prevented them from reproaching St. Amand. He could not bear, however, their cold and altered looks; he left their house; and though for several days he would not even see Julie, yet her beauty and her art gradually resumed their empire over him. They were married at Courtroi, and to the joy of the vain Julie, departed to the gay metropolis of France. But, before their departure, before his marriage, St. Amand endeavoured to appease his conscience by obtaining for Monsieur le Tisseur a much more lucrative and honourable office than that he now held. Rightly judging that Malines could no longer be a pleasant residence for them, and much less for Lucille, the duties of the post were to be fulfilled in another town; and knowing that Monsieur le Tisseur's delicacy would revolt at receiving such a favour from his hands, he kept the nature of his negotiation a close secret, and suffered the honest citizen to believe that his own merits alone had entitled him to so unexpected a promotion.

Time went on. This quiet and simple history of humble affections took its date in a stormy epoch of the world—the dawning Revolution of France. The family of Lucille had been little more than a year settled in their new residence, when Dumouriez led his army into the Netherlands. But how meanwhile had that year passed for Lucille? I have said that her spirit was naturally high; that though so tender, she was not weak; her very pilgrimage to Cologne alone, and at the timid age of seventeen, proved that there was a strength in her nature no less than a devotion in her love. The sacrifice she had made brought its own reward. She believed St. Amand was happy, and she would not give way to the selfishness of grief; she had still duties to perform; she could still comfort her parents and cheer their age; she could still be all the world to them: she felt this, and was consoled. Only once during the year had she heard of Julie; she had been seen by a mutual friend at Paris, gay, brilliant, courted, and admired; of St. Amand she heard nothing.

My tale, dear Gertrude, does not lead me through the harsh scenes of war. I do not tell you of the slaughter and the siege, and the blood that inundated those fair lands—the great battle-field of Europe. The people of the Netherlands in general were with the cause of Dumouriez, but the town in which Le Tisseur dwelt offered some faint resistance to his arms. Le Tisseur himself, despite his age, girded on his sword; the town was carried, and the fierce and licentious troops of the conqueror poured, flushed with their easy victory, through its streets. Le Tisseur's house was filled with drunken and rude troopers; Lucille herself trembled in the fierce gripe of one of those dissolute soldiers, more bandit than soldier, whom the subtle Dumouriez had united to his army, and by whose blood he so often saved that of his nobler band; her shrieks, her cries were vain, when suddenly the troopers gave way; "the Captain! brave Captain!" was shouted forth; the insolent soldier felled by a powerful arm, sunk senseless at the feet of Lucille; and a glorious form, towering above its fellows,—even through its glittering garb, even in that dreadful hour, remembered at a glance by Lucille, stood at her side; her protector—her guardian!—Thus once more she beheld St. Amand!

The house was cleared in an instant—the door barred. Shouts, groans, wild snatches of exulting song, the clang of arms, the tramp of horses, the hurrying footsteps, the deep music, sounded loud, and blended terribly without. Lucille heard them not,—she was on that breast which **never** should have deserted her.

Effectually to protect his friends, St. Amand took up his quarters at their house; **and for** two days he was once more under the same roof **as** Lucille. He never recurred voluntarily to Julie; he answered **Lucille's** timid inquiry after her health, briefly, and with coldness, **but he** spoke with all the enthusiasm of a long-pent and ardent spirit, **of the** new profession he had embraced. Glory seemed now to be his only mistress; and the vivid delusion of the first bright dreams **of** the Revolution filled his mind, broke from his tongue, and lighted **up** those dark eyes which Lucille had redeemed to day.

She saw him depart at the head of his troop; she saw his proud **crest** glancing in the sun; she saw his steed winding through the narrow street; she saw that his last glance reverted to her, where she stood at the door; and, as he waved his **adieu, she** fancied that there was on his face that look of deep **and** grateful tenderness, which reminded her of the one bright epoch of her life.

She was right; **St.** Amand had long since in bitterness repented of a transient **infatuation,** had long since distinguished the **true** Florimel **from** the false, and felt that, in Julie, Lucille's wrongs were avenged. But in the hurry and heat of war he plunged that regret—the keenest of all—which embodies the bitter words, "TOO LATE!"

Years passed away, and in the **resumed** tranquillity of Lucille's life, the brilliant apparition **of** St. Amand appeared as something dreamed of, not seen. The star of Napoleon had risen above the horizon; the romance of his early career had commenced; and the campaign of Egypt had been the herald of those brilliant and meteoric successes which flashed forth from the gloom of the Revolution **of France.**

You are aware, dear Gertrude, how many in the French as well as **the** English troops, returned home from Egypt, blinded with the ophthalmia **of** that arid soil. Some of the young men in Lucille's town, who **had** joined Napoleon's army, came back darkened by that fearful affliction, and Lucille's alms, and Lucille's aid, and Lucille's sweet voice, were ever at hand for those poor sufferers, whose common misfortune touched **so** thrilling a chord of her heart.

Her father was now dead, and she had only her mother to cheer amidst the ills of age. As one evening they sat at work together, Madame le Tisseur said, after a pause—

"I wish, dear Lucille, thou couldst be persuaded to marry Justin; he loves thee well, and now that thou art yet young, and hast many years before thee, thou shouldst remember that when I die thou wilt be alone."

"Ah cease, dearest mother, I never can marry now; and as for love—once taught in the bitter school in which I have learned the knowledge of myself—I cannot be deceived again."

"My Lucille, you do not know yourself: never was a woman loved, if Justin does not love you; and never did lover feel with more real warmth how worthily he loved."

And this was true; and not of Justin alone, for Lucille's modest virtues, her kindly temper, and a certain undulating and feminine grace, which accompanied all her movements, had secured her as many conquests as if she had been beautiful. She had rejected all offers of marriage with a shudder; without even the throb of a flattered vanity. One memory, sadder, was also dearer, to her than all things; and something sacred in its recollections made her deem it even a crime to think of effacing the past by a new affection.

"I believe," continued Madame le Tisseur, angrily, "that thou still thinkest fondly of him, from whom only in the world thou couldst have experienced ingratitude."

"Nay, mother," said Lucille, with a blush and a slight sigh, "Eugene is married to another."

While thus conversing, they heard a gentle and timid knock at the door—the latch was lifted. "This," said the rough voice of a *commissionaire* of the town, "this, monsieur, is the house of *Madame le Tisseur*, and *voilà mademoiselle!*" A tall figure, with a shade over his eyes, and wrapped in a long military cloak, stood in the room. A thrill shot across Lucille's heart. He stretched out his arms. "Lucille," said that melancholy voice, which had made the music of her first youth—"where art thou, Lucille? Alas! she does not recognize St. Amand."

Thus was it, indeed. By a singular fatality, the burning suns and the sharp dust of the plains of Egypt had smitten the young soldier, in the flush of his career, with a second—and this time, with an irremediable—blindness! He had returned to France to find his hearth lonely: Julie was no more—a sudden fever had cut her off in the midst of youth; and he had sought his way to Lucille's house, to see if one hope yet remained to him in the world!

And when, days afterwards, humbly and sadly he re-urged a former suit, did Lucille shut her heart to its prayer? Did her pride remember its wound—did she revert to his desertion—did she reply to the whisper of her yearning love, "*thou hast been before forsaken?*"

That voice, and those darkened eyes, pled to **her** with a pathos not to be resisted; "**I am** once more necessary to him," was all her thought—"if **I reject** him, who will tend him?" In that thought was the motive **of her** conduct; in that thought gushed back upon her soul all the springs of checked, but unconquered, unconquerable love! In that thought she stood beside him at the altar, and **pledged**, with a yet holier devotion than she might have felt of yore, **the vow** of her imperishable truth.

And Lucille found, in the future, a reward which the common world could never comprehend. With his blindness returned all the feelings she had first awakened in St. Amand's solitary heart; again he yearned for her step—again he missed even a moment's absence from his side—again her voice chased the shadow from his brow— and **in** her presence was a sense of shelter and of sunshine. He no longer sighed for the blessing he had lost; he reconciled himself to fate, and entered into that serenity of mood which mostly characterizes the blind. Perhaps after we have seen the actual world, and experienced its hollow pleasures, we can resign ourselves the better to its exclusion; and as the cloister, which repels the ardour of our hope, is sweet to our remembrance, so the darkness loses its terror, when experience has wearied us with the glare and travail of **the** day. It was something, too, as they advanced in life, to feel the chains that bound him to Lucille strengthening daily, and to cherish in his overflowing heart the sweetness of increasing gratitude; it was something **that** he could **not see** years wrinkle that open brow, or dim the tenderness of that touching smile;—it was something that to him she was beyond the reach of time, and preserved to the verge of a grave (which received them **both** within a few days of each other) in all the bloom of her unwithering affection—in all the freshness of **a** heart that never could grow old!

Gertrude, who had broken in upon Trevylyan's story by a **thousand** anxious interruptions, and a thousand pretty apologies for interrupting, was charmed with a tale in which true love was made happy at last, although she did not forgive St. Amand his ingratitude, and although she declared, with a critical shake of the head, that "it was very unnatural that the mere beauty of Julie, or the mere want of it in Lucille, should have produced such an effect upon him, if he had ever *really* **loved** Lucille **in** his blindness."

As they **passed** through Malines, the town assumed an interest in Gertrude's eyes, to which it scarcely of itself was entitled. She looked wistfully at **the** broad market-place; at a corner of which was one of those **out**-of-door groups of quiet and noiseless revellers, which Dutch art has raised from the Familiar to the Picturesque;

and then glancing to the town of St. Rembauld, she fancied, amidst the silence of noon, that she yet heard the plaintive cry of the blind orphan—"Fido, Fido, why hast thou deserted me?"

CHAPTER V.

ROTTERDAM,—THE CHARACTER OF THE DUTCH.—THEIR RESEMBLANCE TO THE GERMANS.—A DISPUTE BETWEEN VANE AND TREVYLYAN, AFTER THE MANNER OF THE ANCIENT NOVELISTS, AS TO WHICH IS PREFERABLE, THE LIFE OF ACTION OR THE LIFE OF REPOSE.—TREVYLYAN'S CONTRAST BETWEEN LITERARY AMBITION AND THE AMBITION OF PUBLIC LIFE.

OUR travellers arrived at Rotterdam on a bright and sunny day. There is a cheerfulness about the operations of Commerce—a life—a bustle—an action which always exhilarate the spirits at the first glance. Afterwards they fatigue us; we get too soon behind the scenes, and find the base and troublous passions which move the puppets and conduct the drama.

But Gertrude, in whom ill health had not destroyed the vividness of impression that belongs to the inexperienced, was delighted at the cheeriness of all around her. As she leaned lightly on Trevylyan's arm, he listened with a forgetful joy to her questions and exclamations at the stir and liveliness of a city, from which was to commence their pilgrimage along the Rhine. And indeed the scene was rife with the spirit of that people at once so active and so patient—so daring on the sea—so cautious on the land. Industry was visible everywhere; the vessels in the harbour—the crowded boat, putting off to land—the throng on the quay, all looked bustling and spoke of commerce. The city itself, on which the skies shone fairly through light and fleecy clouds, wore a cheerful aspect. The church of St. Lawrence rising above the clean, neat houses, and on one side, trees thickly grouped, gaily contrasted at once the waters and the city.

"I like this place," said Gertrude's father, quietly; "it has an air of comfort."

"And an absence of Grandeur," said Trevylyan.

"A commercial people are one great middle class in their habits and train of mind," replied Vane; "and grandeur belongs to the extremes,—an impoverished population, and a wealthy despot."

They went to see the statue of Erasmus, and the house in which he was born. Vane had a certain admiration for Erasmus which his companions did **not** share; he liked the quiet irony of the sage, and his knowledge **of the** world; and, besides, Vane was of that time of life when philosophers become objects of interest. **At** first they are teachers; secondly, friends; and it **is only a few who** arrive at the third stage, and find them deceivers. **The Dutch are a singular people.** Their literature is neglected, but it has some **of the German vein in** its **strata,**—the patience, the learning, the homely **delineation,** and even some traces of the mixture of the humorous and the terrible, which form that genius for the grotesque so especially German,—you find this in their legends and ghost-stories. But in Holland activity destroys, in Germany indolence nourishes, romance.

They stayed a day or two at Rotterdam, and then proceeded up **the** Rhine to Gorcum. The banks were flat and tame, and nothing **could** be less impressive of its native majesty than this part of the course of the great River.

"I never felt before," whispered Gertrude, **tenderly,** "how much there was **of** consolation **in** your presence; for **here I am** at last on the Rhine—the blue Rhine, and how disappointed I should be if you were **not** by my **side!**"

"But my Gertrude, **you** must wait till we have passed **Cologne,** before *the glories* of the Rhine burst upon you."

"It reverses life, my child," said the moralizing Vane; "and **the** stream flows through dulness **at** first, reserving its poetry for our perseverance."

"I will not allow your **doctrine,**" said Trevylyan, as the ambitious ardour of his native disposition **stirred** within him. "Life has always action; it is our own fault **if it ever** be dull: youth has its enterprise, manhood its schemes; and even if infirmity creep upon age, the mind, the mind still triumphs over the mortal clay, and in the quiet hermitage, among books, and from thoughts, keeps **the** great wheel within everlastingly in motion. No, the **better** class of spirits have always an antidote to the insipidity of a common career, they have ever energy at will——"

"**And never** happiness!" answered **Vane, after** a pause, as he **gazed** on the proud countenance of Trevylyan, with that kind of **calm,** half-pitying interest which belonged to a character deeply imbued with the philosophy of a **sad** experience, acting upon an unimpassioned heart. "And in truth, Trevylyan, it would please me if I could but teach you the folly **of** preferring the exercise **of** that energy, of which you speak, to **the** golden luxuries of REST. What ambition can ever bring an adequate reward? Not, surely, the ambition of letters—the desire of intellectual renown!"

"True," said Trevylyan, quietly; "that dream I have long renounced; there is nothing palpable in literary fame—it scarcely perhaps soothes the vain,—it assuredly chafes the proud. In my earlier years I attempted some works, which gained what the world, perhaps rightly, deemed a sufficient meed of reputation; yet it was not sufficient to recompense myself for the fresh hours I had consumed, for the sacrifices of pleasure I had made. The subtle aims that had inspired me were not perceived; the thoughts that had seemed new and beautiful to me, fell flat and lustreless on the soul of others. If I was approved, it was often for what I condemned myself! and I found that the trite commonplace and the false wit charmed, while the truth fatigued, and the enthusiasm revolted. For men of that genius to which I make no pretension, who have dwelt apart in the obscurity of their own thoughts, gazing upon stars that shine not for the dull sleepers of the world, it must be a keen sting to find the product of their labour confounded with a class, and to be mingled up in men's judgment with the faults or merits of a tribe. Every great genius must deem himself original and alone in his conceptions. It is not enough for him that these conceptions should be approved as good, unless they are admitted as inventive, if they mix him with the herd he has shunned, not separate him in fame as he has been separated in soul. Some Frenchman, the oracle of his circle, said of the poet of the Phêdre, 'Racine and the other imitators of Corneille;' and Racine, in his wrath, nearly forswore tragedy for ever. It is in vain to tell the author that the public is the judge of his works. The author believes himself above the public, or he would never have written, and," continued Trevylyan, with enthusiasm, "he *is* above them; their fiat may crush his glory, but never his self-esteem. He stands alone and haughty amidst the wrecks of the temple he imagined he had raised 'TO THE FUTURE,' and retaliates neglect with scorn. But is this, the life of scorn, a pleasurable state of existence? Is it one to be cherished? Does even the moment of fame counterbalance the years of mortification? And what is there in literary fame itself present and palpable to its heir? His work is a pebble thrown into the deep; the stir lasts for a moment, and the wave closes up, to be susceptible no more to the same impression. The circle may widen to other lands and other ages, but around *him* it is weak and faint. The trifles of the day, the low politics, the base intrigues, occupy the tongue, and fill the thought of his contemporaries; he is less known than a mountebank, or a new dancer; his glory comes not home to him; it brings no present, no perpetual reward, like the applauses that wait the actor, or the actor-like mummer of the senate; and this which vexes, also lowers him; his noble nature begins to nourish the base vices of jealousy, and the unwillingness to admire. Goldsmith is forgotten in the presence of a puppet; he feels it, and is mean; he expresses it, and is ludicrous. It is well to say that great minds will not stoop to jealousy; in the greatest minds, it is most frequent.[1] Few authors are ever so aware of the admiration they excite, as to afford to be generous; and this melancholy truth revolts us with our own ambition. Shall we be demigods in our closet, at the price of sinking below mortality in the world? No! it was from this deep sentiment of the unrealness of literary fame, of dissatisfaction at the fruits it produced, of fear for the meanness it engendered, that I resigned betimes all love for its career; and if by the restless desire that haunts men who think much, to write ever, I should be urged hereafter to literature, I will sternly teach myself to persevere in the indifference to its fame."

"You say as I would say," answered Vane, with his tranquil smile; "and your experience corroborates my theory. Ambition, then, is not the root of happiness. Why more in action than in letters?"

"Because," said Trevylyan, "in action we commonly gain in our life all the honour we deserve: the public judge of men better and more rapidly than of books. And he who takes to himself in action a high and pure ambition, associates it with so many objects, that, unlike literature, the failure of one is balanced by the success of the other. He, the creator of deeds, not resembling the creator of books, stands not alone; he is eminently social; he has many comrades, and without their aid he could not accomplish his designs. This divides and mitigates the impatient jealousy against others. He works for a cause, and knows early that he cannot monopolize its whole glory; he shares what he is aware it is impossible to engross. Besides, action leaves him no time for brooding over disappointment. The author has consumed his youth in a work,—it fails in glory. Can he write another work? Bid him call back another youth! But in action, the labour of the mind is from day to day. A week replaces what a week has lost, and all the aspirant's fame is of the present. It is lipped by the Babel of the living world; he is ever on the stage, and the spectators are ever ready to applaud. Thus perpetually in the service of others, self ceases to

---

[1] See the long list of names furnished by D'Israeli, in that most exquisite work, *The Literary Character*, vol. ii. p. 75. Plato, Xenophon, Chaucer, Corneille, Voltaire, Dryden, the Caracci, Domenico Venetiano, murdered by his envious friend, and the gentle Castillo fainting away at the genius of Murillo.

be his world; he has no leisure to brood over real or imaginary wrongs, the excitement whirls on the machine till it is worn out——"

"And kicked aside," said Vane, "with the broken lumber of men's other tools, in the chamber of their son's forgetfulness. Your man of action lasts but for an hour; the man of letters lasts for ages."

"We live not for ages," answered Trevylyan; "our life is on earth, and not in the grave."

"But even grant," continued Vane, "and I for one will concede the point, that posthumous fame is not worth the living agonies that obtain it, how are you better off in your poor and vulgar career of action? Would you assist the rulers?—servility! The people?—folly! If you take the great philosophical view which the worshippers of the past rarely take, but which, unknown to them, is their sole excuse, viz., that the changes which *may* benefit the future unsettle the present; and that it is not the wisdom of practical legislation to risk the peace of our contemporaries in the hope of obtaining happiness for their posterity—to what suspicions, to what charges are you exposed! You are deemed the foe of all liberal opinion, and you read your curses in the eyes of a nation. But take the side of the people. What caprice—what ingratitude! You have professed so much in theory, that you can never accomplish sufficient in practice. Moderation becomes a crime; to be prudent is to be perfidious. New demagogues, without temperance, because without principle, outstrip you in the moment of your greatest services. The public is the grave of a great man's deeds; it is never sated; its maw is eternally open; it perpetually craves for more. Where, in the history of the world, do you find the gratitude of a people? You find fervour, it is true, but not gratitude; the fervour that exaggerates a benefit at one moment, but not the gratitude that remembers it the next year. Once disappoint them, and all your actions, all your sacrifices, are swept from their remembrance for ever; they break the windows of the very house they have given you, and melt down their medals into bullets. Who serves man, ruler or peasant, serves the ungrateful; and all the ambitious are but types of a Wolsey or a De Witt."

"And what," said Trevylyan, "consoles a man in the ills that flesh is heir to, in that state of obscure repose, that serene inactivity to which you would confine him? Is it not his conscience? Is it not his self-acquittal, or his self-approval?"

"Doubtless," replied Vane.

"Be it so," answered the high-souled Trevylyan; "the same consolation awaits us in action as in repose. We sedulously pursue what

F 2

we deem to be true glory. **We are maligned; but our soul acquits us.** Could it do **more** in the scandal and the prejudice that assail us in private life? **You** are silent; but note **how much deeper** should be the **comfort,** how much loftier the **self-esteem;** for if calumny attack us in a wilful obscurity, what have we **done to refute** the **calumny?** How have we served **our** species? Have we **'scorned delight** and loved laborious days?' Have we made the utmost of the **'** talent' confided **to** our care? Have we done those good deeds **to our** race upon which we can retire,—an 'Estate of Beneficence,' **—from** the malice of the world, **and** feel that our deeds are our defenders? This is the consolation **of** virtuous actions; is it so of—even a virtuous—indolence?"

"You speak as a preacher," said Vane; "I merely as a calculator. **You** of virtue in affliction, I of a life in ease."

"Well, then, if the consciousness of perpetual endeavour to advance our race be not alone happier than the **life of** ease, let us see what this vaunted **ease** really is. Tell me, **is it** not another name for *ennui?* This state of quiescence, this **object**less, dreamless torpor, this transition *du lit à la table, de la table* ***au lit*;** what more dreary and monotonous existence can you devise? **Is it** pleasure in this inglorious existence to think that you are serving pleasure? **Is** it freedom to be the slave to self? For I hold," continued Trevylyan, "that this jargon of 'consulting happiness,' this cant of living for ourselves, is but a mean as well as a false philosophy. Why this eternal reference to self? Is self alone to be consulted? Is even our happiness, did it truly consist in repose, really the great end **of** life? I doubt if we cannot ascend higher. I doubt if we cannot say with a great moralist, 'if virtue be not estimable in itself, we can see nothing estimable in following it for the sake of a bargain.' **But,** in fact, repose is the poorest of all delusions; the very act of recurring to self, brings about us all those ills of self from which, in the turmoil of the world, we can escape. We become hypochon**driacs.** Our very health grows an object of painful possession. We **are so** desirous to be well (for what is retirement without health!) that we **are** ever fancying ourselves ill; and, like the man in the 'Spectator,' **we** weigh ourselves daily, and live but by grains and scruples. Retirement is happy only for the poet, for to him it is *not* retirement. He secedes from one world but to gain another, and he finds not *ennui* in seclusion: why?—not because seclusion hath *repose,* but because it hath *occupation.* In one word, then, I say of action and of indolence, grant the same ills to both, and to action there is the readier escape or the nobler consolation."

Vane shrugged his shoulders. "Ah, my dear friend," said he,

tapping his snuff-box with benevolent superiority, "you are much younger than I am!"

But these conversations, which Trevylyan and Vane often held together, dull as I fear this specimen must seem to the reader, had an inexpressible charm for Gertrude. She loved the lofty and generous vein of philosophy which Trevylyan embraced, and which, while it suited his ardent nature, contrasted a demeanour commonly hard and cold to all but herself. And young and tender as she was, his ambition infused its spirit into her fine imagination, and that passion for enterprise which belongs inseparably to romance. She loved to muse over his future lot, and in fancy to share its toils and to exult in its triumphs. And if sometimes she asked herself whether a career of action might not estrange him from her, she had but to turn her gaze upon his watchful eye,—and lo, he was by her side or at her feet!

CHAPTER VI.

GORCUM.—THE TOUR OF THE VIRTUES: A PHILOSOPHER'S TALE.

IT was a bright and cheery morning as they glided by Gorcum. The boats pulling to the shore full of fishermen and peasants in their national costume; the breeze, freshly rippling the waters; the lightness of the blue sky; the loud and laughing voices from the boats;—all contributed to raise the spirit, and fill it with that indescribable gladness which is the physical sense of life.

The tower of the church, with its long windows and its round dial, rose against the clear sky; and on a bench under a green bush facing the water sat a jolly Hollander, refreshing the breezes with the fumes of his national weed.

"How little it requires to make a journey pleasant, when the companions are our friends!" said Gertrude as they sailed along. "Nothing can be duller than these banks; nothing more delightful than this voyage."

"Yet what tries the affections of people for each other so severely as a journey together?" said Vane. "That perpetual companionship from which there is no escaping; that confinement, in all our moments of ill-humour and listlessness, with persons who want us to look amused—Ah, it is a severe ordeal for friendship to pass through! A post-chaise must have jolted many an intimacy to death."

"You speak feelingly, dear father," said Gertrude laughing; "and, I suspect, with a slight desire to be sarcastic upon us. Yet, seriously, I should think that travel must be like life, and that good persons must be always agreeable companions to each other."

"Good persons, my Gertrude!" answered Vane with a smile. "Alas! I fear the good weary each other quite as much as the bad. What say you, Trevylyan,—would Virtue be a pleasant companion from Paris to Petersburg? Ah, I see you intend to be on Gertrude's side of the question. Well now if I tell you a story, since stories are so much the fashion with you, in which you shall find that the Virtues themselves actually made the experiment of a tour, will you promise to attend to the moral?"

"Oh, dear father, anything for a story," cried Gertrude; "especially from you who have not told us one all the way. Come, listen, Albert; nay, listen to your new rival."

And, pleased to see the vivacity of the invalid, Vane began as follows:—

THE TOUR OF THE VIRTUES.

A PHILOSOPHER'S TALE.

Once upon a time, several of the Virtues, weary of living for ever with the Bishop of Norwich, resolved to make a little excursion; accordingly, though they knew everything on earth was very ill prepared to receive them, they thought they might safely venture on a tour from Westminster Bridge to Richmond: the day was fine, the wind in their favour, and as to entertainment,—why there seemed, according to Gertrude, to be no possibility of any disagreement among the Virtues.

They took a boat at Westminster Stairs, and just as they were about to push off, a poor woman, all in rags, with a child in her arms, implored their compassion. Charity put her hand into her reticule, and took out a shilling. Justice, turning round to look after the luggage, saw the folly which Charity was about to commit. "Heavens!" cried Justice, seizing poor Charity by the arm, "what are you doing? Have you never read Political Economy? Don't you know that indiscriminate almsgiving is only the encouragement to Idleness, the mother of Vice? You a Virtue, indeed!—I'm ashamed of you. Get along with you, good woman;—yet stay, there is a ticket for soup at the Mendicity Society: they'll see if you're a proper object of compassion." But Charity is quicker than Justice, and slipping her hand behind her, the poor woman got the shilling and the ticket for soup too. Economy and Generosity saw the double gift. "What waste!" cried Economy, frowning; "what, a ticket and a shilling! *either* would have sufficed."

"Either!" said Generosity, "fie! Charity should have given the poor creature half-a-crown, and Justice a dozen tickets!" So the next ten minutes were consumed in a quarrel between the four Virtues, which would have lasted all the way to Richmond, if Courage had not advised them to get on shore and fight it out. Upon this, the Virtues suddenly perceived they had a little forgotten themselves, and Generosity offering the first apology, they made it up, and went on very agreeably for the next mile or two.

The day now grew a little overcast, and a shower seemed at hand. Prudence, who had on a new bonnet, suggested the propriety of putting to shore for half an hour; Courage was for braving the rain, but, as most of the Virtues are ladies, Prudence carried it. Just as they were about to land, another boat cut in before them very uncivilly, and gave theirs such a shake, that Charity was all but overboard. The company on board the uncivil boat, who evidently thought the Virtues extremely low persons, for they had nothing very fashionable about their exterior, burst out laughing at Charity's discomposure, especially as a large basket full of buns, which Charity carried with her for any hungry-looking children she might encounter at Richmond, fell pounce into the water. Courage was all on fire; he twisted his moustache, and would have made an onset on the enemy, if, to his great indignation, Meekness had not forestalled him, by stepping mildly into the hostile boat and offering both cheeks to the foe. This was too much even for the incivility of the boatmen; they made their excuses to the Virtues, and Courage, who is no bully, thought himself bound discontentedly to accept them. But oh! if you had seen how Courage used Meekness afterwards, you could not have believed it possible that one Virtue could be so enraged with another. This quarrel between the two threw a damp on the party; and they proceeded on their voyage, when the shower was over, with anything but cordiality. I spare you the little squabbles that took place in the general conversation—how Economy found fault with all the villas by the way; and Temperance expressed becoming indignation at the luxuries of the City barge. They arrived at Richmond, and Temperance was appointed to order the dinner; meanwhile Hospitality, walking in the garden, fell in with a large party of Irishmen, and asked them to join the repast.

Imagine the long faces of Economy and Prudence, when they saw the addition to the company. Hospitality was all spirits, he rubbed his hands and called for champagne with the tone of a younger brother. Temperance soon grew scandalized, and Modesty herself coloured at some of the jokes; but Hospitality, who was now half seas over, called the one a milksop, and swore at the other as a prude. Away went the hours; it was time to return, and they made down to the water-side thoroughly out of temper with one another, Economy and Generosity quarrelling all the way about the bill and the waiters. To make up the sum of their mortification, they passed a boat where all the company were in the best possible spirits, laughing and whooping like mad; and discovered these jolly companions to be two or three agreeable Vices, who had put themselves under the management of Good Temper. So you see, Gertrude, that even the Virtues may fall at loggerheads with each other, and pass a very sad time of it, if they happen to be of opposite dispositions, and have forgotten to take Good Temper along with them.

"Ah!" said Gertrude, "but you have overloaded your boat; too many Virtues might contradict one another, but not a few."

"*Voilà ce que je veux dire*," said Vane. "But listen to the sequel of my tale, which now takes a new moral."

At the end of the voyage, and after a long, sulky silence, Prudence said, with a thoughtful air, "My dear friends, I have been thinking that as long as we keep so entirely together, never mixing with the rest of the world, we shall waste our lives in quarrelling amongst ourselves, and run the risk of being still less liked and sought after than we already are. You know that we are none of us popular; every one is quite contented to see us represented in a vaudeville, or described in an essay. Charity, indeed, has her name often taken in vain at a bazaar, or a subscription; and the miser as often talks of the duty he owes to *me*, when he sends the stranger from his door, or his grandson to gaol: but still we only resemble so many wild beasts, whom everybody likes to see, but nobody cares to possess. Now, I propose, that we should all separate and take up our abode with some mortal or other for a year, with the power of changing at the end of that time should we not feel ourselves comfortable; that is, should we not find that we do all the good we intend: let us try the experiment, and on this day twelvemonths let us all meet, under the largest oak in Windsor Forest, and recount what has befallen us." Prudence ceased, as she always does when she has said enough; and, delighted at the project, the Virtues agreed to adopt it on the spot. They were enchanted at the idea of setting up for themselves, and each not doubting his or her success: for Economy in her heart thought Generosity no Virtue at all, and Meekness looked on Courage as little better than a heathen.

Generosity, being the most eager and active of all the Virtues, set off first on his journey. Justice followed, and kept up with him, though at a more even pace. Charity never heard a sigh, or saw a squalid face, but she stayed to cheer and console the sufferer;—a kindness which somewhat retarded her progress.

Courage espied a travelling carriage, with a man and his wife in it quarrelling most conjugally, and he civilly begged he might be permitted to occupy the vacant seat opposite the lady. Economy still lingered, inquiring for the cheapest inns. Poor Modesty looked round and sighed, on finding herself so near to London, where she was almost wholly unknown; but resolved to bend her course thither for two reasons: first, for the novelty of the thing; and, secondly, not liking to expose herself to any risks by a journey on the Continent. Prudence, though the first to project, was the last to execute; and therefore resolved to remain where she was for that night, and take daylight for her travels.

The year rolled on, and the Virtues, punctual to the appointment, met under the oak-tree; they all came nearly at the same time, excepting Economy, who had got into a return post-chaise, the horses to which, having been forty miles in the course of the morning, had foundered by the way, and retarded her journey till night set in. The Virtues looked sad and sorrowful, as people are wont to do after a long and fruitless journey; and, somehow or other, such was the wearying effect of their intercourse with the world, that they appeared wonderfully diminished in size.

"Ah, my dear Generosity," said Prudence with a sigh, "as you were the first to set out on your travels, pray let us hear your adventures first."

"You must know, my dear sisters," said Generosity, "that I had not gone many miles from you before I came to a small country town, in which a marching regiment was quartered, and at an open window I beheld, leaning over a gentleman's chair, the most beautiful creature imagination ever pictured; her eyes shone out like two suns of perfect happiness, and she was almost cheerful enough to have passed for Good Temper herself. The gentleman, over whose chair she leaned, was her husband; they had been married six weeks; he was a lieutenant with a hundred pounds a-year besides his pay. Greatly affected by their poverty, I instantly determined, without a second thought, to ensconce myself in the heart of this charming girl. During the first hour in my new residence I made many wise reflections, such as—that Love never was so perfect as when accompanied by Poverty; what a vulgar error it was to call the unmarried state 'Single *Blessedness*;' how wrong it was of us Virtues never to have tried the marriage bond; and what a falsehood it was to say that husbands neglected their wives, for never was there anything in nature so devoted as the love of a husband—six weeks married!

"The next morning, before breakfast, as the charming Fanny was waiting for her husband, who had not yet finished his toilette, a poor, wretched-looking object appeared at the window, tearing her hair and wringing her hands; her husband had that morning been dragged to prison, and her seven children had fought for the last mouldy crust. Prompted by me, Fanny, without inquiring further into the matter, drew from her silken purse a five-pound note, and gave it to the beggar, who departed more amazed than grateful. Soon after the lieutenant appeared,—'What the d——l, another bill!' muttered he, as he tore the yellow wafer from a large, square, folded, bluish piece of paper. 'Oh, ah! confound the fellow, *he* must be paid. I must trouble you, Fanny, for fifteen pounds to pay this saddler's bill.'

"'Fifteen pounds, love?' stammered Fanny, blushing.

"'Yes, dearest, the fifteen pounds I gave you yesterday.'

"'I have only ten pounds,' said Fanny, hesitatingly, 'for such a poor, wretched-looking creature was here just now, that I was obliged to give her five pounds.'

"'Five pounds? good Heavens!' exclaimed the astonished husband; 'I shall have no more money this three weeks.' He frowned, he bit his lips, nay, he even wrung his hands, and walked up and down the room; worse still, he broke forth with—'Surely, madam, you did not suppose, when you married a lieutenant in a marching regiment, that he could afford to indulge in the whim of giving five pounds to every mendicant who held out her hand to you? You did not, I say, madam, imagine—' but the bridegroom was interrupted by the convulsive sobs of his wife: it was their first quarrel, they were but six weeks married; he looked at her for one moment sternly, the next he was at her feet. 'Forgive me, dearest Fanny,—forgive me, for I cannot forgive myself. I was too great a wretch to say what I did; and do believe, my own Fanny, that while I may be too poor to indulge you in it, I do from my heart admire so noble, so disinterested, a generosity.' Not a little proud did I feel to have been the cause of this exemplary husband's admiration for his amiable wife, and sincerely did I rejoice at having taken up my abode with these *poor* people. But not to tire you, my dear sisters, with the minutiæ of detail, I shall briefly say that things did not long remain in this delightful position; for, before many months had elapsed, poor Fanny had to bear with her husband's increased and more frequent storms of passion, unfollowed by any halcyon and honeymoon suings for forgiveness: for at my instigation every shilling went; and when there were no more to go, her trinkets, and even her clothes followed. The lieutenant became a complete brute, and even allowed his unbridled tongue to call me—me, sisters, *me!*—'heartless Extravagance.' His despicable brother-officers, and their gossiping wives, were no better; for they did nothing but animadvert upon my Fanny's ostentation and absurdity, for by such names had they the impertinence to call *me*. Thus grieved to the soul to find myself the cause of all poor Fanny's misfortunes, I resolved at the end of the year to leave her, being thoroughly convinced that, however amiable and praiseworthy I might be in myself, I was totally unfit to be bosom friend and adviser to the wife of a lieutenant in a marching regiment, with only a hundred pounds a-year besides his pay."

The Virtues groaned their sympathy with the unfortunate Fanny; and Prudence, turning to Justice, said, "I long to hear what you have been doing, for I am certain you cannot have occasioned harm to any one."

Justice shook her head and said, "Alas! I find that there are times and places when even I do better not to appear, as a short account of my adventures will prove to you. No sooner had I left you than I instantly repaired to India, and took up my abode with a Brahmin. I was much shocked by the dreadful inequalities of condition that reigned in the several castes, and I longed to relieve the poor Pariah from his ignominious destiny,—accordingly I set seriously to work on reform. I insisted upon the iniquity of abandoning men from their birth to an irremediable state of contempt, from which no virtue could exalt them. The Brahmins looked upon *my* Brahmin with ineffable horror. They called *me* the most wicked of vices; they saw no distinction between Justice and Atheism. I uprooted their society—that was sufficient crime. But the worst was, that the Pariahs themselves regarded me with suspicion; they thought it unnatural in a Brahmin to care for a Pariah! And one called me 'Madness;' another, 'Ambition;' and a third, 'The Desire to innovate.' My poor Brahmin led a miserable life of it; when one day, after observing, at my dictation, that he thought a Pariah's life as much entitled to respect as a cow's, he was hurried away by the priests and secretly broiled on the altar, as a fitting reward for his sacrilege. I fled hither in great tribulation, persuaded that in some countries even Justice may do harm."

"As for me," said Charity, not waiting to be asked, "I grieve to say that I was silly enough to take up my abode with an old lady in

Dublin, who never **knew** what discretion was, and always acted from impulse; my instigation was irresistible, and the money she gave in her drives through **the** suburbs of Dublin was so lavishly spent, **that** it kept all the rascals of the city in idleness and whisky. I found, to my great horror, that I was a main cause of a terrible epidemic, and that to give alms without discretion was to spread poverty without **help.** I left the city when my year was out, and, as ill-luck would have it, just at the time when I was most wanted."

"And oh," cried Hospitality, "I went to Ireland also. I fixed my abode with a squireen; I ruined him in a year, and only left him because he had no longer a hovel to keep me in."

"**As** for myself," said Temperance, "I entered the breast of **an** English legislator, and he brought in a bill against ale-houses; the consequence was, that the labourers took **to** gin, and I have been forced to confess, that Temperance may **be** too zealous when she dictates too vehemently to others."

"Well," said Courage, keeping more in the back-ground than he had ever done before, and looking rather ashamed of himself, "that travelling carriage I got into belonged to a German general and his wife, who were returning to their own country. Growing very cold as we proceeded, she wrapped me up in a *polonaise;* but the cold increasing, I inadvertently crept into her bosom; once there I could not get out, and from thenceforward the poor general had considerably the worst of it. She became so provoking, that I wondered how he could refrain from an explosion. To do him justice, he did at last threaten to get out of the carriage; upon which, roused by me, she collared him—and conquered. When he got to his own district things grew worse, for if any aide-de-camp offended her she insisted that he might be publicly reprimanded; and should the poor general **refuse,** she would with her own hands confer a caning upon the delinquent. The additional force she had gained in me was **too** much **odds** against the poor general, and he died of **a** broken **heart,** six months after my *liaison* with his wife. She after **this** became so dreaded and detested, that a conspiracy was formed **to** poison her; *this* daunted even me, so I left her without delay,—*et **me** voici!*"

"Humph!" said Meekness, with an air of triumph; "**I**, at least, have been more successful than you. On seeing much in the papers of the cruelties practised by the Turks on the Greeks, I thought my presence would enable the poor sufferers to bear their misfortunes calmly. I went to Greece, then, at a moment when a well-planned and practicable scheme of emancipating themselves from the Turkish yoke was arousing their youth. Without confining myself to one individual, I flitted from breast to breast; I meekened the whole nation; my remonstrances against the insurrection succeeded, and I had the satisfaction of leaving a whole people ready to be killed, or strangled, with the most Christian resignation in the world."

The Virtues, who had been a little cheered by the opening self-complacency of Meekness, would not, to her great astonishment, allow that she had succeeded a whit more happily than her sisters, and called next upon Modesty for her confession.

"You know," said that amiable young lady, "that I went to London in search of a situation. I spent three months of the twelve in going from house to house, but I could not get a single person to receive me. The ladies declared they never saw so old-fashioned a gawkey, and civilly recommended me to their abigails; the abigails turned me round with a stare, and then pushed me down to the kitchen and the fat scullion-maids; who assured me, that 'in the respectable families they had the honour to live in, they had never even heard of my name.' One young housemaid just from the country did indeed receive me with some sort of civility; but she very soon lost me in the servants' hall. I now took refuge with the other sex, as the least uncourteous. I was fortunate enough to find a young gentleman of remarkable talents, who welcomed me with open arms. He was full of learning, gentleness, and honesty. I had only one rival—Ambition. We both contended for an absolute empire over him. Whatever Ambition suggested, I damped. Did Ambition urge him to begin a book, I persuaded him it was not worth publication. Did he get up, full of knowledge, and instigated by my rival to make a speech (for he was in parliament), I shocked him with the sense of his assurance—I made his voice droop and his accents falter. At last, with an indignant sigh, my rival left him; he retired into the country, took orders, and renounced a career he had fondly hoped would be serviceable to others; but finding I did not suffice for his happiness, and piqued at his melancholy, I left him before the end of the year, and he has since taken to drinking!"

The eyes of the Virtues were all turned to Prudence. She was their last hope—"I am just where I set out," said that discreet Virtue; "I have done neither good nor harm. To avoid temptation, I went and lived with a hermit, to whom I soon found that I could be of no use beyond warning him not to overboil his peas and lentils, not to leave his door open when a storm threatened, and not to fill his pitcher too full at the neighbouring spring. I am thus the only one of you that never did harm; but only because I am the only one of you that never had an opportunity of doing it! In a word," continued Prudence, thoughtfully,—"in a word, my friends, circumstances are necessary to the Virtues themselves. Had, for instance, Economy changed with Generosity, and gone to the poor lieutenant's wife, and had I lodged with the Irish squireen instead of Hospitality, what misfortunes would have been saved to both! Alas! I perceive we lose all our efficacy when we are misplaced; and *then*, though in reality Virtues, we operate as Vices. Circumstances must be favourable to our exertions, and harmonious with our nature; and we lose our very divinity unless Wisdom direct our footsteps to the home we should inhabit, and the dispositions we should govern."

The story was ended, and the travellers began to dispute about its moral. Here let us leave them.

CHAPTER VII.

COLOGNE.—THE TRACES OF THE ROMAN YOKE.—THE CHURCH OF ST. MARIA.—TREVYLYAN'S REFLECTIONS ON THE MONASTIC LIFE.—THE TOMB OF THE THREE KINGS.—AN EVENING EXCURSION ON THE RHINE.

ROME—magnificent Rome! wherever the pilgrim wends, the traces of thy dominion greet his eyes. Still, in the heart of the bold German race, is graven the print of the eagle's claws; and amidst the haunted regions of the Rhine we pause to wonder at the great monuments of the Italian yoke.

At Cologne our travellers rested for some days. They were in the city to which the camp of Marcus Agrippa had given birth: that spot had resounded with the armed tread of the legions of Trajan. In that city, Vitellius, Sylvanus, were proclaimed emperors. By that church, did the latter receive his death.

As they passed round the door, they saw some peasants loitering on the sacred ground; and when they noted the delicate cheek of Gertrude, they uttered their salutations with more than common respect. Where they then were, the building swept round in a circular form; and at its base it is supposed, by tradition, to retain something of the ancient Roman masonry. Just before them rose the spire of a plain and unadorned church—singularly contrasting the pomp of the old, with the simplicity of the innovating, creed.

The Church of St. Maria occupies the site of the Roman Capitol;

and the place retains the Roman name; and still something in the aspect of the people betrays the hereditary blood.

Gertrude, whose nature was strongly impressed with *the venerating character*, was fond of visiting the old Gothic churches, which, with so eloquent a moral, unite the living with the dead.

"Pause for a moment," said Trevylyan, before they entered the church of St. Mary. "What recollections crowd upon us! On the site of the Roman Capitol, a Christian church and a convent are erected! By whom? The mother of Charles Martel—the Conqueror of the Saracen—the arch-hero of Christendom itself! And to these scenes and calm retreats, to the cloisters of the convent once belonging to this church, fled the bruised spirit of a royal sufferer—the victim of Richelieu—the unfortunate and ambitious Mary de Medicis. Alas! the cell and the convent are but a vain emblem of that desire to fly to God which belongs to Distress; the solitude soothes, but the monotony recalls, regret. And for my own part, in my frequent tours through Catholic countries, I never saw the still walls in which monastic vanity hoped to shut out the world, but a melancholy came over me! What hearts at war with themselves!—what unceasing regrets!—what pinings after the past!— what long and beautiful years devoted to a moral grave, by a momentary rashness—an impulse—a disappointment! But in these churches the lesson is more impressive and less sad. The weary heart has ceased to ache—the burning pulses are still—the troubled spirit has flown to the only rest which is not a deceit. Power and love—hope and fear—avarice—ambition, they are quenched at last! Death is the only monastery—the tomb is the only cell."

"Your passion is ever for active life," said Gertrude. "You allow no charm to solitude, and contemplation to you seems torture. If any great sorrow ever come upon you, you will never retire to seclusion as its balm. You will plunge into the world, and lose your individual existence in the universal rush of life."

"Ah, talk not of sorrow!" said Trevylyan, wildly,—"let us enter the church."

They went afterwards to the celebrated cathedral, which is considered one of the noblest of the architectural triumphs of Germany; but it is yet more worthy of notice from the Pilgrim of Romance than the searcher after antiquity, for here, behind the grand altar, is the Tomb of the Three Kings of Cologne—the three worshippers, whom tradition humbled to our Saviour. Legend is rife with a thousand tales of the relics of this tomb. The Three Kings of Cologne are the tutelary names of that golden superstition, which has often more votaries than the religion itself from which it springs:

and to Gertrude the simple story of Lucille sufficed to make her for the moment credulous of the sanctity of the spot. Behind the tomb three Gothic windows cast their "dim, religious light" over the tesselated pavement and along the Ionic pillars. They found some of the more credulous believers in the authenticity of the relics kneeling before the tomb, and they arrested their steps, fearful to disturb the superstition which is never without something of sanctity when contented with prayer, and forgetful of persecution. The bones of the Magi are still supposed to consecrate the tomb, and on the higher part of the monument the artist has delineated their adoration to the infant Saviour.

That evening came on with a still and tranquil beauty, and as the sun hastened to its close they launched their boat for an hour or two's excursion upon the Rhine. Gertrude was in that happy mood when the quiet of nature is enjoyed like a bath for the soul, and the presence of him she so idolized deepened that stillness into a more delicious and subduing calm. Little did she dream as the boat glided over the water, and the towers of Cologne rose in the blue air of evening, how few were those hours that divided her from the tomb! But, in looking back to the life of one we have loved, how dear is the thought that the latter days were the days of light, that the cloud never chilled the beauty of the setting sun, and that if the years of existence were brief, all that existence has most tender, most sacred, was crowded into that space! Nothing dark, then, or bitter, rests with our remembrance of the lost: *we* are the mourners, but pity is not for the mourned—our grief is purely selfish; when we turn to its object, the hues of happiness are round it, and that very love which is the parent of our woe was the consolation—the triumph—of the departed!

The majestic Rhine was calm as a lake; the splashing of the oar only broke the stillness, and, after a long pause in their conversation, Gertrude, putting her hand on Trevylyan's arm, reminded him of a promised story: for he too had moods of abstraction, from which, in her turn, she loved to lure him; and his voice to her had become a sort of want.

"Let it be," said she, "a tale suited to the hour; no fierce tradition—nay, no grotesque fable, but of the tenderer dye of superstition. Let it be of love, of woman's love—of the love that defies the grave: for surely even after death it lives; and heaven would scarcely be heaven if memory were banished from its blessings."

"I recollect," said Trevylyan, after a slight pause, "a short German legend, the simplicity of which touched me much when I heard it; but," added he with a slight smile, "so much more faithful appears in the legend the love of the woman than that of the man, that I at least ought scarcely to recite it."

"Nay," said Gertrude tenderly, "the fault of the inconstant only heightens our gratitude to the faithful."

CHAPTER VIII.

THE SOUL IN PURGATORY; OR, LOVE STRONGER THAN DEATH.

THE angels strung their harps in Heaven, and their music went up like a stream of odours to the pavilions of the Most High. But the harp of Seralim was sweeter than that of his fellows, and the Voice of the Invisible One (for the angels themselves know not the glories of Jehovah—only far in the depths of Heaven they see one Unsleeping Eye watching for ever over Creation) was heard saying—

"Ask a gift for the love that burns in thy song, and it shall be given thee."

And Seralim answered—

"There are in that place which men call Purgatory, and which is the escape from Hell, but the painful porch of Heaven, many souls that adore Thee, and yet are punished justly for their sins; grant me the boon to visit them at times, and solace their suffering by the hymns of the harp that is consecrated to Thee!"

And the Voice answered—

"Thy prayer is heard, O gentlest of the angels! and it seems good to Him who chastises but from love. Go! Thou hast thy will."

Then the angel sang the praises of God; and when the song was done he rose from his azure throne at the right hand of Gabriel, and, spreading his rainbow wings, he flew to that melancholy orb which, nearest to earth, echoes with the shrieks of souls that by torture become pure. There the unhappy ones see from afar the bright courts they are hereafter to obtain, and the shapes of glorious beings, who, fresh from the Fountains of Immortality, walk amidst the gardens of Paradise, and feel that their happiness hath no morrow;—and this thought consoles amidst their torments, and makes the true difference between Purgatory and Hell.

Then the angel folded his wings, and, entering the crystal gates, sat down upon a blasted rock and struck his divine lyre, and a peace fell over the wretched; the demon ceased to torture, and the victim to wail. As sleep to the mourners of earth was the song of the angel to the souls of the purifying star: one only voice amidst the general stillness seemed not lulled by the angel; it was the voice of a woman, and it continued to cry out with a sharp cry—

"Oh, Adenheim, Adenheim! mourn not for the lost!"

The angel struck chord after chord, till his most skilful melodies were exhausted; but still the solitary voice, unheeding—unconscious of—the sweetest harp of the angel choir, cried out——

"Oh, Adenheim, Adenheim! mourn not for the lost!"

Then Seralim's interest was aroused, and approaching the spot whence the voice came, he saw the spirit of a young and beautiful girl chained to a rock, and the demons lying idly by. And Seralim said to the demons, "Doth the song lull ye thus to rest?"

And they answered, "Her care for another is bitterer than all our torments; therefore are we idle."

Then the angel approached the spirit, and said in a voice which stilled her cry—for in what state do we outlive sympathy? "Wherefore, O daughter of earth! wherefore wailest thou with the same plaintive wail? and why doth the harp that soothes the most guilty of thy companions, fail in its melody with thee?"

"Oh, radiant stranger," answered the poor spirit, "thou speakest to one who on earth loved God's creatures more than God; therefore is she thus justly sentenced. But I know that my poor Adenheim mourns ceaselessly for me, and the thought of his sorrow is more intolerable to me than all that the demons can inflict."

"And how knowest thou that he laments thee?" asked the angel.

"Because I know with what agony I should have mourned for *him*," replied the spirit, simply.

The divine nature of the angel was touched; for love is the nature of the sons of heaven. "And how," said he, "can I minister to thy sorrow?"

A transport seemed to agitate the spirit, and she lifted up her mistlike and impalpable arms, and cried—

"Give me—oh, give me to return to earth, but for one little hour, that I may visit my Adenheim; and that, concealing from him my present sufferings, I may comfort him in his own."

"Alas!" said the angel, turning away his eyes—for angels may not weep in the sight of others—"I could, indeed, grant thee thi boon, but thou knowest not the penalty. For the souls in Purgatory may return to Earth, but heavy is the sentence that awaits thei return. In a word, for one hour on earth thou must add a thousan years to the tortures of thy confinement here!"

"Is that all?" cried the spirit; "willingly, then, will I brave the doom. Ah, surely they love not in heaven, or thou wouldest know, O Celestial Visitor, that one hour of consolation to the one we love is worth a thousand ages of torture to ourselves! Let me comfort and convince my Adenheim; no matter what becomes of me."

Then the angel looked on high, and he saw in far-distant regions, which in that orb none else could discern, the rays that parted from the all-guarding Eye; and heard the VOICE of the Eternal One bidding him act as his pity whispered. He looked on the spirit, and her shadowy arms stretched pleadingly towards him; he uttered the word that loosens the bars of the gate of Purgatory; and lo, the spirit had re-entered the human world.

It was night in the halls of the Lord of Adenheim, and he sat at the head of his glittering board; loud and long was the laugh, and merry the jest that echoed round; and the laugh and the jest of the Lord of Adenheim were louder and merrier than all.

And by his right side sat a beautiful lady; and ever and anon he turned from others to whisper soft vows in her ear.

"And oh," said the bright dame of Falkenberg, "thy words what ladye can believe?—Didst thou not utter the same oaths, and promise the same love, to Ida, the fair daughter of Loden, and now but three little months have closed upon her grave?"

"By my halidom," quoth the young Lord of Adenheim, "thou dost thy beauty marvellous injustice. Ida! Nay, thou mockest me; *I* love the daughter of Loden! why how then should I be worthy thee? A few gay words, a few passing smiles—behold all the love Adenheim ever bore to Ida. Was it my fault if the poor fool misconstrued such common courtesy? Nay, dearest lady, this heart is virgin to thee."

"And what!" said the lady of Falkenberg, as she suffered the arm of Adenheim to encircle her slender waist, "didst thou not grieve for her loss?"

"Why, verily, yes, for the first week; but in thy bright eyes I found ready consolation."

At this moment, the Lord of Adenheim thought he heard a deep sigh behind him; he turned, but saw nothing, save a slight mist that gradually faded away, and vanished in the distance. Where was the necessity for Ida to reveal herself?

*   *   *   *   *
   *   *   *   *
*   *   *   *   *

"And thou didst not, then, do thine errand to thy lover?" said Seralim, as the spirit of the wronged Ida returned to Purgatory.

"Bid the demons recommence their torture," was poor Ida's answer.

"And was it for this that thou added a thousand years to thy doom?"

"Alas!" answered Ida, "after the single hour I have endured on Earth, there seems to be but little terrible in a thousand fresh years of Purgatory!"[1]

"What! is the story ended?" asked Gertrude.

"Yes."

"Nay, surely the thousand years were not added to poor Ida's doom; and Seralim bore her back with him to heaven?"

"The legend saith no more. The writer was contented to show us the perpetuity of woman's love;——"

"And its reward," added Vane.

"It was not *I* who drew that last conclusion, Albert," whispered Gertrude.

CHAPTER IX.

THE SCENERY OF THE RHINE ANALOGOUS TO THE GERMAN LITERARY GENIUS.—THE DRACHENFELS.

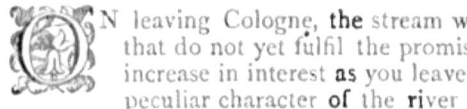N leaving Cologne, the stream winds round among banks that do not yet fulfil the promise of the Rhine; but they increase in interest as you leave Surdt and Godorf. The peculiar character of the river does not, however, really appear, until by degrees the Seven Mountains, and "THE CASTLED CRAG OF DRACHENFELS" above them all, break upon the eye. Around Neider Cassel and Rheidt, the vines lie thick and clustering: and, by the shore, you see from place to place the islands stretching their green length along, and breaking the exulting tide. Village rises upon village, and viewed from the distance as you sail, the pastoral errors that enamoured us of the village life, crowd thick and fast upon us. So still do these hamlets seem, so sheltered from the passions of the world; as if the passions were not like winds —only felt where they breathe, and invisible save by their effects! Leaping into the broad bosom of the Rhine come many a stream and rivulet upon either side. Spire upon spire rises and sinks as you sail on. Mountain and city—the solitary island—the castled

---

[1] This story is principally borrowed from a foreign soil. It seemed to the author worthy of being transferred to an English one, although he fears that much of its singular beauty in the original has been lost by the way.

steep—like the dreams of ambition, suddenly appear, proudly swell, and dimly fade away.

"You begin now," said Trevylyan, "to understand the character of the German literature. The Rhine is an emblem of its luxuriance, its fertility, its romance. The best commentary to the German genius is a visit to the German scenery. The mighty gloom of the Hartz, the feudal towers that look over vines and deep valleys on the legendary Rhine; the gigantic remains of antique power, profusely scattered over plain, mount, and forest; the thousand mixed recollections that hallow the ground; the stately Roman, the stalwart Goth, the chivalry of the feudal age, and the dim brotherhood of the ideal world, have here alike their record and their remembrance. And over such scenes wanders the young German student. Instead of the pomp and luxury of the English traveller, the thousand devices to cheat the way, he has but his volume in his hand, his knapsack at his back. From such scenes he draws and hives all that various store which after years ripen to invention. Hence the florid mixture of the German muse—the classic, the romantic, the contemplative, the philosophic, and the superstitious. Each the result of actual meditation over different scenes. Each the produce of separate but confused recollections. As the Rhine flows, so flows the national genius, by mountain and valley—the wildest solitude—the sudden spires of ancient cities—the mouldered castle—the stately monastery—the humble cot. Grandeur and homeliness, history and superstition, truth and fable, succeeding one another so as to blend into a whole.

"But," added Trevylyan a moment afterwards, "the Ideal is passing slowly away from the German mind, a spirit for the more active and the more material literature is springing up amongst them. The revolution of mind gathers on, preceding stormy events; and the memories that led their grandsires to contemplate, will urge the youth of the next generation to dare and to act."[1]

Thus conversing, they continued their voyage, with a fair wave and beneath a lucid sky.

The vessel now glided beside the Seven Mountains and the Drachenfels.

The sun slowly setting cast his yellow beams over the smooth waters. At the foot of the mountains lay a village deeply sequestered in shade; and above, the Ruin of the Drachenfels caught the richest beams of the sun. Yet thus alone, though lofty, the ray cheered not the gloom that hung over the giant rock: it stood on

---

[1] Is not this prediction already fulfilled?—1849.

high, like some great name on which the light of glory may shine, but which is associated with a certain melancholy, from the solitude to which its very height above the level of the herd condemned its owner!

CHAPTER X.

THE LEGEND OF ROLAND.—THE ADVENTURES OF NYMPHALIN ON THE ISLAND OF NONNEWËRTH.—HER SONG.—THE DECAY OF THE FAIRY-FAITH IN ENGLAND.

N the shore opposite the Drachenfels stand the Ruins of Rolandseck,—they are the shattered crown of a lofty and perpendicular mountain, consecrated to the memory of the brave Roland; below, the trees of an island to which the lady of Roland retired, rise thick and verdant from the smooth tide.

Nothing can exceed the eloquent and wild grandeur of the whole scene. That spot is the pride and beauty of the Rhine.

The legend that consecrates the tower and the island is briefly told; it belongs to a class so common to the Romaunts of Germany. Roland goes to the wars. A false report of his death reaches his betrothed. She retires to the convent in the isle of Nonnewërth, and takes the irrevocable veil. Roland returns home, flushed with glory and hope, to find that the very fidelity of his affianced had placed an eternal barrier between them. He built the castle that bears his name, and which overlooks the monastery, and dwelt there till his death; happy in the power at least to gaze, even to the last, upon those walls which held the treasure he had lost.

The willows droop in mournful luxuriance along the island, and harmonize with the memory that, through the desert of a thousand years, love still keeps green and fresh. Nor hath it permitted even those additions of fiction which, like mosses, gather by time over the truth that they adorn, yet adorning conceal, to mar the simple tenderness of the legend.

All was still in the island of Nonnewërth; the lights shone through the trees from the house that contained our travellers. On one smooth spot where the islet shelves into the Rhine, met the wandering fairies.

"Oh, Pipalee! how beautiful!" cried Nymphalin, as she stood enraptured by the wave; a star-beam shining on her, with her yellow hair "dancing its ringlets in the whistling wind." "For the first time since our departure I do not miss the green fields of England."

"Hist!" said Pipalee under her breath; "I hear fairy steps—they must be the steps of strangers."

"Let us retreat into this thicket of weeds," said Nymphalin, somewhat alarmed; "the good lord-treasurer is already asleep there. They whisked into what to them was a forest, for the reeds were two feet high, and there, sure enough, they found the lord-treasurer stretched beneath a bulrush, with his pipe beside him: for since he had been in Germany he had taken to smoking; and indeed wild thyme, properly dried, makes very good tobacco for a fairy. They also found Nip and Trip sitting very close together. Nip playing with her hair, which was exceedingly beautiful.

"What do you do here?" said Pipalee, shortly; for she was rather an old maid, and did not like fairies to be too close to each other.

"Watching my lord's slumber," said Nip.

"Pshaw!" said Pipalee.

"Nay," quoth Trip, blushing like a sea-shell; "there is no harm in *that*, I'm sure."

"Hush!" said the queen, peeping through the reeds.

And now forth from the green bosom of the earth came a tiny train; slowly, two by two, hand in hand, they swept from a small aperture, shadowed with fragrant herbs, and formed themselves into a ring: then came other fairies, laden with dainties, and presently two beautiful white mushrooms sprang up, on which their viands were placed, and lo, there was a banquet! Oh, how merry they were! what gentle peals of laughter, loud as a virgin's sigh! what jests! what songs! Happy race! if mortals could see you as often as I do, in the soft nights of summer, they would never be at a loss for entertainment. But as our English fairies looked on, they saw that these foreign elves were of a different race from themselves; they were taller and less handsome, their hair was darker, they wore mustaches, and had something of a fiercer air. Poor Nymphalin was a little frightened; but presently soft music was heard floating along, something like the sound we suddenly hear of a still night when a light breeze steals through rushes, or wakes a ripple in some shallow brook dancing over pebbles. And lo, from the aperture of the earth came forth a fay, superbly dressed, and of a noble presence. The queen started back, Pipalee rubbed her eyes, Trip looked over Pipalee's shoulder, and Nip, pinching her arm, cried out amazed, "By the last new star, that is Prince von Fayzenheim!"

Poor Nymphalin gazed again, and her little heart beat under her bee's-wing bodice as if it would break. The prince had a melancholy air, and he sat apart from the banquet, gazing abstractedly on the Rhine.

"Ah!" whispered Nymphalin to herself, "does he think of me?"

Presently the prince drew forth a little flute, hollowed from a small reed, and began to play a mournful air. Nymphalin listened with delight; it was one he had learned in her dominions.

When the air was over, the prince rose, and, approaching the banqueters, despatched them on different errands; one to visit the dwarf of the Drachenfels, another to look after the grave of Musæus, and a whole detachment to puzzle the students of Heidelberg. A few launched themselves upon willow leaves on the Rhine, to cruise about in the starlight, and another band set out a hunting after the gray-legged moth. The prince was left alone; and now Nymphalin, seeing the coast clear, wrapped herself up in a cloak made out of a withered leaf;—and only letting her eyes glow out from the hood, she glided from the reeds, and the prince turning round, saw a dark fairy figure by his side. He drew back, a little startled, and placed his hand on his sword, when Nymphalin circling round him, sang the following words:—

THE FAIRY'S REPROACH.

I.

By the glow-worm's lamp in the dewy brake;
By the gossamer's airy net;
By the shifting skin of the faithless snake;
Oh, teach me to forget:
For none, ah none,
Can teach so well that human spell
As Thou, false one!

II.

By the fairy dance on the greensward smooth;
By the winds of the gentle west;
By the loving stars, when their soft looks soothe
The waves on their mother's breast;
Teach me thy lore!
By which, like withered flowers,
The leaves of buried Hours
Blossom no more!

III.

By the tent in the violet's bell;
By the may on the scented bough;
By the lone green isle where my sisters dwell;
And thine own forgotten vow;
Teach me to live,
Nor feed on thoughts that pine
For love so false as thine!
—Teach me thy lore,
And one thou lov'st no more
Will bless thee and forgive!

"Surely," said Fayzenheim, faltering, "surely I know that voice!"

And Nymphalin's cloak dropped off her shoulder. "My English fairy!" and Fayzenheim knelt beside her.

I wish you had seen the fay kneel, for you would have sworn it was so like a human lover, that you would never have sneered at love afterwards. Love is so fairy-like a part of us, that even a fairy cannot make it differently from us,—that is to say, when we love truly.

There was great joy in the island that night among the elves. They conducted Nymphalin to their palace within the earth, and feasted her sumptuously; and Nip told their adventures with so much spirit, that he enchanted the merry foreigners. But Fayzenheim talked apart to Nymphalin, and told her how he was lord of that island, and how he had been obliged to return to his dominions by the law of his tribe, which allowed him to be absent only a certain time in every year; "But, my queen, I always intended to revisit thee next spring."

"Thou need'st not have left us so abruptly," said Nymphalin, blushing.

"But do *thou* never leave me!" said the ardent fairy; "be mine, and let our nuptials be celebrated on these shores. Wouldst thou sigh for thy green island? No! for *there* the fairy altars are deserted, the faith is gone from the land; thou art among the last of an unhonoured and expiring race. Thy mortal poets are dumb, and Fancy, which was thy priestess, sleeps hushed in her last repose. New and hard creeds have succeeded to the fairy lore. Who steals through the starlit boughs on the nights of June to watch the roundels of thy tribe? The wheels of commerce, the din of trade, have silenced to mortal ear the music of thy subjects' harps! And the noisy habitations of men, harsher than their dreaming sires, are gathering round the dell and vale where thy co-mates linger:—a few years, and where will be the green solitudes of England?"

The queen sighed, and the prince, perceiving that he was listened to, continued—

"Who, in thy native shores, among the children of men, now claims the fairy's care? What cradle wouldst thou tend? On what maid wouldst thou shower thy rosy gifts? What bard wouldst thou haunt in his dreams? Poesy is fled the island, why shouldst thou linger behind? Time hath brought dull customs, that laugh at thy gentle being. Puck is buried in the harebell, he has left no offspring, and none mourn for his loss; for night, which is the fairy season, is busy and garish as the day. What hearth is desolate after the curfew? What house bathed in stillness at the hour in which thy revels commence? Thine empire among men has passed from thee, and thy race are vanishing from the crowded soil. For, despite our diviner nature, our existence is linked with man's. Their neglect is our disease, their forgetfulness our death. Leave then those dull, yet troubled scenes, that are closing round the fairy rings of thy native isle. These mountains, this herbage, these gliding waves, these mouldering ruins, these starred rivulets, be they, O beautiful fairy! thy new domain. Yet in these lands our worship lingers; still can we fill the thought of the young bard, and mingle with his yearnings after the Beautiful, the Unseen. Hither come the pilgrims of the world, anxious only to gather from these scenes the legends of Us; ages will pass away ere the Rhine shall be desecrated of our haunting presence. Come then, my queen, let this palace be thine own, and the moon that glances over the shattered towers of the Dragon Rock witness our nuptials and our vows!"

In such words the fairy prince courted the young queen, and while she sighed at their truth she yielded to their charm. Oh! still may there be one spot on the earth where the fairy feet may press the legendary soil—still be there one land where the faith of The Bright Invisible hallows and inspires! Still glide thou, O majestic and solemn Rhine, among shades and valleys, from which the wisdom of belief can call the creations of the younger world!

CHAPTER XI.

WHEREIN THE READER IS MADE SPECTATOR WITH THE ENGLISH FAIRIES OF THE SCENES AND BEINGS THAT ARE BENEATH THE EARTH.

DURING the heat of next day's noon, Fayzenheim took the English visitors through the cool caverns that wind amidst the mountains of the Rhine. There, a thousand wonders awaited the eyes of the fairy queen. I speak not of the Gothic arch and aisle into which the hollow earth forms itself, or the stream that rushes with a mighty voice through the dark chasm, or the silver columns that shoot aloft, worked by the gnomes from the mines of the mountains of Taunus; but of the strange inhabitants that from time to time they came upon. They found in one solitary cell, lined with dried moss, two misshapen elves, of a larger size than common, with a plebeian working-day aspect, who were chatting noisily together, and making a pair of boots: these were the Hausmannen or domestic elves, that dance into tradesmen's houses of a night, and play all sorts of undignified tricks. They were very civil to the queen, for they are good-natured creatures on the whole, and once had many relations in Scotland. They then, following the course of a noisy rivulet, came to a hole, from which the sharp head of a fox peeped out. The queen was frightened. "Oh, come on," said the fox, encouragingly, " I am one of the fairy race, and many are the gambols we of the brute-elves play in the German world of romance." "Indeed, Mr. Fox," said the prince, "you only speak the truth ; and how is Mr. Bruin?" "Quite well, my prince ; but tired of his seclusion, for indeed our race can do little or nothing now in the world, and lie here in our old age, telling stories of the past, and recalling the exploits we did in our youth ; which, madam, you may see in all the fairy histories in the prince's library."

"Your own love adventures, for instance, Master Fox," said the prince.

The fox snarled angrily, and drew in his head.

"You have displeased your friend," said Nymphalin.

"Yes—he likes no allusions to the amorous follies of his youth. Did you ever hear of his rivalry with the dog for the cat's good graces?"

"No—that must be very amusing."

"Well, my queen, when we rest by and by, I will relate to you the history of the fox's wooing."

The next place they came to was a vast Runic cavern, covered with dark inscriptions of a forgotten tongue ; and sitting on a huge stone they found a dwarf with long yellow hair, his head leaning on his breast, and absorbed in meditation.

"This is a spirit of a wise and powerful race," whispered Fayzenheim, "that has often battled with the fairies ; but he is of the kindly tribe."

Then the dwarf lifted his head with a mournful air ; and gazed upon the bright shapes before him, lighted by the pine-torches that the prince's attendants carried.

"And what dost thou muse upon ? O descendant of the race of Laurin !" said the prince.

"Upon TIME !" answered the dwarf gloomily. "I see a River, and its waves are black, flowing from the clouds, and none knoweth its source. It rolls deeply on, aye and evermore, through a green valley, which it slowly swallows up, washing away tower and town, and vanquishing all things ; and the name of the River is TIME."

Then the dwarf's head sunk on his bosom, and he spoke no more.

The fairies proceeded:—"Above us," said the prince, "rises one of the loftiest mountains of the Rhine; for mountains are the Dwarf's home. When the Great Spirit of all made earth, he saw that the hollows of the rocks and hills were tenantless; and yet, that a mighty kingdom and great palaces were hid within them; a dread and dark solitude: but lighted at times from the starry eyes of many jewels; and there, was the treasure of the human world—gold and silver—and great heaps of gems, and a soil of metals. So God made a race for this vast empire, and gifted them with the power of thought, and the soul of exceeding wisdom; so that they want not the merriment and enterprise of the outer world: but musing in these dark caves is their delight. Their existence rolls away in the luxury of thought; only from time to time they appear in the world, and betoken woe or weal to men; according to their nature—for they are divided into two tribes, the benevolent and the wrathful." While the prince spoke, they saw glaring upon them from a ledge in the upper rock a grisly face with a long matted beard. The prince gathered himself up, and frowned at the evil dwarf, for such it was; but with a wild laugh the face abruptly disappeared, and the echo of the laugh rang with a ghastly sound through the long hollows of the earth.

The queen clung to Fayzenheim's arm. "Fear not, my queen," said he; "the evil race have no power over our light and aërial nature: with men only they war; and he whom we have seen was, in the old ages of the world, one of the deadliest visitors to mankind."

But now they came winding by a passage to a beautiful recess in the mountain empire; it was of a circular shape of amazing height, in the midst of it played a natural fountain of sparkling waters, and around it were columns of massive granite, rising in countless vistas, till lost in the distant shade. Jewels were scattered round, and brightly played the fairy torches on the gem, the fountain, and the pale silver, that gleamed at frequent intervals from the rocks. "Here let us rest," said the gallant fairy, clapping his hands— "what, ho! music and the feast."

So the feast was spread by the fountain's side; and the courtiers scattered rose-leaves, which they had brought with them, for the prince and his visitor; and amidst the dark kingdom of the dwarfs broke the delicate sound of fairy lutes. "We have not these evil beings in England," said the queen, as low as she could speak; "they rouse my fear, but my interest also. Tell me, dear prince, of what nature was the intercourse of the evil dwarf with man?"

"You know," answered the prince, "that to every species of living thing there is something in common; the vast chain of sympathy runs through all creation. By that which they have in common with the beast of the field or the bird of the air, men govern the inferior tribes; they appeal to the common passions of fear and emulation when they tame the wild steed; to the common desire of greed and gain when they snare the fishes of the stream, or allure the wolves to the pitfall by the bleating of the lamb. In their turn, in the older ages of the world, it was by the passions which men had in common with the demon race that the fiends commanded or allured them. The dwarf whom you saw, being of that race which is characterized by the ambition of power and the desire of hoarding, appealed then in his intercourse with men to the same characteristics in their own bosoms; to ambition or to avarice. And thus were his victims made! But, not now, dearest Nymphalin," continued the prince, with a more lively air—"not now will we speak of those gloomy beings. Ho, there! cease the music, and come hither all of ye—to listen to a faithful and homely history of the Dog, the Cat, the Griffin, and the Fox."

CHAPTER XII.

THE WOOING OF MASTER FOX.[1]

YOU are aware, my dear Nymphalin, that in the time of which I am about to speak there was no particular enmity between the various species of brutes; the dog and the hare chatted very agreeably together, and all the world knows that the wolf, unacquainted with mutton, had a particular affection for the lamb. In these happy days, two most respectable cats, of very old family, had an only daughter: never was kitten more amiable or more seducing; as she grew up she manifested so many charms, that in a little while she became noted as the greatest beauty in the neighbourhood: need I to you, dearest Nymphalin, describe

---

[1] In the excursions of the fairies, it is the object of the author to bring before the reader a rapid phantasmagoria of the various beings that belong to the German superstitions, so that the work may thus describe the outer and the inner world of the land of the Rhine. The tale of the Fox's Wooing has been composed to give the English reader an idea of a species of novel not naturalized amongst us, though frequent among the legends of our Irish neighbours; in which the brutes are the only characters drawn—drawn too, with shades of distinction as nice and subtle as if they were the creatures of the civilized world.

her perfection? **Suffice** it to say that her skin was of the most delicate tortoise shell, that her paws were smoother than velvet, that her whiskers were twelve inches long at the least, and that her eyes had a gentleness altogether astonishing in a cat. But if the young beauty had suitors in plenty during the lives of monsieur and madame, you may suppose the number was not diminished when, at the age of two years and a half, she was left an orphan, and sole heiress to all the hereditary property. In fine, she was the richest marriage in the whole country. Without troubling you, dearest queen, with the adventures of the rest of her lovers, with their suit, and their rejection, **I come** at once to the two rivals most sanguine of success—the dog and the fox.

Now the dog was a handsome, honest, straightforward, affectionate fellow. "For my part," said he, "I don't wonder at my cousin's refusing Bruin the bear, and Gauntgrim the wolf: to be sure they give themselves great airs, and call themselves '*noble*,' but what then? Bruin is always in the sulks, and Gauntgrim always in a passion; a cat of any sensibility would lead a miserable life with them: as for **me,** I am very good-tempered when I'm not put out; and I have **no fault** except that of being angry if disturbed at my meals. I am **young** and good-looking, fond of play and amusement, and altogether **as** agreeable **a** husband as a cat could **find in a** summer's day. If she **marries me,** well and good; she may **have** her property **settled on herself:**—if not, I shall bear her no malice; and **I** hope **I sha'n't be too much** in love to forget that there are other cats in the world."

With that the dog threw his tail **over his** back, and set off to his mistress with a gay face on the matter.

Now the fox heard the dog talking thus to himself—for the fox **was** always peeping about, in holes and corners, and he burst out a-laughing when the dog was out of sight.

"Ho, ho, my fine fellow!" said he; "not so fast, if **you** please: you've got the fox for a rival, let me tell you."

The fox, as you very well know, is a beast that can never do anything without a manœuvre; and as, from his cunning, he was generally very lucky in anything he undertook, he did not doubt for a moment that he should **put** the dog's nose out **of** joint. Reynard was aware that in love **one** should, if possible, be the first in the field, and he therefore resolved **to get** the start of the dog and arrive before him at **the** cat's residence. But this was no easy matter; for though Reynard could run faster than the dog for a little way, he was **no** match for him in a journey of some distance. "However," **said** Reynard, "those good-natured creatures are never very wise;

and I think I know already what will make him bait on his way."

With that, the fox trotted pretty fast by a short cut in the woods, and getting before the dog, laid himself down by a hole in the earth, and began to howl most piteously.

The dog, hearing the noise, was very much alarmed; "See now," said he, "if the poor fox has not got himself into some scrape! Those cunning creatures are always in mischief; thank Heaven, it never comes into my head to be cunning!" And the good-natured animal ran off as hard as he could to see what was the matter with the fox.

"Oh dear!" cried Reynard; "what shall I do, what shall I do! my poor little sister has fallen into this hole, and I can't get her out—she'll certainly be smothered." And the fox burst out a-howling more piteously than before.

"But, my dear Reynard," quoth the dog very simply, "why don't you go in after your sister?"

"Ah, you may well ask that," said the fox; "but, in trying to get in, don't you perceive that I have sprained my back, and can't stir? Oh dear! what shall I do if my poor little sister is smothered!"

"Pray don't vex yourself," said the dog; "I'll get her out in an instant:" and with that he forced himself with great difficulty into the hole.

Now, no sooner did the fox see that the dog was fairly in, than he rolled a great stone to the mouth of the hole, and fitted it so tight, that the dog, not being able to turn round and scratch against it with his fore-paws, was made a close prisoner.

"Ha, ha," cried Reynard, laughing outside; "amuse yourself with my poor little sister, while I go and make your compliments to Mademoiselle the Cat."

With that Reynard set off at an easy pace, never troubling his head what became of the poor dog. When he arrived in the neighbourhood of the beautiful cat's mansion, he resolved to pay a visit to a friend of his, an old magpie that lived in a tree, and was well acquainted with all the news of the place. "For," thought Reynard, "I may as well know the blind side of my mistress that is to be, and get round it at once."

The magpie received the fox with great cordiality, and inquired what brought him so great a distance from home.

"Upon my word," said the fox, "nothing so much as the pleasure of seeing your ladyship, and hearing those agreeable anecdotes you tell with so charming a grace: but, to let you into a secret—be sure it don't go farther——"

"On the word of a magpie," interrupted the bird.

"Pardon me for doubting you," continued the fox; "I should have recollected that a pie was a proverb for discretion. But, as I was saying, you know her majesty the lioness?"

"Surely," said the magpie, bridling.

"Well; she was pleased to fall in—that is to say—to—to—take a caprice to your humble servant, and the lion grew so jealous that I thought it prudent to decamp. A jealous lion is no joke, let me assure your ladyship. But mum's the word."

So great a piece of news delighted the magpie. She could not but repay it in kind, by all the news in her budget. She told the fox all the scandal about Bruin and Gauntgrim, and she then fell to work on the poor young cat. She did not spare her foibles, you may be quite sure. The fox listened with great attention, and he learned enough to convince him, that however much the magpie might exaggerate, the cat was very susceptible to flattery, and had a great deal of imagination.

When the magpie had finished, she said, "But it must be very unfortunate for you to be banished from so magnificent a court as that of the lion?"

"As to that," answered the fox, "I console myself for my exile with a present his majesty made me on parting, as a reward for my anxiety for his honour and domestic tranquillity; namely, three hairs from the fifth leg of the amoronthologosphorus. Only think of that, ma'am!"

"The what?" cried the pie, cocking down her left ear.

"The amoronthologosphorus."

"La!" said the magpie; "and what is that very long word, my dear Reynard?"

"The amoronthologosphorus is a beast that lives on the other side of the river Cylinx; it has five legs, and on the fifth leg there are three hairs, and whoever has those three hairs can be young and beautiful for ever."

"Bless me! I wish you would let me see them," said the pie, holding out her claw.

"Would that I could oblige you, ma'am; but it's as much as my life's worth to show them to any but the lady I marry. In fact, they only have an effect on the fair sex, as you may see by myself, whose poor person they utterly fail to improve: they are, therefore, intended for a marriage present, and his majesty the lion thus generously atoned to me for relinquishing the tenderness of his queen. One must confess that there was a great deal of delicacy in the gift. But you'll be sure not to mention it."

"A magpie gossip, indeed!" quoth the old blab.

The fox then wished the magpie good night, and retired to a hole to sleep off the fatigues of the day, before he presented himself to the beautiful young cat.

The next morning, Heaven knows how! it was all over the place that Reynard the fox had been banished from court for the favour shown him by her majesty, and that the lion had bribed his departure with three hairs that would make any lady whom the fox married young and beautiful for ever.

The cat was the first to learn the news, and she became all curiosity to see so interesting a stranger, possessed of "qualifications" which, in the language of the day, "would render any animal happy!" She was not long without obtaining her wish. As she was taking a walk in the wood the fox contrived to encounter her. You may be sure that he made her his best bow; and he flattered the poor cat with so courtly an air that she saw nothing surprising in the love of the lioness.

Meanwhile let us see what became of his rival, the dog.

"Ah, the poor creature!" said Nymphalin; "it is easy to guess that he need not be buried alive to lose all chance of marrying the heiress."

"Wait till the end," answered Fayzenheim. "When the dog found that he was thus entrapped, he gave himself up for lost. In vain he kicked with his hind-legs against the stone—he only succeeded in bruising his paws; and at length he was forced to lie down, with his tongue out of his mouth, and quite exhausted. "However," said he, after he had taken breath, "it won't do to be starved here, without doing my best to escape; and if I can't get out one way, let me see if there is not a hole at the other end." Thus saying, his courage, which stood him in lieu of cunning, returned, and he proceeded on in the same straightforward way in which he always conducted himself. At first the path was exceedingly narrow, and he hurt his sides very much against the rough stones that projected from the earth. But by degrees the way became broader, and he now went on with considerable ease to himself, till he arrived in a large cavern, where he saw an immense griffin sitting on his tail, and smoking a huge pipe.

The dog was by no means pleased at meeting so suddenly a creature that had only to open his mouth to swallow him up at a morsel; however he put a bold face on the danger, and walking respectfully up to the griffin, said, "Sir, I should be very much obliged to you if you would inform me the way out of these holes into the upper world."

The griffin took the pipe out of his mouth, and looked at the dog very sternly.

"Ho, wretch!" said he, "how comest thou hither? I suppose thou wantest to steal my treasure: but I know how to treat such vagabonds as you, and I shall certainly eat you up."

"You can do that if you choose," said the dog; "but it would be very unhandsome conduct in an animal so much bigger than myself. For my own part, I never attack any dog that is not of equal size: I should be ashamed of myself if I did. And as to your treasure, the character I bear for honesty is too well known to merit such a suspicion."

"Upon my word," said the griffin, who could not help smiling for the life of him, "you have a singularly free mode of expressing yourself;—and how, I say, came you hither?"

Then the dog, who did not know what a lie was, told the griffin his whole history,—how he had set off to pay his court to the cat, and how Reynard the fox had entrapped him into the hole.

When he had finished, the griffin said to him, "I see, my friend, that you know how to speak the truth; I am in want of just such a servant as you will make me, therefore stay with me and keep watch over my treasure when I sleep."

"Two words to that," said the dog. "You have hurt my feelings very much by suspecting my honesty, and I would much sooner go back into the wood and be avenged on that scoundrel the fox, than serve a master who has so ill an opinion of me. I pray you, therefore, to dismiss me, and to put me in the right way to my cousin the cat."

"I am not a griffin of many words," answered the master of the cavern, "and I give you your choice—be my servant, or be my breakfast; it is just the same to me. I give you time to decide till I have smoked out my pipe."

The poor dog did not take so long to consider. "It is true," thought he, "that it is a great misfortune to live in a cave with a griffin of so unpleasant a countenance: but, probably, if I serve him well and faithfully, he'll take pity on me some day, and let me go back to earth, and prove to my cousin what a rogue the fox is; and as to the rest, though I would sell my life as dear as I could, it is impossible to fight a griffin with a mouth of so monstrous a size."— In short, he decided to stay with the griffin.

"Shake a paw on it," quoth the grim smoker; and the dog shook paws.

"And now," said the griffin, "I will tell you what you are to do—look here;" and moving his tail, he showed the dog a great heap of gold and silver, in a hole in the ground, that he had covered with the folds of his tail; and also, what the dog thought more valuable, a great heap of bones of very tempting appearance.

"Now," said the griffin, "during the day, I can take very good care of these myself; but at night it is very necessary that I should go to sleep: so when I sleep, you must watch over them instead of me."

"Very well," said the dog. "As to the gold and silver, I have no objection; but I would much rather that you would lock up the bones, for I'm often hungry of a night, and——"

"Hold your tongue," said the griffin.

"But, sir," said the dog, after a short silence, "surely nobody ever comes into so retired a situation! Who are the thieves, if I may make bold to ask?"

"Know," answered the griffin, "that there are a great many serpents in this neighbourhood, they are always trying to steal my treasure; and if they catch me napping, they, not contented with theft, would do their best to sting me to death. So that I am almost worn out for want of sleep."

"Ah!" quoth the dog, who was fond of a good night's rest, "I don't envy you your treasure, sir."

At night, the griffin, who had a great deal of penetration, and saw that he might depend on the dog, lay down to sleep in another corner of the cave; and the dog, shaking himself well, so as to be quite awake, took watch over the treasure. His mouth watered exceedingly at the bones, and he could not help smelling them now and then; but he said to himself,—"A bargain's a bargain, and since I have promised to serve the griffin, I must serve him as an honest dog ought to serve."

In the middle of the night he saw a great snake creeping in by the side of the cave, but the dog set up so loud a bark that the griffin awoke, and the snake crept away as fast as he could. Then the griffin was very much pleased, and he gave the dog one of the bones to amuse himself with; and every night the dog watched the treasure, and acquitted himself so well that not a snake, at last, dared to make its appearance; so the griffin enjoyed an excellent night's rest.

The dog now found himself much more comfortable than he expected. The griffin regularly gave him one of the bones for supper; and, pleased with his fidelity, made himself as agreeable a master as a griffin could be. Still, however, the dog was secretly very anxious to return to earth; for having nothing to do during the day but to doze on the ground, he dreamed perpetually of his cousin the cat's charms; and, in fancy, he gave the rascal Reynard as hearty a worry as a fox may well have the honour of receiving from a dog's paws. He awoke panting—alas! he could not realize his dreams.

One night, as he was watching as usual over the treasure, he was greatly surprised to see a beautiful little black and white dog enter the cave; and it came fawning to our honest friend, wagging its tail with pleasure.

"Ah! little one," said our dog, whom, to distinguish, I will call the watch-dog, "you had better make the best of your way back again. See, there is a great griffin asleep in the other corner of the cave, and if he wakes, he will either eat you up or make you his servant, as he has made me."

"I know what you would tell me," says the little dog; "and I have come down here to deliver you. The stone is now gone from the mouth of the cave, and you have nothing to do but to go back with me. Come, brother, come."

The dog was very much excited by this address. "Don't ask me, my dear little friend," said he; "you must be aware that I should be too happy to escape out of this cold cave, and roll on the soft turf once more: but if I leave my master, the griffin, those cursed serpents, who are always on the watch, will come in and steal his treasure—nay, perhaps, sting him to death." Then the little dog came up to the watch-dog, and remonstrated with him greatly, and licked him caressingly on both sides of his face; and, taking him by the ear, endeavoured to draw him from the treasure: but the dog would not stir a step, though his heart sorely pressed him. At length the little dog, finding it all in vain, said, "Well then, if I must leave, good-bye; but I have become so hungry in coming down all this way after you, that I wish you would give me one of those bones; they smell very pleasantly, and one out of so many could never be missed."

"Alas!" said the watch-dog, with tears in his eyes, "how unlucky I am to have eat up the bone my master gave me, otherwise you should have had it and welcome. But I can't give you one of these, because my master has made me promise to watch over them all, and I have given him my paw on it. I am sure a dog of your respectable appearance will say nothing farther on the subject."

Then the little dog answered pettishly, "Pooh, what nonsense you talk! surely a great griffin can't miss a little bone, fit for me;" and nestling his nose under the watch-dog, he tried forthwith to bring up one of the bones.

On this the watch-dog grew angry, and, though with much

reluctance, he seized the little dog by the nape of the neck and threw him off, but without hurting him. Suddenly the little dog changed into a monstrous serpent, bigger even than the griffin himself, and the watch-dog barked with all his might. The griffin rose in a great hurry, and the serpent sprang upon him ere he was well awake. I wish, dearest Nymphalin, you could have seen the battle between the griffin and the serpent, how they coiled and twisted, and bit and darted their fiery tongues at each other. At length, the serpent got uppermost, and was about to plunge his tongue into that part of the griffin which is unprotected by his scales, when the dog, seizing him by the tail, bit him so sharply, that he could not help turning round to kill his new assailant, and the griffin, taking advantage of the opportunity, caught the serpent by the throat with both claws, and fairly strangled him. As soon as the griffin had recovered from the nervousness of the conflict, he heaped all manner of caresses on the dog for saving his life. The dog told him the whole story, and the griffin then explained, that the dead snake was the king of the serpents, who had the power to change himself into any shape he pleased. "If he had tempted you," said he, "to leave the treasure but for one moment, or to have given him any part of it, ay, but a single bone, he would have crushed you in an instant, and stung me to death ere I could have waked; but none, no not the most venomous thing in creation, has power to hurt the honest!"

"That has always been my belief," answered the dog; "and now, sir, you had better go to sleep again, and leave the rest to me."

"Nay," answered the griffin, "I have no longer need of a servant; for now that the king of the serpents is dead, the rest will never molest me. It was only to satisfy his avarice that his subjects dared to brave the den of the griffin."

Upon hearing this the dog was exceedingly delighted; and raising himself on his hind-paws, he begged the griffin most movingly to let him return to earth, to visit his mistress the cat, and worry his rival the fox.

"You do not serve an ungrateful master," answered the griffin. "You shall return, and I will teach you all the craft of our race, which is much craftier than the race of that pettifogger the fox, so that you may be able to cope with your rival."

"Ah, excuse me," said the dog, hastily, "I am equally obliged to you; but I fancy honesty is a match for cunning any day; and I think myself a great deal safer in being a dog of honour than if I knew all the tricks in the world."

"Well," said the griffin, a little piqued at the dog's bluntness, "do as you please; I wish you all possible success."

Then the griffin opened a secret door in the side of the cabin, and the dog saw a broad path that led at once into the wood. He thanked the griffin with all his heart, and ran wagging his tail into the open moonlight. "Ah, ah! master fox," said he, "there's no trap for an honest dog that has not two doors to it, cunning as you think yourself."

With that he curled his tail gallantly over his left leg, and set off on a long trot to the cat's house. When he was within sight of it, he stopped to refresh himself by a pool of water, and who should be there but our friend the magpie.

"And what do *you* want, friend?" said she, rather disdainfully, for the dog looked somewhat out of case after his journey.

"I am going to see my cousin the cat," answered he.

"*Your* cousin! marry come up," said the magpie; "don't you know she is going to be married to Reynard the fox? This is not a time for her to receive the visits of a brute like you."

These words put the dog in such a passion, that he very nearly bit the magpie for her uncivil mode of communicating such bad news. However he curbed his temper, and, without answering her, went at once to the cat's residence.

The cat was sitting at the window, and no sooner did the dog see her than he fairly lost his heart; never had he seen so charming a cat before: he advanced, wagging his tail, and with his most insinuating air; when the cat, getting up, clapped the window in his face—and lo! Reynard the fox appeared in her stead.

"Come out, thou rascal?" said the dog, showing his teeth: "come out, I challenge thee to single combat; I have not forgiven thy malice, and thou seest that I am no longer shut up in the cave, and unable to punish thee for thy wickedness."

"Go home, silly one!" answered the fox, sneering; "thou hast no business here, and as for fighting thee—bah!" Then the fox left the window and disappeared. But the dog, thoroughly enraged, scratched lustily at the door, and made such a noise, that presently the cat herself came to the window.

"How now!" said she, angrily; "what means all this rudeness? Who are you, and what do you want at my house?"

"O, my dear cousin," said the dog, "do not speak so severely. Know that I have come here on purpose to pay you a visit; and, whatever you do, let me beseech you not to listen to that villain Reynard—you have no conception what a rogue he is!"

"What!" said the cat, blushing; "do you dare to abuse your

betters in this fashion? I see you have a design on me. Go, this instant, or——"

"Enough, madam," said the dog, proudly; "you need not speak twice to me—farewell."

And he turned away very slowly, and went under a tree, where he took up his lodgings for the night. But the next morning there was an amazing commotion in the neighbourhood; a stranger, of a very different style of travelling from that of the dog, had arrived at the dead of the night, and fixed his abode in a large cavern, hollowed out of a steep rock. The noise he had made in flying through the air was so great, that it had awakened every bird and beast in the parish; and Reynard, whose bad conscience never suffered him to sleep very soundly, putting his head out of the window, perceived, to his great alarm, that the stranger was nothing less than a monstrous griffin.

Now the griffins are the richest beasts in the world; and that's the reason they keep so close under ground. Whenever it does happen that they pay a visit above, it is not a thing to be easily forgotten.

The magpie was all agitation—what could the griffin possibly want there? She resolved to take a peep at the cavern, and, accordingly, she hopped timorously up the rock, and pretended to be picking up sticks for her nest.

"Holla, ma'am!" cried a very rough voice, and she saw the griffin putting his head out of the cavern. "Holla! you are the very lady I want to see; you know all the people about here—eh?"

"All the best company, your lordship, I certainly do," answered the magpie, dropping a curtsey.

Upon this the griffin walked out; and smoking his pipe leisurely in the open air, in order to set the pie at her ease, continued—

"Are there any respectable beasts of good families settled in this neighbourhood?"

"O, most elegant society, I assure your lordship," cried the pie. "I have lived here myself these ten years, and the great heiress, the cat yonder, attracts a vast number of strangers."

"Humph—heiress, indeed! much *you* know about heiresses!" said the griffin. "There is only one heiress in the world, and that's my daughter."

"Bless me! has your lordship a family? I beg you a thousand pardons. But I only saw your lordship's own equipage last night, and did not know you brought any one with you."

"My daughter went first, and was safely lodged before I arrived. She did not disturb you, I dare say, as I did; for she sails along like a swan; but I have the gout in **my left** claw, and **that's the** reason I puff and groan **so** in taking a journey."

"Shall I drop in upon Miss Griffin, and see how she is after her journey?" said the pie, advancing.

"I thank you, no. I don't intend her to be seen while I stay here—it unsettles her; and I'm afraid of the young beasts running away with her if they once heard how handsome she was: she's the living picture of me, but she's monstrous giddy! Not that I should care much if she did go off with a beast of degree, were I not obliged to **pay** her portion, which is prodigious; and I don't like parting with money, ma'am, when I've once got it. Ho, ho, ho!"

"You are too witty, my lord. But if you refused your consent?" said the pie, anxious to know **the** whole family history of so grand a seigneur.

"I should have to pay the dowry all the same. It was left her by her uncle the dragon. But don't let this go any farther."

"Your lordship may depend on my secrecy. I wish your lordship a very good morning."

Away flew the pie, and she did not stop **till she** got **to the cat's** house. The cat and the fox were at breakfast, and the **fox had his** paw on his heart. "Beautiful scene!" cried the pie; the cat coloured, and bade the pie **take a** seat.

Then off went the pie's tongue, glib, glib, glib, chatter, chatter, chatter. She related to them the whole story of the griffin and his daughter, and a great deal more besides, that the griffin had never told her.

The cat listened attentively. Another young heiress in the neighbourhood might be **a** formidable rival. "But is the griffiness handsome?" said she.

"Handsome!" cried the pie; **"oh!** if you could have seen the **father!**—such a mouth, such eyes, such a complexion; and he **declares** she's the living picture of himself! But what do you say, Mr. Reynard? you, who have been so much in the world, have, perhaps, seen the young lady!"

"Why, I can't say I have," answered the fox, waking from a reverie; "but she must be wonderfully rich. I dare say that fool, the dog, will be making up to her."

"Ah! by the way," said the pie, **"what** a fuss he made at your door yesterday; why would you not admit him, my dear?"

"Oh!" said the cat, demurely, "Mr. Reynard says that he is a **dog** of very bad character, quite a fortune-hunter; and hiding the most dangerous disposition to bite under an appearance of good nature. I hope he won't be quarrelsome with you, dear Reynard!"

"With me? O the poor wretch, no!—he might bluster a little; but he knows that if I'm once angry I'm a devil at biting;—but one should not boast of oneself."

In the evening Reynard felt a strange desire to go and see the griffin smoking his pipe; but what could he do? There was the dog under the opposite tree evidently watching for him, and Reynard had no wish to prove himself that devil at biting which he declared he was. At last he resolved to have recourse to stratagem to get rid of the dog.

A young buck of a rabbit, a sort of provincial fop, had looked in upon his cousin the cat, to pay her his respects, and Reynard, taking him aside, said, "You see that shabby-looking dog under the tree? He has behaved very ill to your cousin the cat, and you certainly ought to challenge him—forgive my boldness—nothing but respect for your character induces me to take so great a liberty; you know I would chastise the rascal myself, but what a scandal it would make! If I were already married to your cousin, it would be a different thing. But you know what a story that cursed magpie would hatch out of it!"

The rabbit looked very foolish: he assured the fox that he was no match for the dog; that he was very fond of his cousin, to be sure; but he saw no necessity to interfere with her domestic affairs;—and, in short, he tried all he possibly could to get out of the scrape: but the fox so artfully played on his vanity—so earnestly assured him that the dog was the biggest coward in the world, and would make a humble apology, and so eloquently represented to him the glory he would obtain for manifesting so much spirit, that at length the rabbit was persuaded to go out and deliver the challenge.

"I'll be your second," said the fox; "and the great field on the other side the wood, two miles hence, shall be the place of battle: there we shall be out of observation. You go first, I'll follow in half an hour—and I say—hark!—in case he does accept the challenge, and you feel the least afraid, I'll be in the field, and take it off your paws with the utmost pleasure; rely on *me*, my dear sir!"

Away went the rabbit. The dog was a little astonished at the temerity of the poor creature; but on hearing that the fox was to be present, willingly consented to repair to the place of conflict. This readiness the rabbit did not at all relish; he went very slowly to the field, and seeing no fox there, his heart misgave him, and while the dog was putting his nose to the ground to try if he could track the coming of the fox, the rabbit slipped into a burrow, and left the dog to walk back again.

Meanwhile the fox was already at the rock; he walked very softfootedly, and looked about with extreme caution, for he had a vague notion that a griffin-papa would not be very civil to foxes.

Now there were two holes in the rock—one below, one above, an upper story and an under; and while the fox was peering about, he saw a great claw from the upper rock beckoning to him.

"Ah, ah!" said the fox, "that's the wanton young griffiness, I'll swear."

He approached, and a voice said—

"Charming Mr. Reynard! Do you not think you could deliver an unfortunate griffiness from a barbarous confinement in this rock?"

"Oh heavens!" cried the fox, tenderly, "what a beautiful voice! and, ah, my poor heart, what a lovely claw! Is it possible that I hear the daughter of my lord, the great griffin?"

"Hush, flatterer! not so loud, if you please. My father is taking an evening stroll, and is very quick of hearing. He has tied me up by my poor wings in the cavern, for he is mightily afraid of some beast running away with me. You know I have all my fortune settled on myself."

"Talk not of fortune," said the fox; "but how can I deliver you? Shall I enter and gnaw the cord?"

"Alas!" answered the griffiness, "it is an immense chain I am bound with. However, you may come in and talk more at your ease."

The fox peeped cautiously all round, and seeing no sign of the griffin, he entered the lower cave and stole upstairs to the upper story; but as he went on, he saw immense piles of jewels and gold, and all sorts of treasure, so that the old griffin might well have laughed at the poor cat being called an heiress. The fox was greatly pleased at such indisputable signs of wealth, and he entered the upper cave, resolved to be transported with the charms of the griffiness.

There was, however, a great chasm between the landing-place and the spot where the young lady was chained, and he found it impossible to pass; the cavern was very dark, but he saw enough of the figure of the griffiness to perceive, in spite of her petticoat, that she was the image of her father, and the most hideous heiress that the earth ever saw!

However, he swallowed his disgust, and poured forth such a heap of compliments that the griffiness appeared entirely won. He implored her to fly with him the first moment she was unchained.

"That is impossible," said she; "for my father never unchains me except in his presence, and then I cannot stir out of his sight."

"The wretch!" cried Reynard, "what is to be done?"

"Why, there is only one thing I know of," answered the griffiness, "which is this—I always make his soup for him, and if I could mix something in it that would put him fast to sleep before he had time to chain me up again, I might slip down and carry off all the treasure below on my back."

"Charming!" exclaimed Reynard; "what invention! what wit! I will go and get some poppies directly."

"Alas!" said the griffiness, "poppies have no effect upon griffins. The only thing that can ever put my father fast to sleep is a nice young cat boiled up in his soup; it is astonishing what a charm that has upon him! But where to get a cat?—it must be a maiden cat too!"

Reynard was a little startled at so singular an opiate. "But," thought he, "griffins are not like the rest of the world, and so rich an heiress is not to be won by ordinary means,"

"I do know a cat—a maiden cat," said he, after a short pause; "but I feel a little repugnance at the thought of having her boiled in the griffin's soup. Would not a dog do as well?"

"Ah, base thing!" said the griffiness, appearing to weep, "you are in love with the cat, I see it; go and marry her, poor dwarf that she is, and leave me to die of grief."

In vain the fox protested that he did not care a straw for the cat; nothing could now appease the griffiness, but his positive assurance that, come what would, poor puss should be brought to the cave, and boiled for the griffin's soup.

"But how will you get her here?" said the griffiness.

"Ah, leave that to me," said Reynard. "Only put a basket out of the window, and draw it up by a cord; the moment it arrives at the window, be sure to clap your claw on the cat at once, for she is terribly active."

"Tush!" answered the heiress; "a pretty griffiness I should be if I did not know how to catch a cat!"

"But this must be when your father is out?" said Reynard.

"Certainly: he takes a stroll every evening at sunset."

"Let it be to-morrow, then," said Reynard, impatient for the treasure.

This being arranged, Reynard thought it time to decamp. He stole down the stairs again, and tried to filch some of the treasure by the way: but it was too heavy for him to carry, and he was forced to acknowledge to himself that it was impossible to get the treasure without taking the griffiness (whose back seemed prodigiously strong) into the bargain.

He returned home to the cat, and when he entered her house, and saw how ordinary everything looked after the jewels in the griffin's cave, he quite wondered how he had ever thought the cat had the least pretensions to good looks.

However, he concealed his wicked design, and his mistress thought he had never appeared so amiable.

"Only guess," said he, "where I have been?—to our new neighbour the griffin; a most charming person, thoroughly affable, and quite the air of the court. As for that silly magpie, the griffin saw her character at once; and it was all a hoax about his daughter: he has no daughter at all. You know, my dear, hoaxing is a fashionable amusement among the great. He says he has heard of nothing but your beauty, and on my telling him we were going to be married, he has insisted upon giving a great ball and supper in honour of the event. In fact, he is a gallant old fellow and dying to see you. Of course, I was obliged to accept the invitation."

"You could not do otherwise," said the unsuspecting young creature, who, as I before said, was very susceptible to flattery.

"And only think how delicate his attentions are," said the fox. "As he is very badly lodged for a beast of his rank, and his treasure takes up the whole of the ground floor, he is forced to give the fête in the upper story, so he hangs out a basket for his guests, and draws them up with his own claw. How condescending! But the great are so amiable!"

The cat, brought up in seclusion, was all delight at the idea of seeing such high life, and the lovers talked of nothing else all the next day;—when Reynard, towards evening, putting his head out of the window, saw his old friend the dog lying as usual and watching him very grimly. "Ah, that cursed creature! I had quite forgotten him; what is to be done now? he would make no bones of me if he once saw me set foot out of doors."

With that, the fox began to cast in his head how he should get rid of his rival, and at length he resolved on a very notable project: he desired the cat to set out first, and wait for him at a turn in the road a little way off. "For," said he, "if we go together we shall certainly be insulted by the dog; and he will know that, in the presence of a lady, the custom of a beast of my fashion will not suffer me to avenge the affront. But when I am alone, the creature is such a coward that he would not dare say his soul's his own: leave the door open and I'll follow immediately."

The cat's mind was so completely poisoned against her cousin that she implicitly believed this account of his character, and accordingly, with many recommendations to her lover not to sully his dignity by getting into any sort of quarrel with the dog, she set off first.

The dog went up to her very humbly, and begged her to allow him to say a few words to her; but she received him so haughtily, that his spirit was up; and he walked back to the tree more than ever enraged against his rival. But what was his joy when he saw that the cat had left the door open! "Now, wretch," thought he, "you cannot escape me!" So he walked briskly in at the back door. He was greatly surprised to find Reynard lying down in the straw, panting as if his heart would break, and rolling his eyes in the pangs of death.

"Ah, friend," said the fox, with a faltering voice, "you are avenged, my hour is come; I am just going to give up the ghost: put your paw upon mine, and say you forgive me."

Despite his anger, the generous dog could not set tooth on a dying foe.

"You have served me a shabby trick," said he; "you have left me to starve in a hole, and you have evidently maligned me with my cousin: certainly I meant to be avenged on you; but if you are really dying, that alters the affair."

"Oh, oh!" groaned the fox very bitterly; "I am past help; the poor cat is gone for Doctor Ape, but he'll never come in time. What a thing it is to have a bad conscience on one's death-bed! But, wait till the cat returns, and I'll do you full justice with her before I die."

The good-natured dog was much moved at seeing his mortal enemy in such a state, and endeavoured as well as he could to console him.

"Oh, oh!" said the fox; "I am so parched in the throat—I am burning;" and he hung his tongue out of his mouth, and rolled his eyes more fearfully than ever.

"Is there no water here?" said the dog, looking round.

"Alas, no!—yet stay—yes, now I think of it, there is some in that little hole in the wall; but how to get at it!—it is so high that I can't, in my poor weak state, climb up to it; and I dare not ask such a favour of one I have injured so much."

"Don't talk of it," said the dog: "but the hole's very small, I could not put my nose through it."

"No; but if you just climb up on that stone, and thrust your paw into the hole, you can dip it into the water, and so cool my poor parched mouth. Oh, what a thing it is to have a bad conscience!"

The dog sprang upon the stone, and getting on his hind legs, thrust his front paw into the hole; when suddenly Reynard pulled a string that he had concealed under the straw, and the dog found his paw caught tight to the wall in a running noose.

"Ah, rascal!" said he, turning round; but the fox leaped up gaily from the straw, and fastening the string with his teeth to a nail in the other end of the wall, walked out, crying, "Good-bye, my dear friend; have a care how you believe hereafter in sudden conversions!"—So he left the dog on his hind-legs to take care of the house.

Reynard found the cat waiting for him where he had appointed, and they walked lovingly together till they came to the cave. It was now dark, and they saw the basket waiting below; the fox assisted the poor cat into it. "There is only room for one," said he, "you must go first!"—up rose the basket; the fox heard a piteous mew, and no more.

"So much for the griffin's soup!" thought he.

He waited patiently for some time, when the griffiness, waving her claw from the window, said cheerfully, "All's right, my dear Reynard; my papa has finished his soup, and sleeps as sound as a rock! All the noise in the world would not wake him now, till he has slept off the boiled cat—which won't be these twelve hours. Come and assist me in packing up the treasure; I should be sorry to leave a single diamond behind."

"So should I," quoth the fox. "Stay, I'll come round by the lower hole: why, the door's shut! pray, beautiful griffiness, open it to thy impatient adorer."

"Alas, my father has hid the key! I never know where he places it; you must come up by the basket; see, I will lower it for you."

The fox was a little loth to trust himself in the same conveyance that had taken his mistress to be boiled; but the most cautious grow rash when money's to be gained, and avarice can trap even a fox. So he put himself as comfortably as he could into the basket, and up he went in an instant. It rested, however, just before it reached the window, and the fox felt, with a slight shudder, the claw of the griffiness stroking his back.

"Oh, what a beautiful coat!" quoth she, caressingly.

"You are too kind," said the fox; "but you can feel it more at your leisure when I am once up. Make haste, I beseech you."

"Oh, what a beautiful bushy tail! Never did I feel such a tail!"

"It is entirely at your service, sweet griffiness," said the fox; "but pray let me in. Why lose an instant?"

"No, never did I feel such a tail! No wonder you are so successful with the ladies."

"Ah, beloved griffiness, my tail is yours to eternity, but you pinch it a little too hard."

Scarcely had he said this, when down dropped the basket, but not with the fox in it ; he found himself caught by the tail, and dangling half way down the rock, by the help of the very same sort of pulley wherewith he had snared the dog. I leave you to guess his consternation ; he yelped out as loud as he could,—for it hurts a fox exceedingly to be hanged by his tail with his head downwards,—when the door of the rock opened, and out stalked the griffin himself, smoking his pipe, with a vast crowd of all the fashionable beasts in the neighbourhood.

"Oho, brother," said the bear, laughing fit to kill himself ; "who ever saw a fox hanged by the tail before?"

"You'll have need of a physician," quoth Doctor Ape.

"A pretty match, indeed ; a griffiness for such a creature as you!" said the goat, strutting by him.

The fox grinned with pain, and said nothing. But that which hurt him most was the compassion of a dull fool of a donkey, who assured him with great gravity that he saw nothing at all to laugh at in his situation !

"At all events," said the fox, at last, "cheated, gulled, betrayed as I am, I have played the same trick to the dog. Go and laugh at him, gentlemen ; he deserves it as much as I can, I assure you."

"Pardon me," said the griffin, taking the pipe out of his mouth ; "one never laughs at the honest."

"And see," said the bear, "here he is."

And indeed the dog had, after much effort, gnawed the string in two, and extricated his paw : the scent of the fox had enabled him to track his footsteps, and here he arrived, burning for vengeance and finding himself already avenged.

But his first thought was for his dear cousin. "Ah, where is she?" he cried movingly ; "without doubt that villain Reynard has served her some scurvy trick."

"I fear so indeed, my old friend," answered the griffin, "but don't grieve : after all, she was nothing particular. You shall marry my daughter the griffiness, and succeed to all the treasure ; ay, and all the bones that you once guarded so faithfully."

"Talk not to me," said the faithful dog. "I want none of your treasure ; and, though I don't mean to be rude, your griffiness may go to the devil. I will run over the world but I will find my dear cousin."

"See her then," said the griffin ; and the beautiful cat, more beautiful than ever, rushed out of the cavern, and threw herself into the dog's paws.

A pleasant scene this for the fox!—he had skill enough in the female heart to know that it may excuse many little infidelities,—but to be boiled alive for a griffin's soup!—no, the offence was inexpiable!

"You understand me, Mr. Reynard," said the griffin, "I have no daughter, and it was me you made love to. Knowing what sort of a creature a magpie is, I amused myself with hoaxing her,—the fashionable amusement at court, you know."

The fox made a mighty struggle, and leaped on the ground, leaving his tail behind him. It did not grow again in a hurry.

"See," said the griffin, as the beasts all laughed at the figure Reynard made running into the wood, "the dog beats the fox, with the ladies, after all; and cunning as he is in everything else, the fox is the last creature that should ever think of making love!"

"Charming!" cried Nymphalin, clasping her hands; "it is just the sort of story I like."

"And I suppose, sir," said Nip, pertly, "that the dog and the cat lived very happily ever afterwards? Indeed the nuptial felicity of a dog and cat is proverbial!"

"I dare say they lived much the same as any other married couple," answered the prince.

CHAPTER XIII.

THE TOMB OF A FATHER OF MANY CHILDREN.

THE feast being now ended, as well as the story, the fairies wound their way homeward by a different path, till at length a red steady light glowed through the long basaltic arches upon them, like the Demon Hunters' fires in the Forest of Pines.

The prince sobered in his pace. "You approach," said he, in a grave tone, "the greatest of our temples; you will witness the tomb of a mighty founder of our race!" An awe crept over the queen, in spite of herself. Tracking the fires in silence, they came to a vast space, in the midst of which was a lone gray block of stone, such as the traveller finds amidst the dread silence of Egyptian Thebes.

And on this stone lay the gigantic figure of a man—dead, but not death-like, for invisible spells had preserved the flesh and the long hair for untold ages; and beside him lay a rude instrument of music, and at his feet was a sword and a hunter's spear; and above, the rock wound, hollowed and roofless, to the upper air, and daylight came through, sickened and pale, beneath red fires that burnt everlastingly around him, on such simple altars as belong to a savage race. But the place was not solitary, for many motionless, but not lifeless, shapes sat on large blocks of stone beside the tomb. There was the wizard, wrapped in his long black mantle, and his face covered with his hands—there was the uncouth and deformed dwarf, gibbering to himself—there sat the household elf—there glowed from a gloomy rent in the wall, with glittering eyes and shining scale, the enormous dragon of the North. An aged crone in rags, leaning on a staff, and gazing malignantly on the visitors, with bleared but fiery eyes, stood opposite the tomb of the gigantic dead. And now the fairies themselves completed the group! But all was dumb and unutterably silent; the silence that floats over some antique city of the desert, when, for the first time for a hundred centuries, a living foot enters its desolate remains; the silence that belongs to the dust of eld,—deep, solemn, palpable, and sinking into the heart with a leaden and death-like weight. Even the English fairy spoke not; she held her breath, and gazing on the tomb, she saw, in rude vast characters,

THE TEUTON.

"*We* are all that remain of his religion!" said the prince, as they turned from the dread temple.

CHAPTER XIV.

THE FAIRY'S CAVE, AND THE FAIRY'S WISH.

IT was evening; and the fairies were dancing beneath the twilight star.

"And why art thou sad, my violet?" said the prince, "for thine eyes seek the ground!"

"Now that I have found thee," answered the queen, "and now that I feel what happy love is to a fairy, I sigh over that love which I have lately witnessed among mortals, but the bud of whose happiness already conceals the worm. For well didst thou say, my prince, that we are linked with a mysterious affinity to mankind, and whatever is pure and gentle amongst them speaks at once to our sympathy, and commands our vigils."

"And most of all," said the German fairy, "are they who love under our watch; for love is the golden chain that binds all in the universe: love lights up alike the star and the glow-worm; and wherever there is love in men's lot, lies the secret affinity with men, and with things divine."

"But with the human race," said Nymphalin, "there is no love that outlasts the hour, for either death ends, or custom alters: when the blossom comes to fruit, it is plucked and seen no more; and therefore, when I behold true love sentenced to an early grave, I comfort myself that I shall not at least behold the beauty dimmed, and the softness of the heart hardened into stone. Yet, my prince, while still the pulse can beat, and the warm blood flow, in that beautiful form, which I have watched over of late, let me not desert her; still let my influence keep the sky fair, and the breezes pure; still let me drive the vapour from the moon, and the clouds from the faces of the stars; still let me fill her dreams with tender and brilliant images, and glass in the mirror of sleep, the happiest visions of fairy land; still let me pour over her eyes that magic, which suffers them to see no fault in one in whom she has garnered up her soul! And as death comes slowly on, still let me rob the spectre of its terror, and the grave of its sting;—so that, all gently and unconscious to herself, life may glide into the Great Ocean where the shadows lie; and the spirit without guile, may be severed from its mansion without pain!"

The wish of the fairy was fulfilled.

CHAPTER XV.

THE BANKS OF THE RHINE.—FROM THE DRACHENFELS TO BROHL: AN INCIDENT THAT SUFFICES IN THIS TALE FOR AN EPOCH.

FROM the Drachenfels commences the true glory of the Rhine; and, once more, Gertrude's eyes conquered the languor that crept gradually over them as she gazed on the banks around.

Fair blew the breeze, and freshly curled the waters; and Gertrude did not feel the vulture that had fixed its talons within her breast. The Rhine widens, like a broad lake, between the Drachenfels and Unkel; villages are scattered over the extended plain on the left; on the right is the Isle of Werth and the houses of Oberwinter; the hills are covered with vines; and still Gertrude turned back with a lingering gaze to the lofty crest of the Seven Hills.

On, on—and the spires of Unkel rose above a curve in the banks, and on the opposite shore stretched those wondrous basaltic columns which extend to the middle of the river, and when the Rhine runs low, you may see them like an engulfed city beneath the waves. You then view the ruins of Okkenfels, and hear the voice of the pastoral Gasbach pouring its waters into the Rhine. From amidst the clefts of the rocks the vine peeps luxuriantly forth, and gives a richness and colouring to what Nature, left to herself, intended for the stern.

"But turn your eye backward to the right," said Trevylyan; "those banks were formerly the special haunt of the bold robbers of the Rhine, and from amidst the entangled brakes that then covered the ragged cliffs, they rushed upon their prey. In the gloomy canvas of those feudal days what vigorous and mighty images were crowded! A robber's life amidst these mountains, and beside this mountain stream, must have been the very poetry of the spot carried into action."

They rested at Brohl, a small town between two mountains. On the summit of one you see the gray remains of Rheinech. There is something weird and preternatural about the aspect of this place; its soil betrays signs that, in the former ages (from which even tradition is fast fading away), some volcano here exhausted its fires. The stratum of the earth is black and pitchy, and the springs beneath it are of a dark and graveolent water. Hear the stream of the Brohlbach falls into the Rhine, and in a valley rich with oak and pine, and full of caverns, which are not without their traditionary inmates, stands the castle of Schweppenbourg, which our party failed not to visit.

Gertrude felt fatigued on their return, and Trevylyan sat by her in the little inn, while Vane went forth, with the curiosity of science, to examine the strata of the soil.

They conversed in the frankness of their plighted troth upon those topics which are only for lovers: upon the bright chapter in the history of their love; their first meeting; their first impressions; the little incidents in their present journey—incidents noticed by themselves alone; that life *within* life which two persons know together,—which one knows not without the other,—which ceases to both the instant they are divided.

"I know not what the love of others may be," said Gertrude, "but ours seems different from all of which I have read. Books tell us of jealousies and misconstructions, and the necessity of an absence, the sweetness of a quarrel; but *we*, dearest Albert, have had no experience of these passages in love. *We* have never misunderstood each other; we have no reconciliation to look back to. When was there ever occasion for me to ask forgiveness from you? Our love is made up only of one memory—unceasing kindness! A harsh word, a wronging thought, never broke in upon the happiness we have felt and feel."

"Dearest Gertrude," said Trevylyan, "that character of our love is caught from you; you, the soft, the gentle, have been its pervading genius; and the well has been smooth and pure, for you were the spirit that lived within its depths."

And to such talk succeeded silence still more sweet—the silence of the hushed and overflowing heart. The last voices of the birds—the sun slowly sinking in the west—the fragrance of descending dews—filled them with that deep and mysterious sympathy which exists between Love and Nature.

It was after such a silence—a long silence, that seemed but as a moment—that Trevylyan spoke, but Gertrude answered not; and, yearning once more for her sweet voice, he turned and saw that she had fainted away.

This was the first indication of the point to which her increasing debility had arrived. Trevylyan's heart stood still, and then beat violently; a thousand fears crept over him, he clasped her in his arms, and bore her to the open window. The setting sun fell upon her countenance, from which the play of the young heart and warm fancy had fled, and in its deep and still repose the ravages of disease were darkly visible. What were then his emotions! his heart was like stone; but he felt a rush as of a torrent to his temples: his eyes grew dizzy—he was stunned by the greatness of his despair. For the last week he had taken hope for his companion; Gertrude had seemed so much stronger, for her happiness had given her a false support; and though there had been moments when, watching the bright hectic come and go, and her step linger, and the breath heave short, he had felt the hope suddenly cease, yet never had he known till now that fulness of anguish, that dread certainty of the worst, which the calm, fair face before him struck into his soul: and mixed with this agony as he gazed was all the passion of the most ardent love. For there she lay in his arms, the gentle breath rising from lips where the rose yet lingered, and the long, rich hair, soft and silken as an infant's, stealing from its confinement: every thing that belonged to Gertrude's beauty was so inexpressively soft, and pure, and youthful! Scarcely seventeen, she seemed much younger than she was; her figure had sunken from its roundness, but still how light, how lovely were its wrecks! the neck whiter than snow,—the fair small hand! Her weight was scarcely felt in the arms of her lover,—and he—what a contrast!—was in all the **pride** and **flower** of glorious manhood! his **was** the lofty brow, the wreathing hair, the haughty eye, the elastic form; and upon this frail, perishable thing had he fixed all his heart, all the hopes of his youth, the **pride** of his manhood, his schemes, his energies, his ambition!

"Oh, Gertrude!" **cried he,** "is it—is it thus—is there indeed **no** hope?"

And Gertrude now slowly recovering, **and opening** her eyes upon Trevylyan's **face, the** revulsion was so great, **his** emotions so overpowering, **that,** clasping her to his bosom, **as if** even death should not tear her away from him, he wept over her in an agony of tears; not those tears that relieve the heart, but the fiery rain of the internal storm, a sign of the fierce tumult that shook the very core of his existence, not a relief.

Awakened to herself, Gertrude, in amazement and **alarm, threw** her arms around his neck, and, looking wistfully into **his face,** implored him to speak to her.

"Was it my illness, love?" said she; and the music **of her voice** only conveyed to him the thought of how soon it would **be dumb to** him for ever. "Nay," she continued, winningly, "it **was but the** heat of the day; I am better now—I am well; there is no **cause to** be alarmed for me;" and, with all the innocent fondness of **extreme** youth, **she kissed** the burning tears from his eyes.

There was a playfulness, an innocence in this poor girl, so **unconscious as** yet of her destiny, which rendered her fate doubly touching; and which **to** the stern Trevylyan, hackneyed by the world, made her irresistible charm; and now as she put aside her hair, and looked up gratefully, yet pleadingly, into his face, he **could** scarce refrain from pouring out to her the confession of his anguish and despair. But the necessity of self-control—the necessity of concealing from *her* a knowledge **which** might only, by impressing her imagination, expedite her doom, while it would embitter to her **mind** the unconscious enjoyment of the hour, nerved **and manned** him. He checked by those violent efforts which only men can make, the evidence of his emotions; and endeavoured, by a rapid torrent of words, to divert her attention from a weakness, the causes of which he **could not** explain. Fortunately Vane soon returned, and Trevylyan, consigning Gertrude to his care, hastily left the room.

Gertrude sunk into a reverie.

"Ah, dear father!" said she, suddenly, and after a pause, **"if I** indeed were worse than I have thought myself of late—if I were to die now, what would Trevylyan feel? Pray God, **I** may live for his sake!"

"My child, do not talk thus: you are better, much better than you were. Ere the autumn ends, Trevylyan's happiness will be your lawful care. Do not think so despondently of yourself."

"I thought not of myself," sighed Gertrude, "but of *him!*"

CHAPTER XVI.

GERTRUDE.—THE EXCURSION TO HAMMERSTEIN.—THOUGHTS.

THE next day they visited the environs of Brohl. Gertrude was unusually silent; for her temper, naturally sunny and enthusiastic, was accustomed to light up everything she saw. Ah, once how bounding was that step! how undulating the young graces of that form! how playfully once danced the ringlets on that laughing cheek! But she clung to Trevylyan's proud form with a yet more endearing tenderness than was her wont, and hung yet more eagerly on his words; her hand sought his, and she often pressed it to her lips, and sighed as she did so. Something that she would not tell seemed passing within her, and sobered her playful mood. But there was this noticeable in Gertrude : whatever took away from her gaiety, increased her tenderness. The infirmities of her frame never touched her temper. She was kind—gentle—loving to the last.

They had crossed to the opposite banks, to visit the Castle of Hammerstein. The evening was transparently serene and clear; and the warmth of the sun yet lingered upon the air, even though the twilight had passed and the moon risen, as their boat returned by a lengthened passage to the village. Broad and straight flows the Rhine in this part of its career. On one side lay the wooded village of Namedy, the hamlet of Fornech, backed by the blue rock of Kruezborner Ley, the mountains that shield the mysterious Brohl: and, on the opposite shore, they saw the mighty rock of Hammerstein, with the green and livid ruins sleeping in the melancholy moonlight. Two towers rose haughtily above the more dismantled wrecks. How changed since the alternate banners of the Spaniard and the Swede waved from their ramparts, in that great war in which the gorgeous Wallenstein won his laurels! And in its mighty calm, flowed on the ancestral Rhine; the vessel reflected on its smooth expanse, and above, girded by thin and shadowy clouds, the moon cast her shadows upon rocks covered with verdure, and brought into a dim light the twin spires of Andernach, tranquil in the distance.

"How beautiful is this hour!" said Gertrude, with a low voice: "surely we do not live enough in the night; one half the beauty of the world is slept away. What in the day can equal the holy calm, the loveliness, and the stillness which the moon now casts over the earth? These," she continued, pressing Trevylyan's hand, "are hours to remember; and *you*,—will you ever forget them?"

Something there is in recollections of such times and scenes that seem not to belong to real life, but are rather an episode in its history; they are like some wandering into a more ideal world; they refuse to blend with our ruder associations; they live in us, apart and alone, to be treasured ever, but not lightly to be recalled. There are none living to whom we can confide them,—who can sympathize with what then we felt? It is this that makes poetry, and that page which we create as a confidant to ourselves, necessary to the thoughts that weigh upon the breast. We write, for our writing is our friend, the inanimate paper is our confessional; we pour forth on it the thoughts that we could tell to no private ear, and are relieved—are consoled. And, if genius has one prerogative dearer than the rest, it is that which enables it to do honour to the dead—to revive the beauty, the virtue that are no more; to wreathe chaplets that outlive the day round the urn which were else forgotten by the world!

When the poet mourns, in his immortal verse, for the dead, tell me not that fame is in his mind! it is filled by thoughts, by emotions that shut out the living. He is breathing to his genius—to that sole and constant friend, which has grown up with him from his cradle —the sorrows too delicate for human sympathy; and when afterwards he consigns the confession to the crowd, it is indeed from the hope of honour;—honour not for himself, but for the being that is no more.

CHAPTER XVII.

LETTER FROM TREVYLYAN TO * * * *.

"COBLENTZ.

"AM obliged to you, my dear friend, for your letter; which, indeed, I have **not,** in the course of our rapid journey, had the leisure, perhaps the heart; to answer before. But we are staying in this town for some days, **and I** write now in the early morning, ere any one else in our hotel **is awake.** Do not tell me of adventure, of politics, of intrigues; my nature is altered. I threw **down** your letter, animated and brilliant as it was, with **a** sick and revolted heart. But I am now in somewhat less dejected spirits. **Gertrude is** better—yes, really better; there is a physician here who gives **me** hope; my care is perpetually to amuse, and never to fatigue her,—never to permit her thoughts to **rest** upon herself. For I have imagined that illness cannot, at least **in** the unexhausted vigour of our years, fasten upon us irremediably unless we feed it with our own belief in its existence. You see **men** of **the most** delicate frames engaged in active and professional **pursuits,** who literally have no time for illness. Let them **become idle—let them** take care of themselves—let them think of **their health—and** they **die!** The rust rots the steel which use preserves; **and,** thank Heaven, although Gertrude, once during our voyage, seemed roused, by an inexcusable imprudence of emotion on my part, into some suspicion of her state, yet it passed away; for she thinks rarely of herself—I am ever in her thoughts and seldom from her side, and you know, too, the sanguine and credulous nature of her disease. But, indeed, I now hope more than I have done **since** I knew her.

"When, after **an excited and adventurous life which had** comprised **so many** changes in so few years, **I found myself at** rest in the bosom **of a** retired and remote part **of** the country, **and** Gertrude and her **father were my** only neighbours, **I was in** that **state of** mind in which **the passions,** recruited **by** solitude, are accessible to the purer and **more divine** emotions. I was struck by Gertrude's beauty; I was **charmed** by her **simplicity.** Worn in the usages and fashions **of the** world, the inexperience, the trustfulness, the exceeding youth **of her** mind, charmed and touched me; but when **I saw** the stamp **of** our national disease **in** her bright eye and transparent cheek, I felt my love chilled **while** my interest was increased.

I fancied myself safe, and I went daily into the danger; I imagined so pure a light could not burn, and I was consumed. Not till my anxiety grew into pain, my interest into terror, did I know the secret of my own heart; and at the moment that I discovered this secret, I discovered also that Gertrude loved me! What a destiny was mine! what happiness, yet what misery! Gertrude was my own—but for what period? I might touch that soft hand—I might listen to the tenderest confession from that silver voice,—but all the while my heart spoke of passion, my reason whispered of death. You know that I am considered of a cold and almost callous nature, that I am not easily moved into affection, but my very pride bowed me here into weakness. There was so soft a demand upon my protection, so constant an appeal to my anxiety. You know that my father's quick temper burns within me, that I am hot, and stern, and exacting; but one hasty word, one thought of myself, here were inexcusable. So brief a time might be left for her earthly happiness,—could I embitter one moment? All that feeling of uncertainty which should in prudence have prevented my love, increased it almost to a preternatural excess. That which it is said mothers feel for an only child in sickness, I feel for Gertrude. *My existence is not!—I exist in her!*

"Her illness increased upon her at home; they have recommended travel. She chose the course we were to pursue, and, fortunately, it was so familiar to me, that I have been enabled to brighten the way. I am ever on the watch that she shall not know a weary hour; you would almost smile to see how I have roused myself from my habitual silence; and to find me—me, the scheming and worldly actor of real life, plunged back into the early romance of my boyhood, and charming the childish delight of Gertrude with the invention of fables and the traditions of the Rhine.

"But I believe I have succeeded in my object; if not, what is left to me? *Gertrude is better!*—In that sentence what visions of hope dawn upon me! I wish you could have seen Gertrude before we left England; you might then have understood my love for her. Not that we have not, in the gay capitals of Europe, paid our brief vows to forms more richly beautiful; not that we have not been charmed by a more brilliant genius,—by a more tutored grace. But there is that in Gertrude which I never saw before; the union of the childish and the intellectual, an ethereal simplicity, a temper that is never dimmed, a tenderness—oh God! let me not speak of her virtues, for they only tell me how little she is suited to the earth.

"You will direct to me at Mayence, whither our course now leads us, and your friendship will find indulgence for a letter that is so little a reply to yours.

"Your sincere friend,
"A. G. TREVYLYAN."

CHAPTER XVIII.

COBLENTZ.—EXCURSION TO THE MOUNTAINS OF TAUNUS; ROMAN TOWER IN THE VALLEY OF EHRENBREITSTEIN.—TRAVEL, ITS PLEASURES ESTIMATED DIFFERENTLY BY THE YOUNG AND THE OLD.—THE STUDENT OF HEIDELBERG; HIS CRITICISMS ON GERMAN LITERATURE.

GERTRUDE had, indeed, apparently rallied during their stay at Coblentz; and a French physician established in the town (who adopted a peculiar treatment for consumption, which had been attended with no ordinary success), gave her father and Trevylyan a sanguine assurance of her ultimate recovery. The time they passed within the white walls of Coblentz was, therefore, the happiest and most cheerful part of their pilgrimage. They visited the various places in its vicinity; but the excursion which most delighted Gertrude was one to the mountains of Taunus.

They took advantage of a beautiful September day; and, crossing the river, commenced their tour from the Thal, or valley of Ehrenbreitstein. They stopped on their way to view the remains of a Roman tower in the valley; for the whole of that district bears frequent witness of the ancient conquerors of the world. The mountains of Taunus are still intersected with the roads which the Romans cut to the mines that supplied them with silver. Roman urns, and inscribed stones, are often found in these ancient places. The stones, inscribed with names utterly unknown—a type of the uncertainty of fame!—the urns, from which the dust is gone—a very satire upon life!

Lone, gray, and mouldering, this tower stands aloft in the valley; and the quiet Vane smiled to see the uniform of a modern Prussian, with his white belt and lifted bayonet, by the spot which had once echoed to the clang of the Roman arms. The soldier was paying a momentary court to a country damsel, whose straw hat and rustic dress did not stifle the vanity of the sex; and this rude and humble gallantry, in that spot, was another moral in the history of human passions. Above, the ramparts of a modern rule frowned down upon the solitary tower, as if in the vain insolence with which present power looks upon past decay; the living race upon ancestral greatness. And indeed, in this respect, rightly!—for modern times have no parallel to that degradation of human dignity stamped upon the ancient world by the long sway of the Imperial Harlot, all slavery herself, yet all tyranny to earth;—and, like her own Messalina, at once a prostitute and an empress!

They continued their course by the ancient baths of Ems, and keeping by the banks of the romantic Lahn, arrived at Holzapfel.

"Ah," said Gertrude, one day, as they proceeded to the springs of the Carlovingian Wiesbaden, "surely perpetual travel with those we love must be the happiest state of existence. If home has its comforts, it also has its cares; but here we are at home with Nature, and the minor evils vanish almost before they are felt."

"True," said Trevylyan, "we escape from 'THE LITTLE,' which is the curse of life; the small cares that devour us up, the grievances of the day. We are feeding the divinest part of our nature,—the appetite to admire."

"But of all things wearisome," said Vane, "a succession of changes is the most. There can be a monotony in variety itself. As the eye aches in gazing long at the new shapes of the kaleidoscope, the mind aches at the fatigue of a constant alternation of objects; and we delightedly return to REST, which is to life what green is to the earth."

In the course of their sojourn among the various baths of Taunus, they fell in, by accident, with a German student of Heidelberg, who was pursuing the pedestrian excursions so peculiarly favoured by his tribe. He was tamer and gentler than the general herd of those young wanderers, and our party were much pleased with his enthusiasm, because it was unaffected. He had been in England, and spoke its language almost as a native.

"Our literature," said he, one day, conversing with Vane, "has two faults—we are too subtle and too homely. We do not speak enough to the broad comprehension of mankind; we are for ever making abstract qualities of flesh and blood. Our critics have turned your Hamlet into an allegory; they will not even allow Shakspeare to paint mankind, but insist on his embodying qualities. They turn poetry into metaphysics, and truth seems to them shallow, unless an allegory, which is false, can be seen at the bottom. Again, too, with our most imaginative works we mix a homeliness that we fancy touching, but which in reality is ludicrous. We eternally step from the sublime to the ridiculous—we want taste."

"But not, I hope, French taste. Do not govern a Goethe, or even a Richter, by a Boileau!" said Trevylyan.

"No, but Boileau's taste was false. Men, who have the reputation for good taste, often acquire it solely because of the want of genius. By taste, I mean a quick tact into the harmony of composition, the art of making the whole consistent with its parts, the *concinnitas*—Schiller alone of our authors has it;—but we are fast mending; and, by following shadows so long we have been led at last to the substance. Our past literature is to us what astrology was to science,—false but ennobling, and conducting us to the true language of the intellectual heaven."

Another time the scenes they passed, interspersed with the ruins of frequent monasteries, leading them to converse on the monastic life, and the various additions time makes to religion, the German said: "Perhaps one of the works most wanted in the world, is the history of Religion. We have several books, it is true, on the subject, but none that supply the want I allude to. A German ought to write it; for it is, probably, only a German that would have the requisite learning. A German only, too, is likely to treat the mighty subject with boldness, and yet with veneration; without the shallow flippancy of the Frenchman, without the timid sectarianism of the English. It would be a noble task, to trace the winding mazes of antique falsehood; to clear up the first glimmerings of divine truth; to separate Jehovah's word from man's invention; to vindicate the All-merciful from the dread creeds of bloodshed and of fear: and, watching in the great Heaven of Truth the dawning of the True Star, follow it—like the Magi of the East—till it rested above the real God. Not indeed presuming to such a task," continued the German, with a slight blush, "I have about me an humble essay, which treats only of one part of that august subject; which, leaving to a loftier genius the history of the true religion, may be considered as the history of a false one;—of such a creed as Christianity supplanted in the north; or such as may perhaps be found among the fiercest of the savage tribes. It is a fiction—as you may conceive; but yet, by a constant reference to the early records of human learning, I have studied to weave it up from truths. If you would like to hear it—it is very short——"

"Above all things," said Vane; and the German drew a manuscript neatly bound, from his pocket.

"After having myself criticised so insolently the faults of our national literature," said he, smiling, "you will have a right to criticise the faults that belong to so humble a disciple of it. But you will see that, though I have commenced with the allegorical or the supernatural, I have endeavoured to avoid the subtlety of conceit, and the obscurity of design, which I blame in the wilder of our authors. As to the style, I wished to suit it to the subject; it ought to be, unless I err, rugged and massive; hewn, as it were, out of the rock of primæval language. But you, madam;—doubtless you do not understand German?"

"Her mother was an Austrian," said Vane; "and she knows at least enough of the tongue to understand you; so pray begin."

Without further preface, the German then commenced the story, which the reader will find translated [1] in the next chapter.

CHAPTER XIX.

THE FALLEN STAR; OR, THE HISTORY OF A FALSE RELIGION.

AND the STARS sat, each on his ruby throne, and watched with sleepless eyes upon the world. It was the night ushering in the new year, a night on which every star receives from the archangel that then visits the universal galaxy, its peculiar charge. The destinies of men and empires are then portioned forth for the coming year, and, unconsciously to ourselves, our fates become minioned to the stars. A hushed and solemn night is that in which the dark Gates of Time open to receive the ghost of the Dead Year, and the young and radiant Stranger rushes forth from the clouded chasms of Eternity. On that night, it is said, that there are given to the spirits that we see not, a privilege and a power; the dead are troubled in their forgotten graves, and men feast and laugh, while demon and angel are contending for their doom.

It was night in heaven; all was unutterably silent, the music of the spheres had paused, and not a sound came from the angels of the stars; and they who sat upon those shining thrones were three thousand and ten, each resembling each. Eternal youth clothed their radiant limbs with celestial beauty, and on their faces was written the dread of calm, that fearful stillness which feels not, sympathizes not with the dooms over which it broods. War, tempest, pestilence, the rise of empires, and their fall, they ordain, they compass, unexultant and uncompassionate. The fell and thrilling crimes

---

[1] Nevertheless I beg to state seriously, that the German student is an impostor; and that he has no right to wrest the parentage of the fiction from the true author.

that stalk abroad when the world sleeps, the paricide with his stealthy step, and horrent brow, and lifted knife; the unwifed mother that glides out and looks behind, and behind, and shudders, and casts her babe upon the river, and hears the wail, and pities not—the splash, and does not tremble;—these the starred kings behold—to these they lead the unconscious step; but the guilt blanches not their lustre, neither doth remorse wither their unwrinkled youth. Each star wore a kingly diadem; round the loins of each was a graven belt, graven with many and mighty signs; and the foot of each was on a burning ball, and the right arm drooped over the knee as they bent down from their thrones; they moved not a limb or feature, save the finger of the right hand, which ever and anon moved slowly pointing, and regulated the fates of men as the hand of the dial speaks the career of time.

One only of the three thousand and ten wore not the same aspect as his crowned brethren; a star, smaller than the rest, and less luminous; the countenance of this star was not impressed with the awful calmness of the others; but there were sullenness and discontent upon his mighty brow.

And this star said to himself,—"Behold! I am created less glorious than my fellows, and the archangel apportions not to me the same lordly destinies. Not for me are the dooms of kings and bards, the rulers of empires, or, yet nobler, the swayers and harmonists of souls. Sluggish are the spirits and base the lot of the men I am ordained to lead through a dull life to a fameless grave. And wherefore?—is it mine own fault, or is it the fault which is not mine, that I was woven of beams less glorious than my brethren? Lo! when the archangel comes, I will bow not my crowned head to his decrees. I will speak, as the ancestral Lucifer before me: *he* rebelled because of his glory, *I* because of my obscurity; *he* from the ambition of pride, and *I* from its discontent."

And while the star was thus communing with himself, the upward heavens were parted as by a long river of light, and adown that stream swiftly, and without sound, sped the archangel visitor of the stars; his vast limbs floated in the liquid lustre, and his outspread wings, each plume the glory of a sun, bore him noiselessly along; but thick clouds veiled his lustre from the eyes of mortals, and while above all was bathed in the serenity of his splendour, tempest and storm broke below over the children of the earth: "He bowed the heavens and came down, and darkness was under his feet."

And the stillness on the faces of the stars became yet more still, and the awfulness was humbled into awe. Right above their thrones paused the course of the archangel; and his wings stretched from east to west, overshadowing with the shadow of light the immensity of space. Then forth, in the shining stillness, rolled the dread music of his voice : and, fulfilling the heraldry of God, to each star he appointed the duty and the charge, and each star bowed his head yet lower as he heard the fiat, while his throne rocked and trembled at the Majesty of the Word. But, at last, when each of the brighter stars had, in succession, received the mandate, and the vice-royalty over the nations of the earth, the purple and diadems of kings; —the archangel addressed the lesser star as he sat apart from his fellows :—

"Behold," said the archangel, "the rude tribes of the north, the fishermen of the river that flows beneath, and the hunters of the forests, that darken the mountain tops with verdure! these be thy charge, and their destinies thy care. Nor deem thou, O Star of the sullen beams, that thy duties are less glorious than the duties of thy brethren; for the peasant is not less to thy master and mine than the monarch; nor doth the doom of empires rest more upon the sovereign than on the herd. The passions and the heart are the dominion of the stars,—a mighty realm; nor less mighty beneath the hide that garbs the shepherd, than under the jewelled robes of the eastern kings."

Then the star lifted his pale front from his breast, and answered the archangel :—

"Lo!" he said, "ages have passed, and each year thou hast appointed me to the same ignoble charge. Release me, I pray thee, from the duties that I scorn; or, if thou wilt that the lowlier race of men be my charge, give unto me the charge not of many, but of one, and suffer me to breathe into him the desire that spurns the valleys of life, and ascends its steeps. If the humble are given to me, let there be amongst them one whom I may lead on the mission that shall abase the proud; for, behold, O Appointer of the Stars, as I have sat for uncounted years upon my solitary throne, brooding over the things beneath, my spirit hath gathered wisdom from the changes that shift below. Looking upon the tribes of earth, I have seen how the multitude are swayed, and tracked the steps that lead weakness into power; and fain would I be the ruler of one who, if abased, shall aspire to rule."

As a sudden cloud over the face of noon was the change on the brow of the archangel.

"Proud and melancholy star," said the herald, "thy wish would war with the courses of the invisible DESTINY, that, throned far above, sways and harmonizes all; the source from which the lesser rivers of fate are eternally gushing through the heart of the universe of things. **Thinkest** thou that thy wisdom, of itself, can lead the peasant to **become a king?**"

And the **crowned star gazed undauntedly on the face of the archangel, and answered,**

"Yea!—grant me but one trial!"

Ere the archangel could reply, the farthest centre of the heaven **was** rent as by a thunderbolt; and the divine herald covered his face **with** his hands, **and a voice low and** sweet, and mild with the consciousness of **unquestionable** power, spoke forth to the repining star.

"The **time has** arrived when **thou** mayest have thy wish. Below **thee,** upon yon solitary plain, sits **a** mortal, gloomy as thyself, who, **born** under thy influence, may be moulded to thy will."

The voice ceased as the voice **of** a dream. Silence **was over the seas of** space, and the archangel, **once more** borne **aloft, slowly** soared away into the farther heaven, to **promulgate the divine** bidding to the stars of far-distant worlds. **But the soul of the discontented** star exulted within itself; and **it said, "I will call forth a** king from the valley of the herdsman, that **shall trample on the** kings subject **to my** fellows, and render the charge of **the contemned** star more glorious than the minions of its favoured brethren; **thus** shall I **revenge neglect**—thus shall I prove **my** claim hereafter **to the** heritage **of the great of earth!"**

* * * * *

* * * * *

At that time, though the world had rolled on for ages, and the pilgrimage of man had passed through various states of existence, which our dim traditionary knowledge has not preserved, yet the condition of our race in the northern hemisphere was then what *we*, in our imperfect lore, have conceived to be among the earliest.

* * * * *

* * * * *

By a rude and vast pile of stones, the **masonry of** arts forgotten, a lonely man sat at midnight, gazing upon the heavens; a storm had just passed from the earth—the clouds had rolled away, and the high stars looked **down upon** the rapid waters **of** the Rhine; and no sound save the roar **of the waves,** and the dripping of the rain from the mighty trees, **was heard** around the ruined pile: the white sheep lay scattered on the **plain,** and slumber w:th them. He sat watching **over** the herd, **lest the** foes of a neighbouring tribe seized them unawares, and thus he communed with himself: "The king sits upon **his** throne, **and is** honoured by a warrior race, and the warrior exults in the trophies he has won; the step of the huntsman is bold upon the mountain-top, and his name is sung at night round the pine-fires, by the lips of the bard; and the bard himself hath honour in the hall. But I, who belong not to the race of kings, and whose limbs can bound not to the rapture of war, nor scale the eyries of the eagle and the haunts of the swift stag; whose hand cannot string the harp, and whose voice is harsh in the song; *I* have neither honour nor command, and men bow not the head as I pass along; yet do I feel within me the consciousness of a great power that should rule my species—not obey. My eye pierces the secret hearts of men—I see their thoughts ere their lips proclaim them; and I scorn, while I see, the weakness and the vices which I never shared—I laugh at the madness of the warrior—I mock within my soul at the tyranny of kings. Surely there is something in man's nature more fitted to command—more worthy of renown, than the sinews of the arm, or the swiftness of the feet, or the accident of birth!"

As Morven, the son of Osslah, thus mused within himself, still looking at the heavens, the solitary man beheld a star suddenly shooting from its place, and speeding through the silent air, till it suddenly paused right over the midnight river, and facing the inmate of the pile of stones.

As he gazed upon the star, strange thoughts grew slowly over him. He drank, as it were, from its solemn aspect, the spirit of a great design. A dark cloud rapidly passing over the earth, snatched the star from his sight; but left to his awakened mind the thoughts and the dim scheme that had come to him as he gazed.

When the sun arose, one of his brethren relieved him of his charge over the herd, and he went away, but not to his father's home. Musingly he plunged into the dark and leafless recesses of the winter forest; and shaped out of his wild thoughts, more palpably and clearly, the outline of his daring hope. While thus absorbed he heard a great noise in the forest, and, fearful lest the hostile tribe of the Alrich might pierce that way, he ascended one of the loftiest pine-trees, to whose perpetual verdure the winter had not denied the shelter he sought, and, concealed by its branches, he looked anxiously forth in the direction whence the noise had proceeded. And IT came—it came with a tramp and a crash, and a crushing tread upon the crunched boughs and matted leaves that strewed the soil—it came—it came, the monster that the world now holds no more—the mighty Mammoth of the North! Slowly it moved in its huge strength along, and its burning eyes glittered through the gloomy shade; its jaws, falling apart, showed the grinders with which it snapped asunder the young oaks of the forest; and the vast tusks, which, curved downward to the midst of its massive limbs, glistened white and ghastly, curdling the blood of one destined hereafter to be the dreadest ruler of the men of that distant age.

The livid eyes of the monster fastened on the form of the herdsman, even amidst the thick darkness of the pine. It paused—it glared upon him—its jaws opened, and a low deep sound, as of gathering thunder, seemed to the son of Osslah as the knell of a dreadful grave. But after glaring on him for some moments, it again, and calmly, pursued its terrible way, crashing the boughs as it marched along, till the last sound of its heavy tread died away upon his ear.[1]

Ere yet, however, Morven summoned the courage to descend the tree, he saw the shining of arms through the bare branches of the wood, and presently a small band of the hostile Alrich came into sight. He was perfectly hidden from them; and listening as they passed him, he heard one say to another,—

"The night covers all things; why attack them by day?"

And he who seemed the chief of the band, answered,

"Right. To-night, when they sleep in their city, we will upon them. Lo! they will be drenched in wine, and fall like sheep into our hands."

"But where, O chief," said a third of the band, "shall our men hide during the day? for there are many hunters among the youth of the Oestrich tribe, and they might see us in the forest unawares, and arm their race against our coming."

"I have prepared for that," answered the chief. "Is not the dark cavern of Oderlin at hand? Will it not shelter us from the eyes of the victims?"

Then the men laughed, and, shouting, they went their way adown the forest.

When they were gone, Morven cautiously descended, and, striking into a broad path, hastened to a vale that lay between the forest and the river in which was the city where the chief of his country dwelt. As he passed by the warlike men, giants in that day, who thronged the streets (if streets they might be called), their half garments parting from their huge limbs, the quiver at their backs, and the hunting spear in their hands, they laughed and shouted out, and, pointing to him, cried, "Morven, the woman! Morven, the cripple! what dost thou among men?"

[1] *The critic* will perceive that this sketch of the beast, whose race has perished is mainly intended to designate the remote period of the world in which the tale is cast.

For the son of Osslah was small in stature and of slender strength, and his step had halted from his birth; but he passed through the warriors unheedingly. At the outskirts of the city he came upon a tall pile in which some old men dwelt by themselves, and counselled the king when times of danger, or when the failure of the season, the famine or the drought, perplexed the ruler, and clouded the savage fronts of his warrior tribe.

They gave the counsels of experience, and when experience failed, they drew in their believing ignorance, assurances, and omens from the winds of heaven, the changes of the moon, and the flights of the wandering birds. Filled (by the voices of the elements, and the variety of mysteries which ever shift along the face of things, unsolved by the wonder which pauses not, the fear which believes, and that eternal reasoning of all experience, which assigns causes to effect) with the notion of superior powers, they assisted their ignorance by the conjectures of their superstition. But as yet they knew no craft and practised no *voluntary* delusion; they trembled too much at the mysteries which had created their faith to seek to belie them. They counselled as they believed, and the bold dream of governing their warriors and their kings by the wisdom of deceit had never dared to cross men thus worn and gray with age.

The son of Osslah entered the vast pile with a fearless step, and approached the place at the upper end of the hall where the old men sat in conclave.

"How, base-born and craven limbed!" cried the eldest, who had been a noted warrior in his day; "darest thou enter unsummoned amidst the secret councils of the wise men? Knowest thou not, scatterling! that the penalty is death?"

"Slay me, if thou wilt," answered Morven, "but hear! As I sat last night in the ruined palace of our ancient kings, tending, as my father bade me, the sheep that grazed around, lest the fierce tribe of Alrich should descend unseen from the mountains upon the herd, a storm came darkly on; and when the storm had ceased, and I looked above on the sky, I saw a star descend from its height towards me, and a voice from the star said, 'Son of Osslah, leave thy herd and seek the council of the wise men, and say unto them, that they take thee as one of their number, or that sudden will be the destruction of them and theirs.' But I had courage to answer the voice, and I said, 'Mock not the poor son of the herdsman. Behold they will kill me if I utter so rash a word, for I am poor and valueless in the eyes of the tribe of Oestrich, and the great in deeds and the gray of hair alone sit in the council of the wise men.'

"Then the voice said, 'Do my bidding, and I will give thee a token that thou **comest from the Powers that sway the** seasons and sail upon the **eagles of the** winds. Say unto the wise men that this very night, if they **refuse** to receive **thee of** their **band,** evil shall fall upon them, and the morrow shall **dawn in** blood.'

"**Then** the voice ceased, and the **cloud** passed over **the** star; and I communed with myself, and came, **O** dread fathers, mournfully unto **you.** For I feared that ye **would** smite me **because of** my bold tongue, and **that** ye would sentence me to the **death, in** that I asked what may scarce be given **even to** the sons of kings."

Then the grim elders looked **one** at the other, and marvelled much, **nor** knew they what answer **they** should make **to** the herdsman's son.

At length one of the **wise men said,** "Surely there must be truth in the son of Osslah, for he **would not** dare to falsify the great lights of Heaven. If he had given **unto men the words** of the star, verily we might doubt the truth. But **who would brave the** vengeance of **the** gods of night?"

Then the elders **shook** their heads approvingly; **but one answered** and said—

"Shall we **take the** herdsman's son as our equal? **No!**" The name of the **man who** thus answered was Darvan, **and his words** were pleasing **to the elders.**

But Morven **spoke out:** "Of a truth, O councillors of kings! I look **not to be an equal with** yourselves. Enough if I tend the gates of your **palace, and serve** you as the **son** of Osslah may serve;" **and** he bowed **his head** humbly as he spoke.

Then **said the chief of** the elders, **for he** was wiser than the others, "But how wilt thou deliver us from **the** evil that is to come? **Doubtless** the star **has** informed thee of **the** service thou canst render **to us if we** take thee into our palace, as well as the ill that will fall on us **if we** refuse."

Morven answered meekly, "Surely, if thou acceptest **thy servant, the star will** teach him that which may requite thee; **but as yet he** knows **only** what he has uttered."

Then the **sages** bade him withdraw, **and** they communed with themselves, **and they** differed much; but though fierce men, and bold at the **war-cry of a** human foe, they shuddered at the prophecy of a star. So **they** resolved to take the son of Osslah, and suffer him to keep the **gate of the** council-hall.

He heard their **decree** and bowed his **head,** and went to the gate, **and sat** down by it in silence.

And **the** sun went down in the west, and the first stars of the twilight began to glimmer, when Morven started from his seat, and a trembling appeared to seize his limbs. His lips foamed; an agony and a fear possessed him; he writhed as a man whom the spear of a foeman has pierced with a mortal wound, and suddenly fell upon his face on the stony earth.

The elders approached him; wondering, they lifted him up. He slowly recovered as from a swoon; his eyes rolled wildly.

"Heard ye not the voice of the star?" he said.

And the chief of the elders answered, "Nay, we heard no sound."

Then Morven sighed heavily.

"To me only the word was given. Summon instantly, O councillors of the king! summon the armed men, and all the youth of the tribe, and let them take the sword and the spear, and follow thy servant. For lo! the star hath announced to him that the foe shall fall into our hands as the wild beast of the forests."

The son of Osslah spoke with the voice of command, and the elders were amazed. "Why pause ye?" he cried. "Do the gods of the night lie? On my head rest the peril if I deceive ye."

Then the elders communed together; and they went forth and summoned the men of arms, and all the young of the tribe; and each man took the sword and the spear, and Morven also. And the son of Osslah walked first, still looking up at the star, and he motioned them to be silent, and move with a stealthy step.

So they went through the thickest of the forest, till they came to the mouth of a great cave, overgrown with aged and matted trees, and it was called the Cave of Oderlin; and he bade the leaders place the armed men on either side the cave, to the right and to the left, among the bushes.

So they watched silently till the night deepened, when they heard a noise in the cave and the sound of feet, and forth came an armed man; and the spear of Morven pierced him, and he fell dead at the mouth of the cave. Another and another, and both fell! Then loud and long was heard the war-cry of Alrich, and forth poured, as a stream over a narrow bed, the river of armed men. And the sons of Oestrich fell upon them, and the foe were sorely perplexed and terrified by the suddenness of the battle and the darkness of the night; and there was a great slaughter.

And when the morning came, the children of Oestrich counted the slain, and found the leader of Alrich and the chief men of the tribe amongst them, and great was the joy thereof. So they went back in triumph to the city, and they carried the brave son of Osslah on their shoulders, and shouted forth, "Glory to the servant of the star."

And Morven dwelt in the council of the wise men.

Now the king of the tribe had one daughter, and she was stately amongst the women of the tribe, and fair to look upon. And Morven gazed upon her with the eyes of love, but he did not dare to speak.

Now the son of Osslah laughed secretly at the foolishness of men; he loved them not, for they had mocked him; he honoured them not, for he had blinded the wisest of their elders. He shunned their feasts and merriment, and lived apart and solitary. The austerity of his life increased the mysterious homage which his commune with the stars had won him, and the boldest of the warriors bowed his head to the favourite of the gods.

One day he was wandering by the side of the river, and he saw a large bird of prey rise from the waters, and give chase to a hawk that had not yet gained the full strength of its wings. From his youth the solitary Morven had loved to watch, in the great forests and by the banks of the mighty stream, the habits of the things which nature has submitted to man; and looking now on the birds, he said to himself, "Thus is it ever; by cunning or by strength each thing wishes to master its kind." While thus moralizing, the larger bird had stricken down the hawk, and it fell terrified and panting at his feet. Morven took the hawk in his hands, and the vulture shrieked above him, wheeling nearer and nearer to its protected prey; but Morven scared away the vulture, and placing the hawk in his bosom he carried it home, and tended it carefully, and fed it from his hand until it had regained its strength; and the hawk knew him, and followed him as a dog. And Morven said, smiling to himself, "Behold, the credulous fools around me put faith in the flight and motion of birds. I will teach this poor hawk to minister to my ends." So he tamed the bird, and tutored it according to its nature; but he concealed it carefully from others, and cherished it in secret.

The king of the country was old and like to die, and the eyes of the tribe were turned to his two sons, nor knew they which was the worthier to reign. And Morven passing through the forest one evening, saw the younger of the two, who was a great hunter, sitting mournfully under an oak, and looking with musing eyes upon the ground.

"Wherefore musest thou, O swift-footed Siror?" said the son of Osslah; "and wherefore art thou sad?"

"Thou canst not assist me," answered the prince, sternly; "take thy way."

"Nay," answered Morven, "thou knowest not what thou sayest; am I not the favourite of the stars?"

"Away, I am no graybeard whom the approach of death makes doting: talk not to me of the stars; I know only the things that my eye sees and my ear drinks in."

"Hush," said Morven, solemnly, and covering his face; "hush! lest the heavens avenge thy rashness. But, behold, the stars have given unto me to pierce the secret hearts of others; and I can tell thee the thoughts of thine."

"Speak out, base-born!"

"Thou art the younger of two, and thy name is less known in war than the name of thy brother: yet wouldst thou desire to be set over his head, and to sit on the high seat of thy father?"

The young man turned pale. "Thou hast truth in thy lips," said he, with a faltering voice.

"Not from me, but from the stars, descends the truth."

"Can the stars grant my wish?"

"They can: let us meet to-morrow." Thus saying, Morven passed into the forest.

The next day, at noon, they met again.

"I have consulted the gods of night, and they have given me the power that I prayed for, but on one condition."

"Name it."

"That thou sacrifice thy sister on their altars; thou must build up a heap of stones, and take thy sister into the wood, and lay her on the pile, and plunge thy sword into her heart; so only shalt thou reign."

The prince shuddered, and started to his feet, and shook his spear at the pale front of Morven.

"Tremble," said the son of Osslah, with a loud voice. "Hark to the gods who threaten thee with death, that thou hast dared to lift thine arm against their servant!"

As he spoke, the thunder rolled above; for one of the frequent storms of the early summer was about to break. The spear dropped from the prince's hand; he sat down, and cast his eyes on the ground.

"Wilt thou do the bidding of the stars, and reign?" said Morven.

"I will!" cried Siror, with a desperate voice.

"This evening, then, when the sun sets, thou wilt lead her hither, alone; I may not attend thee. Now, let us pile the stones."

Silently the huntsman bent his vast strength to the fragments of rock that Morven pointed to him, and they built the altar, and went their way.

And beautiful is the dying of the great sun, when the last song of the birds fades into the lap of silence; when the islands of the cloud are bathed in light, and the first star springs up over the grave of day!

"Whither leadest thou my steps, my brother?" said Orna; "and why doth thy lip quiver? and why dost thou turn away thy face?"

"Is not the forest beautiful; does it not tempt us forth, my sister?"

"And wherefore are those heaps of stone piled together?"

"Let others answer; *I* piled them not."

"Thou tremblest, brother: we will return."

"Not so; by those stones is a bird that my shaft pierced to-day; a bird of beautiful plumage that I slew for thee."

"We are by the pile: where hast thou laid the bird?"

"Here!" cried Siror; and he seized the maiden in his arms, and, casting her on the rude altar, he drew forth his sword to smite her to the heart.

Right over the stones rose a giant oak, the growth of immemorial ages; and from the oak, or from the heavens, broke forth a loud and solemn voice, "Strike not, son of kings! the stars forbear their own: the maiden thou shalt not slay; yet shalt thou reign over the race of Oestrich; and thou shalt give Orna as a bride to the favourite of the stars. Arise, and go thy way!"

The voice ceased: the terror of Orna had overpowered for a time the springs of life; and Siror bore her home through the wood in his strong arms.

"Alas!" said Morven, when, at the next day, he again met the aspiring prince; "alas! the stars have ordained me a lot which my heart desires not: for I, lonely of life, and crippled of shape, am insensible to the fires of love; and ever, as thou and thy tribe know, I have shunned the eyes of women, for the maidens laughed at my halting step and my sullen features; and so in my youth I learned betimes to banish all thoughts of love. But since they told me (as they declared to *thee*), that only through that marriage, thou, O beloved prince! canst obtain thy father's plumed crown, I yield me to their will."

"But," said the prince, "not until I am king can I give thee my sister in marriage; for thou knowest that my sire would smite me to the dust, if I asked him to give the flower of our race to the son of the herdsman Osslah."

"Thou speakest the words of truth. Go home and fear not: but, when thou art king, the sacrifice must be made, and Orna mine. Alas! how can I dare to lift my eyes to her! But so ordain the dread kings of the night!—who shall gainsay their word?"

"The day that sees me king, sees Orna thine," answered the prince.

Morven walked forth, as was his wont, alone; and he said to himself, "The king is old, yet may he live long between me and mine hope!" and he began to cast in his mind how he might shorten the time. Thus absorbed, he wandered on so unheedingly, that night advanced, and he had lost his path among the thick woods, and knew not how to regain his home: so he lay down quietly beneath a tree, and rested till day dawned; then hunger came upon him, and he searched among the bushes for such simple roots as those with which, for he was ever careless of food, he was used to appease the cravings of nature.

He found, among other more familiar herbs and roots, a red berry of a sweetish taste, which he had never observed before. He ate of it sparingly, and had not proceeded far in the wood before he found his eyes swim, and a deadly sickness came over him. For several hours he lay convulsed on the ground expecting death; but the gaunt spareness of his frame, and his unvarying abstinence, prevailed over the poison, and he recovered slowly, and after great anguish: but he went with feeble steps back to the spot where the berries grew, and, plucking several, hid them in his bosom, and by nightfall regained the city.

The next day he went forth among his father's herds, and seizing a lamb, forced some of the berries into his stomach, and the lamb, escaping, ran away, and fell down dead. Then Morven took some more of the berries and boiled them down, and mixed the juice with wine, and he gave the wine in secret to one of his father's servants, and the servant died.

Then Morven sought the king, and coming into his presence alone, he said unto him, "How fares my lord?"

The king sat on a couch, made of the skins of wolves, and his eye was glassy and dim; but vast were his aged limbs, and huge was his stature, and he had been taller by a head than the children of men, and none living could bend the bow he had bent in youth. Gray, gaunt, and worn, as some mighty bones that are dug at times from the bosom of the earth,—a relic of the strength of old.

And the king said, faintly, and with a ghastly laugh,—

"The men of my years fare ill. What avails my strength? Better had I been born a cripple like thee, so should I have had nothing to lament in growing old."

The red flush passed over Morven's brow; but he bent humbly,—

"O king, what if I could give thee back thy youth? what if I could restore to thee the vigour which distinguished thee above the sons of men, when the warriors of Alrich fell like grass before thy sword?"

Then the king uplifted his dull eyes, and he said,—

"What meanest thou, son of Osslah? Surely I hear much of thy great wisdom, and how thou speakest nightly with the stars. Can the gods of the night give unto thee the secret to make the old young?"

"Tempt them not by doubt," said Morven, reverently. "All things are possible to the rulers of the dark hour; and, lo! the star that loves thy servant spake to him at the dead of night, and said, 'Arise, and go unto the king; and tell him that the stars honour the tribe of Oestrich, and remember how the king bent his bow against the sons of Alrich; wherefore, look thou under the stone that lies to the right of thy dwelling—even beside the pine-tree, and thou shalt see a vessel of clay, and in the vessel thou wilt find a sweet liquid, that shall make the king thy master forget his age for ever.' Therefore, my lord, when the morning rose I went forth, and looked under the stone, and behold the vessel of clay; and I have brought it hither to my lord, the king."

"Quick—slave—quick! that I may drink and regain my youth!"

"Nay, listen, O king! farther said the star to me:

"'It is only at night, when the stars have power, that this their gift will avail; wherefore, the king must wait till the hush of the midnight, when the moon is high, and then may he mingle the liquid with his wine. And he must reveal to none that he hath received the gift from the hand of the servant of the stars. For THEY do their work in secret, and when men sleep; therefore they love not the babble of mouths, and he who reveals their benefits shall surely die.'"

"Fear not," said the king, grasping the vessel; "none shall know; and, behold, I will rise on the morrow; and my two sons—wrangling for my crown,—verily I shall be younger than they!"

Then the king laughed loud; and he scarcely thanked the servant of the stars, neither did he promise him reward: for the kings in those days had little thought,—save for themselves.

And Morven said to him, "Shall I not attend my lord? for without me, perchance, the drug might fail of its effect."

"Ay," said the king, "rest here."

"Nay," replied Morven; "thy servants will marvel and talk much, if they see the son of Osslah sojourning in thy palace. So would the displeasure of the gods of night perchance be incurred.

Suffer that the lesser door of the palace be unbarred, so that at the night hour, when the moon is midway in the heavens, I may steal unseen into thy chamber, and mix the liquid with thy wine."

"So be it," said the king. "Thou art wise, though thy limbs are crooked and curt; and the stars might have chosen a taller man." Then the king laughed again; and Morven laughed too, but there was danger in the mirth of the son of Osslah.

The night had begun to wane, and the inhabitants of Oestrich were buried in deep sleep, when, hark! a sharp voice was heard crying out in the streets, "Woe, woe! Awake, ye sons of Oestrich —woe!" Then forth, wild—haggard—alarmed—spear in hand, rushed the giant sons of the rugged tribe, and they saw a man on a height in the middle of the city, shrieking "Woe!" and it was Morven, the son of Osslah! And he said unto them, as they gathered round him, "Men and warriors, tremble as ye hear. The star of the west hath spoken to me, and thus said the star:—'Evil shall fall upon the kingly house of Oestrich,—yea, ere the morning dawn; wherefore, go thou mourning into the streets, and wake the inhabitants to woe!' So I rose and did the bidding of the star." And while Morven was yet speaking, a servant of the king's house ran up to the crowd, crying loudly—"The king is dead!" So they went into the palace and found the king stark upon his couch, and his huge limbs all cramped and crippled by the pangs of death, and his hands clenched as if in menace of a foe—the Foe of all living flesh! Then fear came on the gazers, and they looked on Morven with a deeper awe than the boldest warrior would have called forth; and they bore him back to the council-hall of the wise men, wailing and clashing their arms in woe, and shouting, ever and anon, "Honour to Morven the prophet!" And that was the first time the word PROPHET was ever used in those countries.

At noon, on the third day from the king's death, Siror sought Morven, and he said, "Lo, my father is no more, and the people meet this evening at sunset to elect his successor, and the warriors and the young men will surely choose my brother, for he is more known in war. Fail me not, therefore."

"Peace, boy!" said Morven, sternly; "nor dare to question the truth of the gods of night."

For Morven now began to presume on his power among the people, and to speak as rulers speak, even to the sons of kings. And the voice silenced the fiery Siror, nor dared he to reply.

"Behold," said Morven, taking up a chaplet of coloured plumes, "wear this on thy head, and put on a brave face, for the people like a hopeful spirit, and go down with thy brother to the place where the new king is to be chosen, and leave the rest to the stars. But, above all things, forget not that chaplet; it has been blessed by the gods of night."

The prince took the chaplet and returned home.

It was evening, and the warriors and chiefs of the tribe were assembled in the place where the new king was to be elected. And the voices of the many favoured Prince Voltoch, the brother of Siror, for he had slain twelve foemen with his spear; and verily, in those days, that was a great virtue in a king.

Suddenly there was a shout in the streets, and the people cried out, "Way for Morven the prophet, the prophet!" For the people held the son of Osslah in even greater respect than did the chiefs. Now, since he had become of note, Morven had assumed a majesty of air which the son of the herdsman knew not in his earlier days; and albeit his stature was short, and his limbs halted, yet his countenance was grave and high. He only of the tribe wore a garment that swept the ground, and his head was bare, and his long black hair descended to his girdle, and rarely was change or human passion seen in his calm aspect. He feasted not, nor drank wine, nor was his presence frequent in the streets. He laughed not, neither did he smile, save when alone in the forest,—and then he laughed at the follies of his tribe.

So he walked slowly through the crowd, neither turning to the left nor to the right, as the crowd gave way; and he supported his steps with a staff of the knotted pine.

And when he came to the place where the chiefs were met, and the two princes stood in the centre, he bade the people around him proclaim silence; then mounting on a huge fragment of rock, he thus spake to the multitude:—

"Princes, Warriors, and Bards! ye, O council of the wise men! and ye, O hunters of the forests, and snarers of the fishes of the streams! hearken to Morven, the son of Osslah. Ye know that I am lowly of race, and weak of limb; but did I not give into your hands the tribe of Alrich, and did ye not slay them in the dead of night with a great slaughter? Surely, ye must know this of himself did not the herdsman's son; surely he was but the agent of the bright gods that love the children of Oestrich? three nights since when slumber was on the earth, was not my voice heard in the streets! Did I not proclaim woe to the kingly house of Oestrich! and verily the dark arm had fallen on the bosom of the mighty, that is no more. Could I have dreamed this thing merely in a dream, or was I not as the voice of the bright gods that watch over the tribes of Oestrich? Wherefore, O men and chiefs! scorn not the son of Osslah, but listen to his words; for are they not the wisdom of the stars? Behold, last night, I sat alone in the valley, and the trees were hushed around and not a breath stirred; and I looked upon the star that counsels the son of Osslah; and I said, 'Dread conqueror of the cloud! thou that bathest thy beauty in the streams and piercest the pine-boughs with thy presence; behold thy servant grieved because the mighty one hath passed away, and many foes surround the houses of my brethren; and it is well that they should have a king valiant and prosperous in war, the cherished of the stars. Wherefore, O star! as thou gavest into our hands the warriors of Alrich, and didst warn us of the fall of the oak of our tribe, wherefore I pray thee give unto the people a token that they may choose that king whom the gods of the night prefer!' Then a low voice, sweeter than the music of the bard, stole along the silence. 'Thy love for thy race is grateful to the stars of night: go, then, son of Osslah, and seek the meeting of the chiefs and the people to choose a king, and tell them not to scorn thee because thou art slow to the chase, and little known in war; for the stars give thee wisdom as a recompense for all. Say unto the people that as the wise men of the council shape their lessons by the flight of birds, so by the flight of birds shall a token be given unto them, and they shall choose their kings. For, saith the star of night, the birds are the children of the winds, they pass to and fro along the ocean of the air, and visit the clouds that are the war-ships of the gods. And their music is but broken melodies which they glean from the harps above. Are they not the messengers of the storm? Ere the stream chafes against the bank, and the rain descends, know ye not, by the wail of birds and their low circles over the earth, that the tempest is at hand? Wherefore, wisely do ye deem that the children of the air are the fit interpreters between the sons of men and the lords of the world above. Say then to the people and the chiefs, that they shall take, from among the doves that build their nests in the roof of the palace, a white dove, and they shall let it loose in the air, and verily the gods of the night shall deem the dove as a prayer coming from the people, and they shall send a messenger to grant the prayer and give to the tribes of Oestrich a king worthy of themselves.'

"With that the star spoke no more."

Then the friends of Voltoch murmured among themselves, and they said, "Shall this man dictate to us who shall be king?" But the people and the warriors shouted, "Listen to the star; do we not give or deny battle according as the bird flies,—shall we not by the same token choose him by whom the battle should be led?" And the thing seemed natural to them, for it was after the custom of the tribe. Then they took one of the doves that built in the roof of the palace, and they brought it to the spot where Morven stood, and he, looking up to the stars and muttering to himself, released the bird.

There was a copse of trees at a little distance from the spot, and as the dove ascended, a hawk suddenly rose from the copse and pursued the dove; and the dove was terrified, and soared circling high above the crowd, when lo, the hawk, poising itself one moment on its wings, swooped with a sudden swoop, and, abandoning its prey, alighted on the plumed head of Siror.

"Behold," cried Morven in a loud voice, "behold your king!"

"Hail, all hail the king!" shouted the people. "All hail the chosen of the stars!"

Then Morven lifted his right hand, and the hawk left the prince, and alighted on Morven's shoulder. "Bird of the gods!" said he, reverently, "hast thou not a secret message for my ear?" Then the hawk put its beak to Morven's ear, and Morven bowed his head submissively; and the hawk rested with Morven from that moment and would not be scared away. And Morven said, "The stars have sent me this bird, that, in the day-time when I see them not, we may never be without a councillor in distress."

So Siror was made king, and Morven the son of Osslah was constrained by the king's will to take Orna for his wife; and the people and the chiefs honoured Morven the prophet above all the elders of the tribe.

One day Morven said unto himself, musing, "Am I not already equal with the king! nay, is not the king my servant? did I not place him over the heads of his brothers? am I not, therefore, more fit to reign than he is? shall I not push him from his seat? It is a troublesome and stormy office to reign over the wild men of Oestrich, to feast in the crowded hall, and to lead the warriors to the fray. Surely if I feasted not, neither went out to war, they might say, this is no king, but the cripple Morven; and some of the race of Siror might slay me secretly. But can I not be greater far than kings, and continue to choose and govern them, living as now at my own ease? Verily the stars shall give me a new palace, and many subjects."

Among the wise men was Darvan; and Morven feared him, for his eye often sought the movements of the son of Osslah.

And Morven said, "It were better to *trust* this man than to *blind*, for surely I want a helpmate and a friend." So he said to the wise man as he sat alone watching the setting sun,—

"It seemeth to me, O Darvan! that we ought to build a great

pile in honour of the stars, and the pile should be more glorious than all the palaces of the chiefs and the palace of the king; for are not the stars our masters? And thou and I should be the chief dwellers in this new palace, and we would serve the gods of night and fatten their altars with the choicest of the herd, and the freshest of the fruits of the earth."

And Darvan said, "Thou speakest as becomes the servant of the stars. But will the people help to build the pile, for they are a warlike race and they love not toil?"

And Morven answered, "Doubtless the stars will ordain the work to be done. Fear not."

"In truth thou art a wondrous man, thy words ever come to pass," answered Darvan; "and I wish thou wouldest teach me, friend, the language of the stars."

"Assuredly if thou servest me, thou shalt know," answered the proud Morven; and Darvan was secretly wroth that the son of the herdsman should command the service of an elder and a chief.

And when Morven returned to his wife he found her weeping much. Now she loved the son of Osslah with an exceeding love, for he was not savage and fierce as the men she had known, and she was proud of his fame among the tribe; and he took her in his arms and kissed her, and asked her why she wept. Then she told him that her brother the king had visited her and had spoken bitter words of Morven: "He taketh from me the affection of my people," said Siror, "and blindeth them with lies. And since he hath made me king, what if he take my kingdom from me? Verily a new tale of the stars might undo the old." And the king had ordered her to keep watch on Morven's secrecy, and to see whether truth was in him when he boasted of his commune with the Powers of night.

But Orna loved Morven better than Siror, therefore she told her husband all.

And Morven resented the king's ingratitude, and was troubled much, for a king is a powerful foe; but he comforted Orna, and bade her dissemble, and complain also of him to her brother, so that he might confide to her unsuspectingly whatsoever he might design against Morven.

There was a cave by Morven's house in which he kept the sacred hawk, and wherein he secretly trained and nurtured other birds against future need, and the door of the cave was always barred. And one day he was thus engaged when he beheld a chink in the wall, that he had never noted before, and the sun came playfully in; and while he looked he perceived the sunbeam was darkened, and presently he saw a human face peering in through the chink. And

Morven trembled, for he knew he had been watched. He ran hastily from the cave, but the spy had disappeared amongst the trees, and Morven went straight to the chamber of Darvan and sat himself down. And Darvan did not return home till late, and he started and turned pale when he saw Morven. But Morven greeted him as a brother, and bade him to a feast, which, for the first time, he purposed giving at the full of the moon, in honour of the stars. And going out of Darvan's chamber he returned to his wife, and bade her rend her hair, and go at the dawn of day to the king her brother, and complain bitterly of Morven's treatment, and pluck the black plans from the breast of the king. "For surely," said he, "Darvan hath lied to thy brother, and some evil waits me that I would fain know."

So the next morning Orna sought the king, and she said, "The herdsman's son hath reviled me, and spoken harsh words to me; shall I not be avenged?"

Then the king stamped his feet and shook his mighty sword. "Surely thou shalt be avenged, for I have learned from one of the elders that which convinceth me that the man hath lied to the people, and the base-born shall surely die. Yea, the first time that he goeth alone into the forest my brother and I will fall upon him, and smite him to the death." And with this comfort Siror dismissed Orna.

And Orna flung herself at the feet of her husband. "Fly now, O my beloved!—fly into the forests afar from my brethren, or surely the sword of Siror will end thy days."

Then the son of Osslah folded his arms, and seemed buried in black thoughts; nor did he heed the voice of Orna, until again and again she had implored him to fly.

"Fly!" he said at length. "Nay, I was doubting what punishment the stars should pour down upon our foe. Let warriors fly. Morven the prophet conquers by arms mightier than the sword."

Nevertheless Morven was perplexed in his mind, and knew not how to save himself from the vengeance of the king. Now, while he was musing hopelessly, he heard a roar of waters; and behold the river, for it was now the end of autumn, had burst its bounds, and was rushing along the valley to the houses of the city. And now the men of the tribe, and the women, and the children, came running, and with shrieks to Morven's house, crying, "Behold the river has burst upon us!—Save us, O ruler of the stars!"

Then the sudden thought broke upon Morven, and he resolved to risk his fate upon one desperate scheme.

And he came out from the house calm and sad, and he said, "Ye know not what ye ask; I cannot save ye from this peril: ye have brought it on yourselves."

And they cried, "How? O son of Osslah!—we are ignorant of our crime."

And he answered, "Go down to the king's palace and wait before it, and surely I will follow ye, and ye shall learn wherefore ye have incurred this punishment from the gods." Then the crowd rolled murmuring back, as a receding sea; and when it was gone from the place, Morven went alone to the house of Darvan, which was next his own: and Darvan was greatly terrified, for he was of a great age, and had no children, neither friends, and he feared that he could not of himself escape the waters.

And Morven said to him, soothingly, "Lo, the people love me, and I will see that thou art saved; for verily thou hast been friendly to me, and done me much service with the king."

And as he thus spake, Morven opened the door of the house and looked forth, and saw that they were quite alone; then he seized the old man by the throat, and ceased not his gripe till he was quite dead. And leaving the body of the elder on the floor, Morven stole from the house and shut the gate. And as he was going to his cave he mused a little while, when, hearing the mighty roar of the waves advancing, and far off the shrieks of women, he lifted up his head, and said, proudly, "No! in this hour terror alone shall be my slave; I will use no art save the power of my soul." So, leaning on his pine-staff, he strode down to the palace. And it was now evening, and many of the men held torches, that they might see each other's faces in the universal fear. Red flashed the quivering flames on the dark robes and pale front of Morven; and he seemed mightier than the rest, because his face alone was calm amidst the tumult. And louder and hoarser came the roar of the waters; and swift rushed the shades of night over the hastening tide.

And Morven said in a stern voice, "Where is the king; and wherefore is he absent from his people in the hour of dread?" Then the gate of the palace opened, and, behold, Siror was sitting in the hall by the vast pine-fire, and his brother by his side, and his chiefs around him: for they would not deign to come amongst the crowd at the bidding of the herdsman's son.

Then Morven, standing upon a rock above the heads of the people (the same rock whereon he had proclaimed the king), thus spake:—

"Ye desired to know, O sons of Oestrich! wherefore the river hath burst its bounds, and the peril hath come upon you. Learn, then, that the stars resent as the foulest of human crimes an insult to their servants and delegates below. Ye are all aware of the manner of life of Morven, whom ye have surnamed the Prophet! He harms not man nor beast; he lives alone; and, far from the wild joys of the warrior tribe, he worships in awe and fear the Powers of Night. So is he able to advise ye of the coming danger,—so is he able to save ye from the foe. Thus are your huntsmen swift and your warriors bold; and thus do your cattle bring forth their young, and the earth its fruits. What think ye, and what do ye ask to hear? Listen, men of Oestrich!—they have laid snares for my life; and there are amongst you those who have whetted the sword against the bosom that is only filled with love for you all. Therefore have the stern lords of heaven loosened the chains of the river—therefore doth this evil menace ye. Neither will it pass away until they who dug the pit for the servant of the stars are buried in the same."

Then, by the red torches, the faces of the men looked fierce and threatening; and ten thousand voices shouted forth, "Name them who conspired against thy life, O holy prophet! and surely they shall be torn limb from limb."

And Morven turned aside, and they saw that he wept bitterly; and he said,

"Ye have asked me, and I have answered: but now scarce will ye believe the foe that I have provoked against me; and by the heavens themselves I swear, that if my death would satisfy their fury, nor bring down upon yourselves and your children's children, the anger of the throned stars, gladly would I give my bosom to the knife. Yes," he cried, lifting up his voice, and pointing his shadowy arm towards the hall where the king sat by the pine-fire—"yes, thou whom by my voice the stars chose above thy brother—yes, Siror, the guilty one! take thy sword, and come hither—strike, if thou hast the heart to strike, the Prophet of the Gods!"

The king started to his feet, and the crowd were hushed in a shuddering silence.

Morven resumed:

"Know then, O men of Oestrich! that Siror, and Voltoch his brother, and Darvan the elder of the wise men, have purposed to slay your prophet, even at such hour as when alone he seeks the shade of the forest to devise new benefits for you. Let the king deny it, if he can!"

Then Voltoch, of the giant limbs, strode forth from the hall, and his spear quivered in his hand.

"Rightly hast thou spoken, base son of my father's herdsman! and for thy sins shalt thou surely die; for thou liest when thou speakest of thy power with the stars, and thou laughest at the folly of them who hear thee: wherefore put him to death."

Then the chiefs in the hall clashed their arms, and rushed forth to slay the son of Osslah.

But he, stretching his unarmed hands on high, exclaimed, "Hear him, O dread ones of the night!—hark how he blasphemeth!"

Then the crowd took up the word, and cried, "He blasphemeth —he blasphemeth against the prophet!"

But the king and the chiefs who hated Morven, because of his power with the people, rushed into the crowd; and the crowd were irresolute, nor knew they how to act, for never yet had they rebelled against their chiefs, and they feared alike the prophet and the king.

And Siror cried, "Summon Darvan to us, for he hath watched the steps of Morven, and he shall lift the veil from my people's eyes." Then three of the swift of foot started forth to the house of Darvan.

And Morven cried out with a loud voice, "Hark! thus saith the star who, now riding through yonder cloud, breaks forth upon my eyes—'For the lie that the elder hath uttered against my servant, the curse of the stars shall fall upon him.' Seek, and as ye find him so may ye find ever the foes of Morven and the gods!"

A chill and an icy fear fell over the crowd, and even the cheek of Siror grew pale; and Morven, erect and dark above the waving torches, stood motionless with folded arms. And hark—far and fast came on the war-steeds of the wave—the people heard them marching to the land, and tossing their white manes in the roaring wind.

"Lo, as ye listen," said Morven, calmly, "the river sweeps on. Haste, for the gods will have a victim, be it your prophet or your king."

"Slave!" shouted Siror, and his spear left his hand, and far above the heads of the crowd sped hissing beside the dark form of Morven, and rent the trunk of the oak behind. Then the people, wroth at the danger of their beloved seer, uttered a wild yell, and gathered round him with brandished swords, facing their chieftains and their king. But at that instant, ere the war had broken forth among the tribe, the three warriors returned, and they bore Darvan on their shoulders, and laid him at the feet of the king, and they said tremblingly, "Thus found we the elder in the centre of his own hall." And the people saw that Darvan was a corpse, and that the prediction of Morven was thus verified. "So perish the enemies of Morven and the stars!" cried the son of Osslah. And the people echoed the cry. Then the fury of Siror was at its height, and waving his sword above his head he plunged into the crowd, "Thy blood, baseborn, or mine!"

"So be it!" answered Morven, quailing not. "People, smite the blasphemer! Hark how the river pours down upon your children and your hearths! On, on, or ye perish!"

And Siror fell, pierced by five hundred spears.

"Smite! smite!" cried Morven, as the chiefs of the royal house gathered round the king. And the clash of swords, and the gleam of spears, and the cries of the dying, and the yell of the trampling people, mingled with the roar of the elements, and the voices of the rushing wave.

Three hundred of the chiefs perished that night by the swords of their own tribe. And the last cry of the victors was, "Morven the prophet,—*Morven the king!*"

And the son of Osslah, seeing the waves now spreading over the valley, led Orna his wife, and the men of Oestrich, their women, and their children, to a high mount, where they waited the dawning sun. But Orna sat apart and wept bitterly, for her brothers were no more, and her race had perished from the earth. And Morven sought to comfort her in vain.

When the morning rose, they saw that the river had overspread the greater part of the city, and now stayed its course among the hollows of the vale. Then Morven said to the people, "The star-kings are avenged, and their wrath appeased. Tarry only here until the waters have melted into the crevices of the soil." And on the fourth day they returned to the city, and no man dared to name another, save Morven, as the king.

But Morven retired into his cave and mused deeply; and then assembling the people, he gave them new laws; and he made them build a mighty temple in honour of the stars, and made them heap within it all that the tribe held most precious. And he took unto him fifty children from the most famous of the tribe; and he took also ten from among the men who had served him best, and he ordained that they should serve the stars in the great temple: and Morven was their chief. And he put away the crown they pressed upon him, and he chose from among the elders a new king. And he ordained that henceforth the servants only of the stars in the great temple should elect the king and the rulers, and hold council, and proclaim war; but he suffered the king to feast, and to hunt, and to make merry in the banquet-halls. And Morven built altars in the temple, and was the first who, in the North, sacrificed the beast and the bird, and afterwards human flesh, upon the altars. And he drew auguries from the entrails of the victim, and made schools for the science of the prophet; and Morven's piety was the wonder of the tribe, in that he refused to be a king. And Morven the high priest was ten thousand times mightier than the king. He taught the people to till the ground, and to sow the herb; and by his wisdom, and the valour that his prophecies instilled into men, he conquered all the neighbouring tribes. And the sons of Oestrich spread themselves over a mighty empire, and with them spread the name and the laws of Morven. And in every province which he conquered, he ordered them to build a temple to the stars.

But a heavy sorrow fell upon the fears of Morven. The sister of Siror bowed down her head, and survived not long the slaughter of her race. And she left Morven childless. And he mourned bitterly and as one distraught, for her only in the world had his heart the power to love. And he sat down and covered his face, saying:—

"Lo! I have toiled and travailed; and never before in the world did man conquer what I have conquered. Verily the empire of the iron thews and the giant limbs is no more! I have founded a new power, that henceforth shall sway the lands;—the empire of a plotting brain and a commanding mind. But, behold! my fate is barren, and I feel already that it will grow neither fruit nor tree as a shelter to mine old age. Desolate and lonely shall I pass unto my grave. O Orna! my beautiful! my loved! none were like unto thee, and to thy love do I owe my glory and my life! Would for thy sake, O sweet bird! that nestled in the dark cavern of my heart,—would for thy sake that thy brethren had been spared, for verily with my life would I have purchased thine. Alas! only when I lost thee did I find that thy love was dearer to me than the fear of others!" And Morven mourned night and day, and none might comfort him.

But from that time forth he gave himself solely up to the cares of his calling; and his nature and his affections, and whatever there was yet left soft in him, grew hard like stone; and he was a man without love, and he forbade love and marriage to the priest.

Now, in his latter years, there arose *other* prophets; for the world had grown wiser even by Morven's wisdom, and some did say unto themselves, "Behold Morven, the herdsman's son, is a king of kings: this did the stars for their servant; shall we not also be servants to the star?"

And they wore black garments like Morven, and went about prophesying of what the stars foretold them. And Morven was exceeding wroth; for he, more than other men, knew that the prophets lied; wherefore he went forth against them with the ministers of the temple, and he took them, and burned them by a slow fire: for thus said Morven to the people:—"A true prophet hath honour, but *I* only am a true prophet;—to all false prophets there shall be surely death."

And the people applauded the piety of the son of Osslah.

And Morven educated the wisest of the children in the mysteries of the temple, so that they grew up to succeed him worthily.

And he died full of years and honour; and they carved his effigy on a mighty stone before the temple, and the effigy endured for a thousand ages, and whoso looked on it trembled; for the face was calm with the calmness of unspeakable awe!

And Morven was the first mortal of the North that made Religion the stepping-stone to Power. Of a surety Morven was a great man!

It was the last night of the old year, and the stars sat, each upon his ruby throne, and watched with sleepless eyes upon the world. The night was dark and troubled, the dread winds were abroad, and fast and frequent hurried the clouds beneath the thrones of the kings of night. And ever and anon fiery meteors flashed along the depths of heaven, and were again swallowed up in the grave of darkness. But far below his brethren, and with a lurid haze around his orb, sat the discontented star that had watched over the hunters of the North.

And on the lowest abyss of space there was spread a thick and mighty gloom, from which, as from a caldron, rose columns of wreathing smoke; and still, when the great winds rested for an instant on their paths, voices of woe and laughter, mingled with shrieks, were heard booming from the abyss to the upper air.

And now, in the middest night, a vast figure rose slowly from the abyss, and its wings threw blackness over the world. High upward to the throne of the discontented star sailed the fearful shape, and the star trembled on his throne when the form stood before him face to face.

And the shape said, "Hail, brother!—all hail!"

"I know thee not," answered the star; "thou art not the archangel that visitest the kings of night."

And the shape laughed loud. "I am the fallen star of the morning!—I am Lucifer, thy brother! Hast thou not, O sullen king! served me and mine? and hast thou not wrested the earth from thy Lord who sittest above, and given it to me, by darkening the souls of men with the religion of fear? Wherefore come, brother, come;—thou hast a throne prepared beside my own in the fiery gloom—Come! The heavens are no more for thee?"

Then the star rose from his throne, and descended to the side of Lucifer. For ever hath the spirit of discontent had sympathy with the soul of pride. And they sank slowly down to the gulf of gloom.

It was the first night of the new year, and the stars sat each on his ruby throne, and watched with sleepless eyes upon the world. But sorrow dimmed the bright faces of the kings of night, for they mourned in silence and in fear for a fallen brother.

And the gates of the heaven of heavens flew open with a golden sound, and the swift archangel fled down on his silent wings; and the archangel gave to each of the stars, as before, the message of his Lord; and to each star was his appointed charge. And when the heraldry seemed done there came a laugh from the abyss of gloom, and half-way from the gulf rose the lurid shape of Lucifer the fiend!

"Thou countest thy flock ill, O radiant shepherd! Behold! one star is missing from the three thousand and ten!"

"Back to thy gulf, false Lucifer!—the throne of thy brother hath been filled."

And, lo! as the archangel spake, the stars beheld a young and all-lustrous stranger on the throne of the erring star; and his face was so soft to look upon, that the dimmest of human eyes might have gazed upon its splendour unabashed: but the dark fiend alone was dazzled by its lustre, and, with a yell that shook the flaming pillars of the universe, he plunged backward into the gloom.

Then, far and sweet from the arch unseen, came forth the voice of God,—

"Behold! on the throne of the discontented star sits the star of Hope; and he that breathed into mankind the religion of Fear hath a successor in him who shall teach earth the religion of Love!"

And evermore the star of Fear dwells with Lucifer, and the star of Love keeps vigil in heaven!

CHAPTER XX.

GELNHAUSEN.—THE POWER OF LOVE IN SANCTIFIED PLACES.— A PORTRAIT OF FREDERICK BARBAROSSA.—THE AMBITION OF MEN FINDS NO ADEQUATE SYMPATHY IN WOMEN.

"YOU made me tremble for you more than once," said Gertrude to the student; "I feared you were about to touch upon ground really sacred, but your end redeemed all."

"The false religion always tries to counterfeit the garb, the language, the aspect of the true," answered the German: "for that reason, I purposely suffered my tale to occasion that very fear and anxiety you speak of, conscious that the most scrupulous would be contented when the whole was finished."

This German was one of a new school, of which England as yet knows nothing. We shall see, hereafter, what it will produce.

The student left them at Friedberg, and our travellers proceeded to Gelnhausen,—a spot interesting to lovers; for here Frederick the First was won by the beauty of Gela, and, in the midst of an island vale, he built the Imperial Palace, in honour to the lady of his love. The spot is, indeed, well chosen of itself: the mountains of the Rhinegebürg close it in with the green gloom of woods, and the glancing waters of the Kinz.

"Still, wherever we go," said Trevylyan, "we find all tradition is connected with love; and history, for that reason, hallows less than romance."

"It is singular," said Vane, moralizing, "that love makes but a small part of our actual lives, but is yet the master-key to our sympathies. The hardest of us, who laugh at the passion when they see it palpably before them, are arrested by some dim tradition of its existence in the past. It is as if life had few opportunities of bringing out certain qualities within us, so that they always remain untold and dormant, susceptible to thought, but deaf to action."

"You refine and mystify too much," said Trevylyan, smiling; "none of us have any faculty, any passion, uncalled forth, if we have *really* loved, though but for a day."

Gertrude smiled, and drawing her arm within his, Trevylyan left Vane to philosophize on passion;—a fit occupation for one who had never felt it.

"Here let us pause," said Trevylyan, afterwards, as they visited the remains of the ancient palace, and the sun glittered on the scene, "to recall the old chivalric day of the gallant Barbarossa;—let us suppose him commencing the last great action of his life; let us picture him as setting out for the Holy Land. Imagine him issuing from those walls on his white charger; his fiery eye somewhat dimmed by years, and his hair blanched; but nobler from the impress of time itself;—the clang of arms; the tramp of steeds; banners on high; music pealing from hill to hill; the red cross and the nodding plume; the sun, as now glancing on yonder trees; and thence reflected from the burnished arms of the Crusaders;—but, Gela——"

"Ah," said Gertrude, "*she* must be no more; for she would have outlived her beauty, and have found that glory had now no rival in his breast. Glory consoles men for the death of the loved; but glory is infidelity to the living."

"Nay, not so, dearest Gertrude," said Trevylyan, quickly; "for my darling dream of Fame is the hope of laying its honours at your feet! And if ever, in future years, I should rise above the herd, I should only ask if *your* step were proud, and *your* heart elated."

"I was wrong," said Gertrude, with tears in her eyes; "and, for your sake, I can be ambitious."

Perhaps there, too, she was mistaken; for one of the common disappointments of the heart is, that women have so rarely a sympathy in our better and higher aspirings. Their ambition is not for great things; they cannot understand that desire "which scorns delight, and loves laborious days." If they love us, they usually exact too much. They are jealous of the ambition to which we sacrifice so largely, and which divides us from them; and they leave the stern passion of great minds to the only solitude which affection cannot share. To aspire is to be alone!

CHAPTER XXI.

VIEW OF EHRENBREITSTEIN.—A NEW ALARM IN GERTRUDE'S HEALTH.—TRARBACH.

ANOTHER time our travellers proceeded from Coblentz to Treves, following the course of the Moselle. They stopped on the opposite bank below the bridge that unites Coblentz with the Petersberg, to linger over the superb view of Ehrenbreitstein which you may there behold.

It was one of those calm noonday scenes which impress upon us their own bright and voluptuous tranquillity. There, stood the old herdsman leaning on his staff, and the quiet cattle knee-deep in the gliding waters. Never did stream more smooth and sheen, than was at that hour the surface of the Moselle, mirror the images of the pastoral life. Beyond, the darker shadows of the bridge and of the walls of Coblentz fell deep over the waves, chequered by the tall sails of the craft that were moored around the harbour. But clear against the sun rose the spires and roofs of Coblentz, backed by many a hill sloping away to the horizon. High, dark, and massive, on the opposite bank, swelled the towers and rock of Ehrenbrietstein; a type of that great chivalric spirit—the HONOUR that the rock arrogates for its name,—which demands so many sacrifices of blood and tears, but which ever creates in the restless heart of man a far deeper interest than the more peaceful scenes of life by which it is contrasted. There, still—from the calm waters, and the abodes of common toil and ordinary pleasure—turns the aspiring mind! Still as we gaze on that lofty and immemorial rock we recall the famine and the siege; and own that the more daring crimes of men have a strange privilege in hallowing the very spot which they devastate.

Below, in green curves and mimic bays covered with herbage, the gradual banks mingled with the water; and just where the bridge closed, a solitary group of trees, standing dark in the thickest shadow, gave that melancholy feature to the scene which resembles the one dark thought that often forces itself into our sunniest hours. Their boughs stirred not; no voice of birds broke the stillness of their gloomy verdure; the eye turned from them, as from the sad moral that belongs to existence.

In proceeding to Trarbach, Gertrude was seized with another of those fainting fits which had so terrified Trevylyan before; they stopped an hour or two at a little village, but Gertrude rallied with such apparent rapidity, and so strongly insisted upon proceeding, that they reluctantly continued their way. This event would have thrown a gloom over their journey, if Gertrude had not exerted herself to dispel the impression she had occasioned; and so light, so cheerful, were her spirits, that for the time at least, she succeeded.

They arrived at Trarbach late at noon. This now small and humble town is said to have been the Thronus Bacchi of the ancients. From the spot where the travellers halted to take, as it were, their impression of the town, they saw before them the little hostelry, a poor pretender to the Thronus Bacchi, with the rude sign of the Holy Mother over the door. The peaked roof, the sunk window, the gray walls, chequered with the rude beams of wood so common to the meaner houses on the Continent, bore something of a melancholy and unprepossessing aspect. Right above, with its Gothic windows and venerable spire, rose the church of the town; and, crowning the summit of a green and almost perpendicular mountain, scowled the remains of one of those mighty castles which make the never-failing frown on a German landscape.

The scene was one of quiet and of gloom: the exceeding serenity of the day contrasted, with an almost unpleasing brightness, the poverty of the town, the thinness of the population, and the dreary grandeur of the ruins that overhung the capital of the perished race of the bold Counts of Spanheim.

They passed the night at Trarbach, and continued their journey next day. At Treves, Gertrude was for some days seriously ill; and when they returned to Coblentz, her disease had evidently received a rapid and alarming increase.

CHAPTER XXII.

THE DOUBLE LIFE.—TREVYLYAN'S FATE.—SORROW THE PARENT OF FAME.—NIEDERLAHNSTEIN.—DREAMS.

THERE are two lives to each of us, gliding on at the same time, scarcely connected with each other!—the life of our actions, the life of our minds; the external and the inward history; the movements of the frame, the deep and ever-restless workings of the heart! They who have loved know that there is a diary of the affections, which we might keep for years without having occasion even to touch upon the exterior surface of life, our busy occupations—the mechanical progress of our existence; yet by the last are we judged, the first is never known. History reveals men's deeds, men's outward characters, but *not themselves*. There is a secret self that hath its own life "rounded by a dream," unpenetrated, unguessed. What passed within Trevylyan, hour after hour, as he watched over the declining health of the only being in the world whom his proud heart had been ever destined to love! His real record of the time was marked by every cloud upon Gertrude's brow, every smile of her countenance, every—the faintest—alteration in her disease: yet, to the outward seeming, all this vast current of varying eventful emotion lay dark and unconjectured. He filled up, with wonted regularity, the colourings of existence, and smiled and moved as other men. For still, in the heroism with which devotion conquers self, he sought only to cheer and gladden the young heart on which he had embarked his all; and he kept the dark tempest of his anguish for the solitude of night.

That was a peculiar doom which Fate had reserved for him; and casting him, in after years, on the great sea of public strife, it seemed as if she were resolved to tear from his heart all yearnings for the land. For him there was to be no green or sequestered spot in the valley of household peace. His bark was to know no haven, and his soul not even the desire of rest. For action is that Lethe in which alone we forget our former dreams, and the mind that, too stern not to wrestle with its emotions, seeks to conquer regret, must leave itself

I

no leisure to look behind. Who knows what benefits to the world may have sprung from the sorrows of the benefactor? As the harvest that gladdens mankind in the suns of autumn was called forth by the rains of spring, so the griefs of youth may make the fame of maturity.

Gertrude, charmed by the beauties of the river, desired to continue the voyage to Mayence. The rich Trevylyan persuaded the physician who had attended her to accompany them, and they once more pursued their way along the banks of the feudal Rhine. For what the Tiber is to the classic, the Rhine is to the chivalric, age. The steep rock and the gray dismantled tower, the massive and rude picturesque of the feudal days, constitute the great features of the scene; and you might almost fancy, as you glide along, that you are sailing back adown the river of Time, and the monuments of the pomp and power of old, rising, one after one, upon its shores!

Vane and Du——e, the physician, at the farther end of the vessel, conversed upon stones and strata, in that singular pedantry of science which strips nature to a skeleton, and prowls among the dead bones of the world, unconscious of its living beauty.

They left Gertrude and Trevylyan to themselves, and, "bending o'er the vessel's laving side," they indulged in silence the melancholy with which each was imbued. For Gertrude began to waken, though doubtingly and at intervals, to a sense of the short span that was granted to her life; and over the loveliness around her there floated that sad and ineffable interest which springs from the presentiment of our own death. They passed the rich island of Oberwerth, and Hochheim, famous for its ruby grape, and saw, from his mountain bed, the Lahn bear his tribute of fruits and corn into the treasury of the Rhine. Proudly rose the tower of Niederlahnstein, and deeply lay its shadow along the stream. It was late noon; the cattle had sought the shade from the slanting sun, and, far beyond, the holy castle of Marksburg raised its battlements above mountains covered with the vine. On the water two boats had been drawn alongside each other; and from one, now moving to the land, the splash of oars broke the general stillness of the tide. Fast by an old tower the fishermen were busied in their craft, but the sound of their voices did not reach the ear. It was life, but a silent life; suited to the tranquillity of noon.

"There is something in travel," said Gertrude, "which constantly, even amidst the most retired spots, impresses us with the exuberance of life. We come to those quiet nooks and find a race whose existence we never dreamed of. In their humble path they know the same passions and tread the same career as ourselves. The mountains shut them out from the great world, but their village is a world in itself. And they know and heed no more of the turbulent scenes of remote cities, than our own planet of the inhabitants of the distant stars. What then is death, but the forgetfulness of some few hearts added to the general unconsciousness of our existence that pervades the universe? The bubble breaks in the vast desert of the air without a sound."

"Why talk of death?" said Trevylyan, with a writhing smile; "these sunny scenes should not call forth such melancholy images."

"Melancholy," repeated Gertrude, mechanically. "Yes, death is indeed melancholy when we are loved!"

They stayed a short time at Niederlahnstein, for Vane was anxious to examine the minerals that the Lahn brings into the Rhine; and the sun was waning towards its close as they renewed their voyage. As they sailed slowly on, Gertrude said, "How like a dream is this sentiment of existence, when, without labour or motion, every change of scene is brought before us; and if I am with you, dearest, I do not feel it less resembling a dream, for I have dreamed of you lately more than ever. And dreams have become a part of my life itself."

"Speaking of dreams," said Trevylyan, as they pursued that mysterious subject; "I once during my former residence in Germany fell in with a singular enthusiast, who had taught himself what he termed 'A System of Dreaming.' When he first spoke to me upon it I asked him to explain what he meant, which he did somewhat in the following words."

CHAPTER XXIII.

THE LIFE OF DREAMS.

"I WAS born," said he, "with many of the sentiments of the poet, but without the language to express them; my feelings were constantly chilled by the intercourse of the actual world—my family, mere Germans, dull and unimpassioned—had nothing in common with me; nor did I out of my family find those with whom I could better sympathize. I was revolted by friendships—for they were susceptible to every change; I was disappointed in love—for the truth never approached to my ideal. Nursed early in the lap of Romance, enamoured of the wild and the adventurous, the commonplaces of life were to me inexpressibly tame and joyless. And yet indolence, which belongs to the poetical character, was more inviting than that eager and uncontemplative action which can alone wring enterprise from life. Meditation was my natural element. I loved to spend the noon reclined by some shady stream, and in a half sleep to shape images from the glancing sunbeams; a dim and unreal order of philosophy, that belongs to our nation, was my favourite intellectual pursuit. And I sought amongst the Obscure and the Recondite the variety and emotion I could not find in the Familiar. Thus constantly watching the operations of the inner-mind, it occurred to me at last that sleep having its own world, but as yet a rude and fragmentary one, it might be possible to shape from its chaos all those combinations of beauty, of power, of glory, and of love, which were denied to me in the world in which my frame walked and had its being. So soon as this idea came upon me, I nursed and cherished, and mused over it, till I found that the imagination began to effect the miracle I desired. By brooding ardently, intensely, before I retired to rest, over any especial train of thought, over any ideal creations; by keeping the body utterly still and quiescent during the whole day; by shutting out all living adventure, the memory of which might perplex and interfere with the stream of events that I desired to pour forth into the wilds of sleep, I discovered at last that I could lead in dreams a life solely their own, and utterly distinct from the life of day. Towers and palaces, all my heritage and seigneury, rose before me from the depths of night; I quaffed from jewelled cups the Falernian of imperial vaults; music from harps of celestial tone filled up the crevices of air; and the smiles of immortal beauty flushed like sunlight over all. Thus the adventure and the glory that I could not for my waking life obtain, was obtained for me in sleep. I wandered with the gryphon and the gnome; I sounded the horn at enchanted portals; I conquered in the nightly lists; I planted my standard over battlements huge as the painter's birth of Babylon itself.

"But I was afraid to call forth one shape on whose loveliness to pour all the hidden passion of my soul. I trembled lest my sleep should present me some image which it could never restore, and, waking from which, even the new world I had created might be left desolate for ever. I shuddered lest I should adore a vision which the first ray of morning could smite to the grave.

"In this train of mind I began to ponder whether it might not be possible to connect dreams together; to supply the thread that was wanting; to make one night continue the history of the other, so as to bring together the same shapes and the same scenes, and thus lead a connected and harmonious life, not only in the one half of existence, but in the other, the richer and more glorious, half. No sooner did this idea present itself to me, than I burned to accomplish it. I had before taught myself that Faith is the great creator;

that to believe fervently is to make belief true. So I would not suffer my mind to doubt the practicability of its scheme. I shut myself up then entirely by day, refused books, and hated the very sun, and compelled all my thoughts (and sleep is the mirror of thought) to glide in one direction, the direction of my dreams, so that from night to night the imagination might keep up the thread of action, and I might thus lie down full of the past dream and confident of the sequel. Not for one day only, or for one month, did I pursue this system, but I continued it zealously and sternly till at length it began to succeed. Who shall tell," cried the enthusiast,—I see him now with his deep, bright, sunken eyes, and his wild hair thrown backward from his brow, "the rapture I experienced, when first, faintly and half distinct, I perceived the harmony I had invoked dawn upon my dreams? At first there was only a partial and desultory connection between them; my eye recognized certain shapes, my ear certain tones common to each; by degrees these augmented in number, and were more defined in outline. At length one fair face broke forth from among the ruder forms, and night after night appeared mixing with them for a moment and then vanishing, just as the mariner watches, in a clouded sky, the moon shining through the drifting rack, and quickly gone. My curiosity was now vividly excited, the face, with its lustrous eyes, and seraph features, roused all the emotions that no living shape had called forth. I became enamoured of a dream, and as the statue to the Cyprian was my creation to me; so from this intent and unceasing passion, I at length worked out my reward. My dream became more palpable; I spoke with it; I knelt to it; my lips were pressed to its own; we exchanged the vows of love, and morning only separated us with the certainty that at night we should meet again. Thus then," continued my visionary, "I commenced a history utterly separate from the history of the world, and it went on alternately with my harsh and chilling history of the day, equally regular and equally continuous. And what, you ask, was that history? Methought I was a prince in some Eastern island, that had no features in common with the colder north of my native home. By day I looked upon the dull walls of a German town, and saw homely or squalid forms passing before me; the sky was dim and the sun cheerless. Night came on with her thousand stars, and brought me the dews of sleep. Then suddenly there was a new world; the richest fruits hung from the trees in clusters of gold and purple. Palaces of the quaint fashion of the sunnier climes, with spiral minarets and glittering cupolas, were mirrored upon vast lakes sheltered by the palm-tree and banana. The sun seemed a different orb, so mellow and gorgeous were his beams; birds and winged things of all hues fluttered in the shining air; the faces and garments of men were not of the northern regions of the world, and their voices spoke a tongue which, strange at first, by degrees I interpreted. Sometimes I made war upon neighbouring kings; sometimes I chased the spotted pard through the vast gloom of immemorial forests; my life was at once a life of enterprise and pomp. But above all there was the history of my love! I thought there were a thousand difficulties in the way of attaining its possession. Many were the rocks I had to scale, and the battles to wage, and the fortresses to storm, in order to win her as my bride. But at last" (continued the enthusiast) "she *is* won, she is my own! Time in that wild world, which I visit nightly, passes not so slowly as in this, and yet an hour may be the same as a year. This continuity of existence, this successive series of dreams, so different from the broken incoherence of other men's sleep, at times bewilders me with strange and suspicious thoughts. What if this glorious sleep be a real life, and this dull waking the true repose? Why not? What is there more faithful in the one than in the other? And there have I garnered and collected all of pleasure that I am capable of feeling. I seek no joy in this world—I form no ties, I feast not, nor love, nor make merry—I am only impatient till the hour when I may re-enter my royal realms and pour my renewed delight into the bosom of my bright Ideal. There then have I found all that the world denied me; there have I realized the yearning and the aspiration within me; there have I coined the untold poetry into the Felt—the Seen!"

I found, continued Trevylyan, that this tale was corroborated by inquiry into the visionary's habits. He shunned society; avoided all unnecessary movement or excitement. He fared with rigid abstemiousness, and only appeared to feel pleasure as the day departed, and the hour of return to his imaginary kingdom approached. He always retired to rest punctually at a certain hour, and would sleep so soundly, that a cannon fired under his window would not arouse him. He never, which may seem singular, spoke or moved much in his sleep, but was peculiarly calm, almost to the appearance of lifelessness; but, discovering once that he had been watched in sleep, he was wont afterwards carefully to secure the chamber from intrusion. His victory over the natural incoherence of sleep had, when I first knew him, lasted for some years; possibly what imagination first produced was afterwards continued by habit.

I saw him again a few months subsequent to this confession, and he seemed to be much changed. His health was broken, and his abstraction had deepened into gloom.

I questioned him of the **cause of the alteration, and he answered me** with great reluctance—

"She is dead," said he; "**my realms** are desolate! **A serpent** stung her, and she died in these very **arms**. Vainly, when **I started** from my sleep in horror and despair, **vainly** did I say to myself,—This is but a dream. I shall see her again. A vision cannot die! Hath it flesh that decays? is it not a spirit—bodiless—indissoluble? With what terrible anxiety I awaited the night! Again I slept, and the DREAM **lay** again before me—dead and withered. Even the ideal can **vanish**. I assisted in the burial; **I laid** her in the earth; I heaped the monumental mockery over her form. And never since hath she, or aught like her, revisited my **dreams**. I see her only when I wake; thus to wake is indeed to dream! But," continued the visionary in a solemn voice, "I feel myself departing from this world, and with a fearful **joy; for I think there may** be **a** land beyond even the land of sleep, **where I shall see** her again,—a land in which a vision itself may be restored."

And in truth, concluded Trevylyan, the dreamer died shortly afterwards, suddenly, and **in his** sleep. And never before, perhaps, had Fate so literally **made of a** living man (with his passions and his powers, his ambition and **his** love) the plaything and puppet of a dream!

"Ah," said Vane, who had heard the latter part of Trevylyan's story; "**could the German have** bequeathed **to** us his secret, what a refuge should **we possess from the** ills of earth! The dungeon and disease, **poverty, affliction**, shame, would **cease to be the** tyrants of our lot; **and to** Sleep we should confine **our history** and transfer our emotions."

"Gertrude," whispered the lover, "what **his** kingdom **and his** bride were to the Dreamer, art thou to **me!**"

CHAPTER XXIV.

THE BROTHERS.

THE banks of the Rhine now shelved away into sweeping plains, **and** on their right rose the once imperial **city of** Boppart. In no journey **of** similar length do **you** meet with such striking instances of the mutability and shifts of power. To **find, as** in the Memphian Egypt, **a** city sunk into **a** heap of desolate **ruins;** the hum, the roar, the mart of nations, hushed into the silence of ancestral tombs, is less humbling to our human vanity than to mark, as along the Rhine, the kingly city dwindled into the humble town or the dreary village ; decay without its grandeur, change without the awe of its solitude ! On the site on which Drusus raised his Roman tower, and the kings of the Franks their palaces, trade now dribbles in tobacco-pipes, and transforms into an excellent cotton factory the antique nunnery of Köningsberg ! So be it ; it is the progressive order of things—the world itself will soon be one excellent cotton factory !

"Look !" said Trevylyan, as they sailed on, " at yonder mountain, with its two traditional Castles of Liebenstein and Sternfels."

Massive and huge the ruins swelled above the green rock, at the foot of which lay, in happier security from time and change, the clustered cottages of the peasant, with a single spire rising above the quiet village.

"Is there not, Albert, a celebrated legend attached to those castles?" said Gertrude. "I think I remember to have heard their names in connection with your profession of tale-teller."

"Yes," said Trevylyan, " the story relates to the last lords of those shattered towers, and——"

"You will sit here, nearer to me, and begin," interrupted Gertrude, in her tone of childlike command—"Come."

THE BROTHERS.

A TALE.[1]

You must imagine, then, dear Gertrude (said Trevylyan), a beautiful summer day, and by the same faculty that none possess so richly as yourself, for it is you who can kindle something of that divine spark even in me, you must rebuild those shattered towers in the pomp of old ; raise the gallery and the hall ; man the battlement with warders, and give the proud banners of ancestral chivalry to wave upon the walls. But above, sloping half down the rock, you must fancy the hanging gardens of Liebenstein, fragrant with flowers, and basking in the noonday sun.

On the greenest turf, underneath an oak, there sat three persons, in the bloom of youth. Two of the three were brothers ; the third was an orphan girl, whom the lord of the opposite tower of Sternfels had bequeathed to the protection of his brother, the chief of Liebenstein. The castle itself and the demesne that belonged to it passed

---

[1] This tale is, in reality, founded on the beautiful tradition which belongs to Liebenstein and Sternfels.

away from the female line, and became the heritage of Otho, the orphan's cousin, and the younger of the two brothers now seated on the turf.

"And oh," said the elder, whose name was Warbeck, "you have twined a chaplet for my brother; have you not, dearest Leoline, a simple flower or me?"

The beautiful orphan—(for beautiful she was, Gertrude, as the heroine of the tale you bid me tell ought to be,—should she not have to the dreams of my fancy your lustrous hair, and your sweet smile, and your eyes of blue, that are never, never silent? Ah, pardon me, that in a former tale, I denied the heroine the beauty of your face, and remember that to atone for it, I endowed her with the beauty of your mind)—the beautiful orphan blushed to her temples, and culling from the flowers in her lap the freshest of the roses, began weaving them into a wreath for Warbeck.

"It would be better," said the gay Otho, "to make my sober brother a chaplet of the rue and cypress; the rose is much too bright a flower for so serious a knight."

Leoline held up her hand reprovingly.

"Let him laugh, dearest cousin," said Warbeck, gazing passionately on her changing cheek: "and thou, Leoline, believe that the silent stream runs the deepest."

At this moment, they heard the voice of the old chief, their father, calling aloud for Leoline; for, ever when he returned from the chase, he wanted her gentle presence; and the hall was solitary to him if the light sound of her step, and the music of her voice, were not heard in welcome.

Leoline hastened to her guardian, and the brothers were left alone.

Nothing could be more dissimilar than the features and the respective characters of Otho and Warbeck. Otho's countenance was flushed with the brown hues of health; his eyes were of the brightest hazel: his dark hair wreathed in short curls round his open and fearless brow; the jest ever echoed on his lips, and his step was bounding as the foot of the hunter of the Alps. Bold and light was his spirit; if at times he betrayed the haughty insolence of youth, he felt generously, and though not ever ready to confess sorrow for a fault, he was at least ready to brave peril for a friend.

But Warbeck's frame, though of equal strength, was more slender in its proportions than that of his brother; the fair long hair, that characterized his northern race, hung on either side of a countenance calm and pale, and deeply impressed with thought, even to sadness. His features, more majestic and regular than Otho's, rarely varied in their expression. More resolute even than Otho, he was less impetuous; more impassioned, he was also less capricious.

The brothers remained silent after Leoline had left them. Otho carelessly braced on his sword, that he had laid aside on the grass; but Warbeck gathered up the flowers that had been touched by the soft hand of Leoline, and placed them in his bosom.

The action disturbed Otho; he bit his lip, and changed colour; at length he said, with a forced laugh,

"It must be confessed, brother, that you carry your affection for our fair cousin to a degree that even relationship seems scarcely to warrant."

"It is true," said Warbeck, calmly: "I love her with a **love** surpassing that of blood."

"How!" said Otho, fiercely: "do you dare to think of Leoline as a bride?"

"Dare!" repeated Warbeck, turning yet paler than his wonted hue.

"Yes, I have said the word! Know, Warbeck, that I, too, love Leoline; I, too, claim her as my bride; and never, while I can wield a sword,—never, while I wear the spurs of knighthood, will I render my claim to a living rival. Even," he added (sinking his voice), "though that rival be my brother!"

Warbeck answered not; his very soul seemed stunned; he gazed **long and** wistfully on his brother, and then, turning his face away, **ascended** the rock without uttering a single word.

This silence startled Otho. Accustomed to vent every emotion of his own, he could not comprehend the forbearance of his brother; he knew his high and brave nature too well to imagine that it arose from fear. Might it not be contempt, or might he not, at this moment, intend to seek their father; and, the first to proclaim his love for the orphan, advance, also, the privilege of the elder born? **As these** suspicions flashed across him, the haughty Otho strode **to** his brother's side, and laying his hand on his arm, said,

"Whither goest thou? and dost thou consent to surrender Leoline?"

"Does she love thee, Otho?" answered Warbeck, breaking silence at last; and his voice spoke so deep an anguish, that it arrested the passions of Otho, even at their height.

"It is thou who art now silent," continued Warbeck; "speak, doth she love thee, and has her lip confessed it?"

"I have believed that she loved me," faltered Otho; "but she is of maiden bearing, and her lip, at least, has never told it."

"Enough" said Warbeck, "release your hold."

"Stay," said Otho, his suspicions returning; "stay—yet **one** word; dost thou seek my father? He ever honoured thee more than me: wilt thou own to him thy love, and insist on thy right of birth? By my soul and my hope of heaven, do it, and **one of us** two must fall!"

"Poor boy!" answered Warbeck, bitterly; "how little thou canst read the heart of one who loves truly. Thinkest thou, I would wed her if she loved thee? Thinkest thou I could, even to be blessed myself, give her one moment's pain? Out on the thought—away!"

"Then wilt not thou seek our father?" said Otho, abashed.

"Our father!—has our father the keeping of Leoline's affection?" answered Warbeck; and shaking off his brother's grasp, he sought the way to the castle.

As he entered the hall, he heard the voice of Leoline; she was singing to the old chief one of the simple ballads of the time, that **the** warrior and the hunter loved to hear. He paused lest **he** should break the spell (a spell stronger than a sorcerer's to him), and gazing upon Leoline's beautiful form, his heart sank within him. His brother and himself had each that day, as they sat in the gardens, given her a flower; *his* flower was the fresher and the rarer; his he saw not, but she wore his brother's in her bosom!

The chief, lulled by the music and wearied with the toils of the chase, sank into sleep as the song ended, and Warbeck, coming forward, motioned to Leoline to follow him. He passed into a retired and solitary walk, and when they were a little distance from the castle, Warbeck turned round, and taking Leoline's hand gently, said—

"Let us rest here for one moment, dearest cousin; I have much on my heart to say to thee."

"And what is there," answered Leoline, as they sat on a mossy bank, with the broad Rhine glancing below, "what is there that my kind Warbeck would ask of me? Ah! would it might be some favour, something in poor Leoline's power to grant; for ever from my birth you have been to me most tender, most kind. You, I have often heard them say, taught my first steps to walk; you formed my infant lips into language, and, in after years, when my wild cousin was far away in the forests at the chase, you would brave his gay jest and remain at home, lest Leoline should be weary in the solitude. Ah, would I could repay you!"

Warbeck turned away his cheek; his heart was very full, and it was some moments before he summoned courage to reply.

"My fair cousin," said he, "those were happy days; but they

were the days of childhood. New cares and new thoughts have now come on us. But I am still thy friend, Leoline, and still thou wilt confide in me thy young sorrows and thy young hopes, as thou ever didst. Wilt thou not, Leoline?"

"Canst thou ask me?" said Leoline; and Warbeck, gazing on her face, saw that though her eyes were full of tears, they yet looked steadily upon his; and he knew that she loved him only as a sister.

He sighed, and paused again ere he resumed. "Enough," said he. "Now to my task. Once on a time, dear cousin, there lived among these mountains a certain chief who had two sons, and an orphan like thyself dwelt also in his halls. And the elder son—but no matter, let us not waste words on *him!*—the younger son, then, loved the orphan dearly—more dearly than cousins love; and, fearful of refusal, he prayed the elder one to urge his suit to the orphan. Leoline, my tale is done. Canst thou not love Otho as he loves thee?"

And now lifting his eyes to Leoline, he saw that she trembled violently, and her cheek was covered with blushes.

"Say," continued he, mastering himself; "is not that flower (his present) a token that he is chiefly in thy thoughts?"

"Ah, Warbeck! do not deem me ungrateful, that I wear not yours also; but——"

"Hush!" said Warbeck, hastily; "I am but as thy brother, is not Otho more? He is young, brave, and beautiful. God grant that he may deserve thee, if thou givest him so rich a gift as thy affections."

"I saw less of Otho in my childhood," said Leoline, evasively; "therefore, his kindness of late years seemed stranger to me than thine."

"And thou wilt not then reject him? Thou wilt be his bride?"

"And *thy* sister," answered Leoline.

"Bless thee, mine own dear cousin! one brother's kiss then, and farewell! Otho shall thank thee for himself."

He kissed her forehead calmly, and, turning away, plunged into the thicket; then, nor till then he gave vent to such emotions, as, had Leoline seen them, Otho's suit had been lost for ever; for passionately, deeply as in her fond and innocent heart she loved Otho, the *happiness* of Warbeck was not less dear to her.

When the young knight had recovered his self-possession he went in search of Otho. He found him alone in the wood, leaning with folded arms against a tree, and gazing moodily on the ground. Warbeck's noble heart was touched at his brother's dejection.

"Cheer thee, Otho," said he; "I bring thee no bad tidings; I have seen Leoline—I have conversed with her—nay, start not—she loves thee! she is thine!"

"Generous—generous Warbeck!" exclaimed Otho; and he threw himself on his brother's neck. "No, no," said he, "this must not be; thou hast the elder claim.—I resign her to thee. Forgive me my waywardness, brother, forgive me!"

"Think of the past no more," said Warbeck; "the love of Leoline is an excuse for greater offences than thine: and now, be kind to her; her nature is soft and keen. *I* know her well; for *I* have studied her faintest wish. Thou art hasty and quick of ire; but remember, that a word wounds where love is deep. For my sake, as for hers, think more of her happiness than thine own; now seek her—she waits to hear from thy lips the tale that sounded cold upon mine."

With that he left his brother, and, once more re-entering the castle, he went into the hall of his ancestors. His father still slept; he put his hand on his gray hair, and blessed him; then stealing up to his chamber, he braced on his helm and armour, and thrice kissing the hilt of his sword, said, with a flushed cheek—

"Henceforth be *thou* my bride!" Then passing from the castle, he sped by the most solitary paths down the rock, gained the Rhine, and hailing one of the numerous fishermen of the river, won the opposite shore; and alone, but not sad, for his high heart supported him, and Leoline at least was happy, he hastened to Frankfort.

The town was all gaiety and life, arms clanged at every corner, the sounds of martial music, the wave of banners, the glittering of plumed casques, the neighing of war-steeds, all united to stir the blood and inflame the sense. St. Bertrand had lifted the sacred cross along the shores of the Rhine, and the streets of Frankfort witnessed with what success!

On that same day Warbeck assumed the sacred badge, and was enlisted among the knights of the Emperor Conrad.

We must suppose some time to have elapsed, and Otho and Leoline were not yet wedded; for, in the first fervour of his gratitude to his brother, Otho had proclaimed to his father and to Leoline, the conquest Warbeck had obtained over himself; and Leoline, touched to the heart, would not consent that the wedding should take place immediately. "Let him, at least," said she, "not be insulted by a premature festivity; and give him time, amongst the lofty beauties he will gaze upon in a far country, to forget, Otho, that he once loved her who is the beloved of thee."

The old chief applauded this delicacy; and even Otho, in the first flush of his feelings towards his brother, did not venture to oppose it. They settled, then, that the marriage should take place at the end of a year.

Months rolled away, and an absent and moody gloom settled upon Otho's brow. In his excursions with his gay companions among the neighbouring towns, he heard of nothing but the glory of the Crusaders, of the homage paid to the heroes of the Cross at the courts they visited, of the adventures of their life, and the exciting spirit that animated their war. In fact, neither minstrel nor priest suffered the theme to grow cold ; and the fame of those who had gone forth to the holy strife, gave at once emulation and discontent to the youths who remained behind.

"And my brother enjoys this ardent and glorious life," said the impatient Otho; "while I, whose arm is as strong, and whose heart is as bold, languish here listening to the dull tales of a hoary sire and the silly songs of an orphan girl." His heart smote him at the last sentence, but he had already begun to weary of the gentle love of Leoline. Perhaps when he had no longer to gain a triumph over a rival, the excitement palled ; or perhaps his proud spirit secretly chafed at being conquered by his brother in generosity, even when outshining him in the success of love.

But poor Leoline, once taught that she was to consider Otho her betrothed, surrendered her heart entirely to his control. His wild spirit, his dark beauty, his daring valour, won while they awed her ; and in the fitfulness of his nature were those perpetual springs of hope and fear that are the fountains of ever-agitated love. She saw with increasing grief the change that was growing over Otho's mind ; nor did she divine the cause. "Surely I have not offended him," thought she.

Among the companions of Otho was one who possessed a singular sway over him. He was a knight of that mysterious order of the Temple, which exercised at one time so great a command over the minds of men.

A severe and dangerous wound in a brawl with an English knight had confined the Templar at Frankfort, and prevented his joining the Crusade. During his slow recovery he had formed an intimacy with Otho, and, taking up his residence at the castle of Liebenstein, had been struck with the beauty of Leoline. Prevented by his oath from marriage, he allowed himself a double license in love, and doubted not, could he disengage the young knight from his betrothed, that she would add a new conquest to the many he had already achieved. Artfully therefore he painted to Otho the various attractions of the Holy Cause ; and, above all, he failed not to describe, with glowing colours, the beauties who, in the gorgeous East, distinguished with a prodigal favour the warriors of the Cross. Dowries, unknown in the more sterile mountains of the Rhine, accompanied the hand of these beauteous maidens; and even a prince's daughter was not deemed, he said, too lofty a marriage for the heroes who might win kingdoms for themselves.

"To me," said the Templar, "such hopes are eternally denied. But you, were you not already betrothed, what fortunes might await you!"

By such discourses the ambition of Otho was perpetually aroused; they served to deepen his discontent at his present obscurity, and to convert to distaste the only solace it afforded in the innocence and affection of Leoline.

One night, a minstrel sought shelter from the storm in the halls of Liebenstein. His visit was welcomed by the chief, and he repaid the hospitality he had received by the exercise of his art. He sung of the chase, and the gaunt hound started from the hearth. He sung of love, and Otho, forgetting his restless dreams, approached to Leoline, and laid himself at her feet. Louder then and louder rose the strain. The minstrel sung of war; he painted the feats of the Crusaders; he plunged into the thickest of the battle; the steed neighed; the trump sounded; and you might have heard the ringing of the steel. But when he came to signalize the names of the boldest knights, high among the loftiest sounded the name of Sir Warbeck of Liebenstein. Thrice had he saved the imperial banner; two chargers slain beneath him, he had covered their bodies with the fiercest of the foe. Gentle in the tent and terrible in the fray, the minstrel should forget his craft ere the Rhine should forget its hero. The chief started from his seat. Leoline clasped the minstrel's hand.

"Speak,—you have seen him—he lives—he is honoured?"

"I, myself, am but just from Palestine, brave chief and noble maiden. I saw the gallant knight of Liebenstein at the right hand of the imperial Conrad. And he, ladye, was the only knight whom admiration shone upon without envy, its shadow. Who then" (continued the minstrel, once more striking his harp), "who then would remain inglorious in the hall? Shall not the banners of his sires reproach him as they wave? and shall not every voice from Palestine strike shame into his soul?"

"Right," cried Otho, suddenly, and flinging himself at the feet of his father. "Thou hearest what my brother has done, and thine aged eyes weep tears of joy. Shall *I* only dishonour thine old age with a rusted sword? No! grant me, like my brother, to go forth with the heroes of the Cross!"

"Noble youth," cried the harper, "therein speaks the soul of Sir Warbeck; hear him, Sir knight,—hear the noble youth."

"Heaven cries aloud in his voice," said the Templar, solemnly.

"My son, I cannot chide thine ardour," said the old chief, raising him with trembling hands; "but Leoline, thy betrothed?"

Pale as a statue, with ears that doubted their sense as they drank in the cruel words of her lover, stood the orphan. She did not speak, she scarcely breathed; she sank into her seat, and gazed upon the ground, till, at the speech of the chief, both maiden pride and maiden tenderness restored her consciousness, and she said,—

"*I*, uncle!—Shall *I* bid Otho stay when his wishes bid him depart?"

"He will return to thee, noble ladye, covered with glory," said the harper: but Otho said no more. The touching voice of Leoline went to his soul; he resumed his seat in silence; and Leoline, going up to him, whispered gently, "Act as though I were not;" and left the hall to commune with her heart and to weep alone.

"I can wed her before I go," said Otho, suddenly, as he sat that night in the Templar's chamber.

"Why, that is true! and leave thy bride in the first week—a hard trial!"

"Better than incur the chance of never calling her mine. Dear, kind, beloved Leoline!"

"Assuredly, she deserves all from thee; and, indeed, it is no small sacrifice, at thy years and with thy mien, to renounce for ever all interest among the noble maidens thou wilt visit. Ah, from the galleries of Constantinople what eyes will look down on thee, and what ears, learning that thou art Otho the bridegroom, will turn away, caring for thee no more! A bridegroom without a bride! Nay, man, much as the Cross wants warriors, I am enough thy friend to tell thee, if thou weddest, to stay peaceably at home, and forget in the chase the labours of war, from which thou would strip the ambition of love."

"I would I knew what were best," said Otho, irresolutely. "My brother—ha, shall he for ever excel me?—But Leoline, how will she grieve—she who left him for me!"

"Was that thy fault?" said the Templar, gaily. "It may many times chance to thee again to be preferred to another. Troth, it is a sin under which the conscience may walk lightly enough. But sleep on it, Otho; my eyes grow heavy."

The next day Otho sought Leoline, and proposed to her that their wedding should precede his parting; but so embarrassed was he, so divided between two wishes, that Leoline, offended, hurt, stung by his coldness, refused the proposal at once. She left him lest he should see her weep, and then—then she repented even of her just pride!

But Otho, striving to appease his conscience with the belief that hers now was the *sole* fault, busied himself in preparations for his departure. Anxious to outshine his brother, he departed not as Warbeck, alone and unattended, but levying all the horse, men, and money that his domain of Sternfels—which he had not yet tenanted—would afford, he repaired to Frankfort at the head of a glittering troop.

The Templar, affecting a relapse, tarried behind, and promised to join him at that Constantinople of which he had so loudly boasted. Meanwhile he devoted his whole powers of pleasing to console the unhappy orphan. The force of her simple love was, however, stronger than all his arts. In vain he insinuated doubts of Otho; she refused to hear them: in vain he poured with the softest accents into her ear the witchery of flattery and song: she turned heedlessly away; and only pained by the courtesies that had so little resemblance to Otho, she shut herself up in her chamber, and pined in solitude for her forsaker.

The Templar now resolved to attempt darker arts to obtain power over her, when, fortunately, he was summoned suddenly away by a mission from the Grand Master, of so high import, that it could not be resisted by a passion stronger in his breast than love—the passion of ambition. He left the castle to its solitude; and Otho peopling it no more with his gay companions, no solitude *could* be more unfrequently disturbed.

Meanwhile, though, ever and anon, the fame of Warbeck reached their ears, it came unaccompanied with that of Otho,—of him they heard no tidings: and thus the love of the tender orphan was kept alive by the perpetual restlessness of fear. At length the old chief died, and Leoline was left utterly alone.

One evening as she sat with her maidens in the hall, the ringing of a steed's hoofs was heard in the outer court; a horn sounded, the heavy gates were unbarred, and a knight of a stately mien and covered with the mantle of the Cross, entered the hall; he stopped for one moment at the entrance, as if overpowered by his emotion; in the next he had clasped Leoline to his breast.

"Dost thou not recognize thy cousin Warbeck?" He doffed his casque, and she saw that majestic brow which, unlike Otho's, had never changed or been clouded in its aspect to her.

"The war is suspended for the present," said he. "I learned my father's death, and I have returned home to hang up my banner in the hall, and spend my days in peace."

Time and the life of camps had worked their change upon Warbeck's face; the fair hair, deepened in its shade, was worn from the temples, and disclosed one scar that rather aided the beauty of a countenance that had always something high and martial in its character: but the calm it once wore had settled down into sadness; he conversed more rarely than before, and though he smiled not less often, nor less kindly, the smile had more of thought, and the kindness had forgot its passion. He had apparently conquered a love that was so early crossed, but not that fidelity of remembrance which made Leoline dearer to him than all others, and forbade him to replace the images he had graven upon his soul.

The orphan's lips trembled with the name of Otho, but a certain recollection stifled even her anxiety. Warbeck hastened to forestall her questions.

"Otho was well," he said, "and sojourning at Constantinople; he had lingered there so long that the crusade had terminated without his aid: doubtless now he would speedily return;—a month, a week, nay, a day, might restore him to her side."

Leoline was inexpressibly consoled, yet something remained untold. Why, so eager for the strife of the sacred tomb, had he thus tarried at Constantinople? She wondered, she wearied conjecture, but she did not dare to search farther.

The generous Warbeck concealed from her that Otho led a life of the most reckless and indolent dissipation;—wasting his wealth in the pleasures of the Greek court, and only occupying his ambition with the wild schemes of founding a principality in those foreign climes, which the enterprises of the Norman adventurers had rendered so alluring to the knightly bandits of the age.

The cousins resumed their old friendship, and Warbeck believed that it was friendship alone. They walked again among the gardens in which their childhood had strayed; they sat again on the green turf whereon they had woven flowers; they looked down on the eternal mirror of the Rhine;—ah! could it have reflected the same unawakened freshness of their life's early spring!

The grave and contemplative mind of Warbeck had not been so contented with the honours of war, but that it had sought also those calmer sources of emotion which were yet found among the sages of the East. He had drunk at the fountain of the wisdom of those distant climes, and had acquired the habits of meditation which were indulged by those wiser tribes from which the Crusaders brought back to the North the knowledge that was destined to enlighten their posterity. Warbeck, therefore, had little in common with the ruder chiefs around: he did not summon them to his board, nor attend at their noisy wassails. Often late at night, in yon shattered tower, his lonely lamp shone still over the mighty stream, and his only relief to loneliness was in the presence and the song of his soft cousin.

Months rolled on, when suddenly a vague and fearful rumour reached the castle of Liebenstein. Otho was returning home to the neighbouring tower of Sternfels; but not alone. He brought back with him a Greek bride of surprising beauty, and dowered with almost regal wealth. Leoline was the first to discredit the rumour; Leoline was soon the only one who disbelieved.

Bright in the summer noon flashed the array of horsemen; far up the steep ascent wound the gorgeous cavalcade; the lonely towers of Liebenstien heard the echo of many a laugh and peal of merriment. Otho bore home his bride to the hall of Sternfels.

That night there was a great banquet in Otho's castle; the lights shone from every casement, and music swelled loud and ceaselessly within.

By the side of Otho, glittering with the prodigal jewels of the East, sat the Greek. Her dark locks, her flashing eye, the false colours of her complexion, dazzled the eyes of her guests. On her left hand sat the Templar.

"By the holy rood," quoth the Templar, gaily, though he crossed himself as he spoke, "we shall scare the owls to-night on those grim towers of Liebenstein. Thy grave brother, Sir Otho, will have much to do to comfort his cousin when she sees what a gallant life she would have led with thee."

"Poor damsel!" said the Greek, with affected pity, "doubtless she will now be reconciled to the rejected one. I hear he is a knight of a comely mien."

"Peace!" said Otho, sternly, and quaffing a large goblet of wine.

The Greek bit her lip, and glanced meaningly at the Templar, who returned the glance.

"Nought but a beauty such as thine can win my pardon," said Otho, turning to his bride, and gazing passionately in her face.

The Greek smiled.

Well sped the feast, the laugh deepened, the wine circled, when Otho's eye rested on a guest at the bottom of the board, whose figure was mantled from head to foot, and whose face was covered by a dark veil.

"Beshrew me!" said he, aloud; "but this is scarce courteous at our revel: will the stranger vouchsafe to unmask?"

These words turned all eyes to the figure, and they who sat next it perceived that it trembled violently; at length it rose, and walking slowly, but with grace, to the fair Greek, it laid beside her a wreath of flowers.

"It is a simple gift, ladye," said the stranger, in a voice of such sweetness, that the rudest guest was touched by it. "But it is all I can offer, and the bride of Otho should not be without a gift at my hands. May ye both be happy!"

With these words, the stranger turned and passed from the hall silent as a shadow.

"Bring back the stranger!" cried the Greek, recovering her surprise. Twenty guests sprang up to obey her mandate.

"No, no!" said Otho, waving his hand impatiently. "Touch her not, heed her not, at your peril."

The Greek bent over the flowers to conceal her anger, and from amongst them dropped the broken half of a ring. Otho recognized it at once; it was the half of that ring which he had broken with his betrothed. Alas, he required not such a sign to convince him that that figure, so full of ineffable grace, that touching voice, that simple action so tender in its sentiment, that gift, that blessing, came only from the forsaken and forgiving Leoline!

But Warbeck, alone in his solitary tower, paced to and fro with agitated steps. Deep, undying wrath at his brother's falsehood, mingled with one burning, one delicious hope. He confessed now that he had deceived himself when he thought his passion was no more; was there any longer a bar to his union with Leoline?

In that delicacy which was breathed into him by his love, he had forborne to seek, or to offer her the insult of consolation. He felt that the shock should be borne alone, and yet he pined, he thirsted, to throw himself at her feet.

Nursing these contending thoughts, he was aroused by a knock at his door; he opened it—the passage was thronged by Leoline's maidens; pale, anxious, weeping. Leoline had left the castle, with but one female attendant; none knew whither;—they knew too soon. From the hall of Sternfels she had passed over in the dark and inclement night, to the valley in which the convent of Bornhofen offered to the weary of spirit and the broken of heart a refuge at the shrine of God.

At daybreak, the next morning, Warbeck was at the convent's gate. He saw Leoline: what a change one night of suffering had made in that face, which was the fountain of all loveliness to him! He clasped her in his arms; he wept; he urged all that love could urge: he besought her to accept that heart, which had never wronged her memory by a thought. "Oh, Leoline! didst thou not say once that these arms nursed thy childhood; that this voice soothed thine early sorrows! Ah, trust to them again and for ever. From a love that forsook thee turn to the love that never swerved."

"No," said Leoline; "No. What would the chivalry of which thou art the boast—what would they say of thee, wert thou to wed one affianced and deserted, who tarried years for another, and brought to thine arms only that heart which he had abandoned? No; and even if thou, as I know thou wouldst be, wert callous to such wrong of thy high name, shall I bring to thee a broken heart and bruised spirit? shalt thou wed sorrow and not joy? and shall sighs that will not cease, and tears that may not be dried, be the only dowry of thy bride? Thou, too, for whom all blessings should be ordained? No, forget me; forget thy poor Leoline! She hath nothing but prayers for thee."

In vain Warbeck pleaded; in vain he urged all that passion and truth could urge; the springs of earthly love were for ever dried up in the orphan's heart, and her resolution was immovable—she tore herself from his arms, and the gate of the convent creaked harshly on his ear.

A new and stern emotion now wholly possessed him; though naturally mild and gentle, he cherished anger, when once it was aroused, with the strength of a calm mind. Leoline's tears, her sufferings, her wrongs, her uncomplaining spirit, the change already stamped upon her face, all cried aloud to him for vengeance. "She is an orphan," said he, bitterly; "she hath none to protect, to redress her, save me alone. My father's charge over her forlorn youth descends of right to me. What matters it whether her forsaker be my brother?—he is *her* foe. Hath he not crushed her heart? Hath he not consigned her to sorrow till the grave? And with what insult; no warning, no excuse; with lewd wassailers keeping revel for his new bridals in the hearing—before the sight—of his betrothed! Enough! the time hath come, when, to use his own words, 'One of us two must fall!'" He half drew his sword as he spoke, and thrusting it back violently into the sheath, strode home to his solitary castle. The sound of steeds and of the hunting-horn met him at his portal; the bridal train of Sternfels, all mirth and gladness, were parting for the chase.

That evening a knight in complete armour entered the banquet-hall of Sternfels, and defied Otho, on the part of Warbeck of Liebenstein, to mortal combat.

Even the Templar was startled by so unnatural a challenge; but Otho, reddening, took up the gage, and the day and spot were fixed. Discontented, wroth with himself, a savage gladness seized him;—he longed to wreak his desperate feelings even on his brother.

Nor had he **ever in his** jealous heart forgiven that brother his virtues and his renown.

At the appointed hour the brothers met **as foes.** Warbeck's visor was **up,** and **all the** settled sternness **of** his soul was stamped upon his brow. But **Otho,** more willing **to** brave the arm than to face the front of his brother, kept his visor down ; the Templar stood by him with folded **arms.** It was **a** study in human passions to his mocking mind. Scarce had the first trump sounded **to** this dread conflict, when **a** new actor entered **on** the scene. The rumour of so unprecedented an event had **not** failed to reach the convent of Bornhofen ;—and now, two by **two,** came the sisters of the holy shrine, **and** the armed men made way, **as** with trailing garments and veiled **faces** they swept along **into** the very lists. At that moment one from amongst them left her sisters with **a** slow majestic pace, and paused not till she stood right between **the** brother foes.

"Warbeck," she said in a hollow voice, **that** curdled up his dark spirit as it spoke, "is it thus thou wouldst **prove thy** love, and maintain thy **trust over** the fatherless orphan **whom thy** sire bequeathed to thy care ? Shall I have murder on **my soul ?"** At that question she paused, and those who heard **it were struck dumb and** shuddered. "**The murder** of one man by **the hand of his own** brother !—Away, **Warbeck !** *I command.*"

"**Shall** I forget **thy wrongs,** Leoline ?" said Warbeck.

"**Wrongs !** they **united me** to God ! they are forgiven, they are **no more. Earth** has **deserted** me, but heaven hath taken me to its arms ;—**shall** I murmur at the change ? **And** thou, Otho—(here her voice faltered)—thou, does thy conscience smite thee not ?—wouldst thou atone for robbing me of hope by barring against me the future ? Wretch that I should be, could I dream of mercy—could I dream of comfort, if thy brother fell by thy sword in my cause ? Otho, I **have** pardoned thee, and blessed thee and thine. Once, perhaps, **thou** didst love me ; remember how I loved thee—cast down thine **arms.**"

Otho gazed at the veiled form before **him.** Where had the soft **Leoline learned** to command ?—He **turned** to his brother ; he felt all **that he had** inflicted upon both ; and casting his sword upon the ground, he knelt at the feet of Leoline, and kissed her garment with a devotion that votary never lavished **on a** holier saint.

The spell that lay over the warriors around was broken ; there was one loud cry of congratulation and joy. "And thou, Warbeck !" said Leoline, turning to the spot where, still motionless and haughty, Warbeck stood.

"Have I ever rebelled against **thy will ?**" said he, softly ; and buried the point of his sword in the earth.—"Yet, Leoline, yet," added he, looking at his kneeling brother, "yet art thou already better avenged than by this steel!"

"Thou art! thou art!" cried Otho, smiting his breast; and slowly, and scarce noting the crowd that fell back from his path, Warbeck left the lists.

Leoline said no more; her divine errand was fulfilled. She looked long and wistfully after the stately form of the knight of Liebenstein, and then, with a slight sign, she turned to Otho, "This is the last time we shall meet on earth. Peace be with us all."

She then, with the same majestic and collected bearing, passed on towards the sisterhood; and as, in the same solemn procession, they glided back towards the convent, there was not a man present —no, not even the hardened Templar—who would not, like Otho, have bent his knee to Leoline.

Once more Otho plunged into the wild revelry of the age; his castle was thronged with guests, and night after night the lighted halls shone down athwart the tranquil Rhine. The beauty of the Greek, the wealth of Otho, the fame of the Templar, attracted all the chivalry from far and near. Never had the banks of the Rhine known so hospitable a lord as the knight of Sternfels. Yet gloom seized him in the midst of gladness, and the revel was welcome only as the escape from remorse. The voice of scandal, however, soon began to mingle with that of envy at the pomp of Otho. The fair Greek, it was said, weary of her lord, lavished her smiles on others: the young and the fair were always most acceptable at the castle; and, above all, her guilty love for the Templar scarcely affected disguise. Otho alone appeared unconscious of the rumour; and though he had begun to neglect his bride, he relaxed not in his intimacy with the Templar.

It was noon, and the Greek was sitting in her bower alone with her suspected lover; the rich perfumes of the East mingled with the fragrance of flowers, and various luxuries, unknown till then in those northern shores, gave a soft and effeminate character to the room.

"I tell thee," said the Greek, petulantly, "that he begins to suspect; that I have seen him watch thee, and mutter as he watched, and play with the hilt of his dagger. Better let us fly ere it is too late, for his vengeance would be terrible were it once roused against us. Ah, why did I ever forsake my own sweet land for these barbarous shores! There, love is not considered eternal, nor inconstancy a crime worthy death."

"Peace, pretty one!" said the Templar, carelessly; "thou knowest not the laws of our foolish chivalry. Thinkest thou I could fly from a knight's halls like a thief in the night? Why, verily, even the red cross would not cover such dishonour. If thou fearest that thy dull lord suspects, let us part. The emperor hath sent to me from Frankfort. Ere evening I might be on my way thither."

"And I left to brave the barbarian's revenge alone? Is this thy chivalry?"

"Nay, prate not so wildly," answered the Templar. "Surely, when the object of his suspicion is gone, thy woman's art and thy Greek wiles can easily allay the jealous fiend. Do I not know thee, Glycera? Why thou would'st fool all men—save a Templar."

"And thou, cruel, wouldst thou leave me?" said the Greek, weeping. "How shall I live without thee?"

The Templar laughed slightly. "Can such eyes ever weep without a comforter? But farewell; I must not be found with thee. To-morrow I depart for Frankfort; we shall meet again."

As soon as the door closed on the Templar, the Greek rose, and pacing the room, said, "Selfish, selfish! how could I ever trust him? Yet I dare not brave Otho alone. Surely it was his step that disturbed us in our yesterday's interview. Nay, I will fly. I can never want a companion."

She clapped her hands; a young page appeared; she threw herself on her seat and wept bitterly.

The page approached, and love was mingled with his compassion.

"Why weepest thou, dearest lady?" said he; "is there aught in which Conrad's services—services!—ah, thou hast read his heart —*his devotion* may avail?"

Otho had wandered out the whole day alone; his vassals had observed that his brow was more gloomy than its wont, for he usually concealed whatever might prey within. Some of the most confidential of his servitors he had conferred with, and the conference had deepened the shadow on his countenance. He returned at twilight; the Greek did not honour the repast with her presence. She was unwell, and not to be disturbed. The gay Templar was the life of the board.

"Thou carriest a sad brow to-day, Sir Otho," said he; "good faith, thou hast caught it from the air of Liebenstein."

"I have something troubles me," answered Otho, forcing a smile, "which I would fain impart to thy friendly bosom. The night is clear and the moon is up, let us forth alone into the garden."

The Templar rose, and he forgot not to gird on his sword as he followed the knight.

Otho led the way to one of the most distant terraces that overhung the Rhine.

"Sir Templar," said he, pausing, "answer me one question on thy knightly honour. Was it thy step that left my lady's bower yester-eve at vesper?"

Startled by so sudden a query, the wily Templar faltered in his reply.

The red blood mounted to Otho's brow. "Nay, lie not, sir knight; these eyes, thanks to God! have not witnessed, but these ears have heard from others of my dishonour."

As Otho spoke, the Templar's eye, resting on the water, perceived a boat rowing fast over the Rhine; the distance forbade him to see more than the outline of two figures within it. "She was right," thought he; "perhaps that boat already bears her from the danger."

Drawing himself up to the full height of his tall stature, the Templar replied haughtily—

"Sir Otho of Sternfels, if thou has deigned to question thy vassals, obtain from them only an answer. It is not to contradict such minions that the knights of the Temple pledge their word!"

"Enough," cried Otho, losing patience, and striking the Templar with his clenched hand. "Draw, traitor, draw!"

Alone in his lofty tower Warbeck watched the night deepen over the heavens, and communed mournfully with himself. "To what end," thought he, "have these strong affections, these capacities of love, this yearning after sympathy, been given me? Unloved and unknown I walk to my grave, and all the nobler mysteries of my heart are for ever to be untold."

Thus musing, he heard not the challenge of the warder on the wall, or the unbarring of the gate below, or the tread of footsteps along the winding stair; the door was thrown suddenly open, and Otho stood before him. "Come," he said, in a low voice trembling with passion; "come, I will show thee that which shall glad thine heart. Twofold is Leoline avenged."

Warbeck looked in amazement on a brother he had not met since they stood in arms each against the other's life, and he now saw that the arm that Otho extended to him dripped with blood, trickling drop by drop upon the floor.

"Come," said Otho, "follow me; it is my last prayer. Come, for Leoline's sake, come."

At that name Warbeck hesitated no longer; he girded on his sword, and followed his brother down the stairs and through the castle gate. The porter scarcely believed his eyes when he saw the two brothers, so long divided, go forth at that hour alone, and seemingly in friendship.

Warbeck, arrived at that epoch in the feelings when nothing stuns, followed with silent steps the rapid strides of his brother. The two castles, as you are aware, are scarce a stone's throw from each other. In a few minutes Otho paused at an open space in one of the terraces of Sternfels, on which the moon shone bright and steady. "Behold!" he said, in a ghastly voice, "behold!" and Warbeck saw on the sward the corpse of the Templar, bathed with the blood that even still poured fast and warm from his heart.

"Hark!" said Otho. "He it was who first made me waver in my vows to Leoline; he persuaded me to wed yon whited falsehood. Hark! he, who had thus wronged my real love, dishonoured me with my faithless bride, and thus—thus—thus"—as grinding his teeth, he spurned again and again the dead body of the Templar—"thus Leoline and myself are avenged!"

"And thy wife?" said Warbeck, pityingly.

"Fled—fled with a hireling page. It is well! she was not worth the sword that was once belted on—by Leoline."

The tradition, dear Gertrude, proceeds to tell us that Otho, though often menaced by the rude justice of the day for the death of the Templar, defied and escaped the menace. On the very night of his revenge a long delirious illness seized him; the generous Warbeck forgave, forgot all, save that he had been once consecrated by Leoline's love. He tended him through his sickness, and when he recovered, Otho was an altered man. He forswore the comrades he had once courted, the revels he had once led. The halls of Sternfels were desolate as those of Liebenstein. The only companion Otho sought was Warbeck, and Warbeck bore with him. They had no topic in common, for on one subject Warbeck at least felt too deeply ever to trust himself to speak; yet did a strange and secret sympathy re-unite them. They had at least a common sorrow; often they were seen wandering together by the solitary banks of the river, or amidst the woods, without apparently interchanging word or sign. Otho died first, and still in the prime of youth; and Warbeck was now left companionless. In vain the imperial court wooed him to its pleasures; in vain the camp proffered him the oblivion of renown. Ah! could he tear himself from a spot where morning and night he could see afar, amidst the valley, the roof that sheltered Leoline, and on which every copse, every turf, reminded him of former days? His solitary life, his midnight vigils, strange scrolls about his chamber, obtained him by degrees the repute of cultivating the darker arts; and shunning, he became shunned by, all. But still it was sweet to hear from time to time of the increasing sanctity of her in whom he had treasured up his last thoughts of earth. She it was who healed the sick; she it was who relieved the poor; and the superstition of that age brought pilgrims from afar to the altars that she served.

Many years afterwards, a band of lawless robbers, who, ever and anon, broke from their mountain fastnesses to pillage and to desolate the valleys of the Rhine; who spared neither sex nor age; neither tower nor hut; nor even the houses of God himself; laid waste the territories round Bornhofen, and demanded treasure from the convent. The abbess, of the bold lineage of Rudesheim, refused the sacrilegious demand; the convent was stormed; its vassals resisted; the robbers, enured to slaughter, won the day; already the gates were forced, when a knight at the head of a small but hardy troop, rushed down from the mountain side, and turned the tide of the fray. Wherever his sword flashed, fell a foe. Wherever his war-cry sounded, was a space of dead men in the thick of the battle. The fight was won; the convent saved; the abbess and the sisterhood came forth to bless their deliverer. Laid under an aged oak, he was bleeding fast to death; his head was bare and his locks were gray, but scarcely yet with years. One only of the sisterhood recognized that majestic face; one bathed his parched lips; one held his dying hand; and in Leoline's presence passed away the faithful spirit of the last lord of Liebenstein!

"Oh!" said Gertrude, through her tears; "surely you must have altered the facts,—surely—surely—it must have been impossible for Leoline, with a woman's heart, to have loved Otho more than Warbeck?"

"My child," said Vane, "so think women when they *read* a tale of love, and see *the whole heart* bared before them; but not so act they in real life—when they see only the surface of character, and pierce not its depths—until it is too late!"

CHAPTER XXV.

THE IMMORTALITY OF THE SOUL.—A COMMON INCIDENT NOT BEFORE DESCRIBED.—TREVYLYAN AND GERTRUDE.

THE day now grew cool as it waned to its decline, and the breeze came sharp upon the delicate frame of the sufferer. They resolved to proceed no further; and as they carried with them attendants and baggage, which rendered their route almost independent of the ordinary accommodation, they steered for the opposite shore, and landed at a village beautifully sequestered in a valley, and where they fortunately obtained a lodging not often met with in the regions of the picturesque.

When Gertrude, at an early hour, retired to bed, Vane and Du——e fell into speculative conversation upon the nature of man. Vane's philosophy was of a quiet and passive scepticism; the physician dared more boldly, and rushed from doubt to negation. The attention of Trevylyan, as he sat apart and musing, was arrested in despite of himself. He listened to an argument in which he took no share; but which suddenly inspired him with an interest in that awful subject which, in the heat of youth and the occupations of the world, had never been so prominently called forth before.

"What!" thought he, with unutterable anguish, as he listened to the earnest vehemence of the Frenchman and the tranquil assent of Vane; "if this creed were indeed true,—if there be no other world—Gertrude is lost to me eternally,—through the dread gloom of death there would break forth no star!"

That is a peculiar incident that perhaps occurs to us all at times, but which I have never found expressed in books;—viz. to hear a doubt of futurity at the very moment in which the present is most overcast; and to find at once this world stripped of its delusion, and the next of its consolation. It is perhaps for others, rather than ourselves, that the fond heart requires an Hereafter. The tranquil rest, the shadow, and the silence, the mere pause of the wheel of life, have no terror for the wise, who know the due value of the world—

"After the billows of a stormy sea,
Sweet is at last the haven of repose!"

But not so when that stillness is to divide us eternally from others; when those we have loved with all the passion, the devotion, the watchful sanctity of the weak human heart, are to exist to us no more!—when, after long years of desertion and widowhood on earth, there is to be no hope of re-union in that INVISIBLE beyond the stars; when the torch, not of life only, but of love, is to be quenched in the Dark Fountain; and the grave, that we would fain hope is the great restorer of broken ties, is but the dumb seal of hopeless—utter—inexorable separation! And it is this thought—this sentiment, which makes religion out of woe, and teaches belief to the mourning heart, that in the gladness of united affections felt not the necessity of a heaven! To how many is the death of the beloved, the parent of faith!

Stung by his thoughts, Trevylyan rose abruptly, and stealing from the lowly hostelry, walked forth amidst the serene and deepening night; from the window of Gertrude's room the light streamed calm on the purple air.

With uneven steps and many a pause, he paced to and fro beneath the window, and gave the rein to his thoughts. How intensely he felt the ALL that Gertrude was to him! how bitterly he foresaw the change in his lot and character that her death would work out! For who that met him in later years ever dreamed that emotions so soft, and yet so ardent, had visited one so stern? Who could have believed that time was, when the polished and cold Trevylyan had kept the vigils he now held below the chamber of one so little like himself as Gertrude, in that remote and solitary hamlet; shut in by the haunted mountains of the Rhine, and beneath the moonlight of the romantic North?

While thus engaged, the light in Gertrude's room was suddenly extinguished; it is impossible to express how much that trivial incident affected him! It was like an emblem of what was to come; the light had been the only evidence of life that broke upon that hour, and he was now left alone with the shades of night. Was not this like the herald of Gertrude's own death; the extinction of the only living ray that broke upon the darkness of the world?

His anguish, his presentiment of utter desolation, increased. He groaned aloud; he dashed his clenched hand to his breast—large and cold drops of agony stole down his brow. "Father," he exclaimed with a struggling voice, "let this cup pass from me! Smite my ambition to the root; curse me with poverty, shame, and bodily disease; but leave me this one solace, this one companion of my fate!"

At this moment Gertrude's window opened gently, and he heard her accents steal soothingly upon his ear.

"Is not that your voice, Albert?" said she, softly. "I heard it just as I laid down to rest, and could not sleep while you were thus exposed to the damp night air. You do not answer; surely it is your voice: when did I mistake it for another's?"

Mastering with a violent effort his emotions, Trevylyan answered, with a sort of convulsive gaiety—

"Why come to these shores, dear Gertrude, unless you are honoured with the chivalry that belongs to them? What wind, what blight, can harm me while within the circle of your presence; and what sleep can bring me dreams so dear as the waking thought of you?"

"It is cold," said Gertrude, shivering; "come in, dear Albert, I beseech you, and I will thank you to-morrow." Gertrude's voice was choked by the hectic cough, that went like an arrow to Trevylyan's heart; and he felt that in her anxiety for him she was now exposing her own frame to the unwholesome night.

He spoke no more, but hurried within the house; and when the gray light of morn broke upon his gloomy features, haggard from the want of sleep, it might have seemed, in that dim eye and fast-sinking cheek, as if the lovers were not to be divided—even by death itself.

CHAPTER XXVI.

IN WHICH THE READER WILL LEARN HOW THE FAIRIES WERE RECEIVED BY THE SOVEREIGNS OF THE MINES.—THE COMPLAINT OF THE LAST OF THE FAUNS.—THE RED HUNTSMAN.—THE STORM.—DEATH.

IN the deep valley of Ehrenthal, the metal kings—the Prince of the Silver Palaces, the Gnome Monarch of the dull Lead Mine, the President of the Copper United States, held a court to receive the fairy wanderers from the island of Nonnewërth.

The prince was there, in a gallant hunting suit of oak leaves, in honour to England; and wore a profusion of fairy orders, which had been instituted from time to time, in honour of the human poets that had celebrated the spiritual and ethereal tribes. Chief of these, sweet Dreamer of the Midsummer Night's Dream, was the badge crystallized from the dews that rose above the whispering reeds of Avon, on the night of thy birth—the great epoch of the intellectual world! Nor wert thou, O beloved Musæus! nor thou, dim-dreaming Tieck! nor were ye, the wild imaginer of the bright-haired

Undine, and the wayward spirit that invoked for the gloomy Manfred the Witch of the breathless Alps, and the spirits of earth and air!—nor were ye without the honours of fairy homage! Your memory may fade from the heart of man, and the spells of new enchanters may succeed to the charm you once wove over the face of the common world; but still in the green knolls of the haunted valley and the deep shade of forests, and the starred palaces of air, ye are honoured by the beings of your dreams, as demigods and kings! Your graves are tended by invisible hands, and the places of your birth are hallowed by no perishable worship.

Even as I write;[1] far away amidst the hills of Scotland, and by the forest thou hast clothed with immortal verdure; thou, the waker of "the Harp by lone Glenfillan's spring," art passing from the earth which thou hast "painted with delight." And, such are the chances of mortal fame, our children's children may raise new idols on the site of thy holy altar, and cavil where their sires adored; but for thee the mermaid of the ocean shall wail in her coral caves; and the sprite that lives in the waterfalls shall mourn! Strange shapes shall hew thy monument in the recesses of the lonely rocks; ever by moonlight shall the fairies pause from their roundel when some wild note of their minstrelsy reminds them of thine own;—ceasing from their revelries, to weep for the silence of that mighty lyre, which breathed alike a revelation of the mysteries of spirits and of men!

The King of the Silver Mines sat in a cavern in the valley, through which the moonlight pierced its way and slept in shadow on the soil shining with metals wrought into unnumbered shapes; and below him, on a humbler throne, with a gray beard and downcast eye, sat the aged King of the Dwarfs that preside over the dull realms of lead, and inspire the verse of——, and the prose of——! And there too a fantastic household elf, was the President of the Copper Republic—a spirit that loves economy and the Uses, and smiles sparely on the Beautiful. But, in the centre of the cave, upon beds of the softest mosses, the untrodden growth of ages, reclined the fairy visitors—Nymphalin seated by her betrothed. And round the walls of the cave were dwarf attendants on the sovereigns of the metals, of a thousand odd shapes and fantastic garments. On the abrupt ledges of the rocks the bats, charmed to stillness but not sleep, clustered thickly, watching the scene with fixed and amazed eyes; and one old gray owl, the favourite of the witch of the valley, sat blinking in a corner, listening with all her might that she might bring home the scandal to her mistress.

[1] It was just at the time the author was finishing this work that the great master of his art was drawing to the close of his career.

"And tell me, Prince of the Rhine-Island Fays," said the King of the Silver Mines, "for thou art a traveller, and a fairy that hath seen much, how go men's affairs in the upper world? As to ourself, we live here in a stupid splendour, and only hear the news of the day when our brother of lead pays a visit to the English printing-press, or the President of Copper goes to look at his improvements in steam-engines."

"Indeed," replied Fayzenheim, preparing to speak, like Æneas in the Carthaginian court; "indeed, your majesty, I know not much that will interest you in the present aspect of mortal affairs, except that you are quite as much honoured at this day as when the Roman conqueror bent his knee to you among the mountains of Taunus: and a vast number of little round subjects of yours are constantly carried about by the rich, and pined after with hopeless adoration by the poor. But, begging your majesty's pardon, may I ask what has become of your cousin, the King of the Golden Mines? I know very well that he has no dominion in these valleys, and do not therefore wonder at his absence from your court this night; but I see so little of his subjects on earth that I should fear his empire was well nigh at an end, if I did not recognize everywhere the most servile homage paid to a power now become almost invisible."

The King of the Silver Mines fetched a deep sigh. "Alas, prince," said he, "too well do you divine the expiration of my cousin's empire. So many of his subjects have from time to time gone forth to the world, pressed into military service and never returning, that his kingdom is nearly depopulated. And he lives far off in the distant parts of the earth, in a state of melancholy seclusion; the age of gold has passed, the age of paper has commenced."

"Paper," said Nymphalin, who was still somewhat of a *précieuse;* "paper is a wonderful thing. What pretty books the human people write upon it!"

"Ah! that's what I design to convey," said the silver king. "It is the age less of paper money than paper government: the press is the true bank." The lord treasurer of the English fairies pricked up his ears at the word "bank." For he was the Attwood of the fairies: he had a favourite plan of making money out of bulrushes, and had written four large bees'-wings full upon the true nature of capital.

While they were thus conversing, a sudden sound as of some rustic and rude music broke along the air, and closing its wild burden, they heard the following song:—

THE COMPLAINT OF THE LAST FAUN.

I.

The moon on the Latmos mountain
    Her pining vigil keeps;
And ever the silver fountain
    In the Dorian valley weeps.
But gone are Endymion's dreams;—
    And the crystal lymph
    Bewails the nymph
Whose beauty sleeked the streams!

II.

Round Arcady's oak, its green
    The Bromian ivy weaves;
But no more is the satyr seen
    Laughing out from the glossy leaves.
Hushed is the Lycian lute,
    Still grows the seed
    Of the Mœnale reed,
But the pipe of Pan is mute!

III.

The leaves in the noon-day quiver;—
    The vines on the mountains wave;—
And Tiber rolls his river
    As fresh by the Sylvan's cave;
But my brothers are dead and gone;
    And far away
    From their graves I stray,
And dream of the Past alone!

IV.

And the sun of the north is chill;—
    And keen is the northern gale;—
Alas for the song on the Argive hill;
    And the dance in the Cretan vale!—
The youth of the earth is o'er,
    And its breast is rife
    With the teeming life
Of the golden Tribes no more!

V.

My race are more blest than I,
    Asleep in their distant bed;
'Twere better, be sure, to die
    Than to mourn for the buried Dead;—
To rove by the stranger streams,
    At dusk and dawn
    A lonely faun,
The last of the Grecian's dreams.

As the song ended a shadow crossed the moonlight, that lay white and lustrous before the aperture of the cavern; and Nymphalin, looking up, beheld a graceful, yet grotesque figure standing on the sward without, and gazing on the group in the cave. It was a shaggy form, with a goat's legs and ears; but the rest of its body, and the height of the stature, like a man's. An arch, pleasant, yet malicious smile, played about its lips; and in its hand it held the pastoral pipe of which poets have sung;—they would find it difficult to sing to it!

"And who art thou?" said Fayzenheim, with the air of a hero.

"I am the last lingering wanderer of the race which the Romans worshipped: hither I followed their victorious steps, and in these green hollows have I remained. Sometimes in the still noon, when the leaves of spring bud upon the whispering woods, I peer forth from my rocky lair, and startle the peasant with my strange voice and stranger shape. Then goes he home, and puzzles his thick brain with mopes and fancies, till at length he imagines me, the creature of the south! one of his northern demons, and his poets adapt the apparition to their barbarous lines."

"Ho!" quoth the silver king, "surely thou art the origin of the fabled Satan of the cowled men living whilom in yonder ruins, with its horns and goatish limbs: and the harmless faun has been made the figuration of the most implacable of fiends. But why, O wanderer of the south! lingerest thou in these foreign dells? Why returnest thou not to the bi-forked hill-top of old Parnassus, or the wastes around the yellow course of the Tiber?"

"My brethren are no more," said the poor faun; "and the very faith that left us sacred and unharmed is departed. But here all the spirits not of mortality are still honoured; and I wander, mourning for Silenus; though amidst the vines that should console me for his loss."

"Thou hast known great beings in thy day," said the leaden king, who loved the philosophy of a truism (and the history of whose inspirations I shall one day write).

"Ah, yes," said the faun, "my birth was amidst the freshness of the world when the flush of the universal life coloured all things with divinity; when not a tree but had its Dryad—not a fountain that was without its Nymph. I sat by the gray throne of Saturn, in his old age, ere yet he was discrowned (for he was no visionary ideal, but the arch monarch of the pastoral age): and heard from his lips the history of the world's birth. But those times are gone for ever—they have left harsh successors."

"It is the age of paper," muttered the lord treasurer, shaking his head.

"What ho, for a dance!" cried Fayzenheim, too royal for moralities, and he whirled the beautiful Nymphalin into a waltz. Then forth issued the fairies, and out went the dwarfs. And the faun leaning against an aged elm, ere yet the midnight waned, the elves danced their charmed round to the antique minstrelsy of his pipe—the minstrelsy of the Grecian world!

"Hast thou seen yet, my Nymphalin," said Fayzenheim, in the pauses of the dance, "the recess of the Hartz, and the red form of its mighty hunter?"

"It is a fearful sight," answered Nymphalin: "but with thee I should not fear."

"Away then," cried Fayzenheim; "let us away, at the first cock-crow, into those shaggy dells, for, there, is no need of night to conceal us, and the unwitnessed blush of morn, or the dreary silence of noon, is no less than the moon's reign, the season for the sports of the superhuman tribes."

Nymphalin, charmed with the proposal, readily assented, and at the last hour of night, bestriding the star-beams of the many-titled Friga, away sped the fairy cavalcade to the gloom of the mystic Hartz.

Fain would I relate the manner of their arrival in the thick recesses of the forest; how they found the Red Hunter seated on a fallen pine beside a wide chasm in the earth, with the arching boughs of the wizard oak wreathing above his head as a canopy, and his bow and spear lying idle at his feet. Fain would I tell of the reception which he deigned to the fairies, and how he told them of his ancient victories over man; how he chafed at the gathering invasions of his realm; and how joyously he gloated of some great convulsion[1] in the northern states, which, rapt into moody reveries in those solitary woods, the fierce demon broodingly foresaw. All these fain would I narrate, but they are not of the Rhine, and my story will not brook the delay. While thus conversing with the fiend, noon had crept on and the sky had become overcast and lowering; the giant trees waved gustily to and fro, and the low gatherings of the thunder announced the approaching storm. Then the hunter rose and stretched his mighty limbs, and seizing his spear, he strode rapidly into the forest to meet the things of his own tribe that the tempest wakes from their rugged lair.

A sudden recollection broke upon Nymphalin. "Alas, alas!"

---

[1] Which has come to pass. 1847.

she cried, wringing her hands; "what have I done! In journeying hither with thee, I have forgotten my office. I have neglected my watch over the elements, and my human charge is at this hour, perhaps, exposed to all the fury of the storm."

"Cheer thee, my Nymphalin," said the prince, "we will lay the tempest;" and he waved his sword and muttered the charms which curb the winds and roll back the marching thunder: but for once the tempest ceased not at his spells; and now, as the fairies sped along the troubled air, a pale and beautiful form met them by the way, and the fairies paused and trembled. For the power of that Shape could vanquish even them. It was the form of a Female, with golden hair, crowned with a chaplet of withered leaves; her bosoms, of an exceeding beauty, lay bare to the wind, and an infant was clasped between them, hushed into a sleep so still, that neither the roar of the thunder, nor the livid lightning flashing from cloud to cloud, could even ruffle, much less arouse, the slumberer. And the face of the Female was unutterably calm and sweet (though with a something of severe), there was no line nor wrinkle in her hueless brow; care never wrote its defacing characters upon that everlasting beauty. It knew no sorrow or change; ghost-like and shadowy floated on that Shape through the abyss of Time, governing the world with an unquestioned and noiseless sway. And the children of the green solitudes of the earth, the lovely fairies of my tale, shuddered as they gazed and recognized—the form of DEATH!

DEATH VINDICATED.

"And why," said the beautiful Shape, with a voice soft as the last sighs of a dying babe; "why trouble ye the air with spells? mine is the hour and the empire, and the storm is the creature of my power. Far yonder to the west it sweeps over the sea, and the ship ceases to vex the waves; it smites the forest, and the destined tree, torn from its roots, feels the winter strip the gladness from its boughs no more! The roar of the elements is the herald of eternal stillness to their victims; and they who hear the progress of my power idly shudder at the coming of peace. And thou, O tender daughter of the faery kings! why grievest thou at a mortal's doom? Knowest thou not that sorrow cometh with years, and that to live is to mourn? Blessed is the flower that, nipped in its early spring, feels not the blast that one by one scatters its blossoms around it, and leaves but the barren stem. Blessed are the young whom I clasp to my breast, and lull into the sleep which the storm cannot break, nor the morrow arouse to sorrow or to toil. The heart that is stilled in the bloom of its first emotions,—that turns with its last throb to the eye of love, as yet unlearned in the possibility of change,—has exhausted already the wine of life, and is saved only from the lees. As the mother soothes to sleep the wail of her troubled child, I open my arms to the vexed spirit, and my bosom cradles the unquiet to repose!"

The fairies answered not, for a chill and a fear lay over them, and the Shape glided on; ever as it passed away through the veiling clouds they heard its low voice singing amidst the roar of the storm, as the dirge of the water-sprite over the vessel it hath lured into the whirlpool or the shoals.

CHAPTER XXVII.

THURMBERG.—A STORM UPON THE RHINE.—THE RUINS OF RHEINFELS.—PERIL UNFELT BY LOVE.—THE ECHO OF THE LURLEI-BERG.—ST. GOAR.—CAUB, GUTENFELS, AND PFALZ-GRAFENSTEIN.—A CERTAIN VASTNESS OF MIND IN THE FIRST HERMITS.—THE SCENERY OF THE RHINE TO BACHARACH.

OUR party continued their voyage the next day, which was less bright than any they had yet experienced. The clouds swept on dull and heavy, suffering the sun only to break forth at scattered intervals; they wound round the curving bay which the Rhine forms in that part of its course; and gazed upon the ruins of Thurmberg with the rich gardens that skirt the banks below. The last time Trevylyan had seen those ruins soaring against the sky, the green foliage at the foot of the rocks, and the quiet village sequestered beneath, glassing its roofs and solitary tower upon the wave, it had been with a gay summer troop of light friends, who had paused on the opposite shore during the heats of noon, and, over wine and fruits, had mimicked the groups of Boccaccio, and intermingled the lute, the jest, the momentary love, and the laughing tale.

What a difference now in his thoughts—in the object of the voyage—in his present companions! The feet of years fall noiseless; we heed, we note them not, till tracking the same course we passed long since, we are startled to find how deep the impression they leave behind. To revisit the scenes of our youth is to commune with the ghost of ourselves.

At this time the clouds gathered rapidly along the heavens, and they were startled by the first peal of the thunder. Sudden and swift came on the storm, and Trevylyan trembled as he covered Gertrude's form with the rude boat-cloaks they had brought with them; the small vessel began to rock wildly to and fro upon the waters. High above them rose the vast dismantled Ruins of Rheinfels, the lightning darting through its shattered casements and broken arches, and brightening the gloomy trees that here and there clothed the rocks, and tossed to the angry wind. Swift wheeled the water birds over the river, dipping their plumage in the white foam, and uttering their discordant screams. A storm upon the Rhine has a grandeur it is in vain to paint. Its rocks, its foliage, the feudal ruins that everywhere rise from the lofty heights—speaking in characters of stern decay of many a former battle against time and tempest; the broad and rapid course of the legendary river, all harmonize with the elementary strife; and you feel that to see the Rhine only in the sunshine is to be unconscious of its most majestic aspects. What baronial war had those ruins witnessed! From the rapine of the lordly tyrant of those battlements rose the first Confederation of the Rhine—the great strife between the new time and the old—the town and the castle—the citizen and the chief. Gray and stern those ruins breasted the storm—a type of the antique opinion which once manned them with armed serfs; and, yet in ruins and decay, appeals from the victorious freedom it may no longer resist!

Clasped in Trevylyan's guardian arms, and her head pillowed on his breast, Gertrude felt nothing of the storm save its grandeur; and Trevylyan's voice whispered cheer and courage to her ear. She answered by a smile, and a sigh, but not of pain. In the convulsions of nature we forget our own separate existence, our schemes, our projects, our fears; our dreams vanish back into their cells. One passion only the storm quells not, and the presence of Love mingles with the voice of the fiercest storms, as with the whispers of the southern wind. So she felt, as they were thus drawn close together, and as she strove to smile away the anxious terror from Trevylyan's gaze—a security, a delight: for peril is sweet even to the fears of woman, when it impresses upon her yet more vividly that she is beloved.

"A moment more and we reach the land," murmured Trevylyan.

"I wish it not," answered Gertrude, softly. But ere they got into St. Goar the rain descended in torrents, and even the thick coverings round Gertrude's form were not sufficient protection against it. Wet and dripping she reached the inn: but not then, nor for some days, was she sensible of the shock her decaying health had received.

The storm lasted but a few hours, and the sun afterwards broke forth so brightly, and the stream looked so inviting, that they yielded to Gertrude's earnest wish, and, taking a larger vessel, continued their course: they passed along the narrow and dangerous defile of the Gewirre, and the fearful whirlpool of the "Bank;" and on the shore to the left the enormous rock of Lurlei rose, huge and shapeless, on their gaze. In this place is a singular echo, and one of the boatmen wound a horn, which produced an almost supernatural music—so wild, loud, and oft reverberated was its sound.

The river now curved along in a narrow and deep channel amongst rugged steeps, on which the westering sun cast long and uncouth shadows: and here the hermit, from whose sacred name the town of St. Goar derived its own, fixed his abode and preached the religion of the Cross. "There was a certain vastness of mind," said Vane, "in the adoption of utter solitude, in which the first enthusiasts of our religion indulged. The remote desert, the solitary rock, the rude dwelling hollowed from the cave, the eternal commune with their own hearts, with nature, and their dreams of God, all make a picture of severe and preterhuman grandeur. Say what we will of the necessity and charm of social life, there is a greatness about man when he dispenses with mankind."

"As to that," said Du——e, shrugging his shoulders, "there was probably very good wine in the neighbourhood, and the females' eyes about Oberwesel are singularly blue."

They now approached Oberwesel, another of the once imperial towns, and behind it beheld the remains of the castle of the illustrious family of Schomberg: the ancestors of the old hero of the Boyne. A little further on, from the opposite shore, the castle of Gutenfels rose above the busy town of Kaub.

"Another of those scenes," said Trevylyan, "celebrated equally by love and glory, for the castle's name is derived from that of the beautiful ladye of an emperor's passion; and below, upon a ridge in the steep, the great Gustavus issued forth his command to begin battle with the Spaniards."

"It looks peaceful enough now," said Vane, pointing to the craft that lay along the stream, and the green trees drooping over a curve in the bank. Beyond, in the middle of the stream itself, stands the lonely castle of Pfalzgrafenstein, sadly memorable as a prison to the more distinguished of criminals. How many pining eyes may have turned from those casements to the vine-clad hills of the free shore;

how many indignant hearts have nursed the deep curses of hate in the dungeons below, and longed for the wave that dashed against the gray walls to force its way within and set them free!

Here the Rhine seems utterly bounded, shrunk into one of those delusive lakes into which it so frequently seems to change its course; and as you proceed, it is as if the waters were silently overflowing their channel and forcing their way into the clefts of the mountain shore. Passing the Werth Island on one side, and the castle of Stahleck on the other, our voyagers arrived at Bacharach, which, associating the feudal recollections with the classic, takes its name from the god of the vine; and as Du——e declared with peculiar emphasis, quaffing a large goblet of the peculiar liquor, "richly deserves the honour!"

CHAPTER XXVIII.

THE VOYAGE TO BINGEN.—THE SIMPLE INCIDENTS IN THIS TALE EXCUSED.—THE SITUATION AND CHARACTER OF GERTRUDE.—THE CONVERSATION OF THE LOVERS IN THE TEMPLE.—A FACT CONTRADICTED.—THOUGHTS OCCASIONED BY A MADHOUSE AMONGST THE MOST BEAUTIFUL LANDSCAPES OF THE RHINE.

THE next day they again resumed their voyage, and Gertrude's spirits were more cheerful than usual: the air seemed to her lighter, and she breathed with a less painful effort; once more hope entered the breast of Trevylyan; and, as the vessel bounded on, their conversation was steeped in no sombre hues. When Gertrude's health permitted, no temper was so gay, yet so gently gay, as hers; and now the *naïve* sportiveness of her remarks called a smile to the placid lip of Vane, and smoothed the anxious front of Trevylyan himself; as for Du——e, who had much of the boon companion beneath his professional gravity, he broke out every now and then into snatches of French songs and drinking glees, which he declared were the result of the air of Bacharach. Thus conversing, the ruins of Furstenberg, and the echoing vale of Rheindeibach, glided past their sail. Then the old town of Lorch, on the opposite bank (where the red wine is said first to have been made), with the green island before it in the water. Winding round, the stream showed castle upon castle alike in ruins, and built alike upon scarce accessible steeps. Then came the chapel of St. Clements, and the opposing village of Asmannshausen; the lofty Rossell, built at the extremest verge of the cliff; and now the tower of Hatto, celebrated by Southey's ballad; and the ancient town of Bingen. Here they paused awhile from their voyage, with the intention of visiting more minutely the Rheingau, or valley of the Rhine.

It must occur to every one of my readers that, in undertaking, as now, in these passages in the history of Trevylyan, scarcely so much a tale as an episode in real life, it is very difficult to offer any interest save of the most simple and unexciting kind. It is true that to Trevylyan every day, every hour had its incident; but what are those incidents to others? A cloud in the sky; a smile from the lip of Gertrude; these were to him far more full of events than had been the most varied scenes of his former adventurous career; but the history of the heart is not easily translated into language; and the world will not readily pause from its business to watch the alternations in the cheek of a dying girl.

In the immense sum of human existence, what is a single unit? Every sod on which we tread is the grave of some former being: yet is there something that softens without enervating the heart, in tracing in the life of another those emotions that all of us have known ourselves. For who is there that has not, in his progress through life, felt all its ordinary business arrested, and the varieties of fate commuted into one chronicle of the affections? Who has not watched over the passing away of some being, more to him, at that epoch, than all the world? And this unit, so trivial to the calculation of others, of what inestimable value was it not to him? Retracing in another such recollections, shadowed and mellowed down by time, we feel the wonderful sanctity of human life, we feel what emotions a single being can awake; what a world of hope may be buried in a single grave. And thus we keep alive within ourselves the soft springs of that morality which unites us with our kind, and sheds over the harsh scenes and turbulent contests of earth the colouring of a common love.

There is often, too, in the time of year in which such thoughts are presented to us, a certain harmony with the feelings they awaken. As I write, I hear the last sighs of the departing summer, and the sere and yellow leaf is visible in the green of nature. But, when this book goes forth into the world, the year will have passed through a deeper cycle of decay; and the first melancholy signs of winter have breathed into the Universal Mind that sadness which associates itself readily with the memory of friends, of feelings, that are no more. The seasons, like ourselves, track their course, by something of beauty, or of glory, that is left behind. As the traveller in the land of Palestine sees tomb after tomb rise before him, the landmarks of his way, and the only signs of the holiness of the soil; thus Memory wanders over the most sacred spots in its various world, and traces them but by the graves of the Past.

It was now that Gertrude began to feel the shock her frame had received in the storm upon the Rhine. Cold shiverings frequently seized her; her cough became more hollow, and her form trembled at the slightest breeze.

Vane grew seriously alarmed; he repented that he had yielded to Gertrude's wish of substituting the Rhine for the Tiber or the Arno; and would even now have hurried across the Alps to a warmer clime, if Du——e had not declared that she could not survive the journey, and that her sole chance of regaining her strength was rest. Gertrude herself, however, in the continued delusion of her disease, clung to the belief of recovery, and still supported the hopes of her father, and soothed, with secret talk of the future, the anguish of her betrothed. The reader may remember that, the most touching passage in the ancient tragedians, the most pathetic part of the most pathetic of human poets—the pleading speech of Iphigenia, when imploring for her prolonged life, she impresses you with so soft a picture of its innocence and its beauty, and in this Gertrude resembled the Greek's creation—that she felt, on the verge of death, all the flush, the glow, the loveliness of life. Her youth was filled with hope, and many-coloured dreams; she loved, and the hues of morning slept upon the yet disenchanted earth. The heavens to her were not as the common sky; the wave had its peculiar music to her ear, and the rustling leaves a pleasantness that none, whose heart is not bathed in the love and sense of beauty, could discern. Therefore it was, in future years, a thought of deep gratitude to Trevylyan that she was so little sensible of her danger; that the landscape caught not the gloom of the grave; and that, in the Greek phrase, "death found her sleeping amongst flowers."

At the end of a few days, another of those sudden turns, common to her malady, occurred in Gertrude's health; her youth and her happiness rallied against the encroaching tyrant, and for the ensuing fortnight she seemed once more within the bounds of hope. During this time they made several excursions into the Rheingau, and finished their tour at the ancient Heidelberg.

One morning, in these excursions, after threading the wood of Niederwald, they gained that small and fairy temple, which hanging lightly over the mountain's brow, commands one of the noblest landscapes of earth. There, seated side by side, the lovers looked over the beautiful world below; far to the left lay the happy islets, in the embrace of the Rhine, as it wound along the low and curving meadows that stretch away towards Nieder Ingelheim and Mayence. Glistening in the distance, the opposite Nah swept by the Mause tower, and the ruins of Klopp, crowning the ancient Bingen, into the mother tide. There, on either side the town, were the mountains of St. Roch and Rupert, with some old monastic ruin, saddening in the sun. But nearer, below the temple, contrasting all the other features of landscape, yawned a dark and rugged gulf, girt by cragged elms and mouldering towers, the very prototype of the abyss of time—black and fathomless amidst ruin and desolation.

"I think, sometimes," said Gertrude, "as in scenes like these, we sit together, and, rapt from the actual world, see only the enchantment that distance lends to our view—I think sometimes, what pleasure it will be hereafter to recall these hours. If ever you should love me less, I need only to whisper to you, 'The Rhine,' and will not all the feelings you have now for me return?"

"Ah! there will never be occasion to recall my love for you, it can never decay."

"What a strange thing is life!" said Gertrude; "how unconnected, how desultory seem all its links! Has this sweet pause from trouble, from the ordinary cares of life—has it anything in common with your past career—with your future? You will go into the great world; in a few years hence these moments of leisure and musing will be denied to you; the action that you love and court is a jealous sphere; it allows no wandering, no repose. These moments will then seem to you but as yonder islands that stud the Rhine—the stream lingers by them for a moment, and then hurries on in its rapid course; they vary, but they do not interrupt the tide."

"You are fanciful, my Gertrude; but your simile might be juster. Rather let these banks be as our lives, and this river the one thought that flows eternally by both, blessing each with undying freshness."

Gertrude smiled; and, as Trevylyan's arm encircled her, she sunk her beautiful face upon his bosom, he covered it with his kisses, and she thought at the moment, that, even had she passed death, that embrace could have recalled her to life.

They pursued their course to Mayence, partly by land, partly along the river. One day, as returning from the vine-clad mountains of Johannisberg, which commands the whole of the Rheingau, the most beautiful valley in the world, they proceeded by water to the town of Ellfeld, Gertrude said,

"There is a thought in your favourite poet which you have often repeated, and which I cannot think true,

> 'In nature there is nothing melancholy.'

To me, it seems as if a certain melancholy were inseparable from beauty; in the sunniest noon there is a sense of solitude and stillness which pervades the landscape, and even in the flush of life inspires us with a musing and tender sadness. Why is this?"

"I cannot tell," said Trevylyan, mournfully; "but I allow that it is true."

"It is as if," continued the romantic Gertrude, "the spirit of the world spoke to us in the silence, and filled us with a sense of our mortality—a whisper from the religion that belongs to nature, and is ever seeking to unite the earth with the reminiscences of Heaven. Ah, what without a heaven would be even love!—a perpetual terror of the separation that must one day come! If," she resumed, solemnly, after a momentary pause, and a shadow settled on her young face, "if it be true, Albert, that I must leave you soon——"

"It cannot—it cannot!" cried Trevylyan, wildly; "be still, be silent, I beseech you."

"Look yonder," said Du——e, breaking seasonably in upon the conversation of the lovers; "on that hill to the left, what once was an abbey is now an asylum for the insane. Does it not seem a quiet and serene abode for the unstrung and erring minds that tenant it? What a mystery is there in our conformation!—those strange and bewildered fancies which replace our solid reason, what a moral of our human weakness do they breathe!"

It does indeed induce a dark and singular train of thought, when, in the midst of these lovely scenes, we chance upon this lone retreat for those on whose eyes Nature, perhaps, smiles in vain? *Or is it in vain?* They look down upon the broad Rhine, with its tranquil isles; do their wild illusions endow the river with another name, and people the valleys with no living shapes! Does the broken mirror within reflect back the countenance of real things, or shadows and shapes, crossed, mingled, and bewildered,—the phantasma of a sick man's dreams? Yet, perchance, one memory unscathed by the general ruin of the brain can make even the beautiful Rhine more beautiful than it is to the common eye;—can calm it with the hues of departed love, and bid its possessor walk over its vine-clad mountains with the beings that have ceased to *be!* There, perhaps, the self-made monarch sits upon his throne and claims the vessels as his fleet, the waves and the valleys as his own. There, the enthusiast, blasted by the light of some imaginary creed, beholds the shapes of angels, and watches in the clouds round the setting sun, the pavilions of God. There the victim of forsaken or perished love, mightier than the sorcerers of old, evokes the dead, or recalls the faithless by the philtre of undying fancies. Ah, blessed art thou, the winged power of Imagination that is within us!—conquering even grief—brightening even despair. Thou takest us from the world when reason can no longer bind us to it, and givest to the maniac the inspiration and the solace of the bard! Thou, the parent of the purer love, lingerest like love, when even ourself forsakes us, and lightest up the shattered chambers of the heart with the glory that makes a sanctity of decay!

CHAPTER XXIX.

ELLFELD.—MAYENCE.—HEIDELBERG.—A CONVERSATION BETWEEN VANE AND THE GERMAN STUDENT.—THE RUINS OF THE CASTLE OF HEIDELBERG AND ITS SOLITARY HABITANT.

IT was now the full noon; light clouds were bearing up towards the opposite banks of the Rhine, but over the Gothic Towers of Ellfeld the sky spread blue and clear; the river danced beside the old gray walls with a sunny wave, and close at hand a vessel crowded with passengers, and loud with eager voices, gave a merry life to the scene. On the opposite bank the hills sloped away into the far horizon, and one slight skiff in the midst of the waters broke the solitary brightness of the noonday calm.

The town of Ellfeld was the gift of Otho the First to the Church; not far from thence is the crystal spring that gives its name to the delicious grape of Markbrunner.

"Ah!" quoth Du——e, "doubtless the good bishops of Mayence made the best of the vicinity!"

They stayed some little time at this town, and visited the ruins of Scharfenstein; thence proceeding up the river, they passed Nieder Walluf, called the Gate of the Rheingau, and the luxuriant garden of Schierstein; thence, sailing by the castle-seat of the Prince Nassau Usingen, and passing two long and narrow isles they arrived at Mayence, as the sun shot his last rays upon the waters, gilding the proud cathedral-spire, and breaking the mists that began to gather behind, over the rocks of the Rheingau.

Ever-memorable Mayence!—memorable alike for freedom and for song—within those walls how often woke the gallant music of the Troubadour; and how often beside that river did the heart of the maiden tremble to the lay! Within those walls the stout Walpoden first broached the great scheme of the Hanseatic league; and, more than all, O memorable Mayence, thou canst claim the first invention of the mightiest engine of human intellect,—the great leveller of power,—the Demiurgus of the moral world,—the Press! Here too lived the maligned hero of the greatest drama of modern genius, the traditional Faust, illustrating in himself the fate of his successors in dispensing knowledge—held a monster for his wisdom, and consigned to the penalties of hell as a recompense for the benefits he had conferred on earth!

At Mayence, Gertrude heard so much and so constantly of Heidelberg, that she grew impatient to visit that enchanting town, and as Du——e considered the air of Heidelberg more pure and invigorating than that of Mayence, they resolved to fix within it their temporary residence. Alas! it was the place destined to close their brief and melancholy pilgrimage, and to become to the heart of Trevylyan the holiest spot which the earth contained;—the KAABA of the world. But Gertrude, unconscious of her fate, conversed gaily as their carriage rolled rapidly on, and, constantly alive to every new sensation, she touched with her characteristic vivacity on all they had seen in their previous route. There is a great charm in the observations of one new to the world, if we ourselves have become somewhat tired of "its hack sights and sounds;" we hear in their freshness a voice from our own youth.

In the haunted valley of the Neckar, the most crystal of rivers, stands the town of Heidelberg. The shades of evening gathered round it as their heavy carriage rattled along the antique streets, and not till the next day was Gertrude aware of all the unrivalled beauties that environ the place.

Vane, who was an early riser, went forth alone in the morning to reconnoitre the town; and as he was gazing on the tower of St. Peter, he heard himself suddenly accosted; he turned round and saw the German Student, whom they had met among the mountains of Taunus, at his elbow.

"Monsieur has chosen well in coming hither," said the student: "and I trust our town will not disappoint his expectations."

Vane answered with courtesy, and the German offering to accompany him in his walk, their conversation fell naturally on the life of an university, and the current education of the German people.

"It is surprising," said the student, "that men are eternally inventing new systems of education, and yet persevering in the old. How many years ago is it since Fichte predicted, in the system of Pestalozzi, the regeneration of the German people? What has it done? We admire—we praise, and we blunder on in the very course Pestalozzi proves to be erroneous. Certainly," continued the student, "there must be some radical defect in a system of culture in which genius is an exception, and dulness the result. Yet here, in our German universities, everything proves that education without equitable institutions avails little in the general formation of character. Here the young men of the colleges mix on the most equal terms; they are daring, romantic, enamoured of freedom even to its madness; they leave the university, no political career continues the train of mind they had acquired; they plunge into obscurity; live scattered and separate, and the student inebriated with Schiller sinks into the passive priest or the lethargic baron. His college career, so far from indicating his future life, exactly reverses it: he is brought up in one course in order to proceed in another. And this I hold to be the universal error of education in all countries; they conceive it a certain something to be finished at a certain age. They do not make it a part of the continuous history of life, but a wandering from it."

"You have been in England?" asked Vane.

"Yes; I have travelled over nearly the whole of it on foot. I was poor at that time, and imagining there was a sort of masonry between all men of letters, I inquired at each town for the *savans*, and asked money of them as a matter of course."

Vane almost laughed outright at the simplicity and *naïve* unconsciousness of degradation with which the student proclaimed himself a public beggar.

"And how did you generally succeed?"

"In most cases I was threatened with the stocks, and twice I was consigned by the *juge de paix* to the village police, to be passed to some mystic Mecca they were pleased to entitle 'a parish.' Ah," (continued the German with much *bonhommie*,) "it was a pity to see in a great nation so much value attached to such a trifle as money. But what surprised me greatly was the tone of your poetry. Madame de Staël, who knew perhaps as much of England as she did of Germany, tells us that its chief character is the *chivalresque*; and, excepting only Scott, who, by the way, is *not* English, I did not find one chivalrous poet among you. Yet," continued the student, "between ourselves, I fancy that in our present age of civilization, there is an unexamined mistake in the general mind as to the value of poetry. It delights still as ever, but it has ceased to teach. The prose of the heart enlightens, touches, rouses, far more than poetry. Your most philosophical poets would be commonplace if turned into prose. Verse cannot contain the refining subtle thoughts which a great prose writer embodies; the rhyme eternally cripples it; it properly deals with the common problems of human nature which are now hackneyed, and not with the nice and philosophizing corollaries which may be drawn from them. Thus, though it would seem at first a paradox, commonplace is more the element of poetry than of prose."

This sentiment charmed Vane, who had nothing of the poet about him; and he took the student to share their breakfast at the inn, with a complacency he rarely experienced at the re-meeting with a new acquaintance.

After breakfast, our party proceeded through the town towards the wonderful castle which is its chief attraction, and the noblest wreck of German grandeur.

And now pausing, the mountain yet unscaled, the stately ruin frowned upon them, girt by its massive walls and hanging terraces, round which from place to place clung the dwarfed and various foliage. High at the rear rose the huge mountain, covered, save at its extreme summit, with dark trees, and concealing in its mysterious breast the shadowy beings of the legendary world. But towards the ruins, and up a steep ascent, you may see a few scattered sheep thinly studding the broken ground. Aloft, above the ramparts, rose, desolate and huge, the Palace of the Electors of the Palatinate. In its broken walls you may trace the tokens of the lightning that blasted its ancient pomp, but still leaves in the vast extent of pile a fitting monument of the memory of Charlemagne. Below, in the distance, spread the plain far and spacious, till the shadowy river, with one solitary sail upon its breast, united the melancholy scene of earth with the autumnal sky.

"See," said Vane, pointing to two peasants who were conversing near them on the matters of their little trade, utterly unconscious of the associations of the spot, "see, after all that is said and done about human greatness, it is always the greatness of the few. Ages pass, and leave the poor herd, the mass of men, eternally the same —hewers of wood and drawers of water. The pomp of princes has its ebb and flow, but the peasant sells his fruit as gaily to the stranger on the ruins, as to the emperor in the palace."

"Will it be always so?" said the student.

"Let us hope not, for the sake of permanence in glory," said Trevylyan; "had *a people* built yonder palace, its splendour would never have passed away."

Vane shrugged his shoulders, and Du——e took snuff.

But all the impressions produced by the castle at a distance, are as nothing when you stand within its vast area, and behold the architecture of all ages blended into one mighty ruin! The rich hues of the masonry, the sweeping façades—every description of building which man ever framed for war or for luxury—is here ; all having only the common character—RUIN. The feudal rampart, the yawning foss, the rude tower, the splendid arch,—the strength of a fortress, the magnificence of a palace,—all united, strike upon the soul like the history of a fallen empire in all its epochs.

"There is one singular habitant of these ruins," said the student; "a solitary painter, who has dwelt here some twenty years, companioned only by his Art. No other apartment but that which he tenants is occupied by a human being."

"What a poetical existence !" cried Gertrude, enchanted with a solitude so full of associations.

"Perhaps so," cried the cruel Vane, ever anxious to dispel an illusion ; "but more probably custom has deadened to him all that overpowers ourselves with awe ; and he may tread among these ruins rather seeking to pick up some rude morsel of antiquity, than feeding his imagination with the dim traditions that invest them with so august a poetry."

"Monsieur's conjecture has something of the truth in it," said the German : "but then the painter is a Frenchman."

There is a sense of fatality in the singular mournfulness and majesty which belong to the ruins of Heidelberg; contrasting the vastness of the strength with the utterness of the ruin. It has been twice struck with lightning, and is the wreck of the elements, not of man : during the great siege it sustained, the lightning is supposed to have struck the powder magazine by accident.

What a scene for some great imaginative work ! What a mocking interference of the wrath of nature in the puny contests of men ! One stroke of "the red right arm" above us, crushing the triumph of ages, and laughing to scorn the power of the beleaguers and the valour of the besieged !

They passed the whole day among these stupendous ruins, and felt, when they descended to their inn, as if they had left the caverns of some mighty tomb.

CHAPTER XXX.

NO PART OF THE EARTH REALLY SOLITARY.—THE SONG OF THE FAIRIES—THE SACRED SPOT.—THE WITCH OF THE EVIL WINDS.—THE SPELL AND THE DUTY OF THE FAIRIES.

BUT in what spot of the world is there ever utter solitude? The vanity of man supposes that loneliness is *his* absence? Who shall say what millions of spiritual beings glide invisibly among scenes apparently the most deserted? Or what know we of our own mechanism, that we should deny the possibility of life and motion to things that we cannot ourselves recognize?

At moonlight, in the Great Court of Heidelberg, on the borders of the shattered basin overgrown with weeds, the following song was heard by the melancholy shades that roam at night through the mouldering halls of old, and the gloomy hollows in the mountain of Heidelberg.

SONG OF THE FAIRIES IN THE RUINS OF HEIDELBERG.

> From the woods and the glossy green,
>   With the wild thyme strewn;
> From the rivers whose crisped sheen
>   Is kissed by the trembling moon:—
> While the dwarf looks out from his mountain cave,
>   And the erl king from his lair,
> And the water-nymph from her moaning wave,—
>   We skirr the limber air.
>
> There's a smile on the vine-clad shore,
>   A smile on the castled heights;
> They dream back the days of yore,
>   And they smile at our roundel rites!
>   Our roundel rites!
>
> Lightly we tread these halls around,
>   Lightly tread we;
> Yet, hark! we have scared with a single sound
>   The moping owl on the breathless tree,
>   And the goblin sprites!
> Ha! ha! we have scared with a single sound
>   The old gray owl on the breathless tree,
>   And the goblin sprites!

"They come not," said Pipalee; "yet the banquet is prepared, and the poor queen will be glad of some refreshment."

"What a pity! all the rose-leaves will be over-broiled," said Nip.

"Let us amuse ourselves with the old painter," quoth Trip, springing over the ruins.

"Well said," cried Pipalee and Nip: and all three, leaving my lord-treasurer amazed at their levity, whisked into the painter's apartment. Permitting them to throw the ink over their victim's papers, break his pencils, mix his colours, mislay his nightcap, and go whiz against his face in the shape of a great bat, till the astonished Frenchman began to think the pensive goblins of the place had taken a sprightly fit,—we hasten to a small green spot some little way from the town, in the valley of the Neckar, and by the banks of its silver stream. It was circled round by dark trees, save on that side bordered by the river. The wild flowers sprang profusely from the turf which yet was smooth and singularly green. And there was the German fairy describing a circle round the spot, and making his elvish spells. And Nymphalin sat droopingly in the centre, shading her face, which was bowed down as the head of a water-lily, and weeping crystal tears.

There came a hollow murmur through the trees, and a rush as of a mighty wind, and a dark form emerged from the shadow and approached the spot.

The face was wrinkled and old, and stern with a malevolent and evil aspect. The frame was lean and gaunt, and supported by a staff, and a short gray mantle covered its bended shoulders.

"Things of the moonbeam!" said the form, in a shrill and ghastly voice; "what want ye here? and why charm ye this spot from the coming of me and mine?"

"Dark witch of the blight and blast," answered the fairy, 'THOU that nippest the herb in its tender youth, and eatest up the core of the soft bud; behold, it is but a small spot that the fairies claim from thy demesnes, and on which, through frost and heat, they will keep the herbage green and the air gentle in its sighs!"

"And, wherefore, O dweller in the crevices of the earth! wherefore wouldst thou guard this spot from the curses of the seasons?"

"We know by our instinct," answered the fairy, "that this spot will become the grave of one whom the fairies love; hither, by an unfelt influence, shall we guide her yet living steps; and in gazing upon this spot, shall the desire of quiet and the resignation to death steal upon her soul. Behold, throughout the universe, all things at war with one another;—the lion with the lamb; the serpent with the bird; and even the gentlest bird itself with the moth of the air, or the worm of the humble earth! What then to men, and to the spirits transcending men, is so lovely and so sacred as a being that harmeth none? what so beautiful as Innocence? what so **mournful as its untimely tomb**? **And** shall not **that tomb be sacred**? **shall it** not be our peculiar care? May we **not** mourn **over** it as at the passing away of some fair miracle in Nature; too tender to endure, too rare to be forgotten? It is for this, O dread waker of the blast! that the fairies would consecrate this little spot; for this they would charm away from **its** tranquil turf the wandering ghoul and the evil children of the night. Here, not the ill-omened owl, nor the blind bat, nor the unclean worm, shall come. And thou shouldst have neither will nor power to nip the flowers of spring, nor sear the green herbs of summer. Is it not, dark mother of the evil winds! is it not *our* immemorial office to tend the grave of Innocence, and keep fresh the flowers round the resting-place of Virgin Love?"

Then the witch drew her cloak round her, **and** muttered to herself, and without further answer turned away among the trees and vanished, as the breath of the east wind, which goeth with her as her comrade, scattered the melancholy leaves along her **path**!

CHAPTER XXXI.

GERTRUDE AND TREVYLYAN, WHEN THE FORMER IS **AWAKENED** TO **THE** APPROACH OF DEATH.

HE next day, Gertrude **and her** companions went along the banks of the haunted **Neckar**. She had passed a sleepless and painful night, and her evanescent and child-like spirits had sobered down into a melancholy and thoughtful mood. She leaned back in an open carriage with Trevylyan, ever constant by her side, while Du——e and Vane rode slowly in advance. Tre**vylyan** tried in vain to cheer her, even his attempts (usually so eagerly received) to charm her duller moments by tale or legend, were, in this instance, fruitless. She shook her head gently— pressed his hand, and said, "No, dear Trevylyan—no; even your art fails to-day, but your kindness, never!" and pressing his hand to her lips, she burst passionately into tears.

Alarmed and anxious, he clasped **her to** his breast, and strove to lift her face, as it drooped on its resting-place, and kiss away its tears.

"Oh!" said she, **at** length, "do not despise my weakness, I am overcome by my own thoughts: I look upon the world, and see that it is fair and good; I look upon you, and I see all that I can venerate and adore. Life seems to me so sweet, and the earth so lovely; can you wonder, then, that I should shrink at the thought of death? Nay, interrupt me not, dear Albert; the thought must be borne and braved. I have not cherished, I have not yielded to it through my long-increasing illness, but there have been times when it has forced itself upon me; and now, *now* more palpably than ever. Do not think me weak and childish, I never feared death till I knew you; but to see you no more—never again to touch this dear hand—never to thank you for your love—never to be sensible of your care—to lie down and sleep, *and never, never, once more to dream of you!* Ah! that is a bitter thought! but I will brave it—yes, brave it as one worthy of your regard.

Trevylyan, choked by his emotions, covered his own face with his hands, and, leaning back in the carriage, vainly struggled with his sobs.

"Perhaps," she said, yet ever and anon clinging to the hope that had utterly abandoned *him*, "perhaps, I may yet deceive myself; and my love for you, which seems to me as if it could conquer death, may bear me up against this fell disease;—the hope to live with you —to watch you—to share your high dreams, and oh! above all, to soothe you in sorrow and sickness, as you have soothed me—has not that hope something that may support even this sinking frame? And who shall love thee as I love? who see thee as I have seen? who pray for thee in gratitude and tears as I have prayed? Oh, Albert, so little am I jealous of you, so little do I think of myself in comparison, that I could close my eyes happily on the world, if I knew that what I could be to thee, another will be!"

"Gertrude," said Trevylyan; and lifting up his colourless face, he gazed upon her with an earnest and calm solemnity. "Gertrude, let us be united at once! if Fate must sever us, let her cut the last tie too; let us feel at least that on earth we have been all in all to each other; let us defy death, even as it frowns upon us. Be mine to-morrow—this day—oh God! be mine!"

Over even that pale countenance, beneath whose hues the lamp of life so faintly fluttered, a deep, radiant flash passed one moment, lighting up the beautiful ruin with the glow of maiden youth and impassioned hope, and then died rapidly away.

"No, Albert," she said, sighing; "No! it must not be: far easier would come the pang to you, while yet we are not wholly united; and for my own part, I am selfish, and feel as if I should leave a tenderer remembrance on your heart, thus parted;—tenderer, but not so sad. I would not wish you to feel yourself widowed to my memory; I would not cling like a blight to your fair prospects

of the future. Remember me rather as a dream; **as something
never wholly won, and** therefore asking no fidelity but **that of kind
and forbearing thoughts.** Do you remember one evening **as we**
sailed along the Rhine—ah! happy, happy hour!—that we heard
from the banks a strain of music, not so skilfully played as to be
worth listening to for itself, but, suiting as it did the hour and the
scene, we remained silent, that we might hear it the better; and
when it died insensibly upon the waters, a certain melancholy stole
over **us;** we felt that a something that softened the landscape had
gone, and we conversed less lightly than before? Just so, my own
loved—my own adored Trevylyan, just so is the influence that our
brief love—your poor Gertrude's existence, should bequeath to your
remembrance. A sound—a presence—should haunt you for a little
while, but no more, ere you again become sensible of the glories
that court your way!"

But as Gertrude said this, she turned to Trevylyan, and seeing his
agony, she could refrain no longer; she felt that to soothe was to
insult; and, throwing herself upon his breast, they mingled their
tears together.

CHAPTER XXXII.

A SPOT TO BE BURIED IN.

N their return homeward, Du———e took the third seat **in**
the carriage, and endeavoured, with his usual vivacity, to
cheer the spirits of his companions; and such was the
elasticity of Gertrude's nature, that with her, he, to a
certain degree, succeeded in his kindly attempt. Quickly alive to
the charms of scenery, she entered by degrees into the external
beauties which every turn in the road opened to their view; and the
silvery smoothness of the river, that made the constant attraction of
the landscape; the serenity of the time, and the clearness of **the**
heavens, tended to tranquillize a mind that, like a sun-flower, **so**
instinctively turned from the shadow to the light.

Once Du———e stopped the carriage in a spot of herbage, bedded
among the trees, and said to Gertrude, "We are now in one of the
many places along the Neckar, which your favourite traditions
serve to consecrate. Amidst yonder copses, in the early ages of
Christianity, there dwelt a hermit, who, though young in years, was
renowned for the sanctity of his life. None knew whence he came,
nor for what cause he had limited the circle of life to the seclusion

of his cell. He rarely spoke, save when his ghostly advice, or his kindly prayer, was needed; he lived upon herbs, and the wild fruits which the peasants brought to his cave; and every morning and every evening, he came to this spot to fill his pitcher from the water of the stream. But here he was observed to linger long after his task was done, and to sit gazing upon the walls of a convent which then rose upon the opposite side of the bank, though now even its ruins are gone. Gradually his health gave way beneath the austerities he practised; and one evening he was found by some fishermen insensible on the turf. They bore him for medical aid to the opposite convent; and one of the sisterhood, the daughter of a prince, was summoned to tend the recluse. But when his eyes opened upon hers, a sudden recognition appeared to seize both. He spoke; and the sister threw herself on the couch of the dying man, and shrieked forth a name, the most famous in the surrounding country,—the name of a once noted minstrel, who, in those rude times, had mingled the poet with the lawless chief, and was supposed, years since, to have fallen in one of the desperate frays between prince and outlaw, which were then common; storming the very castle which held her—now the pious nun, then the beauty and presider over the tournament and galliard. In her arms the spirit of the hermit passed away. She survived but a few hours, and left conjecture busy with a history to which it never obtained further clue. Many a troubadour, in later times, furnished forth in poetry the details which truth refused to supply; and the place where the hermit at sunrise and sunset ever came to gaze upon the convent became consecrated by song."

The place invested with this legendary interest was impressed with a singular aspect of melancholy quiet; wild flowers yet lingered on the turf, whose grassy sedges gently overhung the Neckar, that murmured amidst them with a plaintive music. Not a wind stirred the trees; but, at a little distance from the place, the spire of a church rose amidst the copse; and, as they paused, they suddenly heard from the holy building the bell that summons to the burial of the dead. It came on the ear in such harmony with the spot, with the hour, with the breathing calm, that it thrilled to the heart of each with an inexpressible power. It was like the voice of another world—that amidst the solitude of nature summoned the lulled spirit from the cares of this;—it invited, not repulsed, and had in its tone more of softness than of awe.

Gertrude turned, with tears starting to her eyes, and, laying her hand on Trevylyan's, whispered :—"In such a spot, so calm, so sequestered, yet in the neighbourhood of the house of God, would I wish this broken frame to be consigned to rest!"

CHAPTER THE LAST.

THE CONCLUSION OF THIS TALE.

FROM that day Gertrude's spirit resumed its wonted cheerfulness, and for the ensuing week she never reverted to her approaching fate; she seemed once more to have grown unconscious of its limit. Perhaps she sought, anxious for Trevylyan to the last, not to throw additional gloom over their earthly separation; or, perhaps, once steadily regarding the certainty of her doom, its terrors vanished. The chords of thought, vibrating to the subtlest emotions, may be changed by a single incident, or in a single hour; a sound of sacred music, a green and quiet burial-place, may convert the form of death into the aspect of an angel. And therefore wisely, and with a beautiful lore, did the Greeks strip the grave of its unreal gloom; wisely did they body forth the great Principle of Rest by solemn and lovely images—unconscious of the northern madness that made a Spectre of REPOSE!

But while Gertrude's *spirit* resumed its healthful tone, her *frame* rapidly declined, and a few days now could do the ravage of months a little while before.

One evening, amidst the desolate ruins of Heidelberg, Trevylyan, who had gone forth alone to indulge the thoughts which he strove to stifle in Gertrude's presence, suddenly encountered Vane. That calm and almost callous pupil of the adversities of the world was standing alone, and gazing upon the shattered casements and riven tower, through which the sun now cast its slant and parting ray.

Trevylyan, who had never loved this cold and unsusceptible man, save for the sake of Gertrude, felt now almost a hatred creep over him, as he thought in such a time, and with death fastening upon the flower of her house, he could yet be calm, and smile, and muse, and moralize, and play the common part of the world. He strode slowly up to him, and standing full before him, said with a hollow voice and writhing smile: "You amuse yourself pleasantly, sir: this is a fine scene;—and to meditate over griefs a thousand years hushed to rest is better than watching over a sick girl and eating away your heart with fear!"

Vane looked at him quietly, but intently, and made no reply.

"Vane!" continued Trevylyan, with the same preternatural attempt at calm; "Vane, in a few days all will be over, and you and I, the things, the plotters, the false men of the world, will be left alone—left by the sole Being that graces our dull life, that makes by her love, either of us worthy of a thought!"

Vane started, and turned away his face. "You are cruel," said he, with a faltering voice.

"What, man!" shouted Trevylyan, seizing him abruptly by the arm, "can *you* feel? Is your cold heart touched? Come, then," added he, with a wild laugh, "come, let us be friends!"

Vane drew himself aside, with a certain dignity, that impressed Trevylyan even at that hour. "Some years hence," said he, "you will be called cold as I am; sorrow will teach you the wisdom of indifference—it is a bitter school, sir,—a bitter school! But think you that I do indeed see unmoved my last hope shivered—the last tie that binds me to my kind? No, no! I feel it as a man may feel; I cloak it as a man grown gray in misfortune should do! My child is more to me than your betrothed to you; for you are young and wealthy, and life smiles before you; but I—no more—sir—no more."

"Forgive me," said Trevylyan, humbly; "I have wronged you; but Gertrude is an excuse for any crime of love; and now listen to my last prayer—give her to me—even on the verge of the grave. Death cannot seize her in the arms—in the vigils—of a love like mine.'

Vane shuddered. "It were to wed the dead," said he—"No!"

Trevylyan drew back, and without another word, hurried away; he returned to the town; he sought, with methodical calmness, the owner of the piece of ground in which Gertrude had wished to be buried. He purchased it, and that very night he sought the priest of a neighbouring church, and directed it should be consecrated according to the due rite and ceremonial.

The priest, an aged and pious man, was struck by the request, and the air of him who made it.

"Shall it be done forthwith, sir?" said he, hesitating.

"Forthwith," answered Trevylyan, with a calm smile—"a bridegroom, you know, is naturally impatient."

For the next three days, Gertrude was so ill as to be confined to her bed. All that time Trevylyan sat outside her door, without speaking, scarcely lifting his eyes from the ground. The attendants passed to and fro—he heeded them not; perhaps as even the foreign menials turned aside and wiped their eyes, and prayed God to comfort him, he required compassion less at that time than any other. There is a stupefaction in woe, and the heart sleeps without a pang when exhausted by its afflictions.

But on the fourth day Gertrude rose, and was carried down (how changed, yet how lovely ever!) to their common apartment. During those three days the priest had been with her often, and her spirit, full of religion from her childhood, had been unspeakably soothed by his comfort. She took food from the hand of Trevylyan; she smiled upon him as sweetly as of old. She conversed with him, though with a faint voice, and at broken intervals. But she felt no pain; life ebbed away gradually, and without a pang. "My father," she said to Vane, whose features still bore their usual calm, whatever might have passed within, "I know that you will grieve when I am gone more than the world might guess; for I alone know what you were years ago, ere friends left you and fortune frowned, and ere my poor mother died. But do not—do not believe that hope and comfort leave you with me. Till the heaven pass away from the earth, there shall be comfort and hope for all."

They did not lodge in the town, but had fixed their abode on its outskirts, and within sight of the Neckar: and from the window they saw a light sail gliding gaily by, till it passed, and solitude once more rested upon the waters.

"The sail passes from our eyes," said Gertrude, pointing to it, "but still it glides on as happily though we see it no more; and I feel—yes, father, I feel—I know that it is so with *us*. We glide down the river of time from the eyes of men, but we cease not the less to *be!*"

And now, as the twilight descended, she expressed a wish, before she retired to rest, to be left alone with Trevylyan. He was not then sitting by her side, for he would not trust himself to do so; but with his face averted, at a little distance from her. She called him by his name; he answered not nor turned. Weak as she was, she raised herself from the sofa, and crept gently along the floor till she came to him, and sank in his arms.

"Ah, unkind!" she said, "unkind for once! Will you turn away from me? Come, let us look once more on the river: see! the night darkens over it. Our pleasant voyage, the type of our love, is finished; our sail may be unfurled no more. Never again can your voice soothe the lassitude of sickness with the legend and the song—the course is run, the vessel is broken up, night closes over its fragments; but now, in this hour, love me, be kind to me as ever. Still let me be your own Gertrude—still let me close my eyes this night, as before, with the sweet consciousness that I am loved."

"Loved!—O Gertrude! speak not to me thus!"

"Come, that is yourself again!" and she clung with weak arms caressingly to his breast. "And now," she said more solemnly, "let us forget that we are mortal; let us remember only that life is a part, not the whole, of our career; let us feel in this soft hour, and while yet we are unsevered, the presence of The Eternal that is within us, so that it shall not be as death, but as a short absence; and when once the pang of parting is over, you must think only that we are shortly to meet again. What! you turn from me still? See, I do not weep or grieve, I have conquered the pang of our absence; will you be outdone by me? Do you remember, Albert, that you once told me how the wisest of the sages of old, in prison, and before death, consoled his friends with the proof of the immortality of the soul. Is it not a consolation?—does it not suffice; or will you deem it wise from the lips of wisdom, but vain from the lips of love?"

"Hush, hush!" said Trevylyan, wildly; "or I shall think you an angel already."

But let us close this commune, and leave unrevealed the *last* sacred words that ever passed between them upon earth.

When Vane and the physician stole back softly into the room, Trevylyan motioned to them to be still: "She sleeps," he whispered; "hush!" And in truth, wearied out by her own emotions, and lulled by the belief that she had soothed one with whom her heart dwelt now, as ever, she had fallen into sleep, or it may be, insensibility, on his breast. There as she lay, so fair, so frail, so delicate, the twilight deepened into shade, and the first star, like the hope of the future, broke forth upon the darkness of the earth.

Nothing could equal the stillness without, save that which lay breathlessly within. For not one of the group stirred or spoke; and Trevylyan, bending over her, never took his eyes from her face, watching the parted lips, and fancying that he imbibed the breath. Alas, the breath was stilled! from sleep to death she had glided without a sigh: happy, most happy in that death!—cradled in the arms of unchanged love, and brightened in her last thought by the consciousness of innocence and the assurances of heaven!

* * * * *
* * * * *
* * * * *

Trevylyan, after long sojourn on the Continent, returned to England. He plunged into active life, and became what is termed, in this age of little names, a distinguished and noted man. But what was mainly remarkable in his future conduct, was his impatience of rest. He eagerly courted all occupations, even of the most varied and motley kind. Business,—letters,—ambition,—pleasure. He suffered no pause in his career; and leisure to him was as care to others. He lived in the world, as the worldly do, discharging its duties, fostering its affections, and fulfilling its career. But there was a deep and wintry change within him—*the sunlight of his life was gone;* the loveliness of romance had left the earth. The stem was proof as heretofore to the blast, but the green leaves were severed from it for ever, and the bird had forsaken its boughs. Once he had idolized the beauty that is born of song; the glory and the ardour that invest such thoughts as are not of our common clay; but the well of enthusiasm was dried up, and the golden bowl was broken at the fountain. With Gertrude the poetry of existence was gone. As she herself had described her loss, a music had ceased to breathe along the face of things; and though the bark might sail on as swiftly, and the stream swell with as proud a wave, a something that had vibrated on the heart was still, and the magic of the voyage was no more.

And Gertrude sleeps on the spot where she wished her last couch to be made; and far—oh, far dearer is that small spot on the distant banks of the gliding Neckar to Trevylyan's heart, than all the broad lands and fertile fields of his ancestral domain. The turf too preserves its emerald greenness; and it would seem to me that the field flowers spring up by the sides of the simple tomb even more profusely than of old. A curve in the bank breaks the tide of the Neckar; and therefore its stream pauses, as if to linger reluctantly, by that solitary grave, and to mourn among the rustling sedges ere it passes on. And I have thought, when I last looked upon that quiet place,—when I saw the turf so fresh, and the flowers so bright of hue, that aerial hands might *indeed* tend the sod; that it was by no *imaginary* spells that I summoned the fairies to my tale; that in truth, and with vigils constant though unseen, they yet kept from all polluting footsteps, and from the harsher influence of the seasons, the grave of one who so loved their race; and who, in her gentle and spotless virtue, claimed kindred with the beautiful Ideal of the world. Is there one of us who has not known some being for whom it seemed not too wild a phantasy to indulge such dreams?

PAUSANIAS

THE SPARTAN

An unfinished Historical Romance

BY

THE LATE LORD LYTTON

EDITED BY

HIS SON

Dedication.

TO

THE REV. BENJAMIN HALL KENNEDY, D.D.

CANON OF ELY,

AND REGIUS PROFESSOR OF GREEK IN THE UNIVERSITY OF CAMBRIDGE.

My dear Dr. Kennedy,

Revised by your helpful hand, and corrected by your accurate scholarship, to whom may these pages be so fitly inscribed as to that one of their author's earliest and most honoured friends,[1] whose generous assistance has enabled me to place them before the public in their present form?

It is fully fifteen, if not twenty, years since my father commenced the composition of an historical romance on the subject of Pausanias, the Spartan Regent. Circumstances, which need not here be recorded, compelled him to lay aside the work thus begun. But the subject continued to haunt his imagination and occupy his thoughts. He detected in it singular opportunities for effective exercise of the gifts most peculiar to his genius; and repeatedly, in the intervals of other literary labour, he returned to the task which, though again and again interrupted, was never abandoned. To that rare combination of the imaginative and practical faculties which characterized my father's intellect, and received from his life such varied illustration, the story of Pausanias, indeed, briefly as it is told by Thucydides and Plutarch, addressed itself with singular force. The vast conspiracy of the Spartan Regent, had it been successful, would have changed the whole course of Grecian history. To any student of political phenomena, but more especially to one who, during the greater part of his life, had been personally engaged in

---

[1] The late Lord Lytton, in his unpublished autobiographical memoirs, describing his contemporaries at Cambridge, speaks of Dr. Kennedy as "a young giant of learning."—L.

active politics, the story of such a conspiracy could not fail to be attractive. To the student of human nature the character of Pausanias himself offers sources of the deepest interest; and, in the strange career and tragic fate of the great conspirator, an imagination fascinated by the supernatural must have recognized remarkable elements of awe and terror. A few months previous to his death, I asked my father whether he had abandoned all intention of finishing his romance of "Pausanias." He replied, "On the contrary, I am finishing it now," and entered, with great animation, into a discussion of the subject and its capabilities. This reply to my inquiry surprised and impressed me: for, as you are aware, my father was then engaged in the simultaneous composition of two other and very different works, "Kenelm Chillingly" and the "Parisians." It was the last time he ever spoke to me about Pausanias; but from what he then said of it I derived an impression that the book was all but completed, and needing only a few finishing touches to be ready for publication at no distant date.

This impression was confirmed, subsequent to my father's death, by a letter of instructions about his posthumous papers which accompanied his will. In that letter, dated 1856, special allusion is made to Pausanias as a work already far advanced towards its conclusion.

You, to whom, in your kind and careful revision of it, this unfinished work has suggested many questions which, alas, I cannot answer, as to the probable conduct and fate of its fictitious characters, will readily understand my reluctance to surrender an impression seemingly so well justified. I did not indeed cease to cherish it, until reiterated and exhaustive search had failed to recover from the "wallet" wherein Time "puts alms for oblivion," more than those few imperfect fragments which, by your valued help, are here arranged in such order as to carry on the narrative of Pausanias, with no solution of continuity, to the middle of the second volume.

There the manuscript breaks off. Was it ever continued further? I know not. Many circumstances induce me to believe that the conception had long been carefully completed in the mind of its author; but he has left behind him only a very meagre and imperfect indication of the course which, beyond the point where it is broken, his narrative was intended to follow. In presence of this fact I have had to choose between the total suppression of the fragment, and the publication of it in its present form. My choice has not been made without hesitation; but I trust that, from many points of view, the following pages will be found to justify it.

Judiciously (as I cannot but think) for the purposes of his fiction, my father has taken up the story of Pausanias at a period subsequent to the battle of Platæa; when the Spartan Regent, as Admiral of the United Greek Fleet in the waters of Byzantium, was at the summit of his power and reputation. Mr. Grote, in his great work, expresses the opinion (which certainly cannot be disputed by unbiassed readers of Thucydides) that the victory of Platæa was not attributable to any remarkable abilities on the part of Pausanias. But Mr. Grote fairly recognizes as quite exceptional the fame and authority accorded to Pausanias, after the battle, by all the Hellenic States; the influence which his name commanded, and the awe which his character inspired. Not to the mere fact of his birth as an Heracleid, not to the lucky accident (if such it were) of his success at Platæa, and certainly not to his undisputed (but surely by no means uncommon) physical courage, is it possible to attribute the peculiar position which this remarkable man so long occupied in the estimation of his contemporaries. For the little that we know about Pausanias we are mainly dependent upon Athenian writers, who must have been strongly prejudiced against him. Mr. Grote, adopting (as any modern historian needs must do) the narrative so handed down to him, never once pauses to question its estimate of the character of a man who was at one time the glory, and at another the terror, of all Greece. Yet in comparing the summary proceedings taken against Leotychides with the extreme, and seemingly pusillanimous, deference paid to Pausanias by the Ephors long after they possessed the most alarming proofs of his treason, Mr. Grote observes, without attempting to account for the fact, that Pausanias, though only Regent, was far more powerful than any Spartan King. Why so powerful? Obviously, because he possessed uncommon force of character; a force of character strikingly attested by every known incident of his career; and which, when concentrated upon the conception and execution of vast designs (even if those designs be criminal), must be recognized as the special attribute of genius. Thucydides, Plutarch, Diodorus, Grote, all these writers ascribe solely to the administrative incapacity of Pausanias that offensive arrogance which characterized his command at Byzantium, and apparently cost Sparta the loss of her maritime hegemony. But here is precisely one of those problems in public policy and personal conduct which the historian bequeathes to the imaginative writer, and which needs, for its solution, a profound knowledge rather of human nature than of books. For dealing with such a problem, my father, in addition to the intuitive penetration of character and motive, which is common to every great romance writer, certainly possessed two qualifications special to himself: the habit of dealing *practically* with political questions, and experience in the active management of men. His explanation of the policy of Pausanias at Byzantium, if it be not (as I think it is) the right one, is at least the only one yet offered. I venture to think that, historically, it merits attention; as, from the imaginative point of view, it is undoubtedly felicitous. By elevating our estimate of Pausanias as a statesman, it increases our interest in him as a man.

The Author of "Pausanias" does not merely tell us that his hero, when in conference with the Spartan commissioners, displayed "great natural powers which, rightly trained, might have made him not less renowned in council than in war;" but he gives us, though briefly, the arguments used by Pausanias. He presents to us the image, always interesting, of a man who grasps firmly the clear conception of a definite but difficult policy, for success in which he is dependent on the conscious or involuntary coöperation of men impenetrable to that conception, and possessed of a collective authority even greater than his own. To retain Sparta temporarily at the head of Greece was an ambition quite consistent with the more criminal designs of Pausanias; and his whole conduct at Byzantium is rendered more intelligible than it appears in history, when he points out that "for Sparta to maintain her ascendancy two things are needful: first, to continue the war by land, secondly, to disgust the Ionians with their sojourn at Byzantium, to send them with their ships back to their own havens, and so leave Hellas under the sole guardianship of the Spartans and their Peloponnesian allies." And who has not learned, in a later school, the wisdom of the Spartan commissioners? Do not their utterances sound familiar to us? "Increase of dominion is waste of life and treasure. Sparta is content to hold her own. What care we, who leads the Greeks into blows? The fewer blows the better. Brave men fight if they must: wise men never fight if they can help it." Of this scene and some others in the first volume of the present fragment (notably the scene in which the Regent confronts the allied chiefs, and defends himself against the charge of connivance at the escape of the Persian prisoners), I should have been tempted to say that they could not have been written without personal experience of political life; if the interview between Wallenstein and the Swedish ambassadors in Schiller's great trilogy did not recur to my recollection as I write. The language of the ambassadors in that interview is a perfect manual of practical diplomacy; and yet in practical diplomacy Schiller had no personal experience. There are, indeed, no limits to the creative power of genius. But it is perhaps the practical politician who will be most interested by the chapters in which Pausanias explains his policy, or defends his position.

In publishing a romance which its author has left unfinished, I may perhaps be allowed to indicate briefly what I believe to have been the general scope of its design, and the probable progress of its narrative.

The "domestic interest" of that narrative is supplied by the story of Cleonice : a story which, briefly told by Plutarch, suggests one of the most tragic situations it is possible to conceive. The pathos and terror of this dark weird episode in a life which history herself invests with all the character of romance, long haunted the imagination of Byron; and elicited from Goethe one of the most whimsical illustrations of the astonishing absurdity into which criticism sometimes tumbles, when it "o'erleaps itself and falls o' the other—."

Writing of Manfred and its author, he says, "There are, properly speaking, two females whose phantoms for ever haunt him; and which, in this piece also, perform principal parts. One under the name of Astarte, the other without form or actual presence, and merely a voice. Of the horrid occurrence which took place with the former, the following is related :—When a bold and enterprising young man, he won the affections of a Florentine lady. Her husband discovered the amour, and murdered his wife. But the murderer was the same night found dead in the street, and there was no one to whom any suspicion could be attached. Lord Byron removed from Florence, and *these spirits haunted him all his life after*. This romantic incident is rendered highly probable by innumerable allusions to it in his poems. As, for instance, when turning his sad contemplations inwards, he applies to himself the fatal history of the King of Sparta. It is as follows: Pausanias, a Lacedæmonian General, acquires glory by the important victory at Platæa; but afterwards forfeits the confidence of his countrymen by his arrogance, obstinacy, and secret intrigues with the common enemy. This man draws upon himself the heavy guilt of innocent blood, which attends him to his end. For, while commanding the fleet of the allied Greeks in the Black Sea, he is inflamed with a violent passion for a Byzantine maiden. After long resistance, he at length obtains her from her parents; and she is to be delivered up to him at night. She modestly desires the servant to put out the lamp, and, while groping her way in the dark, she overturns it. Pausanias is awakened from his sleep; apprehensive of an attack from murderers he seizes his sword, and destroys his mistress. The horrid sight never leaves him. Her shade pursues him unceasingly; and in vain he implores aid of the gods and the exorcising priests. That poet must have a lacerated heart who selects such a scene from antiquity, appropriates it to himself, and burdens his tragic image with it." [1]

It is extremely characteristic of Byron, that, instead of resenting this charge of murder, he was so pleased by the criticism in which it occurs that he afterwards dedicated "The Deformed Transformed" to Goethe. Mr. Grote repeats the story above alluded to, with all the sanction of his grave authority, and even mentions the name of the young lady; apparently for the sake of adding a few black strokes to his character of Pausanias. But the supernatural part of the legend was, of course, beneath the notice of a nineteenth-century critic; and he passes it by. This part of the story is, however, essential to the psychological interest of it. For whether it be that Pausanias supposed himself, or that contemporary gossips supposed him, to be haunted by the phantom of the woman he had loved and slain, the fact, in either case, affords a lurid glimpse into the inner life of the man;—just as, although Goethe's murder-story about Byron is ludicrously untrue, yet the fact that such a story was circulated, and could be seriously repeated by such a man as Goethe without being resented by Byron himself, offers significant illustration both of what Byron was, and of what he appeared to his contemporaries. Grote also assigns the death of Cleonice to that period in the life of Pausanias when he was in the command of the allies at Byzantium; and refers to it as one of the numerous outrages whereby Pausanias abused and disgraced the authority confided to him. Plutarch, however, who tells the story in greater detail, distinctly fixes the date of its catastrophe subsequent to the return of the Regent to Byzantium, as a solitary volunteer, in the trireme of Hermione. The following is his account of the affair:

"It is related that Pausanias, when at Byzantium, sought, with criminal purpose, the love of a young lady of good family, named Cleonice. The parents yielding to fear, or necessity, suffered him to carry away their daughter. Before entering his chamber, she requested that the light might be extinguished; and in darkness and silence she approached the couch of Pausanias, who was already asleep. In so doing she accidentally upset the lamp. Pausanias, suddenly aroused from slumber, and supposing that some enemy was about to assassinate him, seized his sword, which lay by his bedside, and with it struck the maiden to the ground. She died of her wound; and from that moment repose was banished from the life of Pausanias. A spectre appeared to him every night in his

---

[1] Moore's "Life and Letters of Lord Byron," p. 723.

sleep; and repeated to him in reproachful tones this hexameter verse,

'*Whither I wait thee march, and receive the doom thou deservest,
Sooner or later, but ever, to man crime bringeth disaster.*'

The allies, scandalized by this misdeed, concerted with Cimon, and besieged Pausanias in Byzantium. But he succeeded in escaping. Continually troubled by the phantom, he took refuge, it is said, at Heraclea, in that temple where the souls of the dead are evoked. He appealed to Cleonice and conjured her to mitigate his torment. She appeared to him, and told him that on his return to Sparta he would attain the end of his sufferings; indicating, as it would seem, by these enigmatic words, the death which there awaited him. "This" (adds Plutarch) "is a story told by most of the historians."[1]

I feel no doubt that this version of the story, or at least the general outline of it, would have been followed by the romance had my father lived to complete it. Some modification of its details would doubtless have been necessary for the purposes of fiction. But that the Cleonice of the novel is destined to die by the hand of her lover, is clearly indicated. To me it seems that considerable skill and judgment are shown in the pains taken, at the very opening of the book, to prepare the mind of the reader for an incident which would have been intolerably painful, and must have prematurely ended the whole narrative interest, had the character of Cleonice been drawn otherwise than as we find it in this first portion of the book. From the outset she appears before us under the shadow of a tragic fatality. Of that fatality she is herself intuitively conscious: and with it her whole being is in harmony. No sooner do we recognize her real character than we perceive that, for such a character, there can be no fit or satisfactory issue from the difficulties of her position, in any conceivable combination of earthly circumstances. But she is not of the earth earthly. Her thoughts already habitually hover on the dim frontier of some vague spiritual region in which her love seeks refuge from the hopeless realities of her life; and, recognizing this betimes, we are prepared to see above the hand of her ill-fated lover, when it strikes her down in the dark, the merciful and releasing hand of her natural destiny.

But, assuming the author to have adopted Plutarch's chronology, and deferred the death of Cleonice till the return of Pausanias to Byzantium (the latest date to which he could possibly have deferred it), this catastrophe must still have occurred somewhere in the course, or at the close, of his second volume. There would, in that

[1] Plutarch, "Life of Cimon."

case, have still remained about nine years (and those the most eventful) of his hero's career to be narrated. The premature removal of the heroine from the narrative, so early in the course of it, would therefore, at first sight, appear to be a serious defect in the conception of this romance. Here it is, however, that the credulous gossip of the old biographer comes to the rescue of the modern artist. I apprehend that the Cleonice of the novel would, after her death, have been still sensibly present to the reader's imagination throughout the rest of the romance. She would then have moved through it like a fate, reappearing in the most solemn moments of the story, and at all times apparent, even when unseen, in her visible influence upon the fierce and passionate character, the sombre and turbulent career, of her guilty lover. In short, we may fairly suppose that, in all the closing scenes of the tragedy, Cleonice would have still figured and acted as one of those supernatural agencies which my father, following the example of his great predecessor, Scott, did not scruple to introduce into the composition of historical romance.[1]

Without the explanation here suggested, those metaphysical conversations between Cleonice, Alcman, and Pausanias, which occupy the opening chapters of Book II., might be deemed superfluous. But, in fact, they are essential to the preparation of the catastrophe; and that catastrophe, if reached, would undoubtedly have revealed to any reflective reader their important connection with the narrative which they now appear to retard somewhat unduly.

Quite apart from the unfinished manuscript of this story of Pausanias, and in another portion of my father's papers which have no reference to this story, I have discovered the following, undated, memorandum of the destined contents of the second and third volumes of the work.

PAUSANIAS.
VOL. II.

Lysander—Sparta—Ephors—Decision to recall Pausanias. 60.

Pausanias with Pharnabazes—On the point of success—Xerxes's daughter—Interview with Cleonice—Recalled. 60.

Sparta—Alcman with his family. 60.

Cleonice—Antagoras—Yields to suit of marriage. 60.

Pausanias suddenly reappears as a volunteer—Scenes. 60.

---
[1] "Harold."

DEDICATION.

VOL. III.

Pausanias removes Cleonice, &c.—Conspiracy against him—Up to Cleonice's death. 100.

His expulsion from Byzantium—His despair—His journey into Thrace—Scythians, &c. ?

Heraclea—Ghost. 60.

His return—to Colonæ. ?

Antagoras resolved on revenge—Communicates with Sparta. ?

The * * *—Conference with Alcman—Pausanias depends on Helots, and money. 40.

His return—to death. 120.

This is the only indication I can find of the intended conclusion of the story. Meagre though it be, however, it sufficiently suggests the manner in which the author of the romance intended to deal with the circumstances of Cleonice's death as related by Plutarch. With her forcible removal by Pausanias, or her willing flight with him from the house of her father, it would probably have been difficult to reconcile the general sentiment of the romance in connection with any circumstances less conceivable than those which are indicated in the memorandum. But in such circumstances the step taken by Pausanias might have had no worse motive than the rescue of the woman who loved him from forced union with another; and Cleonice's assent to that step might have been quite compatible with the purity and heroism of her character. In this manner, moreover, a strong motive is prepared for that sentiment of revenge on the part of Antagoras whereby the dramatic interest of the story might be greatly heightened in the subsequent chapters. The intended introduction of the supernatural element is also clearly indicated. But apart from this, fine opportunities for psychological analysis would doubtless have occurred in tracing the gradual deterioration of such a character as that of Pausanias when, deprived of the guardian influence of a hope passionate but not impure, its craving for fierce excitement must have been stimulated by remorseful memories and impotent despairs. Indeed, the imperfect manuscript now printed, contains only the exposition of a tragedy. All the most striking effects, all the strongest dramatic situations, have been reserved for the pages of the manuscript which, alas, are either lost or unwritten.

Who can doubt, for instance, how effectually in the closing scenes of this tragedy the grim image of Alithea might have assumed the place assigned to it by history? All that we now see is the preparation made for its effective presentation in the foreground of such later scenes, by the chapter in the second volume describing the meeting between Lysander and the stern mother of his Spartan chief. In Lysander himself, moreover, we have the germ of a singularly dramatic situation. How would Lysander act in the final struggle which his character and fate are already preparing for him, between patriotism and friendship, his fidelity to Pausanias, and his devotion to Sparta? Is Lysander's father intended for that Ephor, who, in the last moment, made the sign that warned Pausanias to take refuge in the temple which became his living tomb? Probably. Would Themistocles, who was so seriously compromised in the conspiracy of Pausanias, have appeared and played a part in those scenes on which the curtain must remain unlifted? Possibly. Is Alcman the helot who revealed, to the Ephors, the gigantic plots of his master just when those plots were on the eve of execution? There is much in the relations between Pausanias and the Mothon, as they are described in the opening chapters of the romance, which favours, and indeed renders almost irresistible, such a supposition. But then, on the other hand, what genius on the part of the author could reconcile us to the perpetration by his hero of a crime so mean, so cowardly, as that personal perfidy to which history ascribes the revelation of the Regent's far more excusable treasons, and their terrible punishment?

These questions must remain unanswered. The magician can wave his wand no more. The circle is broken, the spells are scattered, the secret lost. The images which he evoked, and which he alone could animate, remain before us incomplete, semi-articulate, unable to satisfy the curiosity they inspire. A group of fragments, in many places broken, you have helped me to restore. With what reverent and kindly care, with what disciplined judgment and felicitous suggestion, you have accomplished the difficult task so generously undertaken, let me here most gratefully attest. Beneath the sculptor's name, allow me to inscribe upon the pedestal your own; and accept this sincere assurance of the inherited esteem and personal regard with which I am,

My dear Dr. Kennedy,
Your obliged and faithful
LYTTON.

CINTRA, 5 July, 1875.

PAUSANIAS, THE SPARTAN.

BOOK I.

CHAPTER I.

N one of the quays which bordered the unrivalled harbour of Byzantium, more than twenty-three centuries before the date at which this narrative is begun, stood two Athenians. In the waters of the haven rode the vessels of the Grecian Fleet. So deep was the basin, in which the tides are scarcely felt,[1] that the prows of some of the ships touched the quays, and the setting sun glittered upon the smooth and waxen surfaces of the prows rich with diversified colours and wrought gilding. To the extreme right of the fleet, and nearly opposite the place upon which the Athenians stood, was a vessel still more profusely ornamented than the rest. On the prow were elaborately carved the heads of the twin deities of the Laconian mariner, Castor and Pollux; in the centre of the deck was a wooden edifice or pavilion having a gilded roof and shaded by purple awnings, an imitation of the luxurious galleys of the Barbarian; while the parasemon, or flag, as it idly waved in the faint breeze of the gentle evening, exhibited the terrible serpent, which, if it was the fabulous type of demigods and heroes, might also be regarded as an emblem of the wily but stern policy of the Spartan State. Such was the galley of the commander of the armament, which (after the reduction of Cyprus) had but lately wrested from the yoke of Persia that link between her European and Asiatic domains, that key of the Bosporus —"the Golden Horn" of Byzantium.[2]

[1] Gibbon, ch. 17.
[2] "The harbour of Constantinople, which may be considered as an arm of the Bosphorus, obtained in a very remote period the denomination of the Golden Horn. The curve which it describes might be compared to the horn of a stag, or, as it should seem, with more propriety to that of an ox."—Gib. c. 17; Strab. l. x.

High above all other Greeks (Themistocles alone excepted) soared the fame of that renowned chief, Pausanias, Regent of Sparta and General of the allied troops at the victorious battle-field of Platæa. The spot on which the Athenians stood was lonely and now unoccupied, save by themselves and the sentries stationed at some distance on either hand. The larger proportion of the crews in the various vessels were on shore; but on the decks idly reclined small groups of sailors, and the murmur of their voices stole, indistinguishably blended, upon the translucent air. Behind rose, one above the other, the Seven Hills, on which long afterwards the Emperor Constantine built a second Rome; and over these heights, even then, buildings were scattered of various forms and dates, here the pillared temples of the Greek colonists, to whom Byzantium owed its origin, there the light roofs and painted domes which the Eastern conquerors had introduced.

One of the Athenians was a man in the meridian of manhood, of a calm, sedate, but somewhat haughty aspect; the other was in the full bloom of youth, of lofty stature, and with a certain majesty of bearing; down his shoulders flowed a profusion of long curled hair,[1] divided in the centre of the forehead, and connected with golden clasps, in which was wrought the emblem of the Athenian nobles— the Grasshopper—a fashion not yet obsolete, as it had become in the days of Thucydides. Still, to an observer, there was something heavy in the ordinary expression of the handsome countenance. His dress differed from the earlier fashion of the Ionians; it dispensed with those loose linen garments which had something of effeminacy in their folds, and was confined to the simple and statue-like grace that characterized the Dorian garb. Yet the clasp that fastened the chlamys upon the right shoulder, leaving the arm free, was of pure gold and exquisite workmanship, and the materials of the simple vesture were of a quality that betokened wealth and rank in the wearer.

"Yes, Cimon," said the elder of the Athenians, "yonder galley itself affords sufficient testimony of the change that has come over the haughty Spartan. It is difficult, indeed, to recognize in this luxurious satrap, who affects the dress, the manners, the very insolence of the Barbarian, that Pausanias who, after the glorious day of Platæa, ordered the slaves to prepare in the tent of Mardonius such a banquet as would have been served to the Persian, while his own Spartan broth and bread were set beside it, in order that he might utter to the chiefs of Greece that noble pleasantry, 'Behold the

---

[1] Ion *apud* Plut.

folly of the Persians, who forsook such splendour to plunder such poverty.'"[1]

"Shame upon his degeneracy, and thrice shame!" said the young Cimon, sternly. "I love the Spartans so well, that I blush for whatever degrades them. And all Sparta is dwarfed by the effeminacy of her chief."

"Softly, Cimon," said Aristides, with a sober smile. "Whatever surprise we may feel at the corruption of Pausanias, he is not one who will allow us to feel contempt. Through all the voluptuous softness acquired by intercourse with these Barbarians, the strong nature of the descendant of the demigod still breaks forth. Even at the distaff I recognize Alcides, whether for evil or for good. Pausanias is one on whom our most anxious gaze must be duly bent. But in this change of his I rejoice; the gods are at work for Athens. See you not that, day after day, while Pausanias disgusts the allies with the Spartans themselves, he throws them more and more into the arms of Athens? Let his madness go on, and ere long the violet-crowned city will become the queen of the seas."

"Such was my own hope," said Cimon, his face assuming a new expression, brightened with all the intelligence of ambition and pride; "but I did not dare own it to myself till you spoke. Several officers of Ionia and the Isles have already openly and loudly proclaimed to me their wish to exchange the Spartan ascendancy for the Athenian."

"And with all your love for Sparta," said Aristides, looking steadfastly and searchingly at his comrade, "you would not then hesitate to rob her of a glory which you might bestow on your own Athens?"

"Ah, am I not Athenian?" answered Cimon, with a deep passion in his voice. "Though my great father perished a victim to the injustice of a faction—though he who had saved Athens from the Mede died in the Athenian dungeon—still, fatherless, I see in Athens but a mother, and if her voice sounded harshly in my boyish years, in manhood I have feasted on her smiles. Yes, I honour Sparta, but I love Athens. You have my answer."

"You speak well," said Aristides, with warmth; "you are worthy of the destinies for which I foresee that the son of Miltiades is reserved. Be wary, be cautious; above all, be smooth, and blend with men of every state and grade. I would wish that the allies themselves should draw the contrast between the insolence of the Spartan chief and the courtesy of the Athenians. What said you to the Ionian officers?"

[1] Herod. ix. 82.

"I said that Athens held there was no difference between to command and to obey, except so far as was best for the interests of Greece; that—as on the field of Platæa, when the Tegeans asserted precedence over the Athenians, we, the Athenian army, at once exclaimed, through your voice, Aristides, 'We come here to fight the Barbarian, not to dispute amongst ourselves; place us where you will':[1]—even so now, while the allies give the command to Sparta, Sparta we will obey. But if we were thought by the Grecian States the fittest leaders, our answer would be the same that we gave at Platæa, 'Not we, but Greece be consulted: place us where you will!'"

"O wise Cimon!" exclaimed Aristides, "I have no caution to bestow on you. You do by intuition that which I attempt by experience. But hark! What music sounds in the distance? the airs that Lydia borrowed from the East?"

"And for which," said Cimon, sarcastically, "Pausanias hath abandoned the Dorian flute."

Soft, airy, and voluptuous were indeed the sounds which now, from the streets leading upwards from the quay, floated along the delicious air. The sailors rose, listening and eager, from the decks; there was once more bustle, life, and animation on board the fleet. From several of the vessels the trumpets woke a sonorous signal-note. In a few minutes the quays, before so deserted, swarmed with the Grecian mariners, who emerged hastily, whether from various houses in the haven, or from the encampment which stretched along it, and hurried to their respective ships. On board the galley of Pausanias there was more especial animation; not only mariners, but slaves, evidently from the Eastern markets, were seen, jostling each other, and heard talking, quick and loud, in foreign tongues. Rich carpets were unfurled and laid across the deck, while trembling and hasty hands smoothed into yet more graceful folds the curtains that shaded the gay pavilion in the centre. The Athenians looked on, the one with thoughtful composure, the other with a bitter smile, while these preparations announced the unexpected, and not undreaded, approach of the great Pausanias.

"Ho, noble Cimon!" cried a young man who, hurrying towards one of the vessels, caught sight of the Athenians and paused. "You are the very person whom I most desired to see. Aristides too!— we are fortunate."

The speaker was a young man of slighter make and lower stature than the Athenians, but well shaped, and with features the partial

---

[1] Plut. in Vit. Arist.

effeminacy of which was elevated by an expression of great vivacity and intelligence. The steed trained for Elis never bore in its proportions the evidence of blood and rare breeding more visibly than the dark brilliant eye of this young man, his broad low transparent brow, expanded nostril and sensitive lip, revealed the passionate and somewhat arrogant character of the vivacious Greek of the Ægean Isles.

"Antagoras," replied Cimon, laying his hand with frank and somewhat blunt cordiality on the Greek's shoulder, "like the grape of your own Chios, you cannot fail to be welcome at all times. But why would you seek us now?"

"Because I will no longer endure the insolence of this rude Spartan. Will you believe it, Cimon—will you believe it, Aristides? Pausanias has actually dared to sentence to blows, to stripes, one of my own men—a free Chian—nay, a Decadarchus.[1] I have but this instant heard it. And the offence—Gods! the *offence!*—was that he ventured to contest with a Laconian, an underling in the Spartan army, which one of the two had the fair right to a wine cask! Shall this be borne, Cimon?"

"Stripes to a Greek!" said Cimon, and the colour mounted to his brow. "Thinks Pausanias that the Ionian race are already his Helots?"

"Be calm," said Aristides; "Pausanias approaches. I will accost him."

"But listen still!" exclaimed Antagoras eagerly, plucking the gown of the Athenian as the latter turned away. "When Pausanias heard of the contest between my soldier and his Laconian, what said he, think you? 'Prior claim; learn henceforth that, where the Spartans are to be found, the Spartans in all matters have the prior claim.'"

"We will see to it," returned Aristides, calmly; "but keep by my side."

And now the music sounded loud and near, and suddenly, as the procession approached, the character of that music altered. The Lydian measures ceased, those who had attuned them gave way to musicians of loftier aspect and simpler garb; in whom might be recognized, not indeed the genuine Spartans, but their free, if subordinate, countrymen of Laconia; and a minstrel, who walked beside them, broke out into a song, partially adapted from the bold and lively strain of Alcæus, the first two lines in each stanza ringing much to that chime, the two latter reduced into briefer compass, as,

[1] Leader of ten men.

with allowance for the differing laws of national rhythm, we thus seek to render the verse :

SONG.

Multitudes, backward ! Way for the Dorian ;
Way for the Lord of rocky Laconia ;
  Heaven to Hercules opened
    Way on the earth for his son.

Steel and fate, blunted, break on his fortitude ;
Two evils only never endureth he—
  Death by a wound in retreating,
    Life with a blot on his name.

Rocky his birthplace ; rocks are immutable ;
So are his laws, and so shall his glory be.
  Time is the Victor of Nations,
    Sparta the Victor of Time.

Watch o'er him heedful on the wide ocean,
Brothers of Helen, luminous guiding stars ;
  Dangerous to Truth are the fickle,
    Dangerous to Sparta the seas.

Multitudes, backward ! Way for the Conqueror ;
Way for the footstep half the world fled before ;
  Nothing that Phœbus can shine on
    Needs so much space as Renown.

Behind the musicians came ten Spartans, selected from the celebrated three hundred who claimed the right to be stationed around the king in battle. Tall, stalwart, sheathed in armour, their shields slung at their backs, their crests of plumage or horsehair waving over their strong and stern features, these hardy warriors betrayed to the keen eye of Aristides their sullen discontent at the part assigned to them in the luxurious procession ; their brows were knit, their lips contracted, and each of them who caught the glance of the Athenians, turned his eyes, as half in shame, half in anger, to the ground.

Coming now upon the quay, opposite to the galley of Pausanias, from which was suspended a ladder of silken cords, the procession halted, and opening on either side, left space in the midst for the commander.

"He comes," whispered Antagoras to Cimon. "By Hercules ! I pray you survey him well. Is it the conqueror of Mardonius, or the ghost of Mardonius himself ?"

The question of the Chian seemed not extravagant to the blunt son of Miltiades, as his eyes now rested on Pausanias.

The pure Spartan race boasted, perhaps, the most superb models of masculine beauty which the land blessed by Apollo could afford.

The laws that regulate marriage ensured a healthful and vigorous progeny. Gymnastic discipline from early boyhood gave ease to the limbs, iron to the muscle, grace to the whole frame. Every Spartan, being born to command, being noble by his birth, lord of the Laconians, Master of the Helots, superior in the eyes of Greece to all other Greeks, was at once a Republican and an Aristocrat. Schooled in the arts that compose the presence, and give calmness and majesty to the bearing, he combined with the mere physical advantages of activity and strength a conscious and yet natural dignity of mien. Amidst the Greeks assembled at the Olympian contests, others showed richer garments, more sumptuous chariots, rarer steeds, but no state could vie with Sparta in the thews and sinews, the aspect and the majesty of the men. Nor were the royal race, the descendants of Hercules, in external appearance unworthy of their countrymen and of their fabled origin.

Sculptor and painter would have vainly tasked their imaginative minds to invent a nobler ideal for the effigies of a hero, than that which the Victor of Platæa offered to their inspiration. As he now paused amidst the group, he towered high above them all, even above Cimon himself. But in his stature there was nothing of the cumbrous bulk and stolid heaviness, which often destroy the beauty of vast strength. Severe and early training, long habits of rigid abstemiousness, the toils of war, and, more than all, perhaps, the constant play of a restless, anxious, aspiring temper, had left, undisfigured by superfluous flesh, the grand proportions of a frame, the very spareness of which had at once the strength and the beauty of one of those hardy victors in the wrestling or boxing match, whose agility and force are modelled by discipline to the purest forms of grace. Without that exact and chiselled harmony of countenance which characterized perhaps the Ionic rather than the Doric race, the features of the royal Spartan were noble and commanding. His complexion was sunburnt, almost to Oriental swarthiness, and the raven's plume had no darker gloss than that of his long hair, which (contrary to the Spartan custom), flowing on either side, mingled with the closer curls of the beard. To a scrutinizing gaze, the more dignified and prepossessing effect of this exterior would perhaps have been counterbalanced by an eye, bright indeed and penetrating, but restless and suspicious, by a certain ineffable mixture of arrogant pride and profound melancholy in the general expression of the countenance, ill according with that frank and serene aspect which best becomes the face of one who would lead mankind. About him altogether—the countenance, the form, the bearing—there was that which woke a vague, profound, and singular interest, an interest somewhat mingled with awe, but not altogether uncalculated to produce that affection which belongs to admiration, save when the sudden frown or disdainful lip repelled the gentler impulse and tended rather to excite fear, or to irritate pride, or to wound self-love.

But if the form and features of Pausanias were eminently those of the purest race of Greece, the dress which he assumed was no less characteristic of the Barbarian. He wore, not the garb of the noble Persian race, which, close and simple, was but a little less manly than that of the Greeks, but the flowing and gorgeous garments of the Mede. His long gown, which swept the earth, was covered with flowers wrought in golden tissue. Instead of the Spartan hat, the high Median cap or tiara crowned his perfumed and lustrous hair, while (what of all was most hateful to Grecian eyes) he wore, though otherwise unarmed, the curved scimitar and short dirk that were the national weapons of the Barbarian. And as it was not customary, nor indeed legitimate, for the Greeks to wear weapons on peaceful occasions and with their ordinary costume, so this departure from the common practice had not only in itself something offensive to the jealous eyes of his comrades, but was rendered yet more obnoxious by the adoption of the very arms of the East.

By the side of Pausanias was a man whose dark beard was already sown with gray. This man, named Gongylus, though a Greek—a native of Eretria, in Eubœa—was in high command under the great Persian king. At the time of the barbarian invasion under Datis and Artaphernes, he had deserted the cause of Greece and had been rewarded with the lordship of four towns in Æolis. Few among the apostate Greeks were more deeply instructed in the language and manners of the Persians; and the intimate and sudden friendship that had grown up between him and the Spartan was regarded by the Greeks with the most bitter and angry suspicion. As if to show his contempt for the natural jealousy of his countrymen, Pausanias, however, had just given to the Eretrian the government of Byzantium itself, and with the command of the citadel had entrusted to him the custody of the Persian prisoners captured in that port. Among these were men of the highest rank and influence at the court of Xerxes; and it was more than rumoured that of late Pausanias had visited and conferred with them, through the interpretation of Gongylus, far more frequently than became the General of the Greeks. Gongylus had one of those countenances which are observed when many of more striking semblance are overlooked. But the features were sharp and the visage lean, the eyes vivid and sparkling as those of the lynx, and the dark pupil seemed yet more dark from the extreme whiteness of the ball, from which it lessened or dilated with the impulse of the spirit which gave it fire. There was in that eye all the subtle craft, the plotting and restless malignity, which usually characterized those Greek renegades who prostituted their native energies to the rich service of the Barbarian; and the lips, narrow and thin, wore that everlasting smile which to the credulous disguises wile, and to the experienced betrays it. Small, spare, and prematurely bent, the Eretrian supported himself by a staff, upon which now leaning, he glanced, quickly and pryingly, around, till his eyes rested upon the Athenians, with the young Chian standing in their rear.

"The Athenian Captains are here to do you homage, Pausanias," said he in a whisper, as he touched with his small lean fingers the arm of the Spartan.

Pausanias turned and muttered to himself, and at that instant Aristides approached.

"If it please you, Pausanias, Cimon and myself, the leaders of the Athenians, would crave a hearing upon certain matters."

"Son of Lysimachus, say on."

"Your pardon, Pausanias," returned the Athenian, lowering his voice, and with a smile—"This is too crowded a council-hall; may we attend you on board your galley?"

"Not so," answered the Spartan haughtily; "the morning to affairs, the evening to recreation. We shall sail in the bay to see the moon rise, and if we indulge in consultations, it will be over our wine-cups. It is a good custom."

"It is a Persian one," said Cimon bluntly.

"It is permitted to us," returned the Spartan coldly, "to borrow from those we conquer. But enough of this. I have no secrets with the Athenians. No matter if the whole city hear what you would address to Pausanias."

"It is to complain," said Aristides with calm emphasis, but still in an undertone.

"Ay, I doubt it not: the Athenians are eloquent in grumbling."

"It was not found so at Platæa," returned Cimon.

"Son of Miltiades," said Pausanias loftily, "your wit outruns your experience. But my time is short. To the matter!"

"If you will have it so, I will speak," said Aristides, raising his voice. "Before your own Spartans, our comrades in arms, I proclaim our causes of complaint. Firstly, then, I demand release and compensation to seven Athenians, free-born and citizens, whom your orders have condemned to the unworthy punishment of standing all day in the open sun with the weight of iron anchors on their shoulders."

"The mutinous knaves!" exclaimed the Spartan. "They introduced into the camp the insolence of their own agora, and were publicly heard in the streets inveighing against myself as a favourer of the Persians."

"It was easy to confute the charge; it was tyrannical to punish words in men whose deeds had raised you to the command of Greece."

"*Their* deeds! Ye Gods, give me patience! By the help of Juno the protectress it was this brain and this arm that—— But I will not justify myself by imitating the Athenian fashion of wordy boasting. Pass on to your next complaint."

"You have placed slaves—yes, Helots—around the springs, to drive away with scourges the soldiers that come for water."

"Not so, but merely to prevent others from filling their vases until the Spartans are supplied."

"And by what right——?" began Cimon, but Aristides checked him with a gesture, and proceeded.

"That precedence is not warranted by custom, nor by the terms of our alliance; and the springs, O Pausanias, are bounteous enough to provide for all. I proceed. You have formally sentenced citizens and soldiers to the scourge. Nay, this very day you have extended the sentence to one in actual command amongst the Chians. Is it not so, Antagoras?"

"It is," said the young Chian, coming forward boldly; "and in the name of my countrymen I demand justice."

"And I also, Uliades of Samos," said a thick-set and burly Greek who had joined the group unobserved, "*I* demand justice. What, by the Gods! Are we to be all equals in the day of battle? 'My good sir, march here;' and, 'My dear sir, just run into that breach;' and yet when we have won the victory and should share the glory, is one state, nay, one man to seize the whole, and deal out iron anchors and tough cowhides to his companions? No, Spartans, this is not your view of the case; you suffer in the eyes of Greece by this misconduct. To Sparta itself I appeal."

"And what, most patient sir," said Pausanias, with calm sarcasm, though his eye shot fire, and the upper lip, on which no Spartan suffered the beard to grow, slightly quivered—"what is *your* contribution to the catalogue of complaints?"

"Jest not, Pausanias; you will find me in earnest," answered Uliades, doggedly, and encouraged by the evident effect that his eloquence had produced upon the Spartans themselves. "I have met with a grievous wrong, and all Greece shall hear of it, if it be not redressed. My own brother, who at Mycale slew four Persians with his own hand, headed a detachment for forage. He and his men were met by a company of mixed Laconians and Helots, their forage taken from them, they themselves assaulted, and my brother, a man who has monies and maintains forty slaves of his own, struck thrice across the face by a rascally Helot. Now, Pausanias, your answer!"

"You have prepared a notable scene for the commander of your forces, son of Lysimachus," said the Spartan, addressing himself to Aristides. "Far be it from me to affect the Agamemnon, but your friends are less modest in imitating the venerable model of Thersites. Enough" (and changing the tone of his voice, the chief stamped his foot vehemently to the ground): "we owe no account to our inferiors; we render no explanation save to Sparta and her Ephors."

"So be it, then," said Aristides, gravely; "we have our answer, and you will hear of our appeal."

Pausanias changed colour. "How?" said he, with a slight hesitation in his tone. "Mean you to threaten me—Me—with carrying the busy tales of your disaffection to the Spartan government?"

"Time will show. Farewell, Pausanias. We will detain you no longer from your pastime."

"But," began Uliades.

"Hush," said the Athenian, laying his hand on the Samian's shoulder. "We will confer anon."

Pausanias paused a moment, irresolute and in thought. His eyes glanced towards his own countrymen, who, true to their rigid discipline, neither spake nor moved, but whose countenances were sullen and overcast, and at that moment his pride was shaken, and his heart misgave him. Gongylus watched his countenance, and once more laying his hand on his arm, said in a whisper—

"He who seeks to rule never goes back."

"Tush, you know not the Spartans."

"But I know Human Nature; it is the same everywhere. You cannot yield to this insolence; to-morrow, of your own accord, send for these men separately and pacify them."

"You are right. Now to the vessel!"

With this, leaning on the shoulder of the Persian, and with a slight wave of his hand towards the Athenians—he did not deign even that gesture to the island officers—Pausanias advanced to the vessel, and slowly ascending, disappeared within his pavilion. The Spartans and the musicians followed; then, spare and swarthy, some half score of Egyptian sailors; last came a small party of Laconians and Helots, who, standing some distance behind Pausanias, had not hitherto been observed. The former were but slightly armed; the latter had forsaken their customary rude and savage garb, and wore long gowns and gay tunics, somewhat in the fashion of the Lydians. With these last there was one of a mien and aspect that strongly differed from the lowering and ferocious cast of countenance common to the Helot race. He was of the ordinary stature, and his frame was not characterized by any appearance of unusual strength; but he trod the earth with a firm step and an erect crest, as if the curse of the slave had not yet destroyed the inborn dignity of the human being. There was a certain delicacy and refinement, rather of thought than beauty, in his clear, sharp, and singularly intelligent features. In contradistinction from the free-born Spartans, his hair was short, and curled close above a broad and manly forehead; and his large eyes of dark blue looked full and bold upon the Athenians with something, if not of defiance, at least of pride in their gaze, as he stalked by them to the vessel.

"A sturdy fellow for a Helot," muttered Cimon.

"And merits well his freedom," said the son of Lysimachus. "I remember him well. He is Alcman, the foster-brother of Pausanias, whom he attended at Platæa. Not a Spartan that day bore himself more bravely."

"No doubt they will put him to death when he goes back to Sparta," said Antagoras. "When a Helot is brave, the Ephors clap the black mark against his name, and at the next crypteia he suddenly disappears."

"Pausanias may share the same fate as his Helot, for all I care," quoth Uliades. "Well, Athenians, what say you to the answer we have received?"

"That Sparta shall hear of it," answered Aristides.

"Ah, but is that all? Recollect the Ionians have the majority in the fleet; let us not wait for the slow Ephors. Let us at once throw off this insufferable yoke, and proclaim Athens the Mistress of the Seas. What say you, Cimon?"

"Let Aristides answer."

"Yonder lie the Athenian vessels," said Aristides. "Those who put themselves voluntarily under our protection we will not reject. But remember we assert no claim; we yield but to the general wish."

"Enough; I understand you," said Antagoras.

"Not quite," returned the Athenian with a smile, "The breach between you and Pausanias is begun, but it is not yet wide enough. You yourselves must do that which will annul all power in the Spartan, and then if ye come to Athens ye will find her as bold against the Doric despot as against the Barbarian foe."

"But speak more plainly. What would you have us do?" asked Uliades, rubbing his chin in great perplexity.

"Nay, nay, I have already said enough. Fare ye well, fellow-countrymen," and leaning lightly on the shoulder of Cimon, the Athenian passed on.

Meanwhile, the splendid galley of Pausanias slowly put forth into the farther waters of the bay. The oars of the rowers broke the surface into countless phosphoric sparkles, and the sound they made, as they dashed amidst the gentle waters, seemed to keep time with the song and the instruments on the deck. The Ionians gazed in silence as the stately vessel, now shooting far ahead of the rest, swept into the centre of the bay. And the moon, just rising, shone full upon the glittering prow, and streaked the rippling billows over which it had bounded, with a light, as it were, of glory.

Antagoras sighed.

"What think you of?" asked the rough Samian.

"Peace," replied Antagoras. "In this hour, when the fair face of Artemis recalls the old legends of Endymion, is it not permitted to man to remember that before the iron age came the golden, before war reigned love?"

"Tush," said Uliades. "Time enough to think of love when we have satisfied vengeance. Let us summon our friends, and hold council on the Spartan's insults."

"Whither goes now the Spartan?" murmured Antagoras abstractedly, as he suffered his companion to lead him away. Then halting abruptly, he struck his clenched hand on his breast.

"O Aphrodite!" he cried; "this night—this night I will seek thy temple. Hear my vows—soothe my jealousy!"

"Ah," grunted Uliades, "if, as men say, thou lovest a fair Byzantine, Aphrodite will have sharp work to cure thee of jealousy, unless she first makes thee blind."

Antagoras smiled faintly, and the two Ionians moved on slowly and in silence. In a few minutes more the quays were deserted, and nothing but the blended murmur, spreading wide and indistinct throughout the camp, and a noisier but occasional burst of merriment from those resorts of obscener pleasure which were profusely scattered along the haven, mingled with the whispers of "the far resounding sea."

CHAPTER II.

ON a couch, beneath his voluptuous awning, reclined Pausanias. The curtains, drawn aside, gave to view the moonlit ocean, and the dim shadows of the shore, with the dark woods beyond, relieved by the distant lights of the city. On one side of the Spartan was a small table, that supported goblets and vases of that exquisite wine which Maronea proffered to the thirst of the Byzantine, and those cooling and delicious fruits which the orchards around the city supplied as amply as the fabled gardens of the Hesperides, were heaped on the other side. Towards the foot of the couch, propped upon cushions piled on the floor, sat Gongylus, conversing in a low, earnest voice, and fixing his eyes steadfastly on the Spartan. The habits of the Eretrian's life, which had brought him in constant contact with the Persians, had infected his very language with the luxuriant extravagance of the East. And the thoughts he uttered made his language but too musical to the ears of the listening Spartan.

"And fair as these climes may seem to you, and rich as are the gardens and granaries of Byzantium, yet to me who have stood on the terraces of Babylon and looked upon groves covering with blossom and fruit the very fortresses and walls of that queen of nations,—to me, who have roved amidst the vast delights of Susa, through palaces whose very porticoes might enclose the limits of a Grecian city,—who have stood, awed and dazzled, in the courts of that wonder of the world, that crown of the East, the marble magnificence of Persepolis—to me, Pausanias, who have been thus admitted into the very heart of Persian glories, this city of Byzantium appears but a village of artisans and fishermen. The very foliage of its forests, pale and sickly, the very moonlight upon these waters, cold and smileless, ah, if thou couldst but see! But pardon me, I weary thee?"

"Not so," said the Spartan, who, raised upon his elbow, listened to the words of Gongylus with deep attention. "Proceed."

"Ah, if thou couldst but see the fair regions which the great king has apportioned to thy countryman Demaratus. And if a domain, that would satiate the ambition of the most craving of your earlier tyrants, fall to Demaratus, what would be the splendid satrapy in which the conqueror of Platæa might plant his throne?"

"In truth, my renown and my power are greater than those ever possessed by Demaratus," said the Spartan musingly.

"Yet," pursued Gongylus, "it is not so much the mere extent of the territories which the grateful Xerxes could proffer to the brave Pausanias—it is not their extent so much that might tempt desire, neither is it their stately forests, nor the fertile meadows, nor the ocean-like rivers, which the gods of the East have given to the race of Cyrus. There, free from the strange constraints which our austere customs and solemn Deities impose upon the Greeks, the beneficent Ormuzd scatters ever-varying delights upon the paths of men. All that art can invent, all that the marts of the universe can afford of the rare and voluptuous, are lavished upon abodes the splendour of which even our idle dreams of Olympus never shadowed forth. There, instead of the harsh and imperious helpmate to whom the joyless Spartan confines his reluctant love, all the beauties of every clime contend for the smile of their lord. And wherever are turned the change-loving eyes of Passion, the Aphrodite of our poets, such as the Cytherean and the Cyprian fable her, seems to recline on the lotus leaf or to rise from the unruffled ocean of delight. Instead of the gloomy brows and the harsh tones of rivals envious of your fame, hosts of friends aspiring only to be followers will catch gladness from your smile or sorrow from your frown. There, no jarring contests with little men, who deem themselves the equals of the great, no jealous Ephor is found, to load the commonest acts of life with fetters of iron custom. Talk of liberty! Liberty in Sparta is but one eternal servitude; you cannot move, or eat, or sleep, save as the law directs. Your very children are wrested from you just in the age when their voices sound most sweet. Ye are not men; ye are machines. Call you this liberty, Pausanias? I, a Greek, have known both Grecian liberty and Persian royalty. Better be chieftain to a king than servant to a mob! But in Eretria, at least, pleasure was not denied. In Sparta the very Graces preside over discipline and war only."

"Your fire falls upon flax," said Pausanias, rising, and with passionate emotion. "And if you, the Greek of a happier state, you who know but by report the unnatural bondage to which the Spartans are subjected, can weary of the very name of Greek, what must be the feelings of one who from the cradle upward has been starved out of the genial desires of life? Even in earliest youth, while yet all other lands and customs were unknown, when it was duly poured into my ears that to be born a Spartan constituted the glory and the bliss of earth, my soul sickened at the lesson, and my reason revolted against the lie. Often when my whole body was lacerated with stripes, disdaining to groan, I yet yearned to strike, and I cursed my savage tutors who denied pleasure even to childhood with all the madness of impotent revenge. My mother herself (sweet name elsewhere) had no kindness in her face. She was the pride of the matronage of Sparta, because of all our women Alithea was the most unsexed. When I went forth to my first crypteia, to watch, amidst the wintry dreariness of the mountains, upon the movements of the wretched Helots, to spy upon their sufferings, to take account of their groans, and if one more manly than the rest dared to mingle curses with his groans, to mark *him* for slaughter, as a wolf that threatened danger to the fold; to lurk, an assassin, about his home, to dog his walks, to fall on him unawares, to strike him from behind, to filch away his life, to bury him in the ravines, so that murder might leave no trace; when upon this initiating campaign, the virgin trials of our youth, I first set forth, my mother drew near, and girding me herself with my grandsire's sword, 'Go forth,' she said, 'as the young hound to the chase, to wind, to double, to leap on the prey, and to taste of blood. See, the sword is bright; show me the stains at thy return.'"

"Is it then true, as the Greeks generally declare," interrupted Gongylus, "that in these campaigns, or crypteias, the sole aim and object is the massacre of Helots?"

"Not so," replied Pausanias; "savage though the custom, it smells not so foully of the shambles. The avowed object is to harden the nerves of our youth. Barefooted, unattended, through cold and storm, performing ourselves the most menial offices necessary to life, we wander for a certain season daily and nightly through the rugged territories of Laconia.[1] We go as boys—we come back as men.[2] The avowed object, I say, is inurement to hardship, but with this is connected the secret end of keeping watch on these half-tamed and bull-like herds of men whom we call the Helots. If any be dangerous, we mark him for the knife. One of them had thrice been a ringleader in revolt. He was wary as well as fierce. He had escaped in three succeeding crypteias. To me, as one of the Heraclidæ, was assigned the honour of tracking and destroying him. For three days and three nights I dogged his footsteps, (for he had caught the scent of the pursuers and fled,) through forest and defile, through valley and crag, stealthily and relentlessly. I followed him close. At last, one evening, having lost sight of all my comrades, I came suddenly upon him as I emerged from a wood. It was a

[1] Plat. Leg. i. p. 633. See also Müller's Dorians, vol. ii. p. 41.
[2] Pueros puberes—neque prius in urbem redire quam viri facti essent.—Justin iii. 3.

broad patch of waste land, through which rushed a stream swollen by the rains, and plunging with a sullen roar down a deep and gloomy precipice, that to the right and left bounded the waste, the stream in front, the wood in the rear. He was reclining by the stream, at which, with the hollow of his hand, he quenched his thirst. I paused to gaze upon him, and as I did so he turned and saw me. He rose, and fixed his eyes on mine, and we examined each other in silence. The Helots are rarely of tall stature, but this was a giant. His dress, that of his tribe, of rude sheep-skins, and his cap made from the hide of a dog increased the savage rudeness of his appearance. I rejoiced that he saw me, and that, as we were alone, I might fight him fairly. It would have been terrible to slay the wretch if I had caught him in his sleep."

"Proceed," said Gongylus, with interest, for so little was known of Sparta by the rest of the Greeks, especially outside the Peloponnesus, that these details gratified his natural spirit of gossiping inquisitiveness.

"'Stand!' said I, and he moved not. I approached him slowly. 'Thou art a Spartan,' said he, in a deep and harsh voice, 'and thou comest for my blood. Go, boy, go, thou art not mellowed to thy prime, and thy comrades are far away. The shears of the Fatal deities hover over the thread not of my life but of thine.' I was struck, Gongylus, by this address, for it was neither desperate nor dastardly, as I had anticipated; nevertheless, it beseemed not a Spartan to fly from a Helot, and I drew the sword which my mother had girded on. The Helot watched my movements, and seized a rude and knotted club that lay on the ground beside him.

"'Wretch,' said I, 'darest thou attack face to face a descendant of the Heraclidæ? In me behold Pausanias, the son of Cleombrotus.'

"'Be it so; in the city one is the god-born, the other the man-enslaved. On the mountains we are equals.'

"'Knowest thou not,' said I, 'that if the Gods condemned me to die by thy hand, not only thou, but thy whole house, thy wife and thy children, would be sacrificed to my ghost?'

"'The earth can hide the Spartan's bones as secretly as the Helot's,' answered my strange foe. 'Begone, young and unfleshed in slaughter as you are; why make war upon me? My death can give you neither gold nor glory. I have never harmed thee or thine. How much of the air and sun does this form take from the descendant of the Heraclidæ?'

"'Thrice hast thou raised revolt among the Helots, thrice at thy voice have they risen in bloody, though fruitless, strife against their masters.'

"'Not at my voice, but at that of the two deities who are the war-gods of slaves—Persecution and Despair.'[1]

"Impatient of this parley, I tarried no longer. I sprang upon the Helot. He evaded my sword, and I soon found that all my agility and skill were requisite to save me from the massive weapon, one blow of which would have sufficed to crush me. But the Helot seemed to stand on the defensive, and continued to back towards the wood from which I had emerged. Fearful lest he would escape me, I pressed hard on his footsteps. My blood grew warm; my fury got the better of my prudence. My foot stumbled; I recovered in an instant, and, looking up, beheld the terrible club suspended over my head; it might have fallen, but the stroke of death was withheld. I misinterpreted the merciful delay; the lifted arm left the body of my enemy exposed. I struck him on the side; the thick hide blunted the stroke, but it drew blood. Afraid to draw back within the reach of his weapon, I threw myself on him, and grappled to his throat. We rolled on the earth together; it was but a moment's struggle. Strong as I was even in boyhood, the Helot would have been a match for Alcides. A shade passed over my eyes; my breath heaved short. The slave was kneeling on my breast, and, dropping the club, he drew a short knife from his girdle. I gazed upon him grim and mute. I was conquered, and I cared not for the rest.

"The blood from his side, as he bent over me, trickled down upon my face.

"'And this blood,' said the Helot, 'you shed in the very moment when I spared your life; such is the honour of a Spartan. Do you not deserve to die?'

"'Yes, for I am subdued, and by a slave. Strike!'

"'There,' said the Helot in a melancholy and altered tone, 'there speaks the soul of the Dorian, the fatal spirit to which the Gods have rendered up our wretched race. We are doomed—doomed—and one victim will not expiate our curse. Rise, return to Sparta, and forget that thou art innocent of murder.'

"He lifted his knee from my breast, and I rose, ashamed and humbled.

"At that instant I heard the crashing of the leaves in the wood, for the air was exceedingly still. I knew that my companions were at hand. 'Fly,' I cried; 'fly. If they come I cannot save thee, royal though I be. Fly.'

[1] When Themistocles sought to extort tribute from the Andrians, he said, "I bring with me two powerful gods—Persuasion and Force." "And on our side," was the answer, "are two deities not less powerful—Poverty and Despair!"

"'And *wouldest* thou save me!' said the Helot in surprise.

"'Ay, with my own life. Canst thou doubt it? Lose not a moment. Fly. Yet stay;' and I tore off a part of the woollen vest that I wore. 'Place this at thy side; staunch the blood, that it may not track thee. Now begone!'

"The Helot looked hard at me, and I thought there were tears in his rude eyes; then catching up the club with as much ease as I this staff, he sped with inconceivable rapidity, despite his wound, towards the precipice on the right, and disappeared amidst the thick brambles that clothed the gorge. In a few moments three of my companions approached. They found me exhausted, and panting rather with excitement than fatigue. Their quick eyes detected the blood upon the ground. I gave them no time to pause and examine. 'He has escaped me—he has fled,' I cried; 'follow,' and I led them to the opposite part of the precipice from that which the Helot had taken. Heading the search, I pretended to catch a glimpse of the goatskin ever and anon through the trees, and I stayed not the pursuit till night grew dark, and I judged the victim was far away."

"And he escaped?"

"He did. The crypteia ended. Three other Helots were slain, but not by me. We returned to Sparta, and my mother was comforted for my misfortune in not having slain my foe by seeing the stains on my grandsire's sword. I will tell thee a secret, Gongylus"—(and here Pausanias lowered his voice, and looked anxiously towards him)—"since that day I have not hated the Helot race. Nay, it may be that I have loved them better than the Dorian."

"I do not wonder at it; but has not your wounded giant yet met with his death?"

"No, I never related what had passed between us to any one save my father. He was gentle for a Spartan, and he rested not till Gylippus—so was the Helot named—obtained exemption from the black list. He dared not, however, attribute his intercession to the true cause. It happened, fortunately, that Gylippus was related to my own foster-brother, Alcman, brother to my nurse; and Alcman is celebrated in Sparta, not only for courage in war, but for arts in peace. He is a poet, and his strains please the Dorian ear, for they are stern and simple, and they breathe of war. Alcman's merits won forgiveness for the offences of Gylippus. May the Gods be kind to his race!"

"Your Alcman seems one of no common intelligence, and your gentleness to him does not astonish me, though it seems often to raise a frown on the brows of your Spartans."

"We have lain on the same bosom." said Pausanias touchingly, "and his mother was kinder to me than my own. You must know that to those Helots who have been our foster-brothers, and whom we distinguish by the name of Mothons, our stern law relaxes. They have no rights of citizenship, it is true, but they cease to be slaves;[1] nay, sometimes they attain not only to entire emancipation, but to distinction. Alcman has bound his fate to mine. But to return, Gongylus. I tell thee that it is not thy descriptions of pomp and dominion that allure me, though I am not above the love of power, neither is it thy glowing promises, though blood too wild for a Dorian runs riot in my veins; but it is my deep loathing, my inexpressible disgust for Sparta and her laws, my horror at the thought of wearing away life in those sullen customs, amid that joyless round of tyrannic duties, in my rapture at the hope of escape, of life in a land which the eye of the Ephor never pierces; this it is, and this alone, O Persian, that makes me (the words must out) a traitor to my country, one who dreams of becoming a dependent on her foe."

"Nay," said Gongylus eagerly; for here Pausanias moved uneasily, and the colour mounted to his brow. "Nay, speak not of dependence. Consider the proposals that you can alone condescend to offer to the great king. Can the conqueror of Plataea, with millions for his subjects, hold himself dependent, even on the sovereign of the East? How, hereafter, will the memories of our sterile Greece and your rocky Sparta fade from your mind; or be remembered only as a state of thraldom and bondage, which your riper manhood has outgrown!"

"I will try to think so, at least," said Pausanias gloomily. "And, come what may, I am not one to recede. I have thrown my shield into a fearful peril; but I will win it back or perish. Enough of this, Gongylus. Night advances. I will attend the appointment you have made. Take the boat, and within an hour I will meet you with the prisoners at the spot agreed on, near the Temple of Aphrodite. All things are prepared?"

"All," said Gongylus, rising, with a gleam of malignant joy on his dark face. "I leave thee, kingly slave of the rocky Sparta, to prepare the way for thee, as Satrap of half the East."

So saying he quitted the awning, and motioned three Egyptian sailors who lay on the deck without. A boat was lowered, and the sound of its oars woke Pausanias from the reverie into which the parting words of the Eretrian had plunged his mind.

---

[1] The appellation of Mothons was not confined to the Helots who claimed the connection of foster-brothers, but was given also to household slaves.

CHAPTER III.

WITH a slow and thoughtful step, Pausanias passed on to the outer deck. The moon was up, and the vessel scarcely seemed to stir, so gently did it glide along the sparkling waters. They were still within the bay, and the shores rose, white and distinct, to his view. A group of Spartans, reclining by the side of the ship, were gazing listlessly on the waters. The Regent paused beside them.

"Ye weary of the ocean, methinks," said he. "We Dorians have not the merchant tastes of the Ionians."[1]

"Son of Cleombrotus," said one of the group, a Spartan whose rank and services entitled him to more than ordinary familiarity with the chief, "it is not the ocean itself that we should dread, it is the contagion of those who, living on the element, seem to share in its ebb and flow. The Ionians are never three hours in the same mind."

"For that reason," said Pausanias, fixing his eyes steadfastly on the Spartan, "for that reason I have judged it advisable to adopt a rough manner with these innovators, to draw with a broad chalk the line between them and the Spartans, and to teach those who never knew discipline the stern duties of obedience. Think you I have done wisely?"

The Spartan, who had risen when Pausanias addressed him, drew his chief a little aside from the rest.

"Pausanias," said he, "the hard Naxian stone best tames and tempers the fine steel;[2] but the steel may break if the workman be not skilful. These Athenians are grown insolent since Marathon, and their soft kindred of Asia have relighted the fires they took of old from the Cecropian Prytaneum. Their sail is more numerous than ours; on the sea they find the courage they lose on land. Better be gentle with those wayward allies, for the Spartan greyhound shows not his teeth but to bite."

"Perhaps you are right. I will consider these things, and appease the mutineers. But it goes hard with my pride, Thrasyllus, to make equals of this soft-tongued race. Why, these Ionians, do they not enjoy themselves in perpetual holidays?—spend days at the banquet?—ransack earth and sea for dainties and for perfumes?—and shall they be the equals of us men, who, from the age of seven to that of

---

[1] No Spartan served as a sailor, or indeed condescended to any trade or calling, but that of war.
[2] Pind. Isth. v. (vi.) 73.

sixty, are wisely taught to make life so barren and toilsome, that we may well have no fear of death? I hate these sleek and merry feast-givers; they are a perpetual insult to our solemn existence."

There was a strange mixture of irony and passion in the Spartan's voice as he thus spoke, and Thrasyllus looked at him in grave surprise.

"There is nothing to envy in the womanlike debaucheries of the Ionian," said he, after a pause.

"Envy! no; we only hate them, Thrasyllus. Yon Eretrian tells me rare things of the East. Time may come when we shall sup on the black broth in Susa."

"The Gods forbid! Sparta never invades. Life with us is too precious, for we are few. Pausanias, I would we were well quit of Byzantium. I do not suspect you, not I; but there are those who look with vexed eyes on those garments, and I, who love you, fear the sharp jealousies of the Ephors, to whose ears the birds carry all tidings."

"My poor Thrasyllus," said Pausanias, laughing scornfully, "think you that I wear these robes, or mimic the Median manners, for love of the Mede? No, no! But there are arts which save countries as well as those of war. This Gongylus is in the confidence of Xerxes. I desire to establish a peace for Greece upon everlasting foundations. Reflect; Persia hath millions yet left. Another invasion may find a different fortune; and even at the best, Sparta gains nothing by these wars. Athens triumphs, not Lacedæmon. I would, I say, establish a peace with Persia. I would that Sparta, not Athens, should have that honour. Hence these flatteries to the Persian—trivial to us who render them, sweet and powerful to those who receive. Remember these words hereafter, if the Ephors make question of my discretion. And now, Thrasyllus, return to our friends, and satisfy them as to the conduct of Pausanias."

Quitting Thrasyllus, the Regent now joined a young Spartan who stood alone by the prow in a musing attitude.

"Lysander, my friend, my only friend, my best-loved Lysander," said Pausanias, placing his hand on the Spartan's shoulder. "And why so sad?"

"How many leagues are we from Sparta?" answered Lysander mournfully.

"And canst thou sigh for the black broth, my friend? Come, how often hast thou said, 'Where Pausanias is, *there* is Sparta!'"

"Forgive me, I am ungrateful," said Lysander with warmth. "My benefactor, my guardian, my hero, forgive me if I have added to your own countless causes of anxiety. Wherever you are there is life, and there glory. When I was just born, sickly and feeble, I was exposed on Taygetus. You, then a boy, heard my faint cry, and took on me that compassion which my parents had forsworn. You bore me to your father's roof, you interceded for my life. You prevailed even on your stern mother. I was saved; and the Gods smiled upon the infant whom the son of the humane Hercules protected. I grew up strong and hardy, and belied the signs of my birth. My parents then owned me; but still you were my fosterer, my saviour, my more than father. As I grew up, placed under your care, I imbibed my first lessons of war. By your side I fought, and from your example I won glory. Yes, Pausanias, even here, amidst luxuries which revolt me more than the Parthian bow and the Persian sword, even amidst the faces of the stranger, I still feel thy presence my home, thyself my Sparta."

The proud Pausanias was touched, and his voice trembled as he replied, "Brother in arms and in love, whatever service fate may have allowed me to render unto thee, thy high nature and thy cheering affection have more than paid me back. Often in our lonely rambles amidst the dark oaks of the sacred Scotitas,[1] or by the wayward waters of Tiasa,[2] when I have poured into thy faithful breast my impatient loathing, my ineffable distaste for the iron life, the countless and wearisome tyrannies of custom which surround the Spartans, often have I found a consoling refuge in thy divine contentment, thy cheerful wisdom. Thou lovest Sparta; why is she not worthier of thy love? Allowed only to be half men, in war we are demigods, in peace, slaves. Thou wouldst interrupt me. Be silent. I am in a wilful mood; thou canst not comprehend me, and I often marvel at thee. Still we are friends, such friends as the Dorian discipline, which makes friendship necessary in order to endure life, alone can form. Come, take up thy staff and mantle. Thou shalt be my companion ashore. I seek one whom alone in the world I love better than thee. To-morrow to stern duties once more. Alcman shall row us across the bay, and as we glide along, if thou wilt praise Sparta, I will listen to thee as the Ionians listen to their tale-tellers. Ho! Alcman, stop the rowers, and lower the boat."

The orders were obeyed, and a second boat soon darted towards the same part of the bay as that to which the one that bore Gongylus had directed its course. Thrasyllus and his companions watched the boat that bore Pausanias and his two comrades, as it bounded, arrow-like, over the glassy sea.

---

[1] Paus. Lac. x.   [2] *Ib.*, c. xviii.

"Whither goes Pausanias?" asked one of the Spartans.
"Back to Byzantium on business," replied Thrasyllus.
"And we?"
"Are to cruise in the bay till his return."
"Pausanias is changed."
"Sparta will restore him to what he was. Nothing thrives out of Sparta. Even man spoils."
"True, sleep is the sole constant friend the same in all climates."

CHAPTER IV.

ON the shore to the right of the port of Byzantium were at that time thickly scattered the villas or suburban retreats of the wealthier and more luxurious citizens. Byzantium was originally colonized by the Megarians, a Dorian race kindred with that of Sparta; and the old features of the pure and antique Hellas were still preserved in the dialect,[1] as well as in the forms of the descendants of the colonists; in their favourite deities, and rites, and traditions; even in the names of places, transferred from the sterile Megara to that fertile coast; in the rigid and helot-like slavery to which the native Bithynians were subjected, and in the attachment of their masters to the oligarchic principles of government. Nor was it till long after the present date, that democracy in its most corrupt and licentious form was introduced amongst them. But like all the Dorian colonies, when once they departed from the severe and masculine mode of life inherited from their ancestors, the reaction was rapid, the degeneracy complete. Even then the Byzantines, intermingled with the foreign merchants and traders that thronged their haven, and womanized by the soft contagion of the East, were voluptuous, timid, and prone to every excess save that of valour. The higher class were exceedingly wealthy, and gave to their vices or their pleasures a splendour and refinement of which the elder states of Greece were as yet unconscious. At a later period, indeed, we are informed that the Byzantine citizens had their habitual residence in the public hostels, and let their houses—not even taking the trouble to remove their wives—to the strangers who crowded their gay capital. And when their general found it necessary to demand

---

[1] "The Byzantine dialect was in the time of Philip, as we know from the decree in Demosthenes, rich in dorisms."—Müller on the Doric Dialect.

their aid on the ramparts, he could only secure their attendance by ordering the taverns and cookshops to be removed to the place of duty. Not yet so far sunk in sloth and debauch, the Byzantines were nevertheless hosts eminently dangerous to the austerer manners of their Greek visitors. The people, the women, the delicious wine, the balm of the subduing climate served to tempt the senses and relax the mind. Like all the Dorians, when freed from primitive restraint, the higher class, that is, the descendants of the colonists, were in themselves an agreeable, jovial race. They had that strong bias to humour, to jest, to satire, which in their ancestral Megara gave birth to the Grecian comedy, and which lurked even beneath the pithy aphorisms and rude merry-makings of the severe Spartan.

Such were the people with whom of late Pausanias had familiarly mixed, and with whose manners he contrasted, far too favourably for his honour and his peace, the habits of his countrymen.

It was in one of the villas we have described, the favourite abode of the rich Diagoras, and in an apartment connected with those more private recesses of the house appropriated to the females, that two persons were seated by a window which commanded a wide view of the glittering sea below. One of these was an old man in a long robe that reached to his feet, with a bald head and a beard in which some dark hairs yet withstood the encroachments of the gray. In his well-cut features and large eyes were remains of the beauty that characterized his race; but the mouth was full and wide, the forehead low though broad, the cheeks swollen, the chin double, and the whole form corpulent and unwieldy. Still there was a jolly, sleek good humour about the aspect of the man that prepossessed you in his favour. This personage, who was no less than Diagoras himself, was reclining lazily upon a kind of narrow sofa cunningly inlaid with ivory, and studying new combinations in that scientific game which Palamedes is said to have invented at the siege of Troy.

His companion was of a very different appearance. She was a girl who to the eye of a northern stranger might have seemed about eighteen, though she was probably much younger, of a countenance so remarkable for intelligence that it was easy to see that her mind had outgrown her years. Beautiful she certainly was, yet scarcely of that beauty from which the Greek sculptor would have drawn his models. The features were not strictly regular, and yet so harmoniously did each blend with each, that to have amended one would have spoilt the whole. There was in the fulness and depth of the large but genial eye, with its sweeping fringe, and straight, slightly chiselled brow, more of Asia than of Greece. The lips, of the

M

freshest red, were somewhat full and pouting, and dimples without number lay scattered round them—lurking places for the loves. Her complexion was clear though dark, and the purest and most virgin bloom mantled, now paler now richer, through the soft surface. At the time we speak of she was leaning against the open door with her arms crossed on her bosom, and her face turned towards the Byzantine. Her robe, of a deep yellow, so trying to the fair women of the North, became well the glowing colours of her beauty—the damask cheek, the purple hair. Like those of the Ionians, the sleeves of the robe, long and loose, descended to her hands, which were marvellously small and delicate. Long earrings, which terminated in a kind of berry, studded with precious stones, then common only with the women of the East; a broad collar, or necklace, of the smaragdus or emerald; and large clasps, medallion-like, where the swan-like throat joined the graceful shoulder, gave to her dress an appearance of opulence and splendour that betokened how much the ladies of Byzantium had borrowed from the fashions of the Oriental world. Nothing could exceed the lightness of her form, rounded, it is true, but slight and girlish, and the high instep, with the slender foot, so well set off by the embroidered sandal, would have suited such dances as those in which the huntress nymphs of Delos moved around Diana. The natural expression of her face, if countenance so mobile and changeful had one expression more predominant than another, appeared to be irresistibly arch and joyous, as of one full of youth and conscious of her beauty; yet, if a cloud came over the face, nothing could equal the thoughtful and deep sadness of the dark abstracted eyes, as if some touch of higher and more animated emotion—such as belongs to pride, or courage, or intellect—vibrated on the heart. The colour rose, the form dilated, the lip quivered, the eye flashed light, and the mirthful expression heightened almost into the sublime. Yet, lovely as Cleonice was deemed at Byzantium, lovelier still as she would have appeared in modern eyes, she failed in what the Greeks generally, but especially the Spartans, deemed an essential of beauty—in height of stature. Accustomed to look upon the virgin but as the future mother of a race of warriors, the Spartans saw beauty only in those proportions which promised a robust and stately progeny, and the reader may remember the well-known story of the opprobrious reproaches, even, it is said, accompanied with stripes, which the Ephors addressed to a Spartan king for presuming to make choice of a wife below the ordinary stature. Cleonice was small and delicate, rather like the Peri of the Persian than the sturdy Grace of the Dorian. But her beauty was her least charm. She had all that feminine fascination of manner, wayward, varying, inexpressible, yet irresistible, which seizes hold of the imagination as well as the senses, and which has so often made willing slaves of the proud rulers of the world. In fact Cleonice, the daughter of Diagoras, had enjoyed those advantages of womanly education wholly unknown at that time to the freeborn ladies of Greece proper, but which gave to the women of some of the isles and Ionian cities their celebrity in ancient story. Her mother was of Miletus, famed for the intellectual cultivation of the sex, no less than for their beauty—of Miletus, the birthplace of Aspasia—of Miletus, from which those remarkable women who, under the name of Hetaeræ, exercised afterwards so signal an influence over the mind and manners of Athens, chiefly derived their origin, and who seem to have inspired an affection, which in depth, constancy, and fervour, approached to the more chivalrous passion of the North. Such an education consisted not only in the feminine and household arts honoured universally throughout Greece, but in a kind of spontaneous and luxuriant cultivation of all that captivates the fancy and enlivens the leisure. If there were something pedantic in their affectation of philosophy, it was so graced and vivified by a brilliancy of conversation, a charm of manner carried almost to a science, a womanly facility of softening all that comes within their circle, of suiting yet refining each complexity and discord of character admitted to their intercourse, that it had at least nothing masculine or harsh. Wisdom, taken lightly or easily, seemed but another shape of poetry. The matrons of Athens, who could often neither read nor write—ignorant, vain, tawdry, and not always faithful, if we may trust to such scandal as has reached the modern time—must have seemed insipid beside these brilliant strangers; and while certainly wanting their power to retain love, must have had but a doubtful superiority in the qualifications that ensure esteem. But we are not to suppose that the Hetaeræ (that mysterious and important class peculiar to a certain state of society, and whose appellation we cannot render by any proper word in modern language) monopolized all the graces of their countrywomen. In the same cities were many of unblemished virtue and repute who possessed equal cultivation and attraction, but whom a more decorous life has concealed from the equivocal admiration of posterity; though the numerous female disciples of Pythagoras throw some light on their capacity and intellect. Among such as these had been the mother of Cleonice, not long since dead, and her daughter inherited and equalled her accomplishments, while her virgin youth, her inborn playfulness of manner, her pure guilelessness, which the secluded habits of the unmarried women at

Byzantium preserved from all contagion, gave to qualities and gifts so little published abroad, the effect as it were of a happy and wondrous inspiration rather than of elaborate culture.

Such was the fair creature whom Diagoras, looking up from his pastime, thus addressed:—

"And so, perverse one, thou canst not love this great hero, a proper person truly, and a mighty warrior, who will eat you an army of Persians at a meal. These Spartan fighting-cocks want no garlic, I warrant you.[1] And yet you can't love him, you little rogue."

"Why, my father," said Cleonice, with an arch smile, and a slight blush, "even if I did look kindly on Pausanias, would it not be to my own sorrow? What Spartan—above all, what royal Spartan—may marry with a foreigner, and a Byzantine?"

"I did not precisely talk of marriage—a very happy state, doubtless, to those who dislike too quiet a life, and a very honourable one, for war is honour itself; but I did not speak of that, Cleonice. I would only say that this man of might loves thee—that he is rich, rich, rich. Pretty pickings at Platæa; and we have known losses, my child, sad losses. And if you do not love him, why, you can but smile and talk as if you did, and when the Spartan goes home, you will lose a tormenter and gain a dowry."

"My father, for shame!"

"Who talks of shame? You women are always so sharp at finding oracles in oak leaves, that one don't wonder Apollo makes choice of your sex for his priests. But listen to me, girl, seriously," and here Diagoras with a great effort raised himself on his elbow, and lowering his voice, spoke with evident earnestness. "Pausanias has life and death, and, what is worse, wealth or poverty in his hands; he can raise or ruin us with a nod of his head, this black-curled Jupiter. They tell me that he is fierce, irascible, haughty; and what slighted lover is not revengeful? For my sake, Cleonice, for your poor father's sake, show no scorn, no repugnance; be gentle, play with him, draw not down the thunderbolt, even if you turn from the golden shower."

While Diagoras spoke, the girl listened with downcast eyes and flushed cheeks, and there was an expression of such shame and sadness on her countenance, that even the Byzantine, pausing and looking up for a reply, was startled by it.

"My child," said he, hesitatingly and absorbed, "do not miscon-

---

[1] Fighting-cocks were fed with garlic, to make them more fierce. The learned reader will remember how Theorus advised Dicæopolis to keep clear of the Thracians with garlic in their mouths.—See the Acharnians of Aristoph.

ceive me. Cursed be the hour when the Spartan saw thee; but since the Fates have so served us, let us not make bad worse. I love thee, Cleonice, more dearly than the apple of my eye; it is for *thee* I fear, for thee I speak. Alas! it is not dishonour I recommend, it is force I would shun."

"Force!" said the girl, drawing up her form with sudden animation. "Fear not that. It is not Pausanias I dread, it is——"

"What then?"

"No matter; talk of this no more. Shall I sing to thee?"

"But Pausanias will visit us this very night."

"I know it. Hark!" and with her finger to her lip, her ear bent downward, her cheek varying from pale to red, from red to pale, the maiden stole beyond the window to a kind of platform or terrace that overhung the sea. There, the faint breeze stirring her long hair, and the moonlight full upon her face, she stood, as stood that immortal priestess who looked along the starry Hellespont for the young Leander; and her ear had not deceived her. The oars were dashing in the waves below, and dark and rapid the boat bounded on towards the rocky shore. She gazed long and steadfastly on the dim and shadowy forms which that slender raft contained, and her eye detected amongst the three the loftier form of her haughty wooer. Presently the thick foliage that clothed the descent shut the boat, nearing the strand, from her view; but she now heard below, mellowed and softened in the still and fragrant air, the sound of the cithara and the melodious song of the Mothon, thus imperfectly rendered from the language of immortal melody.

SONG.

Carry a sword in the myrtle bough,
Ye who would honour the tyrant-slayer;
I, in the leaves of the myrtle bough,
Carry a tyrant to slay myself.

I pluck'd the branch with a hasty hand,
But Love was lurking amidst the leaves;
His bow is bent and his shaft is poised,
And I must perish or pass the bough.

Maiden, I come with a gift to thee,
Maiden, I come with a myrtle wreath;
Over thy forehead, or round thy breast
Bind, I implore thee, my myrtle wreath.[1]

---

[1] Garlands were twined round the neck, or placed upon the bosom ($\dot{v}\pi o\theta v\mu i\alpha\delta\epsilon\varsigma$). See the quotations from Alcæus, Sappho, and Anacreon in Athenæus, book xiii.
c. 17.

From hand to hand by the banquet lights
On with the myrtle bough passes song:
From hand to hand by the silent stars
What with the myrtle wreath passes? **Love.**

I bear the god in a myrtle wreath,
Under the stars let him pass to thee;
Empty his quiver and bind his wings,
Then pass the myrtle wreath back to me.

Cleonice listened breathlessly to the words, and sighed heavily as they ceased. Then, as the foliage rustled below, she turned quickly into the chamber and seated herself at a little distance from Diagoras; to all appearance calm, indifferent and composed. Was it nature, or the arts of Miletus, that taught the young beauty the hereditary artifices of the sex?

"So it is he, then?" said Diagoras, with a fidgety and nervous trepidation. "Well, he chooses strange hours to visit us. But he is right; his visits cannot be too private. Cleonice, you look provokingly at your ease."

Cleonice made no reply, but shifted her position so that the light from the lamp did not fall upon her face, while her father, hurrying to the threshold of his hall to receive his illustrious visitor, soon reappeared with the Spartan Regent, talking as he entered with the volubility of one of the parasites of Alciphron and Athenæus.

"This is most kind, most affable. Cleonice said you would come, Pausanias, though I began to distrust you. The hours seem long to those who expect pleasure."

"And, Cleonice, *you* knew that I should come," said Pausanias, approaching the fair Byzantine; but his step was timid, and there was no pride now in his anxious eye and bended brow.

"You said you would come to-night," said Cleonice, calmly, "and Spartans, according to proverbs, speak the truth."

"When it is to their advantage, yes,"[1] said Pausanias, with a slight curl of his lips; and, as if the girl's compliment to his countrymen had roused his spleen and changed his thoughts, he seated himself moodily by Cleonice, and remained silent.

The Byzantine stole an arch glance at the Spartan, as he thus sat, from the corner of her eyes, and said, after a pause—

"You Spartans ought to speak the truth more than other people, for you say much less. We too have our proverb at Byzantium, and one which implies that it requires some wit to tell fibs."

---

[1] So said Thucydides of the Spartans, many years afterwards. "They give evidence of honour among themselves, but with respect to others, they consider honourable whatever pleases them, and just whatever is to their advantage."—See Thucyd. lib. v.

"Child, child!" exclaimed Diagoras, holding up his hand reprovingly, and directing a terrified look at the Spartan. To his great relief, Pausanias smiled, and replied—

"Fair maiden, we Dorians are said to have a wit peculiar to ourselves, but I confess that it is of a nature that is but little attractive to your sex. The Athenians are blander wooers."

"Do you ever attempt to woo in Lacedæmon, then? Ah, but the maidens there, perhaps, are not difficult to please."

"The girl puts me in a cold sweat!" muttered Diagoras, wiping his brow. And this time Pausanias did not smile; he coloured, and answered gravely—

"And is it, then, a vain hope for a Spartan to please a Byzantine?"

"You puzzle me. That is an enigma; put it to the oracle."

The Spartan raised his eyes towards Cleonice, and, as she saw the inquiring, perplexed look that his features assumed, the ruby lips broke into so wicked a smile, and the eyes that met his had so much laughter in them, that Pausanias was fairly bewitched out of his own displeasure.

"Ah, cruel one!" said he, lowering his voice, "I am not so proud of being Spartan that the thought should console me for thy mockery."

"Not proud of being Spartan! say not so," exclaimed Cleonice. "Who ever speaks of Greece and places not Sparta at her head? Who ever speaks of freedom and forgets Thermopylæ? Who ever burns for glory, and sighs not for the fame of Pausanias and Platæa? Ah, yes, even in jest say not that you are not proud to be a Spartan!"

"The little fool!" cried Diagoras, chuckling, and mightily delighted; "she is quite mad about Sparta—no wonder!"

Pausanias, surprised and moved by the burst of the fair Byzantine, gazed at her admiringly, and thought within himself how harshly the same sentiment would have sounded on the lips of a tall Spartan virgin; but when Cleonice heard the approving interlocution of Diagoras, her enthusiasm vanished from her face, and putting out her lips poutingly, she said, "Nay, father, I repeat only what others say of the Spartans. They are admirable heroes; but from the little I have seen, they are——"

"What?" said Pausanias eagerly, and leaning nearer to Cleonice.

"Proud, dictatorial, and stern as companions."

Pausanias once more drew back.

"There it is again!" groaned Diagoras. "I feel exactly as if I were playing at odd and even with a lion; she does it to vex me. I shall retaliate and creep away."

"Cleonice," said Pausanias, with suppressed emotion, "you trifle with me, and I bear it."

"You are condescending. How would you avenge yourself?"

"How!"

"You would not beat me; you would not make me bear an anchor on the shoulders, as they say you do your soldiers. Shame on you! *you* bear with me! true, what help for you?"

"Maiden," said the Spartan, rising in great anger, "for him who loves and is slighted there is a revenge you have not mentioned."

"For him who *loves!* No, Spartan; for him who shuns disgrace and courts the fame dear to gods and men, there is no revenge upon women. Blush for your threat."

"You madden, but subdue me," said the Spartan as he turned away. He then first perceived that Diagoras had gone—that they were alone. His contempt for the father awoke suspicion of the daughter. Again he approached and said, "Cleonice, I know but little of the fables of poets, yet is it an old maxim often sung and ever belied, that love scorned becomes hate. There are moments when I think I hate thee."

"And yet thou hast never loved me," said Cleonice; and there was something soft and tender in the tone of her voice, and the rough Spartan was again subdued.

"I never loved thee! What, then, is love? Is not thine image always before me?—amidst schemes, amidst perils of which thy very dreams have never presented equal perplexity or phantoms so uncertain, I am occupied but with thee. Surely, as upon the hyacinth is written the exclamation of woe, so on this heart is graven thy name. Cleonice, you who know not what it is to love, you affect to deny or to question mine."

"And what," said Cleonice, blushing deeply, and with tears in her eyes, "what result can come from such a love? You may not wed with the stranger. And yet, Pausanias, yet you know that all other love dishonours the virgin even of Byzantium. You are silent; you turn away. Ah, do not let them wrong you. My father fears your power. If you love me you are powerless; your power has passed to me. Is it not so? I, a weak girl, can rule, command, irritate, mock you, if I will. You may fly me, but not control."

"Do not tempt me too far, Cleonice," said the Spartan, with a faint smile.

"Nay, I will be merciful henceforth, and you, Pausanias, come here no more. Awake to the true sense of what is due to your divine ancestry—your great name. Is it not told of you that, after the fall of Mardonius, you nobly dismissed to her country, unscathed and honoured, the captive Coan lady?[1] Will you reverse at Byzantium the fame acquired at Platæa? Pausanias, spare us; appeal not to my father's fear, still less to his love of gold."

"I cannot, I cannot fly thee," said the Spartan, with great emotion. "You know not how stormy, how inexorable are the passions which burst forth after a whole youth of restraint. When nature breaks the barriers, she rushes headlong on her course. I am no gentle wooer; where in Sparta should I learn the art? But, if I love thee not as these mincing Ionians, who come with offerings of flowers and song, I do love thee with all that fervour of which the old Dorian legends tell. I could brave, like the Thracian, the dark gates of Hades, were thy embrace my reward. Command me as thou wilt—make me thy slave in all things, even as Hercules was to Omphale; but tell me only that I may win thy love at last. Fear not. Why fear me? in my wildest moments a look from thee can control me. I ask but love for love. Without thy love thy beauty were valueless. Bid me not despair."

Cleonice turned pale, and the large tears that had gathered in her eyes fell slowly down her cheeks; but she did not withdraw her hand from his clasp, or avert her countenance from his eyes.

"I do not fear thee," said she, in a very low voice. "I told my father so; but—but—" (and here she drew back her hand and averted her face), "I fear myself."

"Ah, no, no," cried the delighted Spartan, detaining her, "do not fear to trust to thine own heart. Talk not of dishonour. There are" (and here the Spartan drew himself up, and his voice took a deeper swell)—"there are those on earth who hold themselves above the miserable judgments of the vulgar herd—who can emancipate themselves from those galling chains of custom and of country which helotize affection, genius, nature herself. What is dishonour here may be glory elsewhere; and this hand, outstretched towards a mightier sceptre than Greek ever wielded yet, may dispense, not shame and sorrow, but glory and golden affluence to those I love."

"You amaze me, Pausanias. *Now* I fear you. What mean these mysterious boasts? Have you the dark ambition to restore in your own person that race of tyrants whom your country hath helped to sweep away? Can you hope to change the laws of Sparta, and reign there, your will the state?"

"Cleonice, we touch upon matters that should not disturb the ears of women. Forgive me if I have been roused from myself."

[1] Herod. ix.

"At Miletus—so have I heard my mother say—there were women worthy to be the confidants of men."

"But they were women who loved. Cleonice, I should rejoice in an hour when I might pour every thought into thy bosom."

At this moment there was heard on the strand below a single note from the Mothon's instrument, low, but prolonged; it ceased, and was again renewed. The royal conspirator started and breathed hard.

"It is the signal," he muttered; "they wait me. Cleonice," he said aloud, and with much earnestness in his voice, "I had hoped, ere we parted, to have drawn from your lips those assurances which would give me energy for the present and hope in the future. Ah, turn not from me because my speech is plain and my manner rugged. What, Cleonice, what if I could defy the laws of Sparta; what if, instead of that gloomy soil, I could bear thee to lands where heaven and man alike smile benignant on love? Might I not hope then?"

"Do nothing to sully your fame."

"Is it, then, dear to thee?"

"It is a part of thee," said Cleonice falteringly; and as if she had said too much, she covered her face with her hands.

Emboldened by this emotion, the Spartan gave way to his passion and his joy. He clasped her in his arms—his first embrace—and kissed, with wild fervour, the crimsoned forehead, the veiling hands. Then, as he tore himself away, he cast his right arm aloft.

"O Hercules!" he cried, in solemn and kindling adjuration, "my ancestor and my divine guardian, it was not by confining thy labours to one spot of earth, that thou wert borne from thy throne of fire to the seats of the Gods. Like thee I will spread the influence of my arms to nations whose glory shall be my name; and as thy sons, my fathers, expelled from Sparta, returned thither with sword and spear to defeat usurpers and to found the long dynasty of the Heracleids, even so may it be mine to visit that dread abode of torturers and spies, and to build up in the halls of the Atridæ a power worthier of the lineage of the demigod. Again the signal! Fear not, Cleonice, I will not tarnish my fame, but I will exchange the envy of abhorring rivals for the obedience of a world. One kiss more! Farewell!"

Ere Cleonice recovered herself, Pausanias was gone, his wild and uncomprehended boasts still ringing in her ear. She sighed heavily, and turned towards the opening that admitted to the terraces. There she stood watching for the parting of her lover's boat. It was midnight; the air, laden with the perfumes of a thousand fragrant shrubs and flowers that bloom along that coast in the rich luxuriance of nature, was hushed and breathless. In its stillness every sound was audible, the rustling of a leaf, the ripple of a wave. She heard the murmur of whispered voices below, and in a few moments she recognized, emerging from the foliage, the form of Pausanias; but he was not alone. Who were his companions? In the deep lustre of that shining and splendid atmosphere she could see sufficient of the outline of their figures to observe that they were not dressed in the Grecian garb; their long robes betrayed the Persian.

They seemed conversing familiarly and eagerly as they passed along the smooth sands, till a curve in the wooded shore hid them from her view.

"Why do I love him so," said the girl mechanically, "and yet wrestle against that love? Dark forebodings tell me that Aphrodite smiles not on our vows. Woe is me! What will be the end?"

CHAPTER V.

ON quitting Cleonice, Pausanias hastily traversed the long passage that communicated with a square peristyle or colonnade, which again led, on the one hand, to the more public parts of the villa, and, on the other, through a small door left ajar, conducted by a back entrance, to the garden and the sea-shore. Pursuing the latter path, the Spartan bounded down the descent and came upon an opening in the foliage, in which Lysander was seated beside the boat that had been drawn partially on the strand.

"Alone? Where is Alcman?"

"Yonder; you heard his signal?"

"I heard it."

"Pausanias, they who seek you are Persians. Beware!"

"Of what? murder? I am warned."

"Murder to your good name. There are no arms against appearances."

"But I may trust thee?" said the Regent, quickly, "and of Alcman's faith I am convinced."

"Why trust to any man what it were wisdom to reveal to the whole Grecian Council? To parley secretly with the foe is half a treason to our friends."

"Lysander," replied Pausanias, coldly, "you have much to learn before you can be wholly Spartan. Tarry here yet awhile."

"What shall I do with this boy?" muttered the conspirator as he strode on. "I know that he will not betray me, yet can I hope for his aid? I love him so well that I would fain he shared my fortunes. Perhaps by little and little I may lead him on. Meanwhile, his race and his name are so well accredited in Sparta, his father himself an Ephor, that his presence allays suspicion. Well, here are my Persians."

A little apart from the Mothon, who, resting his cithara on a fragment of rock, appeared to be absorbed in reflection, stood the men of the East. There were two of them; one of tall stature and noble presence, in the prime of life; the other more advanced in years, of a coarser make, a yet darker complexion, and of a sullen and gloomy countenance. They were not dressed alike; the taller, a Persian of pure blood, wore a short tunic that reached only to the keees: and the dress fitted to his shape without a single fold. On his round cap or bonnet glittered a string of those rare pearls, especially and immemorially prized in the East, which formed the favourite and characteristic ornament of the illustrious tribe of the Pasargadæ. The other, who was a Mede, differed scarcely in his dress from Pausanias himself, except that he was profusely covered with ornaments; his arms were decorated with bracelets, he wore earrings, and a broad collar of unpolished stones in a kind of filagree was suspended from his throat. Behind the Orientals stood Gongylus, leaning both hands on his staff, and watching the approach of Pausanias with the same icy smile and glittering eye with which he listened to the passionate invectives or flattered the dark ambition of the Spartan. The Orientals saluted Pausanias with a lofty gravity, and Gongylus drawing near, said: "Son of Cleombrotus, the illustrious Ariamanes, kinsman to Xerxes, and of the House of the Achæmenids, is so far versed in the Grecian tongue that I need not proffer my offices as interpreter. In Datis, the Mede, brother to the most renowned of the Magi, you behold a warrior worthy to assist the arms even of Pausanias."

"I greet ye in our Spartan phrase, 'The beautiful to the good,'" said Pausanias, regarding the Barbarians with an earnest gaze. "And I requested Gongylus to lead ye hither in order that I might confer with ye more at ease, than in the confinement to which I regret ye are still sentenced. Not in prisons should be held the conversations of brave men."

"I know," said Ariamanes (the statelier of the Barbarians), in the Greek tongue, which he spoke intelligibly indeed, but with slowness and hesitation, "I know that I am with that hero who refused to dishonour the corpse of Mardonius, and even though a captive I converse without shame with my victor."

"Rested it with me alone, your captivity should cease," replied Pausanias. "War, that has made me acquainted with the valour of the Persians, has also enlightened me as to their character. Your king has ever been humane to such of the Greeks as have sought a refuge near his throne. I would but imitate his clemency."

"Had the great Darius less esteemed the Greeks he would never have invaded Greece. From the wanderers whom misfortune drove to his realms, he learned to wonder at the arts, the genius, the energies of the people of Hellas. He desired less to win their territories than to gain such subjects. Too vast, alas, was the work he bequeathed to Xerxes."

"He should not have trusted to force alone," returned Pausanias. "Greece may be won, but by the arts of her sons, not by the arms of the stranger. A Greek only can subdue Greece. By such profound knowledge of the factions, the interests, the envies and the jealousies of each state as a Greek alone can possess, the mistaken chain that binds them might be easily severed; some bought, some intimidated, and the few that hold out subdued amidst the apathy of the rest."

"You speak wisely, right hand of Hellas," answered the Persian, who had listened to these remarks with deep attention. "Yet had we in our armies your countryman, the brave Demaratus."

"But, if I have heard rightly, ye too often disdained his counsel. Had he been listened to there had been neither a Salamis nor a Platæa.[1] Yet Demaratus himself had been too long a stranger to Greece, and he knew little of any state save that of Sparta. Lives he still?"

"Surely yes, in honour and renown; little less than the son of Darius himself."

"And what reward would Xerxes bestow on one of greater influence than Demaratus; on one who has hitherto conquered every foe, and now beholds before him the conquest of Greece herself?"

"If such a man were found," answered the Persian, "let his

---

[1] After the action at Thermopylæ, Demaratus advised Xerxes to send three hundred vessels to the Laconian coast, and seize the island of Cythera, which commanded Sparta. "The profound experience of Demaratus in the selfish and exclusive policy of his countrymen made him argue that if this were done the fear of Sparta for herself would prevent her joining the forces of the rest of Greece, and leave the latter a more easy prey to the invader."—*Athens, its Rise and Fall*. This advice was overruled by Achæmenes. So again, had the advice of Artemisia, the Carian princess, been taken—to delay the naval engagement of Salamis, and rather to sail to the Peloponnesus—the Greeks, failing of provisions and divided among themselves, would probably have dispersed.

thought run loose, **let** his imagination rove, let him seek only how to find a fitting estimate of the gratitude **of** the king and the vastness of the service."

Pausanias shaded his brow with **his** hand, and mused a few moments; then lifting his eyes to the Persian's watchful but composed countenance, he said, with a slight smile—

"Hard is it, **O** Persian, when the choice is actually before him, **for a** man to renounce his country. There have been hours within this very day when my desires swept afar from Sparta, from all Hellas, and rested on the tranquil pomp of Oriental Satrapies. But now, rude and stern parent though Sparta be to me, I feel still that I am her son; and, while we speak, a throne in stormy Hellas seems the fitting object of a Greek's ambition. In a word, then, I would rise, and yet raise my country. **I would** have at my will a force that may suffice to overthrow in Sparta its grim and unnatural laws, to found amidst its rocks that single **throne** which the son of a demigod should ascend. From that throne **I would** spread my empire over the whole of Greece, Corinth and **Athens** being my tributaries. So that, though men now, and posterity hereafter, may say, 'Pausanias overthrew the Spartan government,' they shall add, 'but Pausanias annexed to the Spartan sceptre the realm **of** Greece. Pausanias was a tyrant, but not a traitor.' How, O Persian, can **these designs accord** with the policy of the Persian king?"

"**Not without** the authority of my master can I answer thee," replied Ariamanes, "so that my answer may be as the king's signet to his decree. But so much at least I say: that it is not the custom of the Persians to interfere with the institutions of those states with which they are connected. Thou desirest to make a monarchy of Greece, with Sparta for its **head.** Be it so; **the** king my master will aid thee so to scheme and **so to** reign, provided thou dost but concede to him a vase of the water from thy fountains, a fragment of **earth** from thy gardens."

"**In other** words," said Pausanias thoughtfully, but with a slight **colour** on his brow, "if I hold my dominions tributary to the king?"

"The dominions that by the king's aid thou wilt have conquered. Is that a hard law?"

"To a Greek and a Spartan the **very** mimicry of allegiance to the foreigner is hard."

The Persian smiled. "Yet, if I understand thee aright, O Chief, **even** kings in Sparta are but subjects to their people. Slave to a crowd at home, or tributary to a throne abroad; slave every hour, **or tributary** for earth and water once a year, which is the freer lot?"

"Thou canst not understand our Grecian notions," replied Pausanias, "nor have I leisure to explain them. But though I may subdue Sparta to myself as to its native sovereign, I will not, even by a type, subdue the land of the Heracleid to the Barbarian."

Ariamanes looked grave; the difficulty raised was serious. And here the craft of Gongylus interposed.

"This may be adjusted, Ariamanes, as befits both parties. Let Pausanias rule in Sparta as he lists, and Sparta stand free of tribute. But for all other states and cities that Pausanias, aided by the great king, shall conquer, let the vase be filled, and the earth be Grecian. Let him but render tribute for those lands which the Persians submit to his sceptre. So shall the pride of the Spartan be appeased, and the claims of the king be satisfied."

"Shall it be so?" said Pausanias.

"Instruct me so to propose to my master, and I will do my best to content him with the exception to the wonted rights of the Persian diadem. And then," continued Ariamanes, "then, Pausanias, Conqueror of Mardonius, Captain at Platæa, thou art indeed a man with whom the lord of Asia may treat as an equal. Greeks before thee have offered to render Greece to the king my master; but they were exiles and fugitives, they had nothing to risk or lose; thou hast fame, and command, and power, and riches, and all——"

"But for a throne," interrupted Gongylus.

"It does not matter what may be my motives," returned the Spartan gloomily, "and were I to tell them, you might not comprehend. But so much by way of explanation. You too have held command?"

"I have."

"If you knew that, when power became to you so sweet that it was as necessary to life itself as food and drink, it would then be snatched from you for ever, and you would serve as a soldier in the very ranks you had commanded as a leader; if you knew that no matter what your services, your superiority, your desires, this shameful fall was inexorably doomed, might you not see humiliation in power itself, obscurity in renown, gloom in the present, despair in the future? And would it not seem to you nobler even to desert the camp than to sink into a subaltern?"

"Such a prospect has in our country made out of good subjects fierce rebels," observed the Persian.

"Ay, ay, I doubt it not," said Pausanias, laughing bitterly. "Well, then, such will be my lot, if I pluck not out a fairer one from the Fatal Urn. As Regent of Sparta, while my nephew is beardless, I am general of her armies, and I have the sway and functions of her king. When he arrives at the customary age, I am a subject, a citizen, a nothing, a miserable fool of memories gnawing my heart away amidst joyless customs and stern austerities, with the recollection of the glories of Plataea and the delights of Byzantium. Persian, I am filled from the crown to the sole with the desire of power, with the tastes of pleasure. I have that within me which before my time has made heroes and traitors, raised demigods to Heaven, or chained the lofty Titans to the rocks of Hades. Something I may yet be; I know not what. But as the man never returns to the boy, so never, never, never once more, can I be again the Spartan subject. Enough; such as I am, I can fulfil what I have said to thee. Will thy king accept me as his ally, and ratify the terms I have proposed?"

"I feel well-nigh assured of it," answered the Persian; "for since thou hast spoken thus boldly, I will answer thee in the same strain. Know, then, that we of the pure race of Persia, we the sons of those who overthrew the Mede, and extended the race of the mountain tribe, from the Scythian to the Arab, from Egypt to Ind, we at least feel that no sacrifice were too great to redeem the disgrace we have suffered at the hands of thy countrymen; and the world itself were too small an empire, too confined a breathing-place for the son of Darius, if this nook of earth were still left without the pale of his dominion."

"This nook of earth? Ay, but Sparta itself must own no lord but me."

"It is agreed."

"If I release thee, wilt thou bear these offers to the king, travelling day and night till thou restest at the foot of his throne?"

"I should carry tidings too grateful to suffer me to loiter by the road."

"And Datis, he comprehends us not; but his eyes glitter fiercely on me. It is easy to see that thy comrade loves not the Greek."

"For that reason he will aid us well. Though but a Mede, and not admitted to the privileges of the Pasargadæ, his relationship to the most powerful and learned of our Magi, and his own services in war, have won him such influence with both priests and soldiers, that I would fain have him as my companion. I will answer for his fidelity to our joint object."

"Enough; ye are both free. Gongylus, you will now conduct our friends to the place where the steeds await them. You will then privately return to the citadel, and give to their pretended escape the probable appearances we devised. Be quick, while it is yet night. One word more. Persian, our success depends upon thy speed. It is while the Greeks are yet at Byzantium, while I yet am in command, that we should strike the blow. If the king consent, through Gongylus thou wilt have means to advise me. A Persian army must march at once to the Phrygian confines, instructed to yield command to me when the hour comes to assume it. Delay not that aid by such vast and profitless recruits as swelled the pomp, but embarrassed the arms, of Xerxes. Armies too large rot by their own unwieldiness into decay. A band of 50,000, composed solely of the Medes and Persians, will more than suffice. With such an army, if my command be undisputed, I will win a second Platæa, but against the Greek."

"Your suggestions shall be law. May Ormuzd favour the bold!"

"Away, Gongylus. You know the rest."

Pausanias followed with thoughtful eyes the receding forms of Gongylus and the Barbarians. "I have passed for ever," he muttered, "the pillars of Hercules. I must go on or perish. If I fall, I die execrated and abhorred; if I succeed, the sound of the choral flutes will drown the hootings. Be it as it may, I do not and will not repent. If the wolf gnaw my entrails, none shall hear me groan." He turned and met the eyes of Alcman, fixed on him so intently, so exultingly, that, wondering at their strange expression, he drew back and said haughtily, "You imitate Medusa, but I am stone already."

"Nay," said the Mothon, in a voice of great humility, "if you are of stone, it is like the divine one which, when borne before armies, secures their victory. Blame me not that I gazed on you with triumph and hope. For, while you conferred with the Persian, methought the murmurs that reached my ear sounded thus: 'When Pausanias shall rise, Sparta shall bend low, and the Helot shall break his chains.'"

"They do not hate me, these Helots?"

"You are the only Spartan they love."

"Were my life in danger from the Ephors——"

"The Helots would rise to a man."

"Did I plant my standard on Taygetus, though all Sparta encamped against it——"

"All the slaves would cut their way to thy side. O Pausanias, think how much nobler it were to reign over tens of thousands who become freemen at thy word, than to be but the equal of 10,000 tyrants."

"The Helots fight well, when well led," said Pausanias, as if to himself. "Launch the boat."

"Pardon me, Pausanias, but is it prudent any longer to trust Lysander? He is the pattern of the Spartan youth, and Sparta is his mistress. He loves her too well not to blab to her every secret."

"O Sparta, Sparta, wilt thou not leave me one friend?" exclaimed Pausanias. "No, Alcman, I will not separate myself from Lysander, till I despair of his alliance. To your oars! be quick."

At the sound of the Mothon's tread upon the pebbles, Lysander, who had hitherto remained motionless, reclining by the boat, rose and advanced towards Pausanias. There was in his countenance, as the moon shining on it cast over his statue-like features a pale and marble hue, so much of anxiety, of affection, of fear, so much of the evident, unmistakable solicitude of friendship, that Pausanias, who, like most men, envied and unloved, was susceptible even of the semblance of attachment, muttered to himself, "No, thou wilt not desert me, nor I thee."

"My friend, my Pausanias," said Lysander, as he approached, "I have had fears—I have seen omens. Undertake nothing, I beseech thee, which thou hast meditated this night."

"And what hast thou seen?" said Pausanias, with a slight change of countenance.

"I was praying the Gods for thee and Sparta, when a star shot suddenly from the heavens. Pausanias, this is the eighth year, the year in which on moonless nights the Ephors watch the heavens."

"And if a star fall they judge their kings," interrupted Pausanias (with a curl of his haughty lip), "to have offended the Gods, and suspend them from their office till acquitted by an oracle at Delphi, or a priest at Olympia. A wise superstition. But, Lysander, the night is not moonless, and the omen is therefore nought."

Lysander shook his head mournfully, and followed his chieftain to the boat, in gloomy silence.

BOOK II.

CHAPTER I.

AT noon the next day, not only the vessels in the harbour presented the same appearance of inactivity and desertion which had characterized the preceding evening, but the camp itself seemed forsaken. Pausanias had quitted his ship for the citadel, in which he took up his lodgment when on shore : and most of the officers and sailors of the squadron were dispersed among the taverns and wine-shops, for which, even at that day, Byzantium was celebrated.

It was in one of the lowest and most popular of these latter resorts, and in a large and rude chamber, or rather outhouse, separated from the rest of the building, that a number of the Laconian Helots were assembled. Some of these were employed as sailors, others were the military attendants on the Regent and the Spartans who accompanied him.

At the time we speak of, these unhappy beings were in the full excitement of that wild and melancholy gaiety which is almost peculiar to slaves in their hours of recreation, and in which reaction of wretchedness modern writers have discovered the indulgence of a native humour. Some of them were drinking deep, wrangling, jesting, laughing in loud discord over their cups. At another table rose the deep voice of a singer, chanting one of those antique airs known but to these degraded sons of the Homeric Archæan, and probably in its origin going beyond the date of the Tale of Troy ; a song of gross and rustic buffoonery, but ever and anon charged with some image or thought worthy of that language of the universal Muses. His companions listened with a rude delight to the rough voice and homely sounds, and now and then interrupted the wassailers at the other tables by cries for silence, which none regarded. Here and there, with intense and fierce anxiety on their faces, small groups were playing at dice ; for gambling is the passion of slaves. And many of these men, to whom wealth could bring no comfort, had secretly amassed large hoards at the plunder of Platæa, from which they had sold to the traders of Ægina gold at the price of brass. The appearance of the rioters was startling and melancholy. They were mostly stunted and undersized, as are generally the progeny of the sons of woe; lean and gaunt with early hardship, the spine of the back curved and bowed by habitual degradation; but with the hard-knit sinews and prominent muscles which are produced by labour and the mountain air; and under shaggy and lowering brows sparkled many a fierce, perfidious, and malignant eye; while as mirth, or gaming, or song, aroused smiles in the various groups, the rude features spoke of passions easily released from the sullen bondage of servitude, and revealed the nature of the animals which thraldom had failed to tame. Here and there however were to be seen forms, unlike the rest, of stately stature, of fair proportions, wearing the divine lineaments of Grecian beauty. From some of these a higher nature spoke out, not in mirth, that last mockery of supreme woe, but in an expression of stern, grave, and disdainful melancholy; others, on the contrary, surpassed the rest in vehemence, clamour, and exuberant extravagance of emotion, as if their nobler physical development only served to entitle them to that base superiority. For health and vigour can make an aristocracy even among Helots. The garments of these merrymakers increased the peculiar effect of their general appearance. The Helots in military excursions naturally relinquished the rough sheep-skin dress that characterized their countrymen at home, the serfs of the soil. The sailors had thrown off, for coolness, the leathern jerkins they habitually wore, and, with their bare arms and breasts, looked as if of a race that yet shivered, primitive and unredeemed, on the outskirts of civilization.

Strangely contrasted with their rougher comrades, were those who, placed occasionally about the person of the Regent, were indulged with the loose and clean robes of gay colours worn by the Asiatic slaves; and these ever and anon glanced at their finery with an air of conscious triumph. Altogether, it was a sight that might well have appalled, by its solemn lessons of human change, the poet who would have beheld in that embruted flock the descendants of the race over whom Pelops and Atreus, and Menelaus, and Agamemnon the king of men, had held their antique sway, and might still more have saddened the philosopher who believed, as Menander has nobly written, 'That Nature knows no slaves.'

Suddenly, in the midst of the confused and uproarious hubbub, the door opened, and Alcman the Mothon entered the chamber. At this sight the clamour ceased in an instant. The party rose, as by a general impulse, and crowded round the new comer.

"My friends," said he, regarding them with the same calm and frigid indifference which usually characterized his demeanour, "you do well to make merry while you may, for something tells me it will not last long. We shall return to Lacedæmon. You look black. So, then, is there no delight in the thought of home?"

"*Home!*" muttered one of the Helots, and the word, sounding drearily on his lips, was echoed by many, so that it circled like a groan.

"Yet ye have your children as much as if ye were free," said Alcman.

"And for that reason it pains us to see them play, unaware of the future," said a Helot of better mien than his comrades.

"But do you know," returned the Mothon, gazing on the last speaker steadily, "that for your children there may not be a future fairer than that which your fathers knew?"

"Tush!" exclaimed one of the unhappy men, old before his time, and of an aspect singularly sullen and ferocious. "Such have been your half-hints and mystic prophecies for years. What good comes of them? Was there ever an oracle for Helots?"

"There was no repute in the oracles even of Apollo," returned Alcman, "till the Apollo-serving Dorians became conquerors. Oracles are the children of victories."

"But there are no victories for us," said the first speaker mournfully.

"Never, if ye despair," said the Mothon loftily. "What," he added after a pause, looking round at the crowd, "what, do ye not see that hope dawned upon us from the hour when thirty-five thousand of us were admitted as soldiers, ay, and as conquerors, at Platæa? From that moment we knew our strength. Listen to me. At Samos once a thousand slaves—mark me, but a thousand,—escaped the yoke—seized on arms, fled to the mountains (we have mountains even in Laconia), descended from time to time to devastate the fields and to harass their ancient lords. By habit they learned war, by desperation they grew indomitable. What became of these slaves? were they cut off? Did they perish by hunger, by the sword, in the dungeon or field? No; those brave men were the founders of Ephesus."[1]

"But the Samians were not Spartans," mumbled the old Helot.

"As ye will, as ye will," said Alcman, relapsing into his usual coldness. "I wish you never to strike unless ye are prepared to die or conquer."

"Some of us are," said the younger Helot.

[1] Malacus ap. Athen. 6.

"Sacrifice a cock to the Fates, then."

"But why think you," asked one of the Helots, "that we shall be so soon summoned back to Laconia?"

"Because while ye are drinking and idling here—drones that ye are—there is commotion in the Athenian bee-hive yonder. Know that Ariamanes the Persian and Datis the Mede have escaped. The allies, especially the Athenians, are excited and angry; and many of them are already come in a body to Pausanias, whom they accuse of abetting the escape of the fugitives."

"Well?"

"Well, and if Pausanias does not give honey in his words,—and few flowers grow on his lips—the bees will sting, that is all. A trireme will be despatched to Sparta with complaints. Pausanias will be recalled—perhaps his life endangered."

"Endangered!" echoed several voices.

"Yes. What is that to you—what care you for his danger? He is a Spartan."

"Ay," cried one; "but he has been kind to the Helots."

"And we have fought by his side," said another.

"And he dressed my wound with his own hand," murmured a third.

"And we have got money under him," growled a fourth.

"And more than all," said Alcman, in a loud voice, "if he lives, he will break down the Spartan government. Ye will not let this man die?"

"Never!" exclaimed the whole assembly. Alcman gazed with a kind of calm and strange contempt on the flashing eyes, the fiery gestures of the throng, and then said, coldly,

"So then ye would fight for one man?"

"Ay, ay, that would we."

"But not for your own liberties, and those of your children unborn?"

There was a dead silence; but the taunt was felt, and its logic was already at work in many of these rugged breasts.

At this moment, the door was suddenly thrown open; and a Helot, in the dress worn by the attendants of the Regent, entered, breathless and panting.

"Alcman! the gods be praised you are here. Pausanias commands your presence. Lose not a moment. And you too, comrades, by Demeter, do you mean to spend whole days at your cups? Come to the citadel; ye may be wanted."

This was spoken to such of the Helots as belonged to the train of Pausanias.

"Wanted—what for?" said one. "Pausanias gives us a holiday while he employs the sleek Egyptians."

"Who that serves Pausanias ever asks that question, or can foresee from one hour to another what he may be required to do?" returned the self-important messenger, with great contempt.

Meanwhile the Mothon, all whose movements were peculiarly silent and rapid, was already on his way to the citadel. The distance was not inconsiderable, but Alcman was swift of foot. Tightening the girdle round his waist, he swung himself, as it were, into a kind of run, which, though not seemingly rapid, cleared the ground with the speed almost rivalling that of the ostrich, from the length of the stride and the extreme regularity of the pace. Such was at that day the method by which messages were despatched from state to state, especially in mountainous countries; and the length of way which was performed, without stopping, by the foot-couriers might startle the best-trained pedestrians in our times. So swiftly indeed did the Mothon pursue his course, that just by the citadel he came up with the Grecian captains who, before he joined the Helots, had set off for their audience with Pausanias. There were some fourteen or fifteen of them, and they so filled up the path which, just there, was not broad, that Alcman was obliged to pause as he came upon their rear.

"And whither so fast, fellow?" said Uliades the Samian, turning round as he heard the strides of the Mothon.

"Please you, master, I am bound to the General."

"Oh, his slave! Is he going to free you?"

"I am already as free as a man who has no city can be."

"Pithy. The Spartan slaves have the dryness of their masters. How, sirrah! do you jostle me?"

"I crave pardon. I only seek to pass."

"Never! to take precedence of a Samian. Keep back."

"I dare not."

"Nay, nay, let him pass," said the young Chian, Antagoras; "he will get scourged if he is too late. Perhaps, like the Persians, Pausanias wears false hair, and wishes the slave to dress it in honour of us."

"Hush!" whispered an Athenian. "Are these taunts prudent?"

Here there suddenly broke forth a loud oath from Uliades, who, lingering a little behind the rest, had laid rough hands on the Mothon, as the latter once more attempted to pass him. With a dexterous and abrupt agility, Alcman had extricated himself from the Samian's grasp, but with a force that swung the captain on his knee. Taking advantage of the position of the foe, the Mothon darted onward, and threading the rest of the party, disappeared through the neighbouring gates of the citadel.

"You saw the insult?" said Uliades between his ground teeth as he recovered himself. "The master shall answer for the slave; and to me, too, who have forty slaves of my own at home!"

"Pooh! think no more of it," said Antagoras gaily; "the poor fellow meant only to save his own hide."

"As if that were of any consequence! my slaves are brought up from the cradle not to know if they have hides or not. You may pinch them by the hour together and they don't feel you. My little ones do it, in rainy weather, to strengthen their fingers. The Gods keep them!"

"An excellent gymnastic invention. But we are now within the citadel. Courage! the Spartan greyhound has long teeth."

Pausanias was striding with hasty steps up and down a long and narrow peristyle or colonnade that surrounded the apartments appropriated to his private use, when Alcman joined him.

"Well, well," cried he, eagerly, as he saw the Mothon, "you have mingled with the common gangs of these worshipful seamen, these new men, these Ionians. Think you they have so far overcome their awe of the Spartan that they would obey the mutinous commands of their officers?"

"Pausanias, the truth must be spoken—Yes!"

"Ye Gods! one would think each of these wranglers imagined he had a whole Persian army in his boat. Why, I have seen the day when, if in any assembly of Greeks a Spartan entered, the sight of his very hat and walking-staff cast a terror through the whole conclave."

"True, Pausanias; but they suspect that Sparta herself will disown her General."

"Ah! say they so?"

"With one voice."

Pausanias paused a moment in deep and perturbed thought.

"Have they dared yet, think you, to send to Sparta?"

"I hear not; but a trireme is in readiness to sail after your conference with the captains."

"So, Alcman, it were ruin to my schemes to be recalled—until— until——"

"The hour to join the Persians on the frontier—yes."

"One word more. Have you had occasion to sound the Helots?"

"But half an hour since. They will be true to you. Lift your right hand, and the ground where you stand will bristle with men who fear death even less than the Spartans."

"Their aid were useless here against the whole Grecian fleet; but in the defiles of Laconia, otherwise. I am prepared then for the worst, even recall."

Here a slave crossed from a kind of passage that led from the outer chambers into the peristyle.

"The Grecian captains have arrived to demand audience."

"Bid them wait," cried Pausanias, passionately.

"Hist! Pausanias," whispered the Mothon. "Is it not best to soothe them—to play with them—to cover the lion with the fox's hide?"

The Regent turned with a frown to his foster-brother, as if surprised and irritated by his presumption in advising; and indeed of late, since Pausanias had admitted the son of the Helot into his guilty intrigues, Alcman had assumed a bearing and tone of equality which Pausanias, wrapped in his dark schemes, did not always notice, but at which from time to time he chafed angrily, yet again permitted it, and the custom gained ground; for in guilt conventional distinctions rapidly vanish, and mind speaks freely out to mind. The presence of the slave, however, restrained him, and after a momentary silence his natural acuteness, great when undisturbed by passion or pride, made him sensible of the wisdom of Alcman's counsel.

"Hold!" he said to the slave. "Announce to the Grecian Chiefs that Pausanias will await them forthwith. Begone. Now, Alcman, I will talk over these gentle monitors. Not in vain have I been educated in Sparta; yet if by chance I fail, hold thyself ready to haste to Sparta at a minute's warning. I must forestall the foe. I have gold, gold; and he who employs most of the yellow orators, will prevail most with the Ephors. Give me my staff; and tarry in yon chamber to the left."

CHAPTER II.

IN a large hall, with a marble fountain in the middle of it, the Greek captains awaited the coming of Pausanias. A low and muttered conversation was carried on amongst them, in small knots and groups, amidst which the voice of Uliades was heard the loudest. Suddenly the hum was hushed, for footsteps were heard without. The thick curtains that at one extreme screened the doorway were drawn aside, and, attended by three of the Spartan knights, amongst whom was Lysander, and by two soothsayers, who were seldom absent, in war or warlike council, from the side of the Royal Heracleid, Pausanias slowly entered the hall. So majestic, grave, and self-collected were the bearing and aspect of the Spartan general, that the hereditary awe inspired by his race was once more awakened, and the angry crowd saluted him, silent and half-abashed. Although the strong passions, and the daring arrogance of Pausanias, did not allow him the exercise of that enduring, systematic, unsleeping hypocrisy which, in relations with the foreigner, often characterized his countrymen, and which, from its outward dignity and profound craft, exalted the vice into genius; yet trained from earliest childhood in the arts that hide design, that control the countenance, and convey in the fewest words the most ambiguous meanings, the Spartan general could, for a brief period, or for a critical purpose, command all the wiles for which the Greek was nationally famous, and in which Thucydides believed that, of all Greeks, the Spartan was the most skilful adept. And now, as, uniting the courtesy of the host with the dignity of the chief, he returned the salute of the officers, and smiled his gracious welcome, the unwonted affability of his manner took the discontented by surprise, and half propitiated the most indignant in his favour.

"I need not ask you, O Greeks," said he, "why ye have sought me. Ye have learnt the escape of Ariamanes and Datis—a strange and unaccountable mischance."

The captains looked round at each other in silence, till at last every eye rested upon Cimon, whose illustrious birth, as well as his known respect for Sparta, combined with his equally well-known dislike of her chief, seemed to mark him, despite his youth, as the fittest person to be speaker for the rest. Cimon, who understood the mute appeal, and whose courage never failed his ambition, raised his head, and, after a moment's hesitation, replied to the Spartan:

"Pausanias, you guess rightly the cause which leads us to your presence. These prisoners were our noblest; their capture the reward of our common valour; they were generals, moreover, of high skill and repute. They had become experienced in our Grecian warfare, even by their defeats. Those two men, should Xerxes again invade Greece, are worth more to his service than half the nations whose myriads crossed the Hellespont. But this is not all. The arms of the Barbarians we can encounter undismayed. It is treason at home which can alone appal us."

There was a low murmur among the Ionians at these words. Pausanias, with well-dissembled surprise on his countenance, turned his eyes from Cimon to the murmurers, and from them again to Cimon, and repeated:

"Treason! son of Miltiades; and from whom?"

"Such is the question that we would put to thee, Pausanias—to thee, whose eyes, as leader of our armies, are doubtless vigilant daily and nightly over the interests of Greece."

"I am not blind," returned Pausanias, appearing unconscious of the irony; "but I am not Argus. If thou hast discovered aught that is hidden from me, speak boldly."

"Thou hast made Gongylus, the Eretrian, governor of Byzantium; for what great services we know not. But he has lived much in Persia."

"For that reason, on this the frontier of her domains, he is better enabled to penetrate her designs and counteract her ambition."

"This Gongylus," continued Cimon, "is well known to have much frequented the Persian captives in their confinement."

"In order to learn from them what may yet be the strength of the king. In this he had my commands."

"I question it not. But, Pausanias," continued Cimon, raising his voice, and with energy, "had he also thy commands to leave thy galley last night, and to return to the citadel?"

"He had. What then?"

"And on his return the Persians disappear—a singular chance, truly. But that is not all. Last night, before he returned to the citadel, Gongylus was perceived, alone, in a retired spot on the outskirts of the city."

"Alone?" echoed Pausanias.

"Alone. If he had companions they were not discerned. This spot was out of the path he should have taken. By this spot, on the soft soil, are the marks of hoofs, and in the thicket close by were found these witnesses," and Cimon drew from his vest a handful of the pearls, only worn by the Eastern captives.

"There is something in this," said Xanthippus, "which requires at least examination. May it please you, Pausanias, to summon Gongylus hither?"

A momentary shade passed over the brow of the conspirator, but the eyes of the Greeks were on him; and to refuse were as dangerous as to comply. He turned to one of his Spartans, and ordered him to summon the Eretrian.

"You have spoken well, Xanthippus. This matter must be sifted."

With that, motioning the captains to the seats that were ranged round the walls and before a long table, he cast himself into a large chair at the head of the table, and waited in silent anxiety the entrance of the Eretrian. His whole trust now was in the craft and penetration of his friend. If the courage or the cunning of Gongylus failed him—if but a word betrayed him—Pausanias was lost. He was girt by men who hated him; and he read in the dark fierce eyes of the Ionians—whose pride he had so often galled, whose revenge he had so carelessly provoked—the certainty of ruin. One hand hidden within the folds of his robe convulsively clinched the flesh, in the stern agony of his suspense. His calm and composed face nevertheless exhibited to the captains no trace of fear.

The draperies were again drawn aside, and Gongylus slowly entered.

Habituated to peril of every kind from his earliest youth, the Eretrian was quick to detect its presence. The sight of the silent Greeks, formally seated round the hall, and watching his steps and countenance with eyes whose jealous and vindictive meaning it required no Œdipus to read, the grave and half-averted brow of Pausanias, and the angry excitement that had prevailed amidst the host at the news of the escape of the Persians—all sufficed to apprise him of the nature of the council to which he had been summoned.

Supporting himself on his staff, and dragging his limbs tardily along, he had leisure to examine, though with apparent indifference, the whole group; and when, with a calm salutation, he arrested his steps at the foot of the table immediately facing Pausanias, he darted one glance at the Spartan so fearless, so bright, so cheering, that Pausanias breathed hard, as if a load were thrown from his breast, and turning easily towards Cimon, said—

"Behold your witness. Which of us shall be questioner, and which judge?"

"That matters but little," returned Cimon. "Before this audience justice must force its way."

"It rests with you, Pausanias," said Xanthippus, "to acquaint the governor of Byzantium with the suspicions he has excited."

"Gongylus," said Pausanias, "the captive Barbarians, Ariamanes and Datis, were placed by me especially under thy vigilance and guard. Thou knowest that, while (for humanity becomes the victor) I ordered thee to vex them by no undue restraints, I nevertheless commanded thee to consider thy life itself answerable for their durance. They have escaped. The captains of Greece demand of thee, as I demanded—by what means—by what connivance? Speak the truth, and deem that in falsehood as well as in treachery, detection is easy, and death certain."

The tone of Pausanias, and his severe look, pleased and reassured all the Greeks, except the wiser Cimon, who, though his suspicions were a little shaken, continued to fix his eyes rather on Pausanias than on the Eretrian.

"Pausanias," replied Gongylus, drawing up his lean frame, as with the dignity of conscious innocence, "that suspicion could fall upon me, I find it difficult to suppose. Raised by thy favour to the command of Byzantium, what have I to gain by treason or neglect? These Persians—I knew them well. I had known them in Susa— known them when I served Darius, being then an exile from Eretria. Ye know, my countrymen, that when Darius invaded Greece I left his court and armies, and sought my native land, to fall or to conquer in its cause. Well, then, I knew these Barbarians. I sought them frequently; partly, it may be, to return to them in their adversity the courtesies shown me in mine. Ye are Greeks; ye will not condemn me for humanity and gratitude. Partly with another motive. I knew that Ariamanes had the greatest influence over Xerxes. I knew that the great king would at any cost seek to regain the liberty of his friend. I urged upon Ariamanes the wisdom of a peace with the Greeks even on their own terms. I told him that when Xerxes sent to offer the ransom, conditions of peace would avail more than sacks of gold. He listened and approved. Did I wrong in this, Pausanias? No; for thou, whose deep sagacity has made thee condescend even to appear half Persian, because thou art all Greek— thou thyself didst sanction my efforts on behalf of Greece."

Pausanias looked with a silent triumph round the conclave, and Xanthippus nodded approval.

"In order to conciliate them, and with too great confidence in their faith, I relaxed by degrees the rigour of their confinement; that was a fault, I own it. Their apartments communicated with a court in which I suffered them to walk at will. But I placed there two sentinels in whom I deemed I could repose all trust—not my own countrymen—not Eretrians—not thy Spartans or Laconians, Pausanias. No; I deemed that if ever the jealousy (a laudable jealousy) of the Greeks should demand an account of my faith and vigilance, my witnesses should be the countrymen of those who have ever the most suspected me. Those sentinels were, the one a Samian, the other a Platæan. These men have betrayed me and Greece. Last night, on returning hither from the vessel, I visited the Persians. They were about to retire to rest, and I quitted them soon, suspecting nothing. This morning they had fled, and with them their abettors, the sentinels. I hastened first to send soldiers in search of them; and, secondly, to inform Pausanias in his galley. If I have erred, I submit me to your punishment. Punish my error, but acquit my honesty."

"And what," said Cimon, abruptly, "led thee far from thy path, between the Heracleid's galley and the citadel, to the fields near the temple of Aphrodite, between the citadel and the bay? Thy colour changes. Mark him, Greeks. Quick; thine answer."

The countenance of Gongylus had indeed lost its colour and hardihood. The loud tone of Cimon—the effect his confusion produced on the Greeks, some of whom, the Ionians less self-possessed and dignified than the rest, half rose, with fierce gestures and muttered exclamations—served still more to embarrass and intimidate him. He cast a hasty look on Pausanias, who averted his eyes. There was a pause. The Spartan gave himself up for lost; but how much more was his fear increased when Gongylus, casting an imploring gaze upon the Greeks, said hesitatingly—

"Question me no farther. I dare not speak;" and as he spoke he pointed to Pausanias.

"It was the dread of thy resentment, Pausanias," said Cimon coldly, "that withheld his confession. Vouchsafe to re-assure him."

"Eretrian," said Pausanias, striking his clenched hand on the table, "I know not what tale trembles on thy lips; but, be it what it may, give it voice, I command thee."

"Thou thyself, thou wert the cause that led me towards the temple of Aphrodite," said Gongylus, in a low voice.

At these words there went forth a general deep-breathed murmur. With one accord every Greek rose to his feet. The Spartan attendants in the rear of Pausanias drew closer to his person; but there was nothing in their faces—yet more dark and vindictive than those of the other Greeks—that promised protection. Pausanias alone remained seated and unmoved. His imminent danger gave him back all his valour, all his pride, all his passionate and profound disdain. With unbleached cheek, with haughty eyes, he met the gaze of the assembly; and then waving his hand as if that gesture sufficed to restrain and awe them, he said—

"In the name of all Greece, whose chief I yet am, whose protector I have once been, I command ye to resume your seats, and listen to the Eretrian. Spartans, fall back. Governor of Byzantium, pursue your tale."

"Yes, Pausanias," resumed Gongylus, "you alone were the cause that drew me from my rest. I would fain be silent, but——"

"Say on," cried Pausanias fiercely, and measuring the space between himself and Gongylus, in doubt whether the Eretrian's head were within reach of his scimitar; so at least Gongylus interpreted that freezing look of despair and vengeance, and he drew back some paces. "I place myself, O Greeks, under your protection; it is dangerous to reveal the errors of the great. Know that, as Governor of Byzantium, many things ye wot not of reach my ears. Hence,

I guard against dangers while ye sleep. Learn, then, that Pausanias is not without the weakness of his ancestor, Alcides; he loves a maiden—a Byzantine—Cleonice, the daughter of Diagoras."

This unexpected announcement, made in so grave a tone, provoked a smile amongst the gay Ionians; but an exclamation of jealous anger broke from Antagoras, and a blush partly of wounded pride, partly of warlike shame, crimsoned the swarthy cheek of Pausanias. Cimon, who was by no means free from the joyous infirmities of youth, relaxed his severe brow, and said, after a short pause—

"Is it, then, among the grave duties of the Governor of Byzantium to watch over the fair Cleonice, or to aid the suit of her illustrious lover?"

"Not so," answered Gongylus; "but the life of the Grecian general is dear, at least, to the grateful Governor of Byzantium. Greeks, ye know that amongst you Pausanias has many foes. Returning last night from his presence, and passing through the thicket, I overheard voices at hand. I caught the name of Pausanias. 'The Spartan,' said one voice, 'nightly visits the house of Diagoras. He goes usually alone. From the height near the temple we can watch well, for the night is clear; if he goes alone, we can intercept his way on his return.' 'To the height!' cried the other. I thought to distinguish the voices, but the trees hid the speakers. I followed the footsteps towards the temple, for it behoved me to learn who thus menaced the chief of Greece. But ye know that the wood reaches even to the sacred building, and the steps gained the temple before I could recognize the men. I concealed myself, as I thought, to watch; but it seems that I was perceived, for he who saw me, and now accuses, was doubtless one of the assassins. Happy I, if the sight of a witness scared him from the crime. Either fearing detection, or aware that their intent that night was frustrated—for Pausanias, visiting Cleonice earlier than his wont, had already resought his galley—the men retreated as they came, unseen, not unheard. I caught their receding steps through the brushwood. Greeks, I have said. Who is my accuser? in him behold the would-be murderer of Pausanias!"

"Liar," cried an indignant and loud voice amongst the captains, and Antagoras stood forth from the circle.

"It is I who saw thee. Darest thou accuse Antagoras of Chios?"

"What at that hour brought Antagoras of Chios to the temple of Aphrodite?" retorted Gongylus.

The eyes of the Greeks turned toward the young captain, and there was confusion on his face. But recovering himself quickly, the Chian answered, "Why should I blush to own it? Aphrodite is no dishonourable deity to the men of the Ionian Isles. I sought the temple at that hour, as is our wont, to make my offering, and record my prayer."

"Certainly," said Cimon. "We must own that Aphrodite is powerful at Byzantium. Who can acquit Pausanias and blame Antagoras?"

"Pardon me—one question," said Gongylus. "Is not the female heart which Antagoras would beseech the goddess to soften towards him that of the Cleonice of whom we spoke? See, he denies it not. Greeks, the Chians are warm lovers, and warm lovers are revengeful rivals."

This artful speech had its instantaneous effect amongst the younger and more unthinking loiterers. Those who at once would have disbelieved the imputed guilt of Antagoras upon motives merely political, inclined to a suggestion that ascribed it to the jealousy of a lover. And his character, ardent and fiery, rendered the suspicion yet more plausible. Meanwhile the minds of the audience had been craftily drawn from the grave and main object of the meeting—the flight of the Persians—and a lighter and livelier curiosity had supplanted the eager and dark resentment which had hitherto animated the circle. Pausanias, with the subtle genius that belonged to him, hastened to seize advantage of this momentary diversion in his favour, and before the Chian could recover his consternation, both at the charge and the evident effect it had produced upon a part of the assembly, the Spartan stretched his hand, and spake.

"Greeks, Pausanias listens to no tale of danger to himself. Willingly he believes that Gongylus either misinterpreted the intent of some jealous and heated threats, or that the words he overheard were not uttered by Antagoras. Possible is it, too, that others may have sought the temple with less gentle desires than our Chian ally. Let this pass. Unworthy such matters of the councils of bearded men; too much reference has been made to those follies which our idleness has given birth to. Let no fair Briseis renew strife amongst chiefs and soldiers. Excuse not thyself, Antagoras; we dismiss all charge against thee. On the other hand, Gongylus will doubtless seem to you to have accounted for his appearance near the precincts of the temple. And it is but a coincidence, natural enough, that the Persian prisoners should have chosen, later in the night, the same spot for the steeds to await them. The thickness of the wood round the temple, and the direction of the place towards the east, points out the neighbourhood as the very one in which the fugitives would appoint the horses. Waste no further time, but provide at once for the pursuit. To you, Cimon, be this care confided. Already have I despatched fifty light-armed men on fleet Thessalian steeds. You, Cimon, increase the number of the pursuers. The prisoners may be yet recaptured. Doth aught else remain worthy of our ears? If so, speak; if not, depart."

"Pausanias," said Antagoras, firmly, "let Gongylus retract, or not, his charge against me, I retain mine against Gongylus. Wholly false is it that in word or deed I plotted violence against thee, though of much—not as Cleonice's lover, but as Grecian captain—I have good reason to complain. Wholly false is it that I had a comrade. I was alone. And coming out from the temple, where I had hung my chaplet, I perceived Gongylus clearly under the starlit skies. He stood in listening attitude close by the sacred myrtle grove. I hastened towards him, but methinks he saw me not; he turned slowly, penetrated the wood, and vanished. I gained the spot on the soft sward which the dropping boughs make ever humid. I saw the print of hoofs. Within the thicket I found the pearls that Cimon has displayed to you. Clear, then, is it that this man lies—clear that the Persians must have fled already—although Gongylus declares that on his return to the citadel he visited them in their prison. Explain this, Eretrian!"

"He who would speak false witness," answered Gongylus, with a firmness equal to the Chian's, "can find pearls at whatsoever hour he pleases. Greeks, this man presses me to renew the charge which Pausanias generously sought to stifle. I have said. And I, Governor of Byzantium, call on the Council of the Grecian Leaders to maintain my authority, and protect their own Chief."

Then arose a vexed and perturbed murmur, most of the Ionians siding with Antagoras, such of the allies as yet clung to the Dorian ascendancy grouping round Gongylus.

The persistence of Antagoras had made the dilemma of no slight embarrassment to Pausanias. Something lofty in his original nature urged him to shrink from supporting Gongylus in an accusation which he believed untrue. On the other hand, he could not abandon his accomplice in an effort, as dangerous as it was crafty, to conceal their common guilt.

"Son of Miltiades," he said after a brief pause, in which his dexterous resolution was formed, "I invoke your aid to appease a contest in which I foresee no result but that of schism amongst ourselves. Antagoras has no witness to support his tale, Gongylus none to support his own. Who shall decide between conflicting testimonies which rest but on the lips of accuser and accused? Hereafter, if the matter be deemed sufficiently grave, let us refer the decision to the oracle that never errs. Time and chance meanwhile may favour us in clearing up the darkness we cannot now penetrate. For you, Governor of Byzantium, it behoves me to say that the escape of prisoners entrusted to your charge justifies vigilance if not suspicion. We shall consult at our leisure whether or not that course suffices to remove you from the government of Byzantium. Heralds, advance; our council is dissolved."

With these words Pausanias rose, and the majesty of his bearing, with the unwonted temper and conciliation of his language, so came in aid of his high office, that no man ventured a dissentient murmur.

The conclave broke up, and not till its members had gained the outer air did any signs of suspicion or dissatisfaction evince themselves; but then, gathering in groups, the Ionians with especial jealousy discussed what had passed, and with their native shrewdness ascribed the moderation of Pausanias to his desire to screen Gongylus and avoid further inquisition into the flight of the prisoners. The discontented looked round for Cimon, but the young Athenian had hastily retired from the throng, and, after issuing orders to pursue the fugitives, sought Aristides in the house near the quay in which he lodged.

Cimon related to his friend what had passed at the meeting, and terminating his recital, said:

"Thou shouldst have been with us. With thee we might have ventured more."

"And if so," returned the wise Athenian with a smile, "ye would have prospered less. Precisely because I would not commit our country to the suspicion of fomenting intrigues and mutiny to her own advantage, did I abstain from the assembly, well aware that Pausanias would bring his minion harmless from the unsupported accusation of Antagoras. Thou hast acted with cool judgment, Cimon. The Spartan is weaving the webs of the Parcæ for his own feet. Leave him to weave on, undisturbed. The hour in which Athens shall assume the sovereignty of the seas is drawing near. Let it come, like Jove's thunder, in a calm sky."

CHAPTER III.

PAUSANIAS did not that night quit the city. After the meeting, he held a private conference with the Spartan Equals, whom custom and the government assigned, in appearance as his attendants, in reality as witnesses if not spies of his conduct. Though every pure Spartan, as compared with the subject Laconian population, was noble, the republic acknowledged two main distinctions in class, the higher, entitled Equals, a word which we might not inaptly and more intelligibly render Peers; the lower, Inferiors. These distinctions, though hereditary, were not immutable. The peer could be degraded, the inferior could become a peer. To the royal person in war three peers were allotted. Those assigned to Pausanias, of the tribe called the Hylleans, were naturally of a rank and influence that constrained him to treat them with a certain deference, which perpetually chafed his pride and confirmed his discontent; for these three men were precisely of the mould which at heart he most despised. Polydorus, the first in rank—for, like Pausanias, he boasted his descent from Hercules—was the personification of the rudeness and bigotry of a Spartan who had never before stirred from his rocky home, and who disdained all that he could not comprehend. Gelon, the second, passed for a very wise man, for he seldom spoke but in monosyllables; yet, probably, his words were as numerous as his ideas. Cleomenes, the third, was as distasteful to the Regent from his merits as the others from their deficiencies. He had risen from the grade of the Inferiors by his valour; blunt, homely, frank, sincere, he never disguised his displeasure at the manner of Pausanias, though, a true Spartan in discipline, he never transgressed the respect which his chief commanded in time of war.

Pausanias knew that these officers were in correspondence with Sparta, and he now exerted all his powers to remove from their minds any suspicion which the disappearance of the prisoners might have left in them.

In this interview he displayed all those great natural powers which, rightly trained and guided, might have made him not less great in council than in war. With masterly precision he enlarged on the growing ambition of Athens, on the disposition in her favour evinced by all the Ionian confederates. "Hitherto," he said truly, "Sparta has uniformly held rank as the first state of Greece; the leadership of the Greeks belongs to us by birth and renown. But see you not that the war is now shifting from land to sea? Sea is not our element; it is that of Athens, of all the Ionian race. If this continue we lose our ascendancy, and Athens becomes the sovereign of Hellas. Beneath the calm of Aristides I detect his deep design. In vain Cimon affects the manner of the Spartan; at heart he is Athenian. This charge against Gongylus is aimed at me. Grant that the plot which it conceals succeed; grant that Sparta share the affected suspicions of the Ionians, and recall me from Byzantium; deem you that there lives one Spartan who could delay for a day the supremacy of Athens? Nought save the respect the

Dorian Greeks at least attach to the General at Platæa could restrain the secret ambition of the city of the demagogues. Deem not that I have been as rash and vain as some hold me for the stern visage I have shown to the Ionians. Trust me that it was necessary to awe them, with a view to maintain our majesty. For Sparta to preserve her ascendancy, two things are needful: first, to continue the war by land; secondly, to disgust the Ionians with their sojourn here, send them with their ships to their own havens, and so leave Hellas under the sole guardianship of ourselves and our Peloponnesian allies. Therefore I say, bear with me in this double design; chide me not if my haughty manner disperse these subtle Ionians. If I bore with them to-day it was less from respect than, shall I say it, my fear lest you should misinterpret me. Beware how you detail to Sparta whatever might rouse the jealousy of her government. Trust to me, and I will extend the dominion of Sparta till it grasp the whole of Greece. We will depose everywhere the revolutionary Demos, and establish our own oligarchies in every Grecian state. We will Laconize all Hellas."

Much of what Pausanias said was wise and profound. Such statesmanship, narrow and congenial, but vigorous and crafty, Sparta taught in later years to her alert politicians. And we have already seen that, despite the dazzling prospects of Oriental dominion, he as yet had separated himself rather from the laws than the interests of Sparta, and still incorporated his own ambition with the extension of the sovereignty of his country over the rest of Greece.

But the peers heard him in dull and gloomy silence; and, not till he had paused and thrice asked for a reply, did Polydorus speak.

"You would increase the dominion of Sparta, Pausanias. Increase of dominion is waste of life and treasure. We have few men, little gold; Sparta is content to hold her own."

"Good," said Gelon, with impassive countenance. "What care we who leads the Greeks into blows? the fewer blows the better. Brave men fight if they must, wise men never fight if they can help it."

"And such is your counsel, Cleomenes?" asked Pausanias, with a quivering lip.

"Not from the same reasons," answered the nobler and more generous Spartan. "I presume not to question your motives, Pausanias. I leave you to explain them to the Ephors and the Gerusia. But since you press me, this I say. First, all the Greeks, Ionian as well as Dorian, fought equally against the Mede, and from the commander of the Greeks all should receive fellowship and courtesy. Secondly, I say if Athens is better fitted than Sparta for the maritime ascendancy, let Athens rule, so that Hellas be saved from the Mede.

Thirdly, O Pausanias, I pray that Sparta may rest satisfied with her own institutions, and not disturb the peace of Greece by forcing them upon other States and thereby enslaving Hellas. What more could the Persian do? Finally, my advice is to suspend Gongylus from his office; to conciliate the Ionians; to remain as a Grecian armament firm and united, and so procure, on better terms, peace with Persia. And then let each State retire within itself, and none aspire to rule the other. A thousand free cities are better guard against the Barbarian than a single State made up of republics overthrown and resting its strength upon hearts enslaved."

"Do you too," said Pausanias, gnawing his nether lip, "Do you too, Polydorus; you too, Gelon, agree with Cleomenes, that, if Athens is better fitted than Sparta for the sovereignty of the seas, we should yield to that restless rival so perilous a power?"

"Ships cost gold," said Polydorus. "Spartans have none to spare. Mariners require skilful captains; Spartans know nothing of the sea."

"Moreover," quoth Gelon, "the ocean is a terrible element. What can valour do against a storm? We may lose more men by adverse weather than a century can repair. Let who will have the seas. Sparta has her rocks and defiles."

"Men and peers," said Pausanias, ill repressing his scorn, "ye little dream what arms ye place in the hands of the Athenians. I have done. Take only this prophecy. You are now the head of Greece. You surrender your sceptre to Athens, and become a second-rate power."

"Never second rate when Greece shall demand armed men," said Cleomenes proudly.

"Armed men, armed men!" cried the more profound Pausanias. "Do you suppose that commerce—that trade—that maritime energy —that fleets which ransack the shores of the world, will not obtain a power greater than mere brute-like valour? But as ye will, as ye will."

"As we speak our forefathers thought," said Gelon.

"And, Pausanias," said Cleomenes gravely, "as we speak, so think the Ephors."

Pausanias fixed his dark eye on Cleomenes, and, after a brief pause, saluted the Equals and withdrew. "Sparta," he muttered as he regained his chamber, "Sparta, thou refusest to be great; but greatness is necessary to thy son. Ah, their iron laws would constrain my soul! but it shall wear them as a warrior wears his armour and adapts it to his body. Thou shalt be queen of all Hellas despite thyself, thine Ephors, and thy laws. Then only will I forgive thee."

CHAPTER IV.

DIAGORAS was sitting outside his door and giving various instructions to the slaves employed on his farm, when, through an arcade thickly covered with the vine, the light form of Antagoras came slowly in sight.

"Hail to thee, Diagoras," said the Chian, "thou art the only wise man I meet with. Thou art tranquil while all else are disturbed; and, worshipping the great Mother, thou carest nought, methinks, for the Persian who invades, or the Spartan who professes to defend."

"Tut," said Diagoras, in a whisper, "thou knowest the contrary: thou knowest that if the Persian comes I am ruined; and, by the gods, I am on a bed of thorns as long as the Spartan stays."

"Dismiss thy slaves," exclaimed Antagoras, in the same undertone; "I would speak with thee on grave matters that concern us both."

After hastily finishing his instructions and dismissing his slaves, Diagoras turned to the impatient Chian, and said:

"Now, young warrior, I am all ears for thy speech."

"Truly," said Antagoras, "if thou wert aware of what I am about to utter, thou wouldst not have postponed consideration for thy daughter, to thy care for a few jars of beggarly olives."

"Hem!" said Diagoras, peevishly. "Olives are not to be despised; oil to the limbs makes them supple; to the stomach it gives gladness. Oil, moreover, bringeth money when sold. But a daughter is the plague of a man's life. First, one has to keep away lovers; and next to find a husband; and when all is done, one has to put one's hand in one's chest, and pay a tall fellow like thee for robbing one of one's own child. That custom of dowries is abominable. In the good old times a bridegroom, as was meet and proper, paid for his bride; now we poor fathers pay him for taking her. Well, well, never bite thy forefinger, and curl up thy brows. What thou hast to say, say."

"Diagoras, I know that thy heart is better than thy speech, and that, much as thou covetest money, thou lovest thy child more. Know, then, that Pausanias—a curse light on him!—brings shame upon Cleonice. Know that already her name hath grown the talk of the camp. Know that his visit to her the night before last was proclaimed in the Council of the Captains as a theme for jest and rude laughter. By the head of Zeus, how thinkest thou to profit by the stealthy wooings of this black-browed Spartan? Knowest thou not that his laws forbid him to marry Cleonice? Wouldst thou have him dishonour her? Speak out to him as thou speakest to men, and tell him that the maidens of Byzantium are not in the control of the General of the Greeks."

"Youth, youth," cried Diagoras, greatly agitated, "wouldst thou bring my gray hairs to a bloody grave? wouldst thou see my daughter reft from me by force—and——"

"How darest thou speak thus, old man?" interrupted the indignant Chian. "If Pausanias wronged a virgin, all Hellas would rise against him."

"Yes, but not till the ill were done, till my throat were cut, and my child dishonoured. Listen. At first indeed, when, as ill-luck would have it, Pausanias, lodging a few days under my roof, saw and admired Cleonice, I did venture to remonstrate, and how think you he took it? 'Never,' quoth he, with his stern quivering lip, 'never did conquest forego its best right to the smiles of beauty. The legends of Hercules, my ancestor, tell thee that to him who labours for men, the gods grant the love of women. Fear not that I should wrong thy daughter—to woo her is not to wrong. But close thy door on me; immure Cleonice from my sight; and nor armed slaves, nor bolts, nor bars shall keep love from the loved one.' Therewith he turned on his heel and left me. But the next day came a Lydian in his train, with a goodly pannier of rich stuffs and a short Spartan sword. On the pannier was written '*Friendship*,' on the sword '*Wrath*,' and Alcman gave me a scrap of parchment, whereon, with the cursed brief wit of a Spartan, was inscribed '*Choose!*' Who could doubt which to take? who, by the Gods, would prefer three inches of Spartan iron in his stomach to a basketful of rich stuffs for his shoulders? Wherefore, from that hour, Pausanias comes as he lists. But Cleonice humours him not, let tongues wag as they may. Easier to take three cities than that child's heart."

"Is it so indeed?" exclaimed the Chian, joyfully; "Cleonice loves him not?"

"Laughs at him to his beard: that is, would laugh if he wore one."

"O Diagoras!" cried Antagoras, "hear me, hear me. I need not remind thee that our families are united by the hospitable ties; that amongst thy treasures thou wilt find the gifts of my ancestors for five generations; that when, a year since, my affairs brought me to Byzantium, I came to thee with the symbols of my right to claim thy hospitable cares. On leaving thee we broke the sacred die. I have one half, thou the other. In that visit I saw and loved Cleonice. Fain would I have told my love, but then my father lived, and I feared lest he should oppose my suit; therefore, as became me, I was silent. On my return home, my fears were confirmed; my father desired that I, a Chian, should wed a Chian. Since I have been with the fleet, news has reached me that the urn holds my father's ashes." Here the young Chian paused. "Alas, alas!" he murmured, smiting his breast, "and I was not at hand to fix over thy doors the sacred branch, to give thee the parting kiss, and receive into my lips thy latest breath. May Hermes, O father, have led thee to pleasant groves!"

Diagoras, who had listened attentively to the young Chian, was touched by his grief, and said pityingly:

"I know thou art a good son, and thy father was a worthy man, though harsh. It is a comfort to think that all does not die with the dead. His money at least survives him."

"But," resumed Antagoras, not heeding this consolation,—"but now I am free: and ere this, so soon as my mourning garment had been lain aside, I had asked thee to bless me with Cleonice, but that I feared her love was gone—gone to the haughty Spartan. Thou reassurest me; and in so doing, thou confirmest the fair omens with which Aphrodite has received my offerings. Therefore, I speak out. No dowry ask I with Cleonice, save such, more in name than amount, as may distinguish the wife from the concubine, and assure her an honoured place amongst my kinsmen. Thou knowest I am rich; thou knowest that my birth dates from the oldest citizens of Chios. Give me thy child, and deliver her thyself at once from the Spartan's power. Once mine, all the fleets of Hellas are her protection, and our marriage torches are the swords of a Grecian army. O Diagoras, I clasp thy knees; put thy right hand in mine. Give me thy child as wife!"

The Byzantine was strongly affected. The suitor was one who, in birth and possessions, was all that he could desire for his daughter; and at Byzantium there did not exist that feeling against intermarriages with the foreigner which prevailed in towns more purely Greek, though in many of them, too, that antique prejudice had worn away. On the other hand, by transferring to Antagoras his anxious charge, he felt that he should take the best course to preserve it untarnished from the fierce love of Pausanias, and there was truth in the Chian's suggestion. The daughter of a Byzantine might be unprotected; the wife of an Ionian captain was safe, even from the power of Pausanias. As these reflections occurred to him, he placed his right hand in the Chian's, and said:

"Be it as thou wilt; I consent to betroth thee to Cleonice. Follow me; thou art free to woo her."

So saying, he rose, and, as if in fear of his own second thoughts, he traversed the hall with hasty strides to the interior of the mansion. He ascended a flight of steps, and, drawing aside a curtain suspended between two columns, Antagoras, who followed timidly behind, beheld Cleonice.

As was the wont in the domestic life of all Grecian states, her handmaids were around the noble virgin. Two were engaged on embroidery, one in spinning, a fourth was reading aloud to Cleonice, and that at least was a rare diversion to women, for few had the education of the fair Byzantine. Cleonice herself was half reclined upon a bench inlaid with ivory and covered with cushions; before her stood a small tripod table on which she leant the arm, the hand of which supported her cheek, and she seemed listening to the lecture of the slave with earnest and absorbed attention, so earnest, so absorbed, that she did not for some moments perceive the entrance of Diagoras and the Chian.

"Child," said the former—and Cleonice started to her feet, and stood modestly before her father, her eyes downcast, her arms crossed upon her bosom—"child, I bid thee welcome my guest-friend, Antagoras of Chios. Slaves, ye may withdraw."

Cleonice bowed her head; and an unquiet, anxious change came over her countenance.

As soon as the slaves were gone, Diagoras resumed—

"Daughter, I present to thee a suitor for thy hand; receive him as I have done, and he shall have my leave to carve thy name on every tree in the garden, with the lover's epithet of 'Beautiful,' attached to it. Antagoras, look up, then, and speak for thyself."

But Antagoras was silent; and a fear unknown to his frank hardy nature came over him. With an arch smile, Diagoras, deeming his presence no longer necessary or expedient, lifted the curtain, and lover and maid were left alone.

Then, with an effort, and still with hesitating accents, the Chian spoke—

"Fair virgin,—not in the groves of Byzantium will thy name be first written by the hand of Antagoras. In my native Chios the myrtle trees are already eloquent of thee. Since I first saw thee, I loved. Maiden, wilt thou be my wife?"

Thrice moved the lips of Cleonice, and thrice her voice seemed to fail her. At length she said,—"Chian, thou art a stranger, and the laws of the Grecian cities dishonour the stranger whom the free citizen stoops to marry."

"Nay," cried Antagoras, "such cruel laws are obsolete in Chios. Nature and custom, and love's almighty goddess, long since have set them aside. Fear not, the haughtiest matron of my native state will not be more honoured than the Byzantine bride of Antagoras."

"Is it in Sparta only that such laws exist?" said Cleonice, half unconsciously, and to the sigh with which she spoke a deep blush succeeded.

"Sparta!" exclaimed Antagoras, with a fierce and jealous pang —"Ah, are thy thoughts then upon the son of Sparta? Were Pausanias a Chian, wouldst thou turn from him scornfully as thou now dost from me?"

"Not scornfully, Antagoras," answered Cleonice (who had indeed averted her face, at his reproachful question; but now turned it full upon him, with an expression of sad and pathetic sweetness), "not scornfully do I turn from thee, though with pain; for what worthier homage canst thou render to woman, than honourable love? Gratefully do I hearken to the suit that comes from thee; but gratitude is not the return that thou wouldst ask, Antagoras. My hand is my father's; my heart, alas, is mine. Thou mayst claim from him the one; the other, neither he can give, nor thou receive."

"Say not so, Cleonice," cried the Chian; "say not, that thou canst not love me, if so I am to interpret thy words. Love brings love with the young. How canst thou yet know thine own heart? Tarry till thou hast listened to mine. As the fire on the altar spreads from offering to offering, so spreads love; its flame envelops all that are near to it. Thy heart will catch the heavenly spark from mine."

"Chian," said Cleonice, gently withdrawing the hand that he sought to clasp, "when as my father's guest-friend thou wert a sojourner within these walls, oft have I heard thee speak, and all thy words spoke the thoughts of a noble soul. Were it otherwise, not thus would I now address thee. Didst thou love gold, and wooed in me but the child of the rich Diagoras, or wert thou one of those who would treat for a wife, as a trader for a slave, invoking Herè, but disdaining Aphrodite, I should bow my head to my doom. But thou, Antagoras, askest love for love; this I cannot give thee. Spare me, O generous Chian. Let not my father enforce his right to my obedience."

"Answer me but one question," interrupted Antagoras in a low voice, though with compressed lips: "Dost thou then love another?"

The blood mounted to the virgin's cheeks, it suffused her brow, her neck, with burning blushes, and then receding, left her face colourless as a statue. Then with tones low and constrained as his own, she pressed her hand on her heart, and replied, "Thou sayest it; I love another."

"And that other is Pausanias? Alas, thy silence, thy trembling, answer me."

Antagoras groaned aloud and covered his face with his hands; but after a short pause, he exclaimed with great emotion, "No, no—say not that thou lovest Pausanias; say not that Aphrodite hath so accursed thee: for to love Pausanias is to love dishonour."

"Hold, Chian! Not so: for my love has no hope. Our hearts are not our own, but our actions are."

Antagoras gazed on her with suspense and awe; for as she spoke her slight form dilated, her lip curled, her cheek glowed again, but with the blush less of love than of pride. In her countenance, her attitude, there was something divine and holy, such as would have beseemed a priestess of Diana.

"Yes," she resumed, raising her eyes, and with a still and mournful sweetness in her upraised features. "What I love is not Pausanias, it is the glory of which he is the symbol, it is the Greece of which he has been the Saviour. Let him depart, as soon he must—let these eyes behold him no more; still there exists for me all that exists now—a name, a renown, a dream. Never for me may the nuptial hymn resound, or the marriage torch be illumined. O goddess of the silver bow, O chaste and venerable Artemis! receive, protect thy servant; and ye, O funereal gods, lead me soon, lead the virgin unreluctant to the shades."

A superstitious fear, a dread as if his earthly love would violate something sacred, chilled the ardour of the young Chian; and for several moments both were silent.

At length, Antagoras, kissing the hem of her robe, said,—

"Maiden of Byzantium,—like thee then, I will love, though without hope. I will not, I dare not, profane thy presence by prayers which pain thee, and seem to me, having heard thee, almost guilty, as if proffered to some nymph circling in choral dance the moonlit mountain-tops of Delos. But ere I depart, and tell thy father that my suit is over, O place at least thy right hand in mine, and swear to me, not the bride's vow of faith and troth, but that vow which a virgin sister may pledge to a brother, mindful to protect and to avenge her. Swear to me, that if this haughty Spartan, contemning alike men, laws, and the household gods, should seek to constrain thy purity to his will; if thou shouldst have cause to tremble at power and force; and fierce desire should demand what gentle love would but reverently implore,—then, Cleonice, seeing how little thy father can defend thee, wilt thou remember Antagoras, and through him, summon around thee all the majesty of Hellas?

Grant me but this prayer, and I leave thee, if in sorrow, yet not with terror."

"Generous and noble Chian," returned Cleonice as her tears fell upon the hand he extended to her,—"why, why do I so ill repay thee? Thy love is indeed that which ennobles the heart that yields it, and her who shall one day recompense thee for the loss of me. Fear not the power of Pausanias: dream not that I shall need a defender, while above us reign the gods, and below us lies the grave. Yet, to appease thee, take my right hand, and hear my oath. If the hour comes when I have need of man's honour against man's wrong, I will call on Antagoras as a brother."

Their hands closed in each other; and not trusting himself to speech, Antagoras turned away his face, and left the room.

CHAPTER V.

FOR some days, an appearance at least of harmony was restored to the contending factions in the Byzantine camp. Pausanias did not dismiss Gongylus from the government of the city; but he sent one by one for the more important of the Ionian complainants, listened to their grievances, and promised redress. He adopted a more popular and gracious demeanour, and seemed, with a noble grace, to submit to the policy of conciliating the allies.

But discontent arose from causes beyond his power, had he genuinely exerted it, to remove. For it was a discontent that lay in the hostility of race to race. Though the Spartan Equals had preached courtesy to the Ionians, the ordinary manner of the Spartan warriors was invariably offensive to the vain and susceptible confederates of a more polished race. A Spartan, wherever he might be placed, unconsciously assumed superiority. The levity of an Ionian was ever displeasing to him. Out of the actual battle-field, they could have no topics in common, none which did not provoke irritation and dispute. On the other hand, most of the Ionians could ill conceal their disaffection, mingled with something of just contempt at the notorious and confessed incapacity of the Spartans for maritime affairs, while a Spartan was yet the commander of the fleet. And many of them, wearied with inaction, and anxious to return home, were willing to seize any reasonable pretext for desertion. In this last motive lay the real strength and safety of Pausanias. And to this end his previous policy of arrogance was not so idle as it had seemed to the Greeks, and appears still in the page of history.

PAUSANIAS, THE SPARTAN. 365

For a Spartan really anxious to preserve the pre-eminence of his country, and to prevent the sceptre of the seas passing to Athens, could have devised no plan of action more sagacious and profound than one which would disperse the Ionians, and the Athenians themselves, and reduce the operations of the Grecian force to that land warfare in which the Spartan pre-eminence was equally indisputable and undisputed. And still Pausanias, even in his change of manner, plotted and intrigued and hoped for this end. Could he once sever from the encampment the Athenians and the Ionian allies, and yet remain with his own force at Byzantium until the Persian army could collect on the Phrygian frontier, the way seemed clear to his ambition. Under ordinary circumstances, in this object he might easily have succeeded. But it chanced that all his schemes were met with invincible mistrust by those in whose interest they were conceived, and on whose co-operation they depended for success. The means adopted by Pausanias in pursuit of his policy were too distasteful to the national prejudices of the Spartan government, to enable him to elicit from the national ambition of that government sufficient sympathy with the object of it. The more he felt himself uncomprehended and mistrusted by his countrymen, the more personal became the character, and the more unscrupulous the course, of his ambition. Unhappily for Pausanias moreover, the circumstances which chafed his pride, also thwarted the satisfaction of his affections; and his criminal ambition was stimulated by that less guilty passion which shared with it the mastery of a singularly turbulent and impetuous soul. Not his the love of sleek, gallant, and wanton youth; it was the love of man in his mature years, but of man to whom love till then had been unknown. In that large and dark and stormy nature all passions once admitted took the growth of Titans. He loved as those long lonely at heart alone can love; he loved as love the unhappy when the unfamiliar bliss of the sweet human emotion descends like dew upon the desert. To him Cleonice was a creature wholly out of the range of experience. Differing in every shade of her versatile humour from the only women he had known, the simple, sturdy, uneducated maids and matrons of Sparta, her softness enthralled him, her anger awed. In his dreams of future power, of an absolute throne and unlimited dominion, Pausanias beheld the fair Byzantine crowned by his side. Fiercely as he loved, and little as the *sentiment* of love mingled with his *passion*, he yet thought not to dishonour a victim, but to elevate a bride. What though the laws of Sparta were against such nuptials, was not the hour approaching when these laws should be trampled under his

armed heel? Since the contract with the Persians, which Gongylus
assured him Xerxes would joyously and promptly fulfil, Pausanias
already felt, in a soul whose arrogance arose from the consciousness
of powers that had not yet found their field, as if he were not the
subject of Sparta, but her lord and king. In his interviews with
Cleonice, his language took a tone of promise and of hope that at
times lulled her fears, and communicated its sanguine colourings of
the future to her own dreams. With the elasticity of youth, her
spirits rose from the solemn despondency with which she had replied
to the reproaches of Antagoras. For though Pausanias spoke not
openly of his schemes, though his words were mysterious, and his
replies to her questions ambiguous and equivocal, still it seemed to
her, seeing in him the hero of all Hellas, so natural that he could
make the laws of Sparta yield to the weight of his authority, or
relax in homage to his renown, that she indulged the belief that his
influence would set aside the iron customs of his country. Was it
too extravagant a reward to the conqueror of the Mede to suffer him
to select at least the partner of his hearth? No, Hope was not dead
in that young breast. Still might she be the bride of him whose
glory had dazzled her noble and sensitive nature, till the faults that
darkened it were lost in the blaze. Thus insensibly to herself her
tones became softer to her stern lover, and her heart betrayed itself
more in her gentle looks. Yet again were there times when doubt
and alarm returned with more than their earlier force—times when,
wrapped in his lurid and absorbing ambition, Pausanias escaped from
his usual suppressed reserve—times when she recalled that night in
which she had witnessed his interview with the strangers of the East,
and had trembled lest the altar should be kindled upon the ruins of
his fame. For Cleonice was wholly, ardently, sublimely Greek,
filled in each crevice of her soul with its lovely poetry, its beautiful
superstition, its heroic freedom. As Greek, she had loved Pausanias,
seeing in him the lofty incarnation of Greece itself. The descendant
of the demigod, the champion of Platæa, the saviour of Hellas—
theme for song till song should be no more—these attributes were
what she beheld and loved ; and not to have reigned by his side
over a world would she have welcomed one object of that evil
ambition which renounced the loyalty of a Greek for the supremacy
of a king.

Meanwhile, though Antagoras had, with no mean degree of generosity, relinquished his suit to Cleonice, he detected with a jealous
vigilance the continued visits of Pausanias, and burned with increasing hatred against his favoured and powerful rival. Though,
in common with all the Greeks out of the Peloponnesus, he was very

imperfectly acquainted with the Spartan constitution, he could not be blinded, like Cleonice, into the belief that a law so fundamental in Sparta, and so general in all the primitive States of Greece, as that which forbade intermarriage with a foreigner, could be cancelled for the Regent of Sparta, and in favour of an obscure maiden of Byzantium. Every visit Pausanias paid to Cleonice but served, in his eyes, as a prelude to her ultimate dishonour. He lent himself, therefore, with all the zeal of his vivacious and ardent character, to the design of removing Pausanias himself from Byzantium. He plotted with the implacable Uliades and the other Ionian captains to send to Sparta a formal mission stating their grievances against the Regent, and urging his recall. But the altered manner of Pausanias deprived them of their just pretext; and the Ionians, more and more under the influence of the Athenian chief, were disinclined to so extreme a measure without the consent of Aristides and Cimon. These two chiefs were not passive spectators of affairs so critical to their ambition for Athens—they penetrated into the motives of Pausanias in the novel courtesy of demeanour that he adopted, and they foresaw that if he could succeed in wearing away the patience of the allies and dispersing the fleet, yet without giving occasion for his own recall, the golden opportunity of securing to Athens the maritime ascendancy would be lost. They resolved, therefore, to make the occasion which the wiles of the Regent had delayed; and towards this object Antagoras, moved by his own jealous hate against Pausanias, worked incessantly. Fearless and vigilant, he was ever on the watch for some new charge against the Spartan chief, ever relentless in stimulating suspicion, aggravating discontent, inflaming the fierce, and arguing with the timid. His less exalted station allowed him to mix more familiarly with the various Ionian officers than would have become the high-born Cimon, and the dignified repute of Aristides. Seeking to distract his mind from the haunting thought of Cleonice, he flung himself with the ardour of his Greek temperament into the social pleasures, which took a zest from the design that he carried into them all. In the banquets, in the sports, he was ever seeking to increase the enemies of his rival, and where he charmed a gay companion, there he often enlisted a bold conspirator.

Pausanias, the unconscious or the careless object of the Ionian's jealous hate, could not resist the fatal charm of Cleonice's presence; and if it sometimes exasperated the more evil elements of his nature, at other times it so lulled them to rest, that had the Fates given him the rightful claim to that single treasure, not one guilty thought might have disturbed the majesty of a soul which, though undisciplined

and uncultured, owed half its turbulence and half its rebellious
pride to its baffled yearnings for human affection and natural joy.
And Cleonice, unable to shun the visits which her weak and covetous father, despite his promised favour to the suit of Antagoras, still
encouraged; and feeling her honour, at least, if not her peace, was
secured by that ascendancy which, with each successive interview
between them, her character more and more asserted over the
Spartan's higher nature, relinquished the tormenting levity of tone
whereby she had once sought to elude his earnestness, or conceal
her own sentiments. An interest in a fate so solemn, an interest
far deeper than mere human love, stole into her heart and elevated
its instincts. She recognized the immense compassion which was
due to the man so desolate at the head of armaments, so dark in the
midst of glory. Centuries roll, customs change, but, ever since the
time of the earliest mother, woman yearns to be the soother.

CHAPTER VI.

IT was the hour of the day when between the two principal
meals of the Greeks men surrendered themselves to idleness or pleasure; when groups formed in the market-
place, or crowded the barbers' shops to gossip and talk
of news; when the tale-teller or ballad-singer collected round him
on the quays his credulous audience; when on playgrounds that
stretched behind the taverns or without the walls the more active
youths assembled, and the quoit was hurled, or mimic battles waged
with weapons of wood, or the Dorians weaved their simple, the
Ionians their more intricate or less decorous dances. At that hour
Lysander, wandering from the circles of his countrymen, walked
musingly by the sea-shore.

"And why," said the voice of a person who had approached him
unperceived, "and why, O Lysander, art thou absent from thy comrades, thou model and theme of the youths of Sparta, foremost in
their manly sports, as in their martial labours?"

Lysander turned and bowed low his graceful head, for he who
accosted him was scarcely more honoured by the Athenians, whom
his birth, his wealth, and his popular demeanour dazzled, than by
the plain sons of Sparta, who, in his simple garb, his blunt and
hasty manner, his professed admiration for all things Spartan, beheld
one Athenian at least congenial to their tastes.

"The child that misses its mother," answered Lysander, "has
small joy with its playmates. And I, a Spartan, pine for Sparta."

"Truly," returned Cimon, "there must be charms in thy noble country of which we other Greeks know but little, if amidst all the luxuries and delights of Byzantium thou canst pine for her rugged hills. And although, as thou knowest well, I was once a sojourner in thy city as ambassador from my own, yet to foreigners so little of the inner Spartan life is revealed, that I pray thee to satisfy my curiosity and explain to me the charm that reconciles thee and thine to institutions which seem to the Ionians at war with the pleasures and the graces of social life."[1]

"Ill can the native of one land explain to the son of another why he loves it," returned Lysander. "That which the Ionian calls pleasure is to me but tedious vanity; that which he calls grace, is to me but enervate levity. Me it pleases to find the day, from sunrise to night, full of occupations that leave no languor, that employ, but not excite. For the morning, our gymnasia, our military games, the chase—diversions that brace the limbs and leave us in peace fit for war—diversions, which, unlike the brawls of the wordy Agora, bless us with the calm mind and clear spirit resulting from vigorous habits, and ensuring jocund health. Noon brings our simple feast, shared in public, enlivened by jest; late at eve we collect in our Leschæ, and the winter nights seem short, listening to the old men's talk of our sires and heroes. To us life is one serene yet active holiday. No Spartan condescends to labour, yet no Spartan can womanize himself by ease. For us, too, differing from you Ionian Greeks, for us women are companions, not slaves. Man's youth is passed under the eyes and in the presence of those from whom he may select, as his heart inclines, the future mother of his children. Not for us your feverish and miserable ambitions, the intrigues of demagogues, the drudgery of the mart, the babble of the populace; we alone know the quiet repose of heart. That which I see everywhere else, the gnawing strife of passion, visits not the stately calm of the Spartan life. We have the leisure, not of the body alone, but

---

[1] Alexander, King of Macedon, had visited the Athenians with overtures of peace and alliance from Xerxes and Mardonius. These overtures were confined to the Athenians alone, and the Spartans were fearful lest they should be accepted. The Athenians, however, generously refused them. Gold, said they, hath no amount, earth no territory how beautiful soever that could tempt the Athenians to accept conditions from the Mede for the servitude of Greece. On this the Persians invaded Attica, and the Athenians, after waiting in vain for promised aid from Sparta, took refuge at Salamis. Meanwhile, they had sent messengers or ambassadors to Sparta, to remonstrate on the violation of their agreement in delaying succour. This chanced at the very time when, by the death of his father Cleombrotus, Pausanias became Regent. Slowly, and after much hesitation, the Spartans sent them aid under Pausanias. Two of the ambassadors were Aristides and Cimon.

of the soul. Equality with us is the all in all, and we know not that jealous anguish—the desire to rise one above the other. We busy ourselves not in making wealth, in ruling mobs, in ostentatious rivalries of state, and gaud, and power—struggles without an object. When we struggle it is for an end. Nothing moves us from our calm, but danger to Sparta, or woe to Hellas. Harmony, peace, and order—these are the graces of our social life. Pity us, O Athenian!"

Cimon had listened with profound attention to a speech unusually prolix and descriptive for a Spartan; and he sighed deeply as it closed. For that young Athenian, destined to so renowned a place in the history of his country, was, despite his popular manners, no favourer of the popular passions. Lofty and calm, and essentially an aristocrat by nature and opinion, this picture of a life unruffled by the restless changes of democracy, safe and aloof from the shifting humours of the multitude, charmed and allured him. He forgot for the moment those counter propensities which made him still Athenian—the taste for magnificence, the love of women, and the desire of rule. His busy schemes slept within him, and he answered:

"Happy is the Spartan who thinks with you. Yet," he added, after a pause, "yet own that there are amongst you many to whom the life you describe has ceased to proffer the charms that enthral you, and who envy the more diversified and exciting existence of surrounding States. Lysander's eulogiums shame his chief Pausanias."

"It is not for me, nor for thee, whose years scarce exceed my own, to judge of our elders in renown," said Lysander, with a slight shade over his calm brow. "Pausanias will surely be found still a Spartan, when Sparta needs him; and the heart of the Heracleid beats under the robe of the Mede."

"Be frank with me, Lysander; thou knowest that my own countrymen often jealously accuse me of loving Sparta too well. I imitate, say they, the manners and dress of the Spartan, as Pausanias those of the Mede. Trust me then, and bear with me, when I say that Pausanias ruins the cause of Sparta. If he tarry here longer in the command he will render all the allied enemies to thy country. Already he has impaired his fame and dimmed his laurels; already, despite his pretexts and excuses, we perceive that his whole nature is corrupted. Recall him to Sparta, while it is yet time—time to reconcile the Greeks with Sparta, time to save the hero of Platæa from the contaminations of the East. Preserve his own glory, dearer to thee as his special friend than to all men, yet dear to me, though an Athenian, from the memory of the deeds which delivered Hellas."

Cimon spoke with the blunt and candid eloquence natural to him, and to which his manly countenance and earnest tone and character for truth gave singular effect.

Lysander remained long silent. At length he said, "I neither deny nor assent to thine arguments, son of Miltiades. The Ephors alone can judge of their wisdom."

"But if we address them, by message, to the Ephors, thou and the nobler Spartans will not resent our remonstrances?"

"All that injures Pausanias Lysander will resent. Little know I of the fables of poets, but Homer is at least as familiar to the Dorian as to the Ionian, and I think with him that between friends there is but one love and one anger."

"Then are the frailties of Pausanias dearer to thee than his fame, or Pausanias himself dearer to thee than Sparta—the erring brother than the venerable mother."

Lysander's voice died on his lips; the reproof struck home to him. He turned away his face, and with a slow wave of his hand seemed to implore forbearance. Cimon was touched by the action and the generous embarrassment of the Spartan; he saw, too, that he had left in the mind he had addressed thoughts that might work as he had designed, and he judged by the effect produced on Lysander what influence the same arguments might effect addressed to others less under the control of personal friendship. Therefore, with a few gentle words, he turned aside, continued his way, and left Lysander alone.

Entering the town, the Athenian threaded his path through some of the narrow lanes and alleys that wound from the quays towards the citadel, avoiding the broader and more frequented streets. The course he took was such as rendered it little probable that he should encounter any of the higher classes, and especially the Spartans, who from their constitutional pride shunned the resorts of the populace. But as he came nearer the citadel stray Helots were seen at times, emerging from the inns and drinking houses, and these stopped short and inclined low if they caught sight of him at a distance, for his hat and staff, his majestic stature, and composed step, made them take him for a Spartan.

One of these slaves, however, emerging suddenly from a house close by which Cimon passed, recognized him, and retreating within abruptly, entered a room in which a man sat alone, and seemingly in profound thought; his cheek rested on one hand, with the other he leaned upon a small lyre, his eyes were bent on the ground, and he started, as a man does dream-like from a reverie, when the Helot touched him and said abruptly, and in a tone of surprise and inquiry,—

"Cimon, the Athenian, is ascending the hill towards the Spartan quarter."

"The Spartan quarter! Cimon!" exclaimed Alcman, for it was he. "Give me thy cap and hide."

Hastily enduing himself in these rough garments, and drawing the cap over his face, the Mothon hurried to the threshold, and, seeing the Athenian at the distance, followed his footsteps, though with the skill of a man used to ambush he kept himself unseen—now under the projecting roofs of the houses, now skirting the wall, which, heavy with buttresses, led towards the outworks of the citadel. And with such success did he pursue his track that when Cimon paused at last at the place of his destination, and gave one vigilant and searching glance around him, he detected no living form.

He had then reached a small space of table-land on which stood a few trees of great age—all that time and the encroachments of the citadel and the town had spared of the sacred grove which formerly surrounded a rude and primitive temple, the gray columns of which gleamed through the heavy foliage. Passing, with a slow and cautious step, under the thick shadow of these trees, Cimon now arrived before the open door of the temple, placed at the east so as to admit the first beams of the rising sun. Through the threshold, in the middle of the fane, the eye rested on the statue of Apollo, raised upon a lofty pedestal and surrounded by a rail—a statue not such as the later genius of the Athenian represented the god of light, and youth, and beauty; not wrought from Parian marble, or smoothest ivory, and in the divinest proportions of the human form, but rude, formal, and roughly hewn from the wood of the yew-tree—some early effigy of the god, made by the simple piety of the first Dorian colonizers of Byzantium. Three forms stood mute by an altar, equally homely and ancient, and adorned with horns, placed a little apart, and considerably below the statue.

As the shadow of the Athenian, who halted at the threshold, fell long and dark along the floor, the figures turned slowly, and advanced towards him. With an inclination of his head Cimon retreated from the temple; and, looking round, saw abutting from the rear of the building a small cell or chamber, which doubtless in former times had served some priestly purpose, but now, doorless, empty, desolate, showed the utter neglect into which the ancient shrine of the Dorian god had fallen amidst the gay and dissolute Byzantians. To this cell Cimon directed his steps; the men he had seen in the temple followed him, and all four, with brief and formal greeting, seated themselves, Cimon on a fragment of some broken column, the others on a bench that stretched along the wall.

"Peers of Sparta," said the Athenian, "ye have doubtless ere this revolved sufficiently the grave matter which I opened to you in a former conference, and in which, to hear your decision, I seek at your appointment these sacred precincts."

"Son of Miltiades," answered the blunt Polydorus, "you inform us that it is the intention of the Athenians to despatch a messenger to Sparta demanding the instant recall of Pausanias. You ask us to second that request. But without our aid the Athenians are masters to do as they will. Why should we abet your quarrel against the Regent?"

"Friend," replied Cimon, "we, the Athenians, confess to no quarrel with Pausanias; what we demand is to avoid all quarrel with him or yourselves. You seem to have overlooked my main arguments. Permit me to re-urge them briefly. If Pausanias remains, the allies have resolved openly to revolt; if you, the Spartans, assist your chief, as methinks you needs must do, you are at once at war with the rest of the Greeks. If you desert him you leave Hellas without a chief, and we will choose one of our own. Meanwhile, in the midst of our dissensions, the towns and states well affected to Persia will return to her sway; and Persia herself falls upon us as no longer an united enemy but an easy prey. For the sake, therefore, of Sparta and of Greece, we entreat you to co-operate with us; or rather, to let the recall of Pausanias be effected more by the wise precaution of the Spartans than by the fierce resolve of the other Greeks. So you save best the dignity of your State, and so, in reality, you best serve your chief. For less shameful to him is it to be recalled by you than to be deposed by us."

"I know not," said Gelon, surlily, "what Sparta hath to do at all with this foreign expedition; we are safe in our own defiles."

"Pardon me, if I remind you that you were scarcely safe at Thermopylæ, and that had the advice Demaratus proffered to Xerxes been taken, and that island of Cithera, which commands Sparta itself, been occupied by Persian troops, as in a future time, if Sparta desert Greece, it may be, you were undone. And, wisely or not, Sparta is now in command at Byzantium, and it behoves her to maintain, with the dignity she assumes, the interests she represents. Grant that Pausanias be recalled, another Spartan can succeed him. Whom of your countrymen would you prefer to that high post, if you, O Peers, aid us in the dismissal of Pausanias?"[1]

* * * * * *

---

[1] This chapter was left unfinished by the author; probably with the intention of recasting it. Such an intention, at least, is indicated by the marginal marks upon the MS.—L.

BOOK III.

CHAPTER I.

THE fountain sparkled to the noonday, the sward around it was sheltered from the sun by vines formed into shadowy arcades, with interlaced leaves for roof. Afar through the vistas thus formed gleamed the blue of a sleeping sea. Under the hills, or close by the margin of the fountain, Cleonice was seated upon a grassy knoll, covered with wild flowers. Behind her, at a little distance, grouped her handmaids, engaged in their womanly work, and occasionally conversing in whispers. At her feet reposed the grand form of Pausanias. Alcman stood not far behind him, his hand resting on his lyre, his gaze fixed upon the upward jet of the fountain.

"Behold," said Cleonice, "how the water soars up to the level of its source!"

"As my soul would soar to thy love," said the Spartan, amorously.

"As thy soul should soar to the stars. O son of Hercules, when I hear thee burst into thy wild flights of ambition, I see not thy way to the stars."

"Why dost thou ever thus chide the ambition which may give me thee?"

"No, for thou mightest then be as much below me as thou art now above. Too humble to mate with the Heracleid, I am too proud to stoop to the Tributary of the Mede."

"Tributary for a sprinkling of water and a handful of earth. Well, my pride may revolt, too, from that tribute. But, alas! what is the tribute Sparta exacts from me now?—personal liberty—freedom of soul itself. The Mede's Tributary may be a king over millions; the Spartan Regent is a slave to the few."

"Cease—cease—cease. I will not hear thee," cried Cleonice, placing her hands on her ears.

Pausanias gently drew them away; and holding them both captive in the large clasp of his own right hand, gazed eagerly into her pure, unshrinking eyes.

"Tell me," he said, "for in much thou art wiser than I am, unjust though thou art. Tell me this. Look onward to the future with a gaze as steadfast as now meets mine, and say if thou canst discover any path, except that which it pleases thee to condemn, which may lead thee and me to the marriage altar!"

Down sank those candid eyes, and the virgin's cheek grew first rosy red, and then pale, as if every drop of blood had receded to the heart.

"Speak!" insisted Pausanias, softening his haughty voice to its meekest tone.

"I cannot see the path to the altar," murmured Cleonice, and the tears rolled down her cheeks.

"And if thou seest it not," returned Pausanias, "art thou brave enough to say—Be we lost to each other for life? I, though man and Spartan, am not brave enough to say that!"

He released her hands as he spoke, and clasped his own over his face. Both were long silent.

Alcman had for some moments watched the lovers with deep interest, and had caught into his listening ears the purport of their words. He now raised his lyre, and swept his hands over the chords. The touch was that of a master, and the musical sounds produced their effect on all. The handmaids paused from their work. Cleonice turned her eyes wistfully towards the Mothon. Pausanias drew his hands from his face, and cried joyously, "I accept the omen. Foster-brother, I have heard that measure to a Hymeneal Song. Sing us the words that go with the melody."

"Nay," said Alcman, gently, "the words are not those which are sung before youth and maiden when they walk over perishing flowers to bridal altars. They are the words which embody a legend of the land in which the heroes of old dwell, removed from earth, yet preserved from Hades."

"Ah," said Cleonice—and a strange expression, calmly mournful, settled on her features—"then the words may haply utter my own thoughts. Sing them to us, I pray thee."

The Mothon bowed his head, and thus began:—

THE ISLE OF SPIRITS.

Many wonders on the ocean
 By the moonlight may be seen;
Under moonlight on the Euxine
 Rose the blessed silver isle,

As Leostratus of Croton,
 At the Pythian God's behest,
Steer'd along the troubled waters
 To the tranquil spirit-land.

In the earthquake of the battle,
  When the Locrians reel'd before
Croton's shock of marching iron,
  Strode a Phantom to their van :

Strode the shade of Locrian Ajax,
  Guarding still the native soil,
And Leotratus, confronting,
  Wounded fell before the spear.

Leech and herb the wound could heal not ;
  Said the Pythian God, "Depart,
Voyage o'er the troubled Euxine
  To the tranquil spirit-land.

"There abides the Locrian Ajax,
  He who gave the wound shall heal ;
Godlike souls are in their mercy
  Stronger yet than in their wrath."

While at ease on lullèd waters
  Rose the blessed silver isle,
Purple vines in lengthening vistas
  Knit the hill-top to the beach.

And the beach had sparry caverns,
  And a floor of golden sands,
And wherever soared the cypress,
  Underneath it bloomed the rose.

Glimmered there amid the vine trees,
  Thoro' cavern, over beach,
Lifelike shadows of a beauty
  Which the living know no more,

Towering statues of great heroes,
  They who fought at Thebes and Troy ;
And with looks that poets dream of
  Beam'd the women heroes loved.

Kingly, forth before their comrades,
  As the vessel touch'd the shore,
Came the stateliest Two, by Hymen
  Ever hallowed into One.

As He strode, the forests trembled
  To the awe that crowned his brow :
As She stepp'd, the ocean dimpled
  To the ray that left her smile.

"Welcome hither, fearless warrior !"
  Said a voice in which there slept
Thunder-sounds to scatter armies,
  As a north-wind scatters leaves.

"Welcome hither, wounded sufferer,"
  Said a voice of music low
As the coo of doves that nestle
  Under summer boughs at noon.

"Who are ye, O shapes of glory?"
  Ask'd the wondering living man:
Quoth the Man-ghost, "This is Helen,
  And the Fair is for the Brave.

"Fairest prize to bravest victor;
  Whom doth Greece her bravest deem?"
Said Leostratus, "Achilles:"
  "Bride and bridegroom then are we."

"Low I kneel to thee, Pelides,
  But, O marvel, she thy bride,
She whose guilt unpeopled Hellas,
  She whose marriage lights fired Troy?"

Frown'd the large front of Achilles,
  Overshadowing sea and sky,
Even as when between Olympus
  And Oceanus hangs storm.

"Know, thou dullard," said Pelides,
  "That on the funereal pyre
Earthly sins are purged from glory,
  And the Soul is as the Name."

If to her in life—a Paris,
  If to me in life—a slave,
Helen's mate is *here* Achilles,
  Mine—the sister of the stars.

Nought of her survives but beauty,
  Nought of me survives but fame;
Here the Beautiful and Famous
  Intermingle evermore."

Then throughout the Blessed Island
  Sang aloud the Race of Light,
"Know, the Beautiful and Famous
  Marry here for evermore!"

"Thy song bears a meaning deeper than its words," said Pausanias; "but if that meaning be consolation, I comprehend it not."

"I do," said Cleonice. "Singer, I pray thee draw near. Let us talk of what my lost mother said was the favourite theme of the grander sages of Miletus. Let us talk of what lies afar and undiscovered amid waters more troubled than the Euxine. Let us speak of the Land of Souls."

"Who ever returned from that land to tell us of it?" said Pausanias. "Voyagers that never voyaged thither save in song."

"Son of Cleombrotus," said Alcman, "hast thou not heard that in one of the cities founded by thine ancestor, Hercules, and named after his own name, there yet dwells a Priesthood that can summon to living eyes the Phantoms of the Dead?"

"No," answered Pausanias, with the credulous wonder common to eager natures which Philosophy has not withdrawn from the realm of superstition.

"But," asked Cleonice, "does it need the Necromancer to convince us that the soul does not perish when the breath leaves the lips? If I judge the burthen of thy song aright, thou art not, O singer, uninitiated in the divine and consoling doctrines which, emanating, it is said, from the schools of Miletus, establish the immortality of the soul, not for Demigods and Heroes only, but for us all; which imply the soul's purification from earthly sins, in some regions less chilling and stationary than the sunless and melancholy Hades."

Alcman looked at the girl surprised.

"Art thou not, maiden," said he, "one of the many female disciples whom the successors of Pythagoras the Samian have enrolled?"

"Nay," said Cleonice, modestly; "but my mother had listened to great teachers of wisdom, and I speak imperfectly the thoughts I have heard her utter when she told me she had no terror of the grave."

"Fair Byzantine," returned the Mothon, while Pausanias, leaning his upraised face on his hand, listened mutely to themes new to his mind and foreign to his Spartan culture. "Fair Byzantine, we in Lacedæmon, whether free or enslaved, are not educated to the subtle learning which distinguishes the intellect of Ionian Sages. But I, born and licensed to be a poet, converse eagerly with all who swell the stores which enrich the treasure-house of song. And thus, since we have left the land of Sparta, and more especially in yon city, the centre of many tribes and of many minds, I have picked up, as it were, desultory and scattered notions, which, for want of a fitting teacher, I bind and arrange for myself as well as I may. And since the ideas that now float through the atmosphere of Hellas are not confined to the great, nay, perhaps are less visible to them, than to those whose eyes are not riveted on the absorbing substances of ambition and power, so I have learned something, I know not how, save that I have listened and reflected. And here, where I have heard what sages conjecture of a world which seems so far off, but to which we are so near that we may reach it in a moment, my interest might indeed be intense. For what is this world to him who came into it a slave!"

"Alcman," exclaimed Pausanias, "the foster-brother of the Heracleid is no more a slave."

The Mothon bowed his head gratefully, but the expression on his face retained the same calm and sombre resignation.

"Alas," said Cleonice, with the delicacy of female consolation, "who in this life is really free? Have citizens no thraldom in custom and law? Are we not all slaves?"

"True. All slaves!" murmured the royal victor. "Envy none, O Alcman. Yet," he continued gloomily, "what is the life beyond the grave which sacred tradition and ancient song holds out to us? Not thy silver island, vain singer, unless it be only for an early race more immediately akin to the Gods. Shadows in the shade are the dead; at the best reviving only their habits when on earth, in phantom-like delusions; aiming spectral darts like Orion at spectral lions; things bloodless and pulseless; existences followed to no purpose through eternity, as dreams are through a night. Who cares so to live again? Not I."

"The sages that now rise around, and speak oracles different from those heard at Delphi," said Alcman, "treat not thus the Soul's immortality. They begin by inquiring how creation rose; they seek to find the primitive element; what that may be they dispute; some say the fiery, some the airy, some the ethereal element. Their language here is obscure. But it is a something which forms, harmonizes, works, and lives on for ever. And of that something is the Soul; creative, harmonious, active, an element in itself. Out of its development here, that soul comes on to a new development elsewhere. If here the beginning lead to that new development in what we call virtue, it moves to light and joy :—if it can only roll on through the grooves it has here made for itself, in what we call vice and crime, its path is darkness and wretchedness."

"In what we call virtue—what we call vice and crime? Ah," said Pausanias, with a stern sneer, "Spartan virtue, O Alcman, is what a Helot may call crime. And if ever the Helot rose and shouted freedom, would he not say, This is virtue? Would the Spartan call it virtue, too, my foster-brother?"

"Son of Cleombrotus," answered Alcman, "it is not for me to vindicate the acts of the master; nor to blame the slave who is of my race. Yet the sage definers of virtue distinguish between the Conscience of a Polity and that of the Individual Man. Self-preservation is the instinct of every community, and all the ordinances ascribed to Lycurgus are designed to preserve the Spartan existence. For what are the pure Spartan race? a handful of men established as lords in the midst of a hostile population. Close by the eyrie thine eagle fathers built in the rocks, hung the silent Amyclæ, a city of foes that cost the Spartans many generations to subdue. Hence thy State was a camp, its citizens sentinels; its children were brought up from the cradle to support the stern life to which necessity devoted the men. Hardship and privation were second nature. Not enough to be brave; vigilance was equally essential. Every Spartan life was precious; therefore came the cunning which characterizes the Spartan; therefore the boy is permitted to steal, but punished if detected; therefore the whole Commonwealth strives to keep aloof from the wars of Greece unless itself be threatened. A single battle in a common cause might suffice to depopulate the Spartan race, and leave it at the mercy of the thousands that so reluctantly own its dominion. Hence the ruthless determination to crush the spirit, to degrade the class of the enslaved Helots; hence its dread lest the slumbering brute force of the Servile find in its own masses a head to teach the consciousness, and a hand to guide the movements, of its power. These are the necessities of the Polity, its vices are the outgrowth of its necessities; and the life that so galls thee, and which has sometimes rendered mad those who return to it from having known another, and the danger that evermore surrounds the lords of a sullen multitude, are the punishments of these vices. Comprehendest thou?"

"I comprehend."

"But individuals have a conscience apart from that of the Community. Every community has its errors in its laws. No human laws, how skilfully soever framed, but give to a national character defects as well as merits, merits as well as defects. Craft, selfishness, cruelty to the subdued, inhospitable frigidity to neighbours, make the defects of the Spartan character. But," added Alcman, with a kind of reluctant anguish in his voice, "the character has its grand virtues, too, or would the Helots not be the masters? Valour indomitable; grand scorn of death; passionate ardour for the State which is so severe a mother to them; antique faith in the sacred altars; sublime devotion to what is held to be duty. Are these not found in the Spartan beyond all the Greeks, as thou seest them in thy friend Lysander; in that soul, stately, pure, compact in its own firm substance as a statue within a temple is in its Parian stone? But what the Gods ask from man is virtue in himself, according as he comprehends it. And, therefore, here all societies are equal; for the Gods pardon in the man the faults he shares with his Community, and ask from him but the good and the beautiful, such as the nature of his Community will permit him to conceive and to accomplish. Thou knowest that there are many kinds of music— for instance, the Doric, the Æolian, the Ionian—in Hellas. The Lydians have their music, the Phrygians theirs too. The Scyth and the Mede doubtless have their own. Each race prefers the music it cultivates, and finds fault with the music of other races. And yet a man who has learned melody and measure, will recognize a music in them all. So it is with virtue, the music of the human soul. It differs in differing races. But he who has learned to know what virtue is can recognize its harmonies, wherever they be heard. And thus the soul that fulfils its own notions of music, and carries them up to its idea of excellence, is the master soul; and in the regions to which it goes, when the breath leaves the lips, it pursues the same, set free from the trammels that confined, and the false judgments that marred it here. For then the soul is no longer Spartan, or Ionian, Lydian, Median, or Scythian. Escaped into the upper air, it is the citizen of universal freedom and universal light. And hence it does not live as a ghost in gloomy shades, being merely a pale memory of things that have passed away; but in its primitive being as an emanation from the one divine principle which penetrates everywhere, vivifies all things, and enjoys in all. This is what I weave together from the doctrines of varying schools; schools that collect from the fields of thought flowers of different kinds which conceal, by adorning it, the ligament that unites them all: this, I say, O Pausanias, is my conception of the soul."

Cleonice rose softly, and taking from her bosom a rose, kissed it fervently, and laid it at the feet of the singer.

"Were this my soul," cried she, "I would ask thee to bind it in the wreath."

Vague and troubled thoughts passed meanwhile through the mind of the Heracleid; old ideas being disturbed and dislodged, the new ones did not find easy settlement in a brain occupied with ambitious schemes and a heart agitated by stormy passions. In much superstitious, in much sceptical, as education had made him the one, and experience but of worldly things was calculated to make him the other, he followed not the wing of the philosophy which passed through heights not occupied by Olympus, and dived into depths where no Tartarus echoed to the wail of Cocytus.

After a pause he said in his perplexity,

"Well mayst thou own that no Delphian oracle tells thee all this. And when thou speakest of the Divine Principle as One, dost thou not, O presumptuous man, depopulate the Halls of Ida? Nay, is it not Zeus himself whom thou dethronest; is not thy Divine Principle the Fate which Zeus himself must obey?"

"There is a young man of Clazomenæ," answered the singer, "named Anaxagoras, who avoiding all active life, though of birth the noblest, gives himself up to contemplation, and whom I have listened to in the city as he passed through it, on his way into Egypt.

And I heard him say, 'Fate is an empty name.'[1] Fate is blind, the Divine is All-seeing."

"How!" cried Cleonice. "An empty name—she! Necessity the All-compelling."

The musician drew from the harp one of the most artful of Sappho's exquisite melodies.

"What drew forth that music?" he asked, smiling. "My hand and my will from a genius not present, not visible. Was that genius a blind fate? no, it was a grand intelligence. Nature is to the Deity what my hand and will are to the unseen genius of the musician. They obey an intelligence and they form a music. If creation proceed from an intelligence, what we call fate is but the consequence of its laws. And Nature operates not in the external world alone, but in the core of all life; therefore in the mind of man obeying only what some supreme intelligence has placed there: therefore in man's mind producing music or discord, according as he has learned the principles of harmony, that is, of good. And there be sages who declare that Intelligence and Love are the same. Yet," added the Mothon, with an aspect solemnly compassionate, "not the love thou mockest by the name of Aphrodite. No mortal eye hath ever seen that love within the known sphere, yet all insensibly feel its reign. What keeps the world together but affection? What makes the earth bring forth its fruits, but the kindness which beams in the sunlight and descends in the dews? What makes the lioness watch over her cubs, and the bird, with all air for its wanderings, come back to the fledglings in its nest? Strike love, the conjoiner, from creation, and creation returns to a void. Destroy love the parental, and life is born but to perish. Where stop the influence of love or how limit its multiform degrees? Love guards the fatherland; crowns with turrets the walls of the freeman. What but love binds the citizens of States together, and frames and heeds the laws that submit individual liberty to the rule of the common good? Love creates, love cements, love enters and harmonises all things. And as like attracts like, so love attracts in the hereafter the loving souls that conceived it here. From the region where it summons them, its opposites are excluded. There ceases war; there ceases pain. There indeed intermingle the beautiful and glorious, but beauty purified from earthly sin, the glorious resting from earthly toil. Ask ye how to know on earth where love is really presiding? Not in Paphos, not in Amathus. Wherever thou seest beauty and good; wherever thou seest life, and that life pervaded with faculties of

---

[1] Anaxagoras was then between 20 and 30 years of age.—See Ritter, vol. ii., for the sentiment here ascribed to him, and a general view of his tenets.

joy, there thou seest love; there thou shouldst recognize the Divinity."

"And where I see misery and hate," said the Spartan, "what should I recognize there?"

"Master," returned the singer, "can the good come without a struggle? Is the beautiful accomplished without strife? Recall the tales of primeval chaos, when, as sang the Ascræan singer, love first darted into the midst; imagine the heave and throe of joining elements; conjure up the first living shapes, born of the fluctuating slime and vapour. Surely they were things incomplete, deformed ghastly fragments of being, as are the dreams of a maniac. Had creative Love stopped there, and then, standing on the height of some fair completed world, had viewed the warring portents, wouldst thou not have said—But these are the works of Evil and Hate? Love did not stop there, it worked on; and out of the chaos once ensouled, this glorious world swung itself into ether, the completed sister of the stars. Again, O my listeners, contemplate the sculptor, when the block from the granite shaft first stands rude and shapeless before him. See him in his earlier strife with the obstinate matter —how uncouth the first outline of limb and feature; unlovelier often in the rugged commencements of shape, than when the dumb mass stood shapeless. If the sculptor had stopped there, the thing might serve as an image for the savage of an abominable creed, engaged in the sacrifice of human flesh. But he pauses not, he works on. Stroke by stroke comes from the stone a shape of more beauty than man himself is endowed with, and in a human temple stands a celestial image.

"Thus is it with the soul in the mundane sphere; it works its way on through the adverse matter. We see its work half completed; we cry, Lo, this is misery, this is hate—because the chaos is not yet a perfected world, and the stone block is not yet a statue of Apollo. But for that reason must we pause?—no, we must work on, till the victory brings the repose.

"All things come into order from the war of contraries—the elements fight and wrestle to produce the wild flower at our feet; from a wild flower man hath striven and toiled to perfect the marvellous rose of the hundred leaves. Hate is necessary for the energies of love, evil for the activity of good; until, I say, the victory is won, until Hate and Evil are subdued, as the sculptor subdues the stone; and then rises the divine image serene for ever, and rests on its pedestal in the Uranian Temple. Lift thine eyes; that temple is yonder. O Pausanias, the sculptor's workroom is the earth."

Alcman paused, and sweeping his hand once more over his lyre, chanted as follows:

> "Dewdrop that weepest on the sharp-barbèd thorn,
> Why didst thou fall from Day's golden chalices?
> 'My tears bathe the thorn,' said the Dewdrop,
> 'To nourish the bloom of the rose.'
>
> "Soul of the Infant, why to calamity
> Comest thou wailing from the calm spirit-source?
> 'Ask of the Dew,' said the Infant,
> 'Why it descends on the thorn!'
>
> "Dewdrop from storm, and soul from calamity
> Vanish soon—whither? let the Dew answer thee;
> 'Have not my tears been my glory?
> Tears drew me up to the sun.'
>
> "What were thine uses, that thou art glorified?
> What did thy tears give, profiting earth or sky?
> 'There, to the thorn-stem a blossom,
> Here, to the Iris a tint.'"

Alcman had modulated the tones of his voice into a sweetness so plaintive and touching, that, when he paused, the hand-maidens had involuntarily risen and gathered round, hushed and noiseless. Cleonice had lowered her veil over her face and bosom; but the heaving of its tissue betrayed her half-suppressed, gentle sob; and the proud mournfulness on the Spartan's swarthy countenance had given way to a soft composure, melancholy still—but melancholy as a lulled, though dark water, over which starlight steals through disparted cloud.

Cleonice was the first to break the spell which bound them all.

"I would go within," she murmured faintly. "The sun, now slanting, strikes through the vine-leaves, and blinds me with its glare."

Pausanias approached timidly, and taking her by the hand, drew her aside, along one of the grassy alleys that stretched onwards to the sea.

The handmaidens tarried behind to cluster nearer round the singer. They forgot he was a slave.

CHAPTER II.

"THOU art weeping still, Cleonice!" said the Spartan, "and I have not the privilege to kiss away thy tears."

"Nay, I weep not," answered the girl, throwing up her veil; and her face was calm, if still sad—the tear yet on the eyelids, but the smile upon the lip—δακρυόεν γελάοισα.

"Thy singer has learned his art from a teacher heavenlier than the Pierides, and its name is Hope."

"But if I understand him aright," said Pausanias, "the Hope that inspires him is a goddess who blesses us little on the earth."

As if the Mothon had overheard the Spartan, his voice here suddenly rose behind them, singing:

> "*There* the Beautiful and Glorious
> Intermingle evermore."

Involuntarily both turned. The Mothon seemed as if explaining to the handmaids the allegory of his marriage song upon Helen and Achilles, for his hand was raised on high, and again, with an emphasis, he chanted:

> "There, throughout the Blessed Islands,
> And amid the Race of Light,
> Do the Beautiful and Glorious
> Intermingle evermore."

"Canst thou not wait, if thou so lovest me?" said Cleonice, with more tenderness in her voice than it had ever yet betrayed to him; "life is very short. Hush!" she continued, checking the passionate interruption that burst from his lips; "I have something I would confide to thee: listen. Know that in my childhood I had a dear friend, a maiden a few years older than myself, and she had the divine gift of trance which comes from Apollo. Often, gazing into space, her eyes became fixed, and her frame still as a statue's; then a shiver seized her limbs, and prophecy broke from her lips. And she told me, in one of these hours, when, as she said, 'all space and all time seemed spread before her like a sunlit ocean,' she told me of my future, so far as its leaves have yet unfolded from the stem of my life. Spartan, she prophesied that I should see thee—and—" Cleonice paused, blushing, and then hurried on, "and she told me that suddenly her eye could follow my fate on the earth no more, that it vanished out of the time and the space on which it gazed, and saying it she wept, and broke into funeral song. And therefore, Pausanias, I say life is very short for me at least—"

"Hold," cried Pausanias; "torture not me, nor delude thyself with the dreams of a raving girl. Lives she near? Let me visit her with thee, and I will prove thy prophetess an impostor."

"They whom the Priesthood of Delphi employ throughout Hellas to find the fit natures for a Pythoness heard of her, and heard herself. She whom thou callest impostor gives the answer to perplexed nations from the Pythian shrine. But wherefore doubt her?—where the sorrow? I feel none. If love does rule the worlds beyond, and

o

does unite souls who love nobly here, yonder we shall meet, O descendant of Hercules, and human laws will not part us there."

"Thou die! die before me! thou, scarcely half my years! And I be left here, with no comfort but a singer's dreamy verse, not even mine ambition! Thrones would vanish out of earth, and turn to cinders in thine urn."

"Speak not of thrones," said Cleonice, with imploring softness, "for the prophetess, too, spake of steps that went towards a throne, and vanished at the threshold of darkness, beside which sate the Furies. Speak not of thrones, dream but of glory and Hellas—of what thy soul tells thee is that virtue which makes life an Uranian music, and thus unites it to the eternal symphony, as the breath of the single flute melts when it parts from the instrument into the great concord of the choir. Knowest thou not that in the creed of the Persians each mortal is watched on earth by a good spirit and an evil one? And they who loved us below, or to whom we have done beneficent and gentle deeds, if they go before us into death, pass to the side of the good spirit, and strengthen him to save and to bless thee against the malice of the bad, and the bad is strengthened in his turn by those whom we have injured. Wouldst thou have all the Greeks whose birthright thou wouldst barter, whose blood thou wouldst shed for barbaric aid to thy solitary and lawless power, stand by the side of the evil Fiend? And what could I do against so many? what could my soul do," added Cleonice with simple pathos, "by the side of the kinder spirit?"

Pausanias was wholly subdued. He knelt to the girl, he kissed the hem of her robe, and for the moment ambition, luxury, pomp, pride fled from his soul, and left there only the grateful tenderness of the man, and the lofty instincts of the hero. But just then—was it the evil spirit that sent him?—the boughs of the vine were put aside, and Gongylus the Eretrian stood before them. His black eyes glittered keen upon Pausanias, who rose from his knee, startled and displeased.

"What brings thee hither, man?" said the Regent, haughtily.

"Danger," answered Gongylus, in a hissing whisper. "Lose not a moment—come."

"Danger!" exclaimed Cleonice, tremblingly, and clasping her hands, and all the human love at her heart was visible in her aspect. "Danger, and to *him!*"

"Danger is but as the breeze of my native air," said the Spartan, smiling; "thus I draw it in and thus breathe it away. I follow thee, Gongylus. Take my greeting, Cleonice—the Good to the Beautiful. Well, then, keep Alcman yet awhile to sing thy kind face to repose, and this time let him tune his lyre to songs of a more Dorian strain—songs that show what a Heracleid thinks of danger."

He waved his hand, and the two men, striding hastily, passed along the vine alley, darkened its vista for a few minutes, then vanishing down the descent to the beach, the wide blue sea again lay lone and still before the eyes of the Byzantine maid.

CHAPTER III.

PAUSANIAS and the Eretrian halted on the shore.

"Now speak," said the Spartan Regent. "Where is the danger?"

"Before thee," answered Gongylus, and his hand pointed to the ocean.

"I see the fleet of the Greeks in the harbour—I see the flag of my galley above the forest of their masts. I see detached vessels skimming along the waves hither and thither as in holiday and sport; but discipline slackens where no foe dares to show himself. Eretrian, I see no danger."

"Yet danger is there, and where danger is thou shouldst be. I have learned from my spies, not an hour since, that there is a conspiracy formed—a mutiny on the eve of an outburst. Thy place now should be in thy galley."

"My boat waits yonder in that creek, overspread by the wild shrubs," answered Pausanias; "a few strokes of the oar, and I am where thou seest. And in truth, without thy summons, I should have been on board ere sunset, seeing that on the morrow I have ordered a general review of the vessels of the fleet. Was that to be the occasion for the mutiny?"

"So it is supposed."

"I shall see the faces of the mutineers," said Pausanias, with a calm visage, and an eye which seemed to brighten the very atmosphere. "Thou shakest thy head; is this all?"

"Thou art not a bird—this moment in one place, that moment in another. There, with yon armament, is the danger thou canst meet. But yonder sails a danger which thou canst not, I fear me, overtake."

"Yonder!" said Pausanias, his eye following the hand of the Eretrian. "I see naught save the white wing of a seagull—perchance, by its dip into the water, it foretells a storm."

"Farther off than the seagull, and seeming smaller than the white spot of its wing, seest thou nothing?"

"A dim speck on the farthest horizon, if mine eyes mistake not."

"The speck of a sail that is bound to Sparta. It carries with it a request for thy recall."

This time the cheek of Pausanias paled, and his voice slightly faltered as he said,

"Art thou sure of this?"

"So I hear that the Samian captain, Uliades, has boasted at noon in the public baths."

"A Samian!—is it only a Samian who hath ventured to address to Sparta a complaint of her General?"

"From what I could gather," replied Gongylus, "the complaint is more powerfully backed. But I have not as yet heard more, though I conjecture that Athens has not been silent, and before the vessel sailed Ionian captains were seen to come with joyous faces from the lodgings of Cimon."

The Regent's brow grew yet more troubled. "Cimon, of all the Greeks out of Laconia, is the one whose word would weigh most in Sparta. But my Spartans themselves are not suspected of privity and connivance in this mission?"

"It is not said that they are."

Pausanias shaded his face with his hand for a moment in deep thought. Gongylus continued—

"If the Ephors recall thee before the Asian army is on the frontier, farewell to the sovereignty of Hellas!"

"Ha!" cried Pausanias, "tempt me not. Thinkest thou I need other tempter than I have here?"—smiting his breast.

Gongylus recoiled in surprise. "Pardon me, Pausanias, but temptation is another word for hesitation. I dreamed not that I could tempt; I did not know that thou didst hesitate."

The Spartan remained silent.

"Are not thy messengers on the road to the great king?—nay, perhaps already they have reached him. Didst thou not say how intolerable to thee would be life henceforth in the iron thraldom of Sparta—and now?"

"And now—I forbid thee to question me more. Thou hast performed thy task, leave me to mine."

He sprang with the spring of the mountain goat from the crag on which he stood—over a precipitous chasm, lighted on a narrow ledge, from which a slip of the foot would have been sure death, another bound yet more fearful, and his whole weight hung suspended by the bough of the ilex which he grasped with a single hand; then from bough to bough, from crag to crag, the Eretrian saw him descending till he vanished amidst the trees that darkened over the fissures at the foot of the cliff.

And before Gongylus had recovered his amaze at the almost preterhuman agility and vigour of the Spartan, and his dizzy sense at the contemplation of such peril braved by another, a boat shot into the sea from the green creek, and he saw Pausanias seated beside Lysander on one of the benches, and conversing with him, as if in calm earnestness, while the ten rowers sent the boat towards the fleet with the swiftness of an arrow to its goal.

"Lysander," said Pausanias, "hast thou heard that the Ionians have offered to me the insult of a mission to the Ephors demanding my recall?"

"No. Who would tell me of insult to thee?"

"But hast thou any conjecture that other Spartans around me, and who love me less than thou, would approve, nay, have approved, this embassy of spies and malcontents?"

"I think none have so approved. I fear some would so approve. The Spartans round thee would rejoice did they know that the pride of their armies, the Victor of Platæa, were once more within their walls."

"Even to the danger of Hellas from the Mede?"

"They would rather all Hellas were Medised than Pausanias the Heracleid."

"Boy, boy," said Pausanias, between his ground teeth, "dost thou not see that what is sought is the disgrace of Pausanias the Heracleid? Grant that I am recalled from the head of this armament, and on the charge of Ionians, and I am dishonoured in the eyes of all Greece. Dost thou remember in the last Olympiad that when Themistocles, the only rival now to me in glory, appeared on the Altis, assembled Greece rose to greet and do him honour? And if I, deposed, dismissed, appeared at the next Olympiad, how would assembled Greece receive me? Couldst thou not see the pointed finger and hear the muttered taunt—That is Pausanias, whom the Ionians banished from Byzantium. No, I must abide here; I must prosecute the vast plans which shall dwarf into shadow the petty genius of Themistocles. I must counteract this mischievous embassy to the Ephors. I must send to them an ambassador of my own. Lysander, wilt thou go, and burying in thy bosom thine own Spartan prejudices, deem that thou canst only serve me by proving the reasons why I should remain here; pleading for me, arguing for me, and winning my suit?"

"It is for thee to command and for me to obey thee," answered Lysander, simply. "Is not that the duty of soldier to chief? When we converse as friends I may contend with thee in speech. When thou sayest, Do this, I execute thine action. To reason with thee would be revolt."

Pausanias placed his clasped hands on the young man's shoulder, and leaving them there, impressively said—

"I select thee for this mission because thee alone can I trust. And of me hast thou a doubt?—tell me."

"If I saw thee taking the Persian gold I should say that the Demon had mocked mine eyes with a delusion. Never could I doubt, unless—unless—"

"Unless what?"

"Thou wert standing under Jove's sky against the arms of Hellas."

"And then, if some other chief bade thee raise thy sword against me, thou art Spartan and wouldst obey?"

"I am Spartan, and cannot believe that I should ever have a cause, or listen to a command, to raise my sword against the chief I now serve and love," replied Lysander.

Pausanias withdrew his hands from the young man's broad shoulder. He felt humbled beside the quiet truth of that sublime soul. His own deceit became more black to his conscience. "Methinks," he said tremulously, "I will not send thee after all—and perhaps the news may be false."

The boat had now gained the fleet, and steering amidst the crowded triremes, made its way towards the floating banner of the Spartan Serpent. More immediately round the General's galley were the vessels of the Peloponnesian allies, by whom he was still honoured. A welcoming shout rose from the seamen lounging on their decks as they caught sight of the renowned Heracleid. Cimon, who was on his own galley at some distance, heard the shout.

"So Pausanias," he said, turning to the officers round him, "has deigned to come on board, to direct, I suppose, the manœuvres for to-morrow."

"I believe it is but the form of a review for manœuvres," said an Athenian officer, "in which Pausanias will inspect the various divisions of the fleet, and if more be intended, will give the requisite orders for a subsequent day. No arrangements demanding much preparation can be anticipated, for Antagoras, the rich Chian, gives a great banquet this day—a supper to the principal captains of the Isles."

"A frank and hospitable reveller is Antagoras," answered Cimon. "He would have extended his invitation to the Athenians—me included—but in their name I declined."

"May I ask wherefore?" said the officer who had before spoken. "Cimon is not held averse to wine-cup and myrtle-bough."

"But things are said over some wine-cups and under some myrtle-boughs," answered Cimon, with a quiet laugh, "which it is imprudence to hear and would be treason to repeat. Sup with me here on deck, friends — a supper for sober companions—sober as the Laconian Syssitia, and let not Spartans say that *our* manners are spoilt by the luxuries of Byzantium."

CHAPTER IV.

IN an immense peristyle of a house which a Byzantine noble, ruined by lavish extravagance, had been glad to cede to the accommodation of Antagoras and other officers of Chios, the young rival of Pausanias feasted the chiefs of the Ægean. However modern civilization may in some things surpass the ancient, it is certainly not in luxury and splendour. And although the Hellenic States had not, at that period, aimed at the pomp of show and the refinements of voluptuous pleasure which preceded their decline; and although they never did carry luxury to the wondrous extent which it reached in Asia, or even in Sicily, yet even at that time a wealthy sojourner in such a city as Byzantium could command an entertainment that no monarch in our age would venture to parade before royal guests, and submit to the criticism of tax-paying subjects.

The columns of the peristyle were of dazzling alabaster, with their capitals richly gilt. The space above was roofless; but an immense awning of purple, richly embroidered in Persian looms—a spoil of some gorgeous Mede—shaded the feasters from the summer sky. The couches on which the banqueters reclined were of citron wood, inlaid with ivory, and covered with the tapestries of Asiatic looms. At the four corners of the vast hall played four fountains, and their spray sparkled to a blaze of light from colossal candelabra, in which burnt perfumed oil. The guests were not assembled at a single table, but in small groups; to each group its tripod of exquisite workmanship. To that feast of fifty revellers no less than seventy cooks had contributed the inventions of their art, but under one great master, to whose care the banquet had been consigned by the liberal host, and who ransacked earth, sky, and sea for dainties more various than this degenerate age ever sees accumulated at a single board. And the epicure who has but glanced over the elaborate page of Athenæus, must own with melancholy self-humiliation that the ancients must have carried the art of flattering the palate to a perfection as absolute as the art which built the Parthenon, and sculptured out of gold and ivory the Olympian Jove. But the first course, with its profusion of birds, flesh, and fishes, its marvellous combinations of forced meats, and inventive poetry of sauces, was now over. And in the interval preceding that second course, in which gastronomy put forth its most exquisite masterpieces, the slaves began to remove the tables, soon to be replaced. Vessels of fragrant waters, in which the banqueters dipped their fingers, were handed round; perfumes, which the Byzantine marts collected from every clime, escaped from their precious receptacles.

Then were distributed the garlands. With these each guest crowned locks that steamed with odours; and in them were combined the flowers that most charm the eye, with bud or herb that most guard from the head the fumes of wine: with hyacinth and flax, with golden asphodel and silver lily, the green of ivy and parsley leaf was thus entwined; and above all the rose, said to convey a delicious coolness to the temples on which it bloomed. And now for the first time wine came to heighten the spirits and test the charm of the garlands. Each, as the large goblet passed to him, poured from the brim, before it touched his lips, his libation to the good spirit. And as Antagoras, rising first, set this pious example, out from the further ends of the hall, behind the fountains, burst a concert of flutes, and the great Hellenic Hymn of the Pæan.

As this ceased, the fresh tables appeared before the banqueters, covered with all the fruits in season, and with those triumphs in confectionery, of which honey was the main ingredient, that well justified the favour in which the Greeks held the bee.

Then, instead of the pure juice of the grape, from which the libation had been poured, came the wines, mixed at least three parts with water, and deliciously cooled.

Up again rose Antagoras, and every eye turned to him.

"Companions," said the young Chian, "it is not held in free States well for a man to seize by himself upon supreme authority. We deem that a magistracy should only be obtained by the votes of others. Nevertheless, I venture to think that the latter plan does not always ensure to us a good master. I believe it was by election that we Greeks have given to ourselves a generalissimo, not contented, it is said, to prove the invariable wisdom of that mode of government; wherefore this seems an occasion to revive the good custom of tyranny. And I propose to do so in my person by proclaiming myself Symposiarch and absolute commander in the

Commonwealth here assembled. But if ye prefer the chance of the die—"

"No, no," cried the guests, almost universally; "Antagoras, the Symposiarch, we submit. Issue thy laws."

"Hearken then, and obey. First, then, as to the strength of the wine. Behold the crater in which there are three Naiades to one Dionysos. He is a match for them; not for more. No man shall put into his wine more water than the slaves have mixed. Yet if any man is so diffident of the god that he thinks three Naiades too much for him, he may omit one or two, and let the wine and the water fight it out upon equal terms. So much for the quality of the drink. As to quantity, it is a question to be deliberated hereafter. And now this cup to Zeus the Preserver."

The toast went round.

"Music, and the music of Lydia!" then shouted Antagoras, and resumed his place on the couch beside Uliades.

The music proceeded, the wines circled.

"Friend," whispered Uliades to the host, "thy father left thee wines, I know. But if thou givest many banquets like this, I doubt if thou wilt leave wines to thy son."

"I shall die childless, perhaps," answered the Chian; "and any friend will give me enough to pay Charon's fee across the Styx."

"That is a melancholy reflection," said Uliades, "and there is no subject of talk that pleases me less than that same Styx. Why dost thou bite thy lip, and choke the sigh? By the Gods! art thou not happy?"

"Happy!" repeated Antagoras, with a bitter smile. "Oh, yes!"

"Good! Cleonice torments thee no more. I myself have gone through thy trials; ay, and oftentimes. Seven times at Samos, five at Rhodes, once at Miletus, and forty-three times at Corinth, have I been an impassioned and unsuccessful lover. Courage; I love still."

Antagoras turned away. By this time the hall was yet more crowded, for many not invited to the supper came, as was the custom with the Greeks, to the Symposium; but these were all of the Ionian race.

"The music is dull without the dancers," cried the host. "Ho, there! the dancing girls. Now would I give all the rest of my wealth to see among these girls one face that yet but for a moment could make me forget—"

"Forget what, or whom?" said Uliades; "not Cleonice?"

"Man, man, wilt thou provoke me to strangle thee?" muttered Antagoras.

Uliades edged **himself** away.

"Ungrateful!" he cried. "What **are a hundred Byzantine girls** to one tried male friend?"

"I will not **be** ungrateful, Uliades, if thou stand by my **side** against the Spartan."

"Thou art, then, bent upon this perilous hazard?"

"Bent on driving Pausanias from Byzantium, or **into** Hades— yes."

"Touch!" said Uliades, holding out his right **hand**. "By Cypris, but these girls dance like the daughters of Oceanus; every step undulates as a wave."

Antagoras motioned to his cup-bearer. "Tell the leader of that dancing choir to come hither." The **cup**-bearer obeyed.

A man **with a** solemn air came to the foot of the Chian's couch, bowing low. He was an Egyptian—one **of** the meanest castes.

"Swarthy friend," said Antagoras, "**didst** thou ever hear of the Pyrrhic dance of the Spartans?"

"Surely, of all dances am I teacher and preceptor."

"Your girls know it, then?"

"Somewhat, from having seen it; but not from **practice**. 'Tis a male dance and a warlike dance, O magnanimous, but, in this instance, untutored, Chian!"

"Hist, and listen." Antagoras whispered. The Egyptian nodded his head, returned to the dancing girls, and when their measure had ceased, gathered them round him.

Antagoras again rose.

"Companions, we are bound now to do homage to our masters— the pleasant, affable and familiar warriors of Sparta."

At this the guests gave way to their applauding laughter.

"And therefore these delicate maidens will present to us that flowing and Amathusian dance, which the Graces taught to Spartan sinews. Ho, there!, begin."

The Egyptian had by this time told **the dancers what** they were expected to do; and they came forward with an affectation of stern dignity, the burlesque humour of which delighted all those lively revellers. And when with adroit mimicry their slight arms and mincing steps mocked that grand and masculine measure so associated with images of Spartan austerity and decorum, the exhibition became so humorously ludicrous, that perhaps a Spartan himself would have been compelled to laugh at it. But the merriment rose to its height, when the Egyptian, who had withdrawn for a few minutes, reappeared with a Median robe and mitred cap, and calling **out in** his barbarous African accent, "Way for the conqueror!" **threw into** his mien and gestures all **the** likeness to Pausanias himself, which a practised mime and posture-master could attain. The laughter of Antagoras alone was not loud—it was low and sullen, as if sobs of rage were stifling it; but his eye watched the effect produced, and it answered the end he had in view.

As the dancers now, while the laughter was at its loudest roar, vanished behind the draperies, the host rose, and his countenance was severe and grave—

"Companions, one cup more, and let it be to Harmodius and Aristogiton. Let the song in their honour come only from the lips of free citizens, of our Ionian comrades. Uliades, begin. I pass to thee a myrtle bough; and under it I pass a sword."

Then he began the famous hymn ascribed to Callistratus, commencing with a clear and sonorous voice, and the guests repeating each stanza after him with the enthusiasm which the words usually produced among the Hellenic republicans:

> I in a myrtle bough the sword will carry,
> As did Harmodius and Aristogiton;
> When they the tyrant slew,
> And back to Athens gave her equal laws.
>
> Thou art in nowise dead, best-loved Harmodius;
> Isles of the Blessed are, they say, thy dwelling,
> There swift Achilles dwells,
> And there, they say, with thee dwells Diomed.
>
> I in a myrtle bough the sword will carry,
> As did Harmodius and Aristogiton,
> When to Athene's shrine
> They gave their sacrifice—a tyrant man.
>
> Ever on earth for both of you lives glory,
> O loved Harmodius, loved Aristogiton,
> For ye the tyrant slew,
> And back to Athens ye gave equal laws.

When the song had ceased, the dancers, the musicians, the attendant slaves had withdrawn from the hall, dismissed by a whispered order from Antagoras.

He, now standing up, took from his brows the floral crown, and first sprinkling them with wine, replaced the flowers by a wreath of poplar. The assembly, a little while before so noisy, was hushed into attentive and earnest silence. The action of Antagoras, the expression of his countenance, the exclusion of the slaves, prepared all present for something more than the convivial address of a Symposiarch.

"Men and Greeks," said the Chian, "on the evening before Teucer led his comrades in exile over the wide waters to found a second Salamis, he sprinkled his forehead with Lyæan dews, being crowned with the poplar leaves—emblems of hardihood and contest;

and, this done, he invited his companions to dispel their cares for the night, that their hearts might with more cheerful hope and bolder courage meet what the morrow might bring to them on the ocean. I imitate the ancient hero, in honour less of him than of the name of Salamis. We, too, have a Salamis to remember, and a second Salamis to found. Can ye forget that, had the advice of the Spartan leader Eurybiades been adopted, the victory of Salamis would never have been achieved? He was for retreat to the Isthmus; he was for defending the Peloponnese, because in the Peloponnesus was the unsocial selfish Sparta, and leaving the rest of Hellas to the armament of Xerxes. Themistocles spoke against the ignoble counsel; the Spartan raised his staff to strike him. Ye know the Spartan manners. 'Strike if you will, but hear me,' cried Themistocles. He was heard, Xerxes was defeated, and Hellas saved. I am not Themistocles; nor is there a Spartan staff to silence free lips. But I too say, Hear me! for a new Salamis is to be won. What was the former Salamis?—the victory that secured independence to the Greeks, and delivered them from the Mede and the Medising traitors. Again we must fight a Salamis. Where, ye say, is the Mede?—not at Byzantium, it is true, in person; but the Medising traitor is here."

A profound sensation thrilled through the assembly.

"Enough of humility do the maritime Ionians practise when they accept the hegemony of a Spartan landsman; enough of submission do the free citizens of Hellas show when they suffer the imperious Dorian to sentence them to punishments only fit for slaves. But when the Spartan appears in the robes of the Mede, when the imperious Dorian places in the government of a city, which our joint arms now occupy, a recreant who has changed an Eretrian birthright for a Persian satrapy; when prisoners, made by the valour of all Hellas, mysteriously escape the care of the Lacedæmonian, who wears their garb, and imitates their manners—say, O ye Greeks, O ye warriors, if there is no second Salamis to conquer!"

The animated words, and the wine already drunk, produced on the banqueters an effect sudden, electrical, universal. They had come to the hall gay revellers; they were prepared to leave the hall stern conspirators.

Their hoarse murmur was as the voice of the sea before a storm.

Antagoras surveyed them with a fierce joy, and, with a change of tone, thus continued: "Ye understand me, ye know already that a delivery is to be achieved. I pass on: I submit to your wisdom the mode of achieving it. While I speak, a swift-sailing vessel bears to Sparta the complaints of myself, of Uliades, and of many Ionian captains here present, against the Spartan general. And although the Athenian chiefs decline to proffer complaints of their own, lest their State, which has risked so much for the common cause, be suspected of using the admiration it excites for the purpose of subserving its ambition, yet Cimon, the young son of the great Miltiades, who has ties of friendship and hospitality with families of high mark in Sparta, has been persuaded to add to our public statement a private letter to the effect, that speaking for himself, not in the name of Athens, he deems our complaints justly founded, and the recall of Pausanias expedient for the discipline of the armament. But can we say what effect this embassy may have upon a sullen and haughty government; against, too, a royal descendant of Hercules; against the general who at Plataea flattered Sparta with a renown to which her absence from Marathon, and her meditated flight from Salamis, gave but disputable pretensions?"

"And," interrupted Uliades, rising, "and—if, O Antagoras, I may crave pardon for standing a moment between thee and thy guests—and this is not all, for even if they recall Pausanias, they may send us another general as bad, and without the fame which somewhat reconciles our Ionian pride to the hegemony of a Dorian. Now, whatever my quarrel with Pausanias, I am less against a man than a principle. I am a seaman, and against the principle of having for the commander of the Greek fleet a Spartan who does not know how to handle a sail. I am an Ionian, and against the principle of placing the Ionian race under the imperious domination of a Dorian. Therefore I say, now is the moment to emancipate our blood and our ocean—the one from an alien, the other from a landsman. And the hegemony of the Spartan should pass away."

Uliades sat down with an applause more clamorous than had greeted the eloquence of Antagoras, for the pride of race and of special calling is ever more strong in its impulses than hatred to a single man. And despite of all that could be said against Pausanias, still these warriors felt awe for his greatness, and remembered that at Plataea, where all were brave, he had been proclaimed the bravest.

Antagoras, with the quickness of a republican Greek, trained from earliest youth to sympathy with popular assemblies, saw that Uliades had touched the right key, and swallowed down with a passionate gulp his personal wrath against his rival, which might otherwise have been carried too far, and have lost him the advantage he had gained.

"Rightly and wisely speaks Uliades," said he. "Our cause is that of our whole race; and clear has that true Samian made it to you all, O Ionians and captains of the seas, that we must not wait for the lordly answer Sparta may return to our embassage. Ye know that while night lasts we must return to our several vessels; an hour more, and we shall be on deck. To-morrow Pausanias reviews the fleet, and we may be some days before we return to land, and can meet in concert. Whether to-morrow or later the occasion for action may present itself, is a question I would pray you to leave to those whom you entrust with the discretionary power to act."

"How act?" cried a Lesbian officer.

"Thus would I suggest," said Antagoras, with well dissembled humility; "let the captains of one or more Ionian vessels perform such a deed of open defiance against Pausanias as leaves to them no option between death and success; having so done, hoist a signal, and sailing at once to the Athenian ships, place themselves under the Athenian leader; all the rest of the Ionian captains will then follow their example. And then, too numerous and too powerful to be punished for a revolt, we shall proclaim a revolution, and declare that we will all sail back to our native havens unless we have the liberty of choosing our own hegemon."

"But," said the Lesbian who had before spoken, "the Athenians as yet have held back and declined our overtures, and without them we are not strong enough to cope with the Peloponnesian allies."

"The Athenians will be compelled to protect the Ionians, if the Ionians in sufficient force demand it," said Uliades. "For as we are nought without them, they are nought without us. Take the course suggested by Antagoras: I advise it. Ye know me, a plain man, but I speak not without warrant. And before the Spartans can either contemptuously dismiss our embassy or send us out another general, the Ionian will be the mistress of the Hellenic seas, and Sparta, the land of oligarchies, will no more have the power to oligarchize democracy. Otherwise, believe me, that power she has now from her hegemony, and that power, whenever it suit her, she will use."

Uliades was chiefly popular in the fleet as a rough good seaman, as a blunt and somewhat vulgar humorist. But whenever he gave advice, the advice carried with it a weight not always bestowed upon superior genius, because from the very commonness of his nature, he reached at the common sense and the common feelings of those whom he addressed. He spoke, in short, what an ordinary man thought and felt. He was a practical man, brave but not over-audacious, not likely to run himself or others into idle dangers, and when he said he had a warrant for his advice, he was believed to speak from his knowledge of the course which the Athenian chiefs, Aristides and Cimon, would pursue if the plan recommended were actively executed.

"I am convinced," said the Lesbian. "And since all are grateful to Athens for that final stand against the Mede, to which all Greece owes her liberties, and since the chief of her armaments here is a man of so modest a virtue, and so clement a justice, as we all acknowledge in Aristides, fitting is it for us Ionians to constitute Athens the maritime sovereign of our race."

"Are ye all of that mind?" cried Antagoras, and was answered by the universal shout, "We are—all!" or if the shout was not universal, none heeded the few whom fear or prudence might keep silent. "All that remains then is to appoint the captain who shall hazard the first danger and make the first signal. For my part, as one of the electors, I give my vote for Uliades, and this is my ballot." He took from his temples the poplar wreath, and cast it into a silver vase on the tripod placed before him.

"Uliades by acclamation!" cried several voices.

"I accept," said the Ionian, "and as Ulysses, a prudent man, asked for a colleague in enterprises of danger, so I ask for a companion in the hazard I undertake, and I select Antagoras."

This choice received the same applauding acquiescence as that which had greeted the nomination of the Ionian.

And in the midst of the applause was heard without the sharp shrill sound of the Phrygian pipe.

"Comrades," said Antagoras, "ye hear the summons to our ships? Our boats are waiting at the steps of the quay, by the Temple of Neptune. Two sentences more, and then to sea. First, silence and fidelity; the finger to the lip, the right hand raised to Zeus Horkios. For a pledge, here is an oath. Secondly, be this the signal: whenever ye shall see Uliades and myself steer our triremes out of the line in which they may be marshalled, look forth and watch breathless, and the instant you perceive that beside our flags of Samos and Chios we hoist the ensign of Athens, draw off from your stations, and follow the wake of our keels, to the Athenian navy. Then, as the Gods direct us, Hark, a second time shrills the fife."

CHAPTER V.

AT the very hour when the Ionian captains were hurrying towards their boats, Pausanias was pacing his decks alone, with irregular strides, and through the cordage and the masts the starshine came fitfully on his troubled features. Long undecided he paused, as the waves sparkled to the stroke of oars, and beheld the boats of the feasters making towards the division of the fleet in which lay the navy of the isles. Farther on, remote and still, anchored the ships of Athens. He clenched his hand, and turned from the sight.

"To lose an empire," he muttered, "and without a struggle ; an empire over yon mutinous rivals, over yon happy and envied Athens : an empire—where its limits?—if Asia puts her armies to my lead, why should not Asia be Hellenized, rather than Hellas be within the tribute of the Mede? Dull—dull stolid Sparta! methinks I could pardon the slavery thou inflictest on my life, didst thou but leave unshackled my intelligence. But each vast scheme to be thwarted, every thought for thine own aggrandizement beyond thy barren rocks, met and inexorably baffled by a selfish aphorism, a cramping saw—'Sparta is wide eno' for Spartans.'—'Ocean is the element of the fickle.'—'What matters the ascendancy of Athens?—it does not cross the Isthmus.'—'Venture nothing where I want nothing.' Why, this is the soul's prison! Ah, had I been born Athenian, I had never uttered a thought against my country. She and I would have expanded and aspired together."

Thus arguing with himself, he at length confirmed his resolve, and with a steadfast step entered his pavilion. There, not on broidered cushions, but by preference on the hard floor, without coverlid, lay Lysander calmly sleeping, his crimson warlike cloak, weather-stained, partially wrapped around him; no pillow to his head but his own right arm.

By the light of the high lamp that stood within the pavilion, Pausanias contemplated the slumberer.

"He says he loves me, and yet can sleep," he murmured bitterly. Then seating himself before a table he began to write, with slowness and precision, whether as one not accustomed to the task or weighing every word.

When he had concluded, he again turned his eyes to the sleeper. "How tranquil! Was my sleep ever as serene? I will not disturb him to the last."

The fold of the curtain was drawn aside, and Alcman entered noiselessly.

"Thou hast obeyed?" whispered Pausanias.

"Yes; the ship is ready, the wind favours. Hast thou decided?"

"I have," said Pausanias, with compressed lips.

He rose, and touched Lysander, lightly, but the touch sufficed; the sleeper woke on the instant, casting aside slumber easily as a garment.

"My Pausanias," said the young Spartan, "I am at thine orders —shall I go? Alas! I read thine eye, and I shall leave thee in peril."

"Greater peril in the council of the Ephors and in the babbling lips of the hoary Gerontes, than amidst the meeting of armaments. Thou wilt take this letter to the Ephors. I have said in it but little; I have said that I confide my cause to thee. Remember that thou insist on the disgrace to me—the Heracleid, and through me to Sparta, that my recall would occasion; remember that thou prove that my alleged harshness is but necessary to the discipline that preserves armies, and to the ascendancy of Spartan rule. And as to the idle tale of Persian prisoners escaped, why thou knowest how even the Ionians could make nothing of that charge. Crowd all sail, strain every oar, no ship in the fleet so swift as that which bears thee. I care not for the few hours' start the talebearers have. Our Spartan forms are slow; they can scarce have an audience ere thou reach. The Gods speed and guard thee, beloved friend. With thee goes all the future of Pausanias."

Lysander grasped his hand in a silence more eloquent than words, and a tear fell on that hand which he clasped. "Be not ashamed of it," he said then, as he turned away, and, wrapping his cloak round his face, left the pavilion. Alcman followed, lowered a boat from the side, and in a few moments the Spartan and the Mothon were on the sea. The boat made to a vessel close at hand—a vessel builded in Cyprus, manned by Bithynians; its sails were all up, but it bore no flag. Scarcely had Lysander climbed the deck than it heaved to and fro, swaying as the anchor was drawn up, then, righting itself, sprang forward, like a hound unleashed for the chase. Pausanias with folded arms stood on the deck of his own vessel, gazing after it, gazing long, till shooting far beyond the fleet, far towards the melting line between sea and sky, it grew less and lesser, and as the twilight dawned, it had faded into space.

The Heracleid turned to Alcman, who, after he had conveyed Lysander to the ship, had regained his master's side.

"What thinkest thou, Alcman, will be the result of all this?"

"The emancipation of the Helots," said the Mothon quietly. "The Athenians are too near thee, the Persians are too far. Wouldst thou have armies Sparta can neither give nor take away from thee, bind to thee a race by the strongest of human ties—make them see in thy power the necessary condition of their freedom."

Pausanias made no answer. He turned within his pavilion, and flinging himself down on the same spot from which he had disturbed Lysander, said, "Sleep here was so kind to him that it may linger where he left it. I have two hours yet for oblivion before the sun rise."

CHAPTER VI.

IF we were enabled minutely to examine the mental organization of men who have risked great dangers, whether by the impulse of virtue, or in the perpetration of crime, we should probably find therein a large preponderance of hope. By that preponderance we should account for those heroic designs which would annihilate prudence as a calculator, did not a sanguine confidence in the results produce special energies to achieve them, and thus create a prudence of its own, being as it were the self-conscious admeasurement of the diviner strength which justified the preterhuman spring. Nor less should we account by the same cause for that audacity which startles us in criminals on a colossal scale, which blinds them to the risks of detection, and often at the bar of justice, while the evidences that ensure condemnation are thickening round them, with the persuasion of acquittal or escape. Hope is thus alike the sublime inspirer or the arch corrupter; it is the foe of terror, the defier of consequences, the buoyant gamester which at every loss doubles the stakes, with a firm hand rattles the dice, and, invoking ruin, cries within itself, "How shall I expend the gain?"

In the character, therefore, of a man like Pausanias, risking so much glory, daring so much peril, strong indeed must have been this sanguine motive power of human action. Nor is a large and active development of hope incompatible with a temperament habitually grave and often profoundly melancholy. For hope itself is often engendered by discontent. A vigorous nature keenly susceptible to joy, and deprived of the possession of the joy it yearns for by circumstances that surround it in the present, is goaded on by its impatience and dissatisfaction; it hopes for the something it has not got, indifferent to the things it possesses, and saddened by the want which it experiences. And therefore it has been well said by philosophers, that real happiness would exclude desire; in other words, not only at the gates of hell, but at the porch of heaven, he who entered would leave hope behind him. For perfect bliss is but supreme content. And if content would say to itself,—"But I hope for something more," it would destroy its own existence.

From his brief slumber the Spartan rose refreshed. The trumpets were sounding near him, and the very sound brightened his aspect, and animated his spirits.

Agreeably to orders he had given the night before, the anchor was raised, the rowers were on their benches, the libation to the Carnean Apollo, under whose special protection the ship was placed, had been poured forth, and with the rising sea and to the blare of trumpets the gorgeous trireme moved forth from the bay.

It moved, as the trumpets ceased, to the note of a sweeter, but not less exciting music. For, according to Hellenic custom, to the rowers was allotted a musician, with whose harmony their oars, when first putting forth to sea, kept time. And on this occasion Alcman superseded the wonted performer by his own more popular song and the melody of his richer voice. Standing by the mainmast, and holding the large harp, which was stricken by the quill, its strings being deepened by a sounding-board, he chanted an Io Pæan to the Dorian god of light and poesy. The harp at stated intervals was supported by a burst of flutes, and the burthen of the verse was caught up by the rowers as in chorus. Thus, far and wide over the shining waves, went forth the hymn.

  Io, Io Pæan! slowly. Song and oar must chime together:
  Io, Io Pæan! by what title call Apollo?
   Clarian? Xanthian? Boëdromian?
   Countless are thy names, Apollo.
    Io Carnëe! Io Carnëe!
    By the margent of Eurotas,
    'Neath the shadows of Täygetus,
    Thee the sons of Lacedæmon
    Name Carneus. Io, Io!
     Io Carnëe! Io Carnëe!

  Io, Io Pæan! quicker. Song and voice must chime together:
  Io Pæan! Io Pæan! King Apollo, Io, Io!
  Io Carnëe!
   For thine altars do the seasons
   Paint the tributary flowers,
   Spring thy hyacinth restores,
   Summer greets thee with the rose,
   Autumn the blue Cyane mingles
   With the coronals of corn,
   And in every wreath thy laurel
   Weaves its everlasting green.
    Io Carnëe! Io Carnëe!
    For the brows Apollo favours
    Spring and winter does the laurel
    Weave its everlasting green.

  Io, Io Pæan! louder. Voice and oar must chime together:
    For the brows Apollo favours
    Even Ocean bears the laurel.
     Io Carnëe! Io Carnëe!

  Io, Io Pæan! stronger. Strong are those who win the laurel.

As the ship of the Spartan commander thus bore out to sea, the other vessels of the armament had been gradually forming themselves into a crescent, preserving still the order in which the allies maintained their several contributions to the fleet, the Athenian ships at the extreme end occupying the right wing, the Peloponnesians massed together at the left.

The Chian galleys adjoined the Samian; for Uliades and Antagoras had contrived that their ships should be close to each other, so that they might take counsel at any moment and act in concert.

And now when the fleet had thus opened its arms as it were to receive the commander, the great trireme of Pausanias began to veer round, and to approach the half moon of the expanded armament. On it came, with its beaked prow, like a falcon swooping down on some array of the lesser birds.

From the stern hung a gilded shield and a crimson pennon. The heavy-armed soldiers in their Spartan mail occupied the centre of the vessel, and the sun shone full upon their armour.

"By Pallas the guardian," said Cimon, "it is the Athenian vessels that the strategus honours with his first visit."

And indeed the Spartan galley now came alongside that of Aristides, the admiral of the Athenian navy.

The soldiers on board the former gave way on either side. And a murmur of admiration circled through the Athenian ship, as Pausanias suddenly appeared. For, as if bent that day on either awing mutiny or conciliating the discontented, the Spartan chief had wisely laid aside the wondrous Median robes. He stood on her stern in the armour he had worn at Platæa, resting one hand upon his shield, which itself rested on the deck. His head alone was uncovered, his long sable locks gathered up into a knot, in the Spartan fashion, a crest as it were in itself to that lofty head. And so imposing were his whole air and carriage, that Cimon, gazing at him, muttered, "What profane hand will dare to rob that demigod of command?"

CHAPTER VII.

PAUSANIAS came on board the vessel of the Athenian admiral, attended by the five Spartan chiefs who have been mentioned before as the warlike companions assigned to him. He relaxed the haughty demeanour which had given so much displeasure, adopting a tone of marked courtesy. He spoke with high and merited praise of the seaman-like appearance of the Athenian crews, and the admirable build and equipment of their vessels.

"Pity only," said he, smiling, "that we have no Persians on the ocean now, and that instead of their visiting us we must go in search of them."

"Would that be wise on our part?" said Aristides. "Is not Greece large enough for Greeks?"

"Greece has not done growing," answered the Spartan; "and the Gods forbid that she should do so. When man ceases to grow in height he expands in bulk; when he stops there too, the frame begins to stoop, the muscles to shrink, the skin to shrivel, and decrepit old age steals on. I have heard it said of the Athenians that they think nothing done while aught remains to do. Is it not truly said, worthy son of Miltiades?"

Cimon bowed his head. "General, I cannot disavow the sentiment. But if Greece entered Asia, would it not be as a river that runs into a sea? it expands, and is merged."

"The river, Cimon, may lose the sweetness of its wave and take the brine of the sea. But the Greek can never lose the flavour of the Greek genius, and could he penetrate the universe, the universe would be Hellenized. But if, O Athenian chiefs, ye judge that we have now done all that is needful to protect Athens, and awe the Barbarian, ye must be longing to retire from the armament and return to your homes."

"When it is fit that we should return, we shall be recalled," said Aristides quietly.

"What, is your State so unerring in its judgment? Experience does not permit me to think so, for it ostracised Aristides."

"An honour," replied the Athenian, "that I did not deserve, but an action that, had I been the adviser of those who sent me forth, I should have opposed as too lenient. Instead of ostracising me, they should have cast both myself and Themistocles into the Barathrum."

"You speak with true Attic honour, and I comprehend that where, in commonwealths constituted like yours, party runs high, and the State itself is shaken, ostracism may be a necessary tribute to the very virtues that attract the zeal of a party and imperil the equality ye so prize. But what can compensate to a State for the evil of depriving itself of its greatest citizens?"

"Peace and freedom," said Aristides. "If you would have the young trees thrive you must not let one tree be so large as to overshadow them. Ah, general at Platæa," added the Athenian, in a benignant whisper, for the grand image before him moved his heart with a mingled feeling of generous admiration and prophetic pity, "ah, pardon me if I remind thee of the ring of Polycrates, and say that Fortune is a queen that requires tribute. Man should tremble most when most seemingly fortune-favoured, and guard most against a fall when his rise is at the highest."

"But it is only at its highest flight that the eagle is safe from the arrow," answered Pausanias.

"And the nest the eagle has forgotten in her soaring is the more exposed to the spoiler."

"Well, my nest is in rocky Sparta; hardy the spoiler who ventures thither. Yet, to descend from these speculative comparisons, it seems that thou hast a friendly and meaning purpose in thy warnings. Thou knowest that there are in this armament men who grudge to me whatever I now owe to Fortune, who would topple me from the height to which I did not climb, but was led by the congregated Greeks, and who, while perhaps they are forging arrow-heads for the eagle, have sent to place poison and a snare in its distant nest. So the Nausicaa is on its voyage to Sparta, conveying to the Ephors complaints against me—complaints from men who fought by my side against the Mede."

"I have heard that a Cyprian vessel left the fleet yesterday, bound to Laconia. I have heard that it does bear men charged by some of the Ionians with representations unfavourable to the continuance of thy command. It bears none from me as the Nauarchus of the Athenians. But——"

"But—what?"

"But I have complained to thyself, Pausanias, in vain."

"Hast thou complained of late, and in vain?"

"Nay."

"Honest men may err; if they amend, do just men continue to accuse?"

"I do not accuse, Pausanias, I but imply that those who do may have a cause, but it will be heard before a tribunal of thine own countrymen, and doubtless thou hast sent to the tribunal those who may meet the charge on thy behalf."

"Well," said Pausanias, still preserving his studied urbanity and lofty smile, "even Agamemnon and Achilles quarrelled, but Greece took Troy not the less. And at least, since Aristides does not denounce me, if I have committed even worse faults than Agamemnon, I have not made an enemy of Achilles. And if," he added after a pause, "if some of these Ionians, not waiting for the return of their envoys, openly mutiny, they must be treated as Thersites was." Then he hurried on quickly, for observing that Cimon's brow lowered, and his lips quivered, he desired to cut off all words that might lead to altercation.

"But I have a request to ask of the Athenian Nauarchus. Will you gratify myself and the fleet by putting your Athenian triremes into play? Your seamen are so famous for their manœuvres, that they might furnish us with sports of more grace and agility than do the Lydian dancers. Landsman though I be, no sight more glads mine eye, than these sea lions of pine and brass, bounding under the yoke of their tamers. I presume not to give thee instructions what to perform. Who can dictate to the seamen of Salamis? But when your ships have played out their martial sport, let them exchange stations with the Peloponnesian vessels, and occupy for the present the left of the armament. Ye object not?"

"Place us where thou wilt, as was said to thee at Platæa," answered Aristides.

"I now leave ye to prepare, Athenians, and greet ye, saying, the Good to the Beautiful."

"A wondrous presence for a Greek commander!" said Cimon, as Pausanias again stood on the stern of his own vessel, which moved off towards the ships of the islands.

"And no mean capacity," returned Aristides. "See you not his object in transplacing us?"

"Ha, truly; in case of mutiny on board the Ionian ships, he separates them from Athens. But woe to him if he thinks in his heart that an Ionian is a Thersites, to be silenced by the blow of a sceptre. Meanwhile let the Greeks see what manner of seamen are the Athenians. Methinks this game ordained to us is a contest before Neptune, and for a crown."

Pausanias bore right on towards the vessels from the Ægæan Isles. Their masts and prows were heavy with garlands, but no music sounded from their decks, no welcoming shout from their crews.

"Son of Cleombrotus," said the prudent Erasinidas, "sullen dogs bite. Unwise the stranger who trusts himself to their kennel. Pass not to those triremes; let the captains, if thou wantest them, come to thee."

Pausanias replied, "Dogs fear the steady eye and spring at the recreant back. Helmsman, steer to yonder ship with the olive tree on the Parasemon, and the image of Bacchus on the guardian standard. It is the ship of Antagoras the Chian captain."

Pausanias turned to his warlike Five. "This time, forgive me, I go alone." And before their natural Spartan slowness enabled them to combat this resolution, their leader was by the side of his rival, alone in the Chian vessel, and surrounded by his sworn foes.

"Antagoras," said the Spartan, "a Chian seaman's ship is his dearest home. I stand on thy deck as at thy hearth, and ask thy hospitality; a crust of thy honied bread, and a cup of thy Chian wine. For from thy ship I would see the Athenian vessels go through their nautical gymnastics."

The Chian turned pale and trembled; his vengeance was braved and foiled. He was powerless against the man who trusted to his honour, and asked to break of his bread and eat of his cup. Pausanias did not appear to heed the embarrassment of his unwilling host, but turning round, addressed some careless words to the soldiers on the raised central platform, and then quietly seated himself, directing his eyes towards the Athenian ships. Upon these all the sails were now lowered. In nice manœuvres the seamen preferred trusting to their oars. Presently one vessel started forth, and with a swiftness that seemed to increase at every stroke.

A table was brought upon deck and placed before Pausanias, and the slaves began to serve to him such light food as sufficed to furnish the customary meal of the Greeks in the earlier forenoon.

"But where is mine host?" asked the Spartan. "Does Antagoras himself not deign to share a meal with his guest?"

On receiving the message, Antagoras had no option but to come forward. The Spartan eyed him deliberately, and the young Chian felt with secret rage the magic of that commanding eye.

Pausanias motioned to him to be seated, making room beside himself. The Chian silently obeyed.

"Antagoras," said the Spartan in a low voice, "thou art doubtless one of those who have already infringed the laws of military discipline and obedience. Interrupt me not yet. A vessel without waiting my permission has left the fleet with accusations against me, thy commander; of what nature I am not even advised. Thou wilt scarcely deny that thou art one of those who sent forth the ship and shared in the accusations. Yet I had thought that if I had ever merited thine ill will, there had been reconciliation between us in the Council Hall. What has chanced since? Why shouldst thou hate me? Speak frankly; frankly have I spoken to thee."

"General," replied Antagoras, "there is no hegemony over men's hearts; thou sayest truly, as man to man, I hate thee. Wherefore? Because as man to man, thou standest between me and happiness. Because thou wooest, and canst only woo to dishonour, the virgin in whom I would seek the sacred wife."

Pausanias slightly recoiled, and the courtesy he had simulated, and which was essentially foreign to his vehement and haughty character, fell from him like a mask. For with the words of Antagoras, jealousy passed within him, and for the moment its agony was such that the Chian was avenged. But he was too habituated to the stateliness of self-control, to give vent to the rage that seized him. He only said with a whitened and writhing lip, "Thou art right; all animosities may yield, save those which a woman's eye can kindle. Thou hatest me—be it so—that is as man to man But as officer to chieftain, I bid thee henceforth beware how thou givest me cause to set this foot on the head that lifts itself to the height of mine."

With that he rose, turned on his heel, and walked towards the stern, where he stood apart gazing on the Athenian triremes, which by this time were in the broad sea. And all the eyes in the fleet were turned towards that exhibition. For marvellous was the ease and beauty with which these ships went through their nautical movements; now as in chase of each other, now approaching as in conflict, veering off, darting aside, threading as it were a harmonious maze, gliding in and out, here, there, with the undulous celerity of the serpent. The admirable build of the ships; the perfect skill of the seamen; the noiseless docility and instinctive comprehension by which they seemed to seize and to obey the unforeseen signals of their Admiral—all struck the lively Greeks that beheld the display, and universal was the thought if not the murmur, There was the power that should command the Grecian seas.

Pausanias was too much accustomed to the sway of masses, not to have acquired that electric knowledge of what circles amongst them from breast to breast, to which habit gives the quickness of an instinct. He saw that he had committed an imprudence, and that in seeking to divert a mutiny, he had incurred a yet greater peril.

He returned to his own ship without exchanging another word with Antagoras, who had retired to the centre of the vessel, fearing to trust himself to a premature utterance of that defiance which the last warning of his chief provoked, and who was therefore arousing the soldiers to louder shouts of admiration at the Athenian skill.

Rowing back towards the wing occupied by the Peloponnesian allies, of whose loyalty he was assured, Pausanias then summoned on board their principal officer, and communicated to him his policy of placing the Ionians not only apart from the Athenians, but under the vigilance and control of Peloponnesian vessels in the immediate neighbourhood. "Therefore," said he, "while the Athenians will occupy this wing, I wish you to divide yourselves; the Lacedæmonian ships will take the way the Athenians abandon, but the Corinthian triremes will place themselves between the ships of the Islands and the Athenians. I shall give further orders towards distributing the Ionian navy. And thus I trust either all chance of a mutiny is cut off, or it will be put down at the first outbreak. Now give orders to your men to take the places thus assigned to you. And having gratified the vanity of our friends the Athenians by their holiday evolutions, I shall send to thank and release them from the fatigue so gracefully borne."

All those with whom he here conferred, and who had no love for Athens or Ionia, readily fell into the plan suggested. Pausanias then despatched a Laconian vessel to the Athenian Admiral, with complimentary messages and orders to cease the manœuvres, and then heading the rest of the Laconian contingent, made slow and stately way towards the station deserted by the Athenians. But pausing once more before the vessels of the Isles, he despatched orders to their several commanders, which had the effect of dividing their array, and placing between them the powerful Corinthian service. In the orders of the vessels he forwarded for this change, he took especial care to dislocate the dangerous contiguity of the Samian and Chian triremes.

The sun was declining towards the west when Pausanias had marshalled the vessels he headed, at their new stations, and the Athenian ships were already anchored close and secured. But there was an evident commotion in that part of the fleet to which the Corinthian galleys had sailed. The Ionians had received with indignant murmurs the command which divided their strength. Under various pretexts each vessel delayed to move; and when the Corinthian ships came to take a vacant space, they found a formidable array,—the soldiers on the platforms armed to the teeth. The confusion was visible to the Spartan chief; the loud hubbub almost reached to his ears. He hastened towards the place; but anxious to continue the gracious part he had so unwontedly played that day, he cleared his decks of their formidable hoplites, lest he might seem to meet menace by menace, and drafting them into other vessels, and accompanied only by his personal serving-men and rowers, he put forth alone, the gilded shield and the red banner still displayed at his stern.

But as he was thus conspicuous and solitary, and midway in the space left between the Laconian and Ionian galleys, suddenly two ships from the latter darted forth, passed through the centre of the Corinthian contingent, and steered with the force of all their rowers, right towards the Spartan's ship.

"Surely," said Pausanias, "that is the Chian's vessel. I recognize the vine tree and the image of the Bromian god; and surely that other one is the Chimera under Uliades, the Samian. They come hither, the Ionian with them, to harangue against obedience to my orders."

"They come hither to assault us," exclaimed Erasinidas; "their beaks are right upon us."

He had scarcely spoken, when the Chian's brass prow smote the gilded shield, and rent the red banner from its staff. At the same time, the Chimera, under Uliades, struck the right side of the Spartan ship, and with both strokes the stout vessel reeled and dived. "Know, Spartan," cried Antagoras, from the platform in the midst of his soldiers, "that we Ionians hold together. He who would separate, means to conquer, us. We disown thy hegemony. If ye would seek us, we are with the Athenians."

With that the two vessels, having performed their insolent and daring feat, veered and shot off with the same rapidity with which they had come to the assault; and as they did so, hoisted the Athenian ensign over their own national standards. The instant that signal was given, from the other Ionian vessels, which had been evidently awaiting it, there came a simultaneous shout; and all, vacating their place and either gliding through or wheeling round the Corinthian galleys, steered towards the Athenian fleet.

The trireme of Pausanias, meanwhile, sorely damaged, part of its side rent away, and the water rushing in, swayed and struggled alone in great peril of sinking.

Instead of pursuing the Ionians, the Corinthian galleys made at once to the aid of the insulted commander.

"Oh," cried Pausanias, in powerless wrath, "Oh, the accursed element! Oh that mine enemies had attacked me on the land!"

"How are we to act?" said Aristides.

"We are citizens of a Republic, in which the majority govern," answered Cimon. "And the majority here tell us how we are to act. Hark to the shouts of our men, as they are opening way for their kinsmen of the Isles."

The sun sank, and with it sank the Spartan maritime ascendancy over Hellas. And from that hour in which the Samian and the Chian insulted the galley of Pausanias, if we accord weight to the authority on which Plutarch must have based his tale, commenced the brief and glorious sovereignty of Athens. Commence when and how it might, it was an epoch most signal in the records of the ancient world for its results upon a civilization to which as yet human foresight can predict no end.

END OF VOLUME I.

PAUSANIAS, THE SPARTAN.
VOLUME II.

BOOK IV.

CHAPTER I.

WE pass from Byzantium, we are in Sparta. In the Archeion, or office of the Ephoralty, sate five men, all somewhat advanced in years. These constituted that stern and terrible authority which had gradually, and from unknown beginnings,[1] assumed a kind of tyranny over the descendants of Hercules themselves. They were the representatives of the Spartan people, elected without reference to rank or wealth,[2] and possessing jurisdiction not only over the Helots and Laconians, but over most of the magistrates. They could suspend or terminate any office, they could accuse the kings and bring them before a court in which they themselves were judges upon trial of life and death. They exercised control over the armies and the embassies sent abroad; and the king, at the head of his forces, was still bound to receive his instructions from this Council of Five. Their duty, in fact, was to act as a check upon the kings, and they were the representatives of that Nobility which embraced the whole Spartan people, in contradistinction to the Laconians and Helots.

The conference in which they were engaged seemed to rivet their most earnest attention. And as the presiding Ephor continued the observations he addressed to them, the rest listened with profound and almost breathless silence.

[1] K. O. Müller (Dorians), Book 3, c. 7, § 2. According to Aristotle, Cicero and others, the Ephoralty was founded by Theopompus subsequently to the mythical time of Lycurgus. To Lycurgus itself it is referred by Xenophon and Herodotus. Müller considers rightly that, though an ancient Doric institution, it was incompatible with the primitive constitution of Lycurgus, and had gradually acquired its peculiar character by causes operating on the Spartan State alone.
[2] Aristot. Pol. ii.

The speaker, named Periclides, was older than the others. His frame, still upright and sinewy, was yet lean almost to emaciation, his face sharp, and his dark eyes gleamed with a cunning and sinister light under his gray brows.

"If," said he, "we are to believe these Ionians, Pausanias meditates some deadly injury to Greece. As for the complaints of his arrogance, they are to be received with due caution. Our Spartans, accustomed to the peculiar discipline of the Laws of Ægimius, rarely suit the humours of Ionians and innovators. The question to consider is not whether he has been too imperious towards Ionians who were but the other day subjected to the Mede, but whether he can make the command he received from Sparta menacing to Sparta herself. We lend him iron, he hath holpen himself to gold."

"Besides the booty at Platæa, they say that he has amassed much plunder at Byzantium," said Zeuxidamus, one of the Ephors, after a pause.

Periclides looked hard at the speaker, and the two men exchanged a significant glance.

"For my part," said a third, a man of a severe but noble countenance, the father of Lysander, and, what was not usual with the Ephors, belonging to one of the highest families of Sparta, "I have always held that Sparta should limit its policy to self-defence; that, since the Persian invasion is over, we have no business with Byzantium. Let the busy Athenians obtain if they will the empire of the sea. The sea is no province of ours. All intercourse with foreigners, Asiatics and Ionians, enervates our men and corrupts our generals. Recall Pausanias—recall our Spartans. I have said."

"Recall Pausanias first," said Periclides, "and we shall then hear the truth, and decide what is best to be done."

"If he has medised, if he has conspired against Greece, let us accuse him to the death," said Agesilaus, Lysander's father.

"We may accuse, but it rests not with us to sentence," said Periclides, disapprovingly.

"And," said a fourth Ephor, with a visible shudder, "what Spartan dare counsel sentence of death to the descendant of the Gods?"

"I dare," replied Agesilaus, "but provided only that the descendant of the Gods had counselled death to Greece. And for that reason, I say that I would not, without evidence the clearest, even harbour the thought that a Heracleid could meditate treason to his country."

Periclides felt the reproof and bit his lips.

"Besides," observed Zeuxidamus, "fines enrich the State."

Periclides nodded approvingly.

An expression of lofty contempt passed over the **brow and** lip of Agesilaus. But with national self-command, he replied gravely, and with equal laconic brevity, "If Pausanias hath committed a trivial error that a fine can expiate, so be it. But talk not of fines till **ye** acquit him of all treasonable connivance with the Mede."

At that moment an officer entered on the conclave, and approaching **the** presiding Ephor, whispered in his ear.

"This is well," exclaimed Periclides aloud. "**A** messenger from Pausanias himself. Your son Lysander has just arrived from Byzantium."

"My son!" exclaimed Agesilaus eagerly, and then checking himself, added calmly, "That is a sign no danger to Sparta threatened Byzantium when he left."

"Let him be admitted," said Periclides.

Lysander entered; and pausing at a little distance from the council board, inclined his head submissively to the Ephors; save a rapid interchange of glances, no separate greeting took place between son and father.

"Thou art welcome," said Periclides. "Thou hast **done thy** duty since thou hast left the city. Virgins will praise thee **as the** brave man; age, more sober, is contented to say thou hast upheld the Spartan name. And thy father without shame may take thy hand."

A warm flush spread **over** the young man's face. He stepped forward with a quick step, **his** eyes beaming with joy. Calm and stately, his father rose, clasped the extended hand, then releasing his own placed it an instant **on** his son's bended head, and reseated himself in silence.

"Thou camest straight from Pausanias?" said Periclides.

Lysander drew from his vest the despatch entrusted to **him, and gave it** to the presiding Ephor. Periclides half rose as **if to take with** more respect what had come from the hand of **the son of** Hercules.

"Withdraw, Lysander," he said, "and wait without while we deliberate on the contents herein."

Lysander obeyed, **and** returned to the outer chamber.

Here he was instantly surrounded by eager, though **not** noisy groups. Some in that chamber were waiting on business connected with the civil jurisdiction of the Ephors. Some had gained admittance for the purpose of greeting their brave countryman, and hearing news of the distant camp from one who had so lately quitted the great Pausanias. For men could talk without restraint of their General, though it was but with reserve and indirectly that they slid in some furtive question as to the health and safety of a brother or a son.

"My heart warms to be amongst ye again," said the simple Spartan youth. "As I came thro' the defiles from the sea-coast, and saw on the height the gleam from the old Temple of Pallas Chalcicœcus, I said to myself, 'Blessed be the Gods that ordained me to live with Spartans or die with Sparta!'"

"Thou wilt see how much we shall make of thee, Lysander," cried a Spartan youth a little younger than himself, one of the superior tribe of the Hylleans. "We have heard of thee at Platæa. It is said that had Pausanias not been there thou wouldst have been called the bravest Greek in the armament."

"Hush," said Lysander, "thy few years excuse thee, young friend. Save our General, we were all equals in the day of battle."

"So thinks not my sister Percalus," whispered the youth archly; "scold her as thou dost me, if thou dare."

Lysander coloured, and replied in a voice that slightly trembled, "I cannot hope that thy sister interests herself in me. Nay, when I left Sparta, I thought—" He checked himself.

"Thought what?"

"That among those who remained behind Percalus might find her betrothed long before I returned."

"Among those who remained *behind!* Percalus! How meanly thou must think of her."

Before Lysander could utter the eager assurance that he was very far from thinking meanly of Percalus, the other bystanders, impatient at this whispered colloquy, seized his attention with a volley of questions, to which he gave but curt and not very relevant answers, so much had the lad's few sentences disturbed the calm tenor of his existing self-possession. Nor did he quite regain his presence of mind until he was once more summoned into the presence of the Ephors.

CHAPTER II.

THE communication of Pausanias had caused an animated discussion in the Council, and led to a strong division of opinion. But the faces of the Ephors, rigid and composed, revealed nothing to guide the sagacity of Lysander, as he re-entered the chamber. He himself, by a strong effort, had recovered the disturbance into which the words of the boy had thrown his mind, and he stood before the Ephors intent upon the object of defending the name, and fulfilling the commands of his chief. So reverent and grateful was the love that he bore to Pausanias, that he scarcely permitted himself even to blame the deviations from Spartan austerity which he secretly mourned in his mind; and as to the grave guilt of treason to the Hellenic cause, he had never suffered the suspicion of it to rest upon an intellect that only failed to be penetrating, where its sight was limited by discipline and affection. He felt that Pausanias had entrusted to him his defence, and though he would fain, in his secret heart, have beheld the Regent once more in Sparta, yet he well knew that it was the duty of obedience and friendship to plead against the sentence of recall which was so dreaded by his chief.

With all his thoughts collected towards that end, he stood before the Ephors, modest in demeanour, vigilant in purpose.

"Lysander," said Periclides, after a short pause, "we know thy affection to the Regent, thy chosen friend; but we know also thy affection for thy native Sparta; where the two may come into conflict, it is, and it must be, thy country which will claim the preference. We charge thee, by virtue of our high powers and authority, to speak the truth on the questions we shall address to thee, without fear or favour."

Lysander bowed his head. "I am in presence of Sparta my mother and Agesilaus my father. They know that I was not reared to lie to either."

"Thou say'st well. Now answer. Is it true that Pausanias wears the robes of the Mede?"

"It is true."

"And has he stated to thee his reasons?"

"Not only to me, but to others."

"What are they?"

"That in the mixed and half medised population of Byzantium, splendour of attire has become so associated with the notion of sovereign power, that the Eastern dress and attributes of pomp are essential to authority; and that men bow before his tiara, who might rebel against the helm and the horsehair. Outward signs have a value, O Ephors, according to the notions men are brought up to attach to them."

"Good," said one of the Ephors. "There is in this departure from our habits, be it right or wrong, no sign then of connivance with the Barbarian."

"Connivance is a thing secret and concealed, and shuns all outward signs."

"But," said Periclides, "what say the other Spartan Captains to this vain fashion, which savours not of the Laws of Ægimius?"

"The first law of Ægimius commands us to fight and to die for the king or the chief who has kingly sway. The Ephors may blame, but the soldier must not question."

"Thou speakest boldly for so young a man," said Periclides harshly.

"I was commanded to speak the truth."

"Has Pausanias entrusted the command of Byzantium to Gongylus the Eretrian, who already holds four provinces under Xerxes?"

"He has done so."

"Know you the reason for that selection?"

"Pausanias says that the Eretrian could not more show his faith to Hellas, than by resigning Eastern satrapies so vast."

"Has he resigned them?"

"I know not; but I presume that when the Persian king knows that the Eretrian is leagued against him with the other Captains of Hellas, he will assign the Satrapies to another."

"And is it true that the Persian prisoners, Ariamanes and Datis, have escaped from the custody of Gongylus?"

"It is true. The charge against Gongylus for that error was heard in a council of confederate captains, and no proof against him was brought forward. Cimon was entrusted with the pursuit of the prisoners. Pausanias himself sent forth fifty scouts on Thessalian horses. The prisoners were not discovered."

"Is it true," said Zeuxidamus, "that Pausanias has amassed much plunder at Byzantium?"

"What he has won as a conqueror was assigned to him by common voice, but he has spent largely out of his own resources in securing the Greek sway at Byzantium."

There was a silence. None liked to question the young soldier farther; none liked to put the direct question, whether or not the Ionian Ambassador could have cause for suspecting the descendant of Hercules of harm against the Greeks. At length Agesilaus said:

"I demand the word, and I claim the right to speak plainly. My son is young, but he is of the blood of Hyllus.

"Son—Pausanias is dear to thee. Man soon dies: man's name lives for ever. Dear to thee if Pausanias is, dearer must be his name. In brief, the Ionian Ambassadors complain of his arrogance towards the Confederates; they demand his recall. Cimon has addressed a private letter to the Spartan host, with whom he lodged here, intimating that it may be best for the honour of Pausanias, and for our weight with the allies, to hearken to the Ionian Embassy. It is a grave question, therefore, whether we should recall the Regent or refuse to hear these charges. Thou art fresh from Byzantium; thou must know more of this matter than we. Loose thy tongue, put aside equivocation. Say thy mind, it is for us to decide afterwards what is our duty to the State."

"I thank thee, my father," said Lysander, colouring deeply at a compliment paid rarely to one so young, "and thus I answer thee:

"Pausanias, in seeking to enforce discipline and preserve the Spartan supremacy, was at first somewhat harsh and severe to these Ionians, who had indeed but lately emancipated themselves from the Persian yoke, and who were little accustomed to steady rule. But of late he has been affable and courteous, and no complaint was urged against him for austerity at the time when this embassy was sent to you. Wherefore was it then sent? Partly, it may be, from motives of private hate, not public zeal, but partly because the Ionian race sees with reluctance and jealousy the Hegemony of Sparta. I would speak plainly. It is not for me to say whether ye will or not that Sparta should retain the maritime supremacy of Hellas, but if ye do will it, ye will not recall Pausanias. No other than the Conqueror of Platæa has a chance of maintaining that authority. Eager would the Ionians be upon any pretext, false or frivolous, to rid themselves of Pausanias. Artfully willing would be the Athenians in especial that ye listened to such pretexts; for, Pausanias gone, Athens remains and rules. On what belongs to the policy of the State it becomes not me to proffer a word, O Ephors. In what I have said I speak what the whole armament thinks and murmurs. But this I may say as soldier to whom the honour of his chief is dear.—The recall of Pausanias may or may not be wise as a public act, but it will be regarded throughout all Hellas as a personal affront to your general; it will lower the royalty of Sparta, it will be an insult to the blood of Hercules. Forgive me, O venerable magistrates. I have fought by the side of Pausanias, and I cannot dare to think that the great Conqueror of Platæa, the man who saved Hellas from the Mede, the man who raised Sparta on that day to a renown which penetrated the farthest corners of the East, will receive from you other return than fame and glory. And fame and glory will surely make that proud spirit doubly Spartan."

Lysander paused, breathing hard and colouring deeply—annoyed with himself for a speech of which both the length and the audacity were much more Ionian than Spartan.

The Ephors looked at each other, and there was again silence.

"Son of Agesilaus," said Periclides, "thou hast proved thy Lacedæmonian virtues too well, and too high and general is thy repute amongst our army, as it is borne to our ears, for us to doubt thy purity and patriotism; otherwise, we might fear that whilst thou speakest in some contempt of Ionian wolves, thou hadst learned the arts of Ionian Agoras. But enough: thou art dismissed. Go to thy home; glad the eyes of thy mother; enjoy the honours thou wilt find awaiting thee amongst thy coevals. Thou wilt learn later whether thou return to Byzantium, or whether a better field for thy valour may not be found in the nearer war with which Arcadia threatens us."

As soon as Lysander left the chamber, Agesilaus spoke :—

"Ye will pardon me, Ephors, if I bade my son speak thus boldly. I need not say I am no vain, foolish father, desiring to raise the youth above his years. But making allowance for his partiality to the Regent, ye will grant that he is a fair specimen of our young soldiery. Probably, as he speaks, so will our young men think. To recall Pausanias is to disgrace our general. Ye have my mind. If the Regent be guilty of the darker charges insinuated—correspondence with the Persian against Greece—I know but one sentence for him—Death. And it is because I would have ye consider well how dread is such a charge, and how awful such a sentence, that I entreat ye not lightly to entertain the one unless ye are prepared to meditate the other. As for the maritime supremacy of Sparta, I hold, as I have held before, that it is not within our councils to strive for it ; it must pass from us. We may surrender it later with dignity ; if we recall our general on such complaints, we lose it with humiliation."

"I agree with Agesilaus," said another, "Pausanias is an Heracleid ; my vote shall not insult him."

"I agree too with Agesilaus," said a third Ephor ; "not because Pausanias is the Heracleid, but because he is the victorious general who demands gratitude and respect from every true Spartan."

"Be it so," said Periclides, who, seeing himself thus outvoted in the council, covered his disappointment with the self-control habitual to his race. "But be we in no hurry to give these Ionian legates their answer to-day. We must deliberate well how to send such a reply as may be most conciliating and prudent. And for the next few days we have an excuse for delay in the religious ceremonials due to the venerable Divinity of Fear, which commence to-morrow. Pass we to the other business before us ; there are many whom we have kept waiting. Agesilaus, thou art excused from the public table to-day if thou wouldst sup with thy brave son at home."

"Nay," said Agesilaus, "my son will go to his pheidition and I to mine—as I did on the day when I lost my first-born."

CHAPTER III.

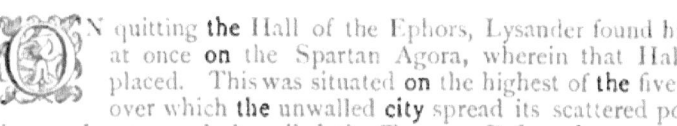N quitting the Hall of the Ephors, Lysander found himself at once on the Spartan Agora, wherein that Hall was placed. This was situated on the highest of the five hills, over which the unwalled city spread its scattered population, and was popularly called the Tower. Before the eyes of the young Spartan rose the statues, rude and antique, of Latona, the Pythian Apollo, and his sister Artemis;—venerable images to Lysander's early associations. The place which they consecrated was called Chorus; for there, in honour of Apollo, and in the most pompous of all the Spartan festivals, the young men were accustomed to lead the sacred dance. The Temple of Apollo himself stood a little in the background, and near to it that of Hera. But more vast than any image of a god was a colossal statue which represented the Spartan people; while on a still loftier pinnacle of the hill than that table-land which enclosed the Agora—dominating, as it were, the whole city—soared into the bright blue sky the sacred Chalciœcus, or Temple of the Brazen Pallas, darkening with its shadow another fane towards the left dedicated to the Lacedæmonian Muses, and receiving a gleam on the right from the brazen statue of Zeus, which was said by tradition to have been made by a disciple of Dædalus himself.

But short time had Lysander to note undisturbed the old familiar scenes. A crowd of his early friends had already collected round the doors of the Archeion, and rushed forward to greet and welcome him. The Spartan coldness and austerity of social intercourse vanished always before the enthusiasm created by the return to his native city of a man renowned for valour; and Lysander's fame had come back to Sparta before himself. Joyously, and in triumph, the young men bore away their comrade. As they passed through the centre of the Agora, where assembled the various merchants and farmers, who, under the name of Periœci, carried on the main business of the Laconian mart, and were often much wealthier than the Spartan citizens, trade ceased its hubbub; all drew near to gaze on the young warrior; and now, as they turned from the Agora, a group of eager women met them on the road, and shrill voices exclaimed: "Go, Lysander, thou hast fought well—go and choose for thyself the maiden that seems to thee the fairest. Go, marry and get sons for Sparta."

Lysander's step seemed to tread on air, and tears of rapture stood in his downcast eyes. But suddenly all the voices hushed; the

crowds drew back ; his friends halted. Close by the great Temple
of Fear, and coming from some place within its sanctuary, there
approached towards the Spartan and his comrades a majestic woman
—a woman of so grand a step and port, that, though her veil as yet
hid her face, her form alone sufficed to inspire awe. All knew her
by her gait ; all made way for Alithea, the widow of a king, the
mother of Pausanias the Regent. Lysander, lifting his eyes from
the ground, impressed by the hush around him, recognized the form
as it advanced slowly towards him, and, leaving his comrades behind,
stepped forward to salute the mother of his chief. She, thus seeing
him, turned slightly aside, and paused by a rude building of immemorial antiquity which stood near the temple. That building was
the tomb of the mythical Orestes, whose bones were said to have
been interred there by the command of the Delphian Oracle. On a
stone at the foot of the tomb sate calmly down the veiled woman,
and waited the approach of Lysander. When he came near, and
alone—all the rest remaining aloof and silent—Alithea removed her
veil, and a countenance grand and terrible as that of a Fate lifted
its rigid looks to the young Spartan's eyes. Despite her age—for
she had passed into middle life before she had borne Pausanias—
Alithea retained all the traces of a marvellous and almost preterhuman beauty. But it was not the beauty of woman. No softness
sate on those lips ; no love beamed from those eyes. Stern, inexorable—not a fault in her grand proportions—the stoutest heart might
have felt a throb of terror as the eye rested upon that pitiless and
imposing front. And the deep voice of the Spartan warrior had a
slight tremor in its tone as it uttered its respectful salutation.

"Draw near, Lysander. What sayest thou of my son?"

"I left him well, and——"

"Does a Spartan mother first ask of the bodily health of an
absent man-child? By the tomb of Orestes and near the Temple of
Fear, a king's widow asks a Spartan soldier what he says of a
Spartan chief."

"All Hellas," replied Lysander, recovering his spirit, "might
answer thee best, Alithea. For all Hellas proclaimed that the
bravest man at Platæa was thy son, my chief."

"And where did my son, thy chief, learn to boast of bravery?
They tell me he inscribed the offerings to the Gods with his name as
the victor of Platæa—the battle won not by one man but assembled
Greece. The inscription that dishonours him by its vainglory will
be erased. To be brave is nought. Barbarians may be brave.
But to dedicate bravery to his native land becomes a Spartan. He
who is everything against a foe should count himself as nothing in
the service of his country."

Lysander remained silent under the gaze of those fixed and imperious eyes.

"Youth," said Alithea, after a short pause, "if thou returnest to Byzantium, say this from Alithea to thy chief:—'From thy childhood, Pausanias, has thy mother feared for thee; and at the Temple of Fear did she sacrifice when she heard that thou wert victorious at Plataea; for in thy heart are the seeds of arrogance and pride; and victory to thine arms may end in ruin to thy name. And ever since that day does Alithea haunt the precincts of that temple. Come back and be Spartan, as thine ancestors were before thee, and Alithea will rejoice and think the gods have heard her. But if thou seest within thyself one cause why thy mother should sacrifice to Fear, lest her son should break the laws of Sparta, or sully his Spartan name, humble thyself, and mourn that thou didst not perish at Plataea. By a temple and from a tomb I send thee warning.' Say this. I have done; join thy friends."

Again the veil fell over the face, and the figure of the woman remained seated at the tomb long after the procession had passed on, and the mirth of young voices was again released.

CHAPTER IV.

THE group that attended Lysander continued to swell as he mounted the acclivity on which his parental home was placed. The houses of the Spartan proprietors were at that day not closely packed together as in the dense population of commercial towns. More like the villas of a suburb, they lay a little apart, on the unequal surface of the rugged ground, perfectly plain and unadorned, covering a large space with ample court-yards, closed in, in front of the narrow streets. And still was in force the primitive law which ordained that doorways should be shaped only by the saw, and the ceilings by the axe; but in contrast to the rudeness of the private houses, at every opening in the street were seen the Doric pillars or graceful stairs of a temple; and high over all dominated the Tower-hill, or Acropolis, with the antique fane of Pallas Chalciœcus.

And so, loud and joyous, the procession bore the young warrior to the threshold of his home. It was an act of public honour to his fair repute and his proven valour. And the Spartan felt as proud of that unceremonious attendance as ever did Roman chief sweeping under arches of triumph in the curule car.

At the threshold of the door stood his mother—for the tidings of his coming had preceded him—and his little brothers and sisters. His step quickened at the sight of these beloved faces.

"Bound forward, Lysander," said one of the train; "thou hast won the right to thy mother's kiss."

"But fail us not at the pheidition before sunset," cried another. "Every one of the obe will send his best contribution to the feast to welcome thee back. We shall have a rare banquet of it."

And so, as his mother drew him within the doors, his arm round her waist, and the children clung to his cloak, to his knees, or sprung up to claim his kiss, the procession set up a kind of chaunted shout, and left the warrior in his home.

"Oh, this is joy, joy!" said Lysander, with sweet tears in his eyes, as he sat in the women's apartment, his mother by his side, and the little ones round him. "Where, save in Sparta, does a man love a home?"

And this exclamation, which might have astonished an Ionian—seeing how much the Spartan civilians merged the individual in the state—was yet true, where the Spartan was wholly Spartan, where, by habit and association, he had learned to love the severities of the existence that surrounded him, and where the routine of duties which took him from his home, whether for exercises or the public tables, made yet more precious the hours of rest and intimate intercourse with his family. For the gay pleasures and lewd resorts of other Greek cities were not known to the Spartan. Not for him were the cook-shops and baths and revels of Ionian idlers. When the State ceased to claim him, he had nothing but his Home.

As Lysander thus exclaimed, the door of the room had opened noiselessly, and Agesilaus stood unperceived at the entrance, and overheard his son. His face brightened singularly at Lysander's words. He came forward and opened his arms.

"Embrace me now, my boy! my brave boy! embrace me now! The Ephors are not here."

Lysander turned, sprang up, and was in his father's arms.

"So thou art not changed. Byzantium has not spoiled thee. Thy name is uttered with praise unmixed with fear. All Persia's gold, all the great king's Satrapies could not medise my Lysander. Ah," continued the father, turning to his wife, "who could have predicted the happiness of this hour? Poor child! he was born sickly. Hera had already given us more sons than we could provide for, ere our lands were increased by the death of thy childless relatives. Wife, wife! when the family council ordained him to be exposed on Taygetus, when thou didst hide thyself lest thy tears should be seen, and my voice trembled as I said, 'Be the laws obeyed,' who could have guessed that the Gods would yet preserve him to be the pride of our house? Blessed be Zeus the saviour and Hercules the warrior!"

"And," said the mother, "blessed be Pausanias, the descendant of Hercules, who took the forlorn infant to his father's home, and who has reared him now to be the example of Spartan youths."

"Ah," said Lysander, looking up into his father's eyes, "if I can ever be worthy of your love, O my father, forget not, I pray thee, that it is to Pausanias I owe life, home, and a Spartan's glorious destiny."

"I forget it not," answered Agesilaus, with a mournful and serious expression of countenance. "And on this I would speak to thee. Thy mother must spare thee awhile to me. Come. I lean on thy shoulder instead of my staff."

Agesilaus led his son into the large hall, which was the main chamber of the house; and pacing up and down the wide and solitary floor, questioned him closely as to the truth of the stories respecting the Regent which had reached the Ephors.

"Thou must speak with naked heart to me," said Agesilaus; "for I tell thee that, if I am Spartan, I am also man and father; and I would serve him, who saved thy life and taught thee how to fight for thy country, in every way that may be lawful to a Spartan and a Greek."

Thus addressed, and convinced of his father's sincerity, Lysander replied with ingenuous and brief simplicity. He granted that Pausanias had exposed himself with a haughty imprudence, which it was difficult to account for, to the charges of the Ionians. "But," he added, with that shrewd observation which his affection for Pausanias rather than his experience of human nature had taught him— "But we must remember that in Pausanias we are dealing with no ordinary man. If he has faults of judgment, which a Spartan rarely commits, he has, O my father, a force of intellect and passion which a Spartan as rarely knows. Shall I tell you the truth? Our State is too small for him. But would it not have been too small for Hercules? Would the laws of Ægimius have permitted Hercules to perform his labours and achieve his conquests? This vast and fiery nature suddenly released from the cramps of our customs, which Pausanias never in his youth regarded save as galling, expands itself, as an eagle long caged would outspread its wings."

"I comprehend," said Agesilaus thoughtfully, and somewhat sadly. "There have been moments in my own life when I regarded Sparta as a prison. In my early manhood I was sent on a mission to Corinth. Its pleasures, its wild tumult of gay licence dazzled and inebriated me. I said, 'This it is to live.' I came back to Sparta sullen and discontented. But then, happily, I saw thy mother at the festival of Diana—we loved each other, we married—and when I was permitted to take her to my home, I became sobered and was a Spartan again. I comprehend. Poor Pausanias! But luxury and pleasure, though they charm awhile, do not fill up the whole of a soul like that of our Heracleid. From these he may recover; but Ambition—that is the true liver of Tantalus, and grows larger under the beak that feeds on it. What is his ambition, if Sparta be too small for him?"

"I think his ambition would be to make Sparta as big as himself." Agesilaus stroked his chin musingly.

"And how?"

"I cannot tell, I can only guess. But the Persian war, if I may judge by what I hear and see, cannot roll away and leave the boundaries of each Greek State the same. Two States now stand forth prominent, Athens and Sparta. Themistocles and Cimon aim at making Athens the head of Hellas. Perhaps Pausanias aims to effect for Sparta what they would effect for Athens."

"And what thinkest thou of such a scheme?"

"Ask me not. I am too young, too inexperienced, and perhaps too Spartan to answer rightly."

"Too Spartan, because thou art too covetous of power for Sparta."

"Too Spartan, because I may be too anxious to keep Sparta what she is."

Agesilaus smiled. "We are of the same mind, my son. Think not that the rocky defiles which enclose us shut out from our minds all the ideas that new circumstance strikes from Time. I have meditated on what thou sayest Pausanias may scheme. It is true that the invasion of the Mede must tend to raise up one State in Greece to which the others will look for a head. I have asked myself, can Sparta be that State? and my reason tells me, No. Sparta is lost if she attempt it. She may become something else, but she cannot be Sparta. Such a State must become maritime, and depend on fleets. Our inland situation forbids this. True we have ports in which the Periœci flourish; but did we use them for a permanent policy the Periœci must become our masters. These five villages would be abandoned for a mart on the sea-shore. This mother of men would be no more. A State that so aspires must have ample wealth at its command. We have none. We might raise tribute from other Greek cities, but for that purpose we must have fleets again, to overawe and compel, for no tribute will be long voluntary. A state that would be the active governor of Hellas must have lives to spare in abundance. We have none, unless we always do hereafter as we did at Platæa, raise an army of Helots—seven Helots to one Spartan. How long, if we did so, would the Helots obey us, and meanwhile how would our lands be cultivated? A State that would be the centre of Greece, must cultivate all that can charm and allure strangers. We banish strangers, and what charms and allures them would womanize us. More than all, a **State** that would obtain the sympathies of the turbulent Hellenic populations, must have the most popular institutions. It must be governed **by a** Demus. We are an Oligarchic Aristocracy—a disciplined **camp of warriors,** not a licentious Agora. Therefore, Sparta cannot **assume the head** of a Greek Confederacy except in the rare seasons of actual war; and the attempt to make her the head of such a confederacy would cause changes so repugnant to our manners and habits, that it would be fraught with destruction to him who made the attempt, **or to us** if he succeeded. Wherefore, to sum up, the ambition of Pausanias is in this impracticable, and must be opposed."

"And Athens," cried Lysander, with a slight pang of natural and national jealousy, "Athens then must wrest from Pausanias the hegemony he now holds for Sparta, and Athens must be what **the** Athenian ambition covets."

"We cannot help **it—she** must; but can it last **?—Impossible.** And woe to her if **she ever** comes in contact with **the bronze of Laconian** shields. But in the meanwhile, what is to be **done with** this **great and awful Heracleid?** They accuse him of medising, **of secret conspiracy with Persia** itself. Can that be possible?"

"If so, **it is but** to use Persia on behalf of Sparta. If he would subdue Greece, it is not for the king, it is for the race of Hercules."

"Ay, ay, ay," cried Agesilaus, shading his **face** with his hand. "All becomes clear to me now. Listen. Did I openly defend Pausanias before the Ephors, I should injure his cause. But when they talk of his betraying Hellas and Sparta, I place before them nakedly and broadly their duty if that charge be true. For if true, O my son, Pausanias must die as criminals die."

"Die—criminal—an Heracleid—king's blood—the victor of Platæa —my friend Pausanias!"

"Rather he than Sparta. What sayest thou?"

"Neither, neither," exclaimed Lysander, wringing **his** hands— "impossible both."

"Impossible both, be it so. I place before the Ephors the terrors of accrediting that charge, in order that they may repudiate it. For the lesser ones it matters not; he is in no danger there, save that of fine. And his gold," added Agesilaus with a curved lip of disdain, "will both condemn and save him. For the rest, I would spare him the dishonour of being publicly recalled, and to say truth, I would save Sparta the peril she might incur from his wrath, if she inflicted on him that slight. But mark me, he himself must resign his command, voluntarily, and return to Sparta. Better so for him and his pride, for he cannot keep the hegemony against the will of the Ionians, whose fleet is so much larger than ours, and it is to his gain if his successor lose it, not he. But better, not only for his pride, but for his glory and his name, that he should come from these scenes of fierce temptation, and, since birth made him a Spartan, learn here again to conform to what he cannot change. I have spoken thus plainly to thee. Use the words I have uttered as thou best may, after thy return to Pausanias, which I will strive to make speedy. But while we talk there goes on danger—danger still of his abrupt recall—for there are those who will seize every excuse for it. Enough of these grave matters: the sun is sinking towards the west, and thy companions await thee at thy feast; mine will be eager to greet me on thy return, and thy little brothers, who go with me to my pheidition, will hear thee so praised that they will long for the crypteia—long to be men, and find some future Platæa for themselves. May the gods forbid it! War is a terrible unsettler. Time saps States as a tide the cliff. War is an inundation, and when it ebbs, a landmark has vanished."

CHAPTER V.

NOTHING so largely contributed to the peculiar character of Spartan society as the uniform custom of taking the principal meal at a public table. It conduced to four objects: the precise status of aristocracy, since each table was formed according to title and rank,—equality among aristocrats, since each at the same table was held the equal of the other—military union, for as they feasted so they fought, being formed into divisions in the field according as they messed together at home; and lastly, that sort of fellowship in public opinion which intimate association amongst those of the same rank and habit naturally occasions. These tables in Sparta were supplied by private contributions; each head of a family was obliged to send a certain portion at his own cost, and according to the number of his children. If his fortune did not allow him to do this, he was excluded from the public tables. Hence a certain fortune was indispensable to the pure Spartan, and this was one reason why it was permitted to expose infants, if the family threatened to be too large for the father's means. The general arrangements were divided into syssitia, according, perhaps, to the number of families, and correspondent to the divisions or obes acknowledged by the State. But these larger sections were again subdivided into companies or clubs of fifteen, vacancies being filled up by ballot; but one vote could exclude. And since, as we have said, the companies were marshalled in the field according to their association at the table, it is clear that fathers of grave years and of high station (station in Sparta increased with years) could not have belonged to the same table as the young men, their sons. Their boys under a certain age they took to their own pheiditia, where the children sat upon a lower bench, and partook of the simplest dishes of the fare.

Though the cheer at these public tables was habitually plain, yet upon occasion it was enriched by presents to the after-course, of game and fruit.

Lysander was received by his old comrades with that cordiality in which was mingled for the first time a certain manly respect, due to feats in battle, and so flattering to the young.

The prayer to the Gods, correspondent to the modern grace, and the pious libations being concluded, the attendant Helots served the black broth, and the party fell to, with the appetite produced by hardy exercise and mountain air.

"What do the allies say to the black broth?" asked a young Spartan.

"They do not comprehend its merits," answered Lysander.

CHAPTER VI.

EVERYTHING in the familiar life to which he had returned delighted the young Lysander. But for anxious thoughts about Pausanias, he would have been supremely blest.

To him the various scenes of his early years brought no associations of the restraint and harshness which revolted the more luxurious nature and the fiercer genius of Pausanias. The plunge into the frigid waters of Eurotas—the sole bath permitted to the Spartans[1] at a time when the rest of Greece had already carried the art of bathing into voluptuous refinement—the sight of the vehement contests of the boys, drawn up as in battle, at the game of football, or in detached engagements, sparing each other so little, that the popular belief out of Sparta was that they were permitted to tear out each other's eyes,[2] but subjecting strength to every skilful art

---

[1] Except occasionally the dry sudorific bath, all warm bathing was strictly forbidden as enervating.

[2] An evident exaggeration. The Spartans had too great a regard for the physical gifts as essential to warlike uses, to permit cruelties that would have blinded

that gymnastics could teach—the mimic war on the island, near the antique trees of the Plane Garden, waged with weapons of wood and blunted iron, and the march regulated to the music of flutes and lyres—nay, even the sight of the stern altar, at which boys had learned to bear the anguish of stripes without a murmur—all produced in this primitive and intensely national intelligence an increased admiration for the ancestral laws, which, carrying patience, fortitude, address and strength to the utmost perfection, had formed a handful of men into the calm lords of a fierce population, and placed the fenceless villages of Sparta beyond a fear of the external assaults and the civil revolutions which perpetually stormed the citadels and agitated the market-places of Hellenic cities. His was not the mind to perceive that much was relinquished for the sake of that which was gained, or to comprehend that there was more which consecrates humanity in one stormy day of Athens, than in a serene century of iron Lacedæmon. But there is ever beauty of soul where there is enthusiastic love of country; and the young Spartan was wise in his own Dorian way.

The religious festival which had provided the Ephors with an excuse for delaying their answer to the Ionian envoys occupied the city. The youths and the maidens met in the sacred chorus; and Lysander, standing by amidst the gazers, suddenly felt his heart beat. A boy pulled him by the skirt of his mantle.

"Lysander, hast thou yet scolded Percalus?" said the boy's voice, archly.

"My young friend," answered Lysander, colouring high, "Percalus hath vouchsafed me as yet no occasion; and, indeed, she alone, of all the friends whom I left behind, does not seem to recognize me."

His eyes, as he spoke, rested with a mute reproach in their gaze on the form of a virgin, who had just paused in the choral dance, and whose looks were bent obdurately on the ground. Her luxuriant hair was drawn upward from cheek and brow, braided into a knot at the crown of the head, in the fashion so trying to those who have neither bloom nor beauty, so exquisitely becoming to those who have both; and the maiden, even amid Spartan girls, was pre-eminently lovely. It is true that the sun had somewhat embrowned the smooth cheek; but the stately throat and the rounded arms were admirably fair—not, indeed, with the pale and dead whiteness which the Ionian women sought to obtain by art, but with the delicate rose-hue of Hebe's youth. Her garment of snow-white wool, fastened over both shoulders with large golden clasps, was without sleeves, fitting not too tightly to the harmonious form, and leaving more

their young warriors. And they even forbade the practice of the pancratium as ferocious and needlessly dangerous to life.

than the ancle free to the easy glide of the dance. Taller than Hellenic women usually were, but about the average height of her Spartan companions, her shape was that which the sculptors give to Artemis. Light and feminine and virginlike, but with all the rich vitality of a divine youth, with a force, not indeed of a man, but such as art would give to the goddess whose step bounds over the mountain top, and whose arm can launch the shaft from the silver bow—yet was there something in the mien and face of Percalus more subdued and bashful than in those of most of the girls around her; and, as if her ear had caught Lysander's words, a smile just now played round her lips, and gave to all the countenance a wonderful sweetness. Then, as it became her turn once more to join in the circling measure she lifted her eyes, directed them full upon the young Spartan, and the eyes said plainly, "Ungrateful! I forget thee! I!"

It was but one glance, and she seemed again wholly intent upon the dance; but Lysander felt as if he had tasted the nectar, and caught a glimpse of the courts of the Gods. No further approach was made by either, although intervals in the evening permitted it. But if on the one hand there was in Sparta an intercourse between the youth of both sexes wholly unknown in most of the Grecian States, and if that intercourse made marriages of love especially more common there than elsewhere, yet, when love did actually exist, and was acknowledged by some young pair, they shunned public notice; the passion became a secret, or confidants to it were few. Then came the charm of stealth:—to woo and to win, as if the treasure were to be robbed by a lover from the Heaven unknown to man. Accordingly Lysander now mixed with the spectators, conversed cheerfully, only at distant intervals permitted his eyes to turn to Percalus, and when her part in the chorus had concluded, a sign, undetected by others, seemed to have been exchanged between them, and, a little while after, Lysander had disappeared from the assembly.

He wandered down the street called the Aphetais, and after a little while the way became perfectly still and lonely, for the inhabitants had crowded to the sacred festival, and the houses lay quiet and scattered. So he went on, passing the ancient temple in which Ulysses is said to have dedicated a statue in honour of his victory in the race over the suitors of Penelope, and paused where the ground lay bare and rugged around many a monument to the fabled chiefs of the heroic age. Upon a crag that jutted over a silent hollow, covered with oleander and arbute and here and there the wild rose, the young lover sat down, waiting patiently; for the eyes of Percalus had told him he should not wait in vain. Afar he saw, in the exceeding clearness of the atmosphere, the Tænarium or Temple of Neptune, unprophetic of the dark connection that shrine would hereafter have with him whom he then honoured as a chief worthy, after death, of a monument amidst those heroes : and the gale that cooled his forehead wandered to him from the field of the Hellanium in which the envoys of Greece had taken council how to oppose the march of Xerxes, when his myriads first poured into Europe.

Alas, all the great passions that distinguish race from race pass away in the tide of generations. The enthusiasm of soul which gives us heroes and demi-gods for ancestors, and hallows their empty tombs ; the vigour of thoughtful freedom which guards the soil from invasion, and shivers force upon the edge of intelligence ; the heroic age and the civilized alike depart ; and he who wanders through the glens of Laconia can scarcely guess where was the monument of Lelex, or the field of the Hellanium. And yet on the same spot where sat the young Spartan warrior, waiting for the steps of the beloved one, may, at this very hour, some rustic lover be seated, with a heart beating with like emotions, and an ear listening for as light a tread. Love alone never passes away from the spot where its footstep hath once pressed the earth, and reclaimed the savage. Traditions, freedom, the thirst for glory, art, laws, creeds, vanish ; but the eye thrills the breast, and hand warms to hand, as before the name of Lycurgus was heard, or Helen was borne a bride to the home of Menelaus. Under the influence of this power, then, something of youth is still retained by nations the most worn with time. But the power thus eternal in nations is shortlived for the individual being. Brief, indeed, in the life of each is that season which lasts for ever in the life of all. From the old age of nations glory fades away ; but in their utmost decrepitude there is still a generation young enough to love. To the individual man, however, glory alone remains when the snows of ages have fallen, and love is but the memory of a boyish dream. No wonder that the Greek genius, half incredulous of the soul, clung with such tenacity to Youth. What a sigh from the heart of the old sensuous world breathes in the strain of Mimnermus, bewailing with so fierce and so deep a sorrow the advent of the years in which man is loved no more !

Lysander's eye was still along the solitary road, when he heard a low musical laugh behind him. He started in surprise, and beheld Percalus. Her mirth was increased by his astonished gaze, till, in revenge, he caught both her hands, and drawing her towards him, kissed, not without a struggle, the lips into serious gravity.

Extricating herself from him, the maiden put on an air of offended dignity, and Lysander, abashed at his own audacity, muttered some broken words of penitence.

"But indeed," he added, as he saw the cloud vanishing from her brow; "indeed thou wert so provoking, and so irresistibly beauteous. And how camest thou here, as if thou hadst dropped from the heavens?"

"Didst thou think," answered Percalus demurely, "that I could be suspected of following thee? Nay; I tarried till I could accompany Euryclea to her home yonder, and then slipping from her by her door, I came across the grass and the glen to search for the arrow shot yesterday in the hollow below thee." So saying, she tripped from the crag by his side into the nooked recess below, which was all out of sight, in case some passenger should pass the road, and where, stooping down, she seemed to busy herself in searching for the shaft amidst the odorous shrubs.

Lysander was not slow in following her footstep.

"Thine arrow is here," said he, placing his hand to his heart.

"Fie! The Ionian poets teach thee these compliments."

"Not so. Who hath sung more of Love and his arrows than our own Alcman?"

"Mean you the Regent's favourite brother?"

"Oh no! The ancient Alcman; the poet whom even the Ephors sanction."

Percalus ceased to seek for the arrow, and they seated themselves on a little knoll in the hollow, side by side, and frankly she gave him her hand, and listened, with rosy cheek and rising bosom, to his honest wooing. He told her truly, how her image had been with him in the strange lands; how faithful he had been to the absent, amidst all the beauties of the Isles and of the East. He reminded her of their early days—how, even as children, each had sought the other. He spoke of his doubts, his fears, lest he should find himself forgotten or replaced; and how overjoyed he had been when at last her eye replied to his.

"And we understood each other so well, did we not, Percalus? Here we have so often met before; here we parted last; here thou knewest I should go; here I knew that I might await thee."

Percalus did not answer at much length, but what she said sufficed to enchant her lover. For the education of a Spartan maid did not favour the affected concealment of real feelings. It could not, indeed, banish what Nature prescribes to women—the modest self-esteem—the difficulty to utter by word, what eye and blush reveal—nor, perhaps, something of that arch and innocent malice, which enjoys to taste the power which beauty exercises before the warm heart will freely acknowledge the power which sways itself. But the girl, though a little wilful and high-spirited, was a candid, pure, and noble creature, and too proud of being loved by Lysander to feel more than a maiden's shame to confess her own.

"And when I return," said the Spartan, "ah then look out and take care; for I shall speak to thy father, gain his consent to our betrothal, and then carry thee away, despite all thy struggles, to the bridesmaid, and these long locks, alas, will fall."

"I thank thee for thy warning, and will find my arrow in time to guard myself," said Percalus, turning away her face, but holding up her hand in pretty menace; "but where is the arrow? I must make haste and find it."

"Thou wilt have time enough, courteous Amazon, in mine absence, for I must soon return to Byzantium."

PERCALUS.—"Art thou so sure of that?"

LYSANDER.—"Why—dost thou doubt it?"

PERCALUS (rising and moving the arbute boughs aside with the tip of her sandal),—"And, unless thou wouldst wait very long for my father's consent, perchance thou mayst have to ask for it very soon—too soon to prepare thy courage for so great a peril."

LYSANDER (perplexed).—"What canst thou mean? By all the Gods, I pray thee speak plain."

PERCALUS.—"If Pausanias be recalled, wouldst thou still go to Byzantium?"

LYSANDER.—"No; but I think the Ephors have decided not so to discredit their General."

PERCALUS (shaking her head incredulously).—"Count not on their decision so surely, valiant warrior; and suppose that Pausanias is recalled, and that some one else is sent in his place whose absence would prevent thy obtaining that consent thou covetest, and so frustrate thy designs on—on—(she added, blushing scarlet)—on these poor locks of mine."

LYSANDER (starting).—"Oh, Percalus, do I conceive thee aright? Hast thou any reason to think that thy father Dorcis will be sent to replace Pausanias—the great Pausanias!"

PERCALUS (a little offended at a tone of expression which seemed to slight her father's pretensions).—"Dorcis, my father, is a warrior whom Sparta reckons second to none; a most brave captain, and every inch a Spartan; but—but—"

LYSANDER.—"Percalus, do not trifle with me. Thou knowest how my fate has been linked to the Regent's. Thou must have intelligence not shared even by my father, himself an Ephor.—What is it?"

PERCALUS.—"Thou wilt be secret, my Lysander, for what I may tell thee I can only learn at the hearth-stone."

LYSANDER.—"Fear me not. Is not all between us a secret?"

PERCALUS.—"Well, then, Periclides and my father, as thou art aware, are near kinsmen. And when the Ionian Envoys first arrived, it was my father who was specially appointed to see to their fitting entertainment. And that same night I overheard Dorcis say to my mother, 'If I could succeed Pausanias, and conclude this war, I should be consoled for not having commanded at Platæa.' And my mother, who is proud for her husband's glory, as a woman should be, said, 'Why not strain every nerve as for a crown in Olympia? Periclides will aid thee—thou wilt win.'"

LYSANDER.—"But that was the first night of the Ionian's arrival."

PERCALUS.—"Since then, I believe that thy father and others of the Ephors overruled Periclides and Zeuxidamus, for I have heard all that passed between my father and mother on the subject. But early this morning, while my mother was assisting to attire me for the festival, Periclides himself called at our house, and before I came from home, my mother, after a short conference with Dorcis, said to me, in the exuberance of her joy, 'Go, child, and call here all the maidens, as thy father ere long will go to outshine all the Grecian chiefs.' So that if my father does go, thou wilt remain in Sparta. Then, my beloved Lysander—and—and—but what ails thee? Is that thought so sorrowful?"

LYSANDER.—"Pardon me, pardon; thou art a Spartan maid; thou must comprehend what should be felt by a Spartan soldier when he thinks of humiliation and ingratitude to his chief. Gods! the man who rolled back the storm of the Mede to be insulted in the face of Hellas by the government of his native city! The blush of shame upon his cheek burns my own."

The warrior bowed his face in his clasped hands.

Not a resentful thought natural to female vanity and exacting affection then crossed the mind of the Spartan girl. She felt at once, by the sympathy of kindred nurture, all that was torturing her lover. She was even prouder of him that he forgot her for the moment to be so truthful to his chief; and abandoning the innocent coyness she had before shown, she put her arm round his neck with a pure and sisterly fondness, and, kissing his brow, whispered soothingly, "It is for me to ask pardon, that I did not think of this—that I spoke so foolishly; but comfort—thy chief is not disgraced even by recall. Let them recall Pausanias, they cannot recall his glory. When, in Sparta, did we ever held a brave man discredited by obedience to the government? None are disgraced who do not disgrace themselves."

"Ah! my Percalus, so I should say; but so will not think Pausanias, nor the allies; and in this slight to him I see the shadow of the Erinnys. But it may not be true yet; nor can Periclides of himself dispose thus of the Lacedæmonian armies."

"We will hope so, dear Lysander," said Percalus, who, born to be man's helpmate, then only thought of consoling and cheering him. "And if thou dost return to the camp, tarry as long as thou wilt, thou wilt find Percalus the same."

"The Gods bless thee, maiden!" said Lysander, with grateful passion, "and blessed be the State that rears such women; elsewhere Greece knows them not."

"And does Greece elsewhere know such men?" asked Percalus, raising her graceful head. "But so late—is it possible? See where the shadows are falling! Thou wilt but be in time for thy pheidition. Farewell."

"But when to meet again?"

"Alas! when we can." She sprang lightly away; then, turning her face as she fled, added, "Look out! thou wert taught to steal in thy boyhood—steal an interview. I will be thy accomplice."

CHAPTER VII.

THAT night, as Agesilaus was leaving the public table at which he supped, Periclides, who was one of the same company, but who had been unusually silent during the entertainment, approached him, and said, "Let us walk towards thy home together; the moon is up, and will betray listeners to our converse should there be any."

"And in default of the moon, thy years, if not yet mine, permit thee a lanthorn, Periclides."

"I have not drunk enough to need it," answered the Chief of the Ephors, with unusual pleasantry; "but as thou art the younger man, I will lean on thine arm, so as to be closer to thine ear."

"Thou hast something secret and grave to say, then?"

Periclides nodded.

As they ascended the rugged acclivity, different groups, equally returning home from the public tables, passed them. Though the sacred festival had given excuse for prolonging the evening meal, and the wine-cup had been replenished beyond the abstemious wont, still each little knot of revellers passed, and dispersed in a sober and decorous quiet which perhaps no other eminent city in Greece could have exhibited; young and old equally grave and noiseless. For the Spartan youth, no fair Hetæræ then opened homes adorned with flowers, and gay with wit, no less than alluring with beauty; but as the streets grew more deserted, there stood in the thick shadow of some angle, or glided furtively by some winding wall, a bridegroom lover, tarrying till all was still, to steal to the arms of the lawful wife, whom for years perhaps he might not openly acknowledge, and carry in triumph to his home.

But not of such young adventurers thought the sage Periclides, though his voice was as low as a lover's "hist!" and his step as stealthy as a bridegroom's tread.

"My friend," said he, "with the faint gray of the dawn there comes to my house a new messenger from the camp, and the tidings he brings change all our decisions. The Festival does not permit us as Ephors to meet in public, or, at least, I think thou wilt agree with me it is more prudent not to do so. All we should do now, should be in strict privacy."

"But hush! from whom the message—Pausanias?"

"No—from Aristides the Athenian."

"And to what effect?"

"The Ionians have revolted from the Spartan hegemony, and ranged themselves under the Athenian flag."

"Gods! what I feared has already come to pass."

"And Aristides writes to me, with whom you remember that he has the hospitable ties, that the Athenians cannot abandon their Ionian allies and kindred who thus appeal to them, and that if Pausanias remain, open war may break out between the two divisions into which the fleet of Hellas is now rent."

"This must not be, for it would be war at sea; we and the Peloponnesians have far the fewer vessels, the less able seamen. Sparta would be conquered."

"Rather than Sparta should be conquered, must we not recall her General?"

"I would give all my lands, and sink out of the rank of Equal, that this had not chanced," said Agesilaus, bitterly.

"Hist! hist! not so loud."

"I had hoped we might induce the Regent himself to resign the command, and so have been spared the shame and the pain of an act that affects the hero-blood of our kings. Could not that be done yet?"

"Dost thou think so? Pausanias resign in the midst of a mutiny? Thou canst not know the man."

"Thou art right—impossible. I see no option now. He must be recalled. But the Spartan hegemony is then gone—gone for ever—gone to Athens."

"Not so. Sparta hath many a worthy son beside this too arrogant Heracleid."

"Yes; but where his genius of command?—where his immense

renown?—where a man, I say, not in Sparta, but in all Greece, fit to cope with Aristides and Cimon in the camp, with Themistocles in the city of our rivals? If Pausanias fails, who succeeds?"

"Be not deceived. What must be, must; it is but a little time earlier than Necessity would have fixed. Wouldst thou take the command?"

"I? The Gods forbid."

"Then, if thou wilt not, I know but one man."

"And who is he?"

"Dorcis."

Agesilaus started, and, by the light of the moon, gazed full upon the face of the chief Ephor.

"Thy kinsman, Dorcis? Ah! Periclides, hast thou schemed this from the first?"

Periclides changed colour at finding himself thus abruptly detected, and as abruptly charged; however, he answered with laconic dryness,—

"Friend, did I scheme the revolt of the Ionians? But if thou knowest a better man than Dorcis, speak. Is he not brave?"

"Yes."

"Skilful?"

"No. Tut! thou art as conscious as I am that thou mightest as well compare the hat on thy brow to the brain it hides as liken the stolid Dorcis to the fiery but profound Heracleid."

"Ay, ay. But there is one merit the hat has which the brow has not—it can do no harm. Shall we send our chiefs to be made worse men by Eastern manners? Dorcis has dull wit, granted; no arts can corrupt it; he may not save the hegemony, but he will return as he went, a Spartan."

"Thou art right again, and a wise man, Periclides. I submit. Thou hast my vote for Dorcis. What else hast thou designed? for I see now that whatever thou designest that wilt thou accomplish; and our meeting on the Archeion is but an idle form."

"Nay, nay," said Periclides, with his austere smile, "thou givest me a wit and a will that I have not. But as chief of the Ephors I watch over the State. And though I design nothing, this I would counsel,—On the day we answer the Ionians, we shall tell them, 'What ye ask, we long since proposed to do.' And Dorcis is already on the seas as successor to Pausanias."

"When will Dorcis leave?" said Agesilaus, curtly.

"If the other Ephors concur, to-morrow night."

"Here we are at my doors, wilt thou not enter?"

"No. I have others yet to see. I knew we should be of the same mind."

Agesilaus made no reply; but as he entered the court-yard of his house, he muttered uneasily,—

"And if Lysander is right, and Sparta is too small for Pausanias, do not we bring back a giant who will widen it to his own girth, and rase the old foundations to make room for the buildings he would add?"

* * * * * * *

(UNFINISHED.)

THE pages covered by the manuscript of this uncompleted story of "Pausanias" are scarcely more numerous than those which its author has filled with the notes made by him from works consulted with special reference to the subject of it. Those notes (upon Greek and Persian antiquities) are wholly without interest for the general public. They illustrate the author's conscientious industry, but they afford no clue to the plot of his romance. Under the sawdust, however, thus fallen in the industrial process of an imaginative work, unhappily unfinished, I have found two specimens of original composition. They are rough sketches of songs expressly composed for "Pausanias;" and, since they are not included in the foregoing portion of it, I think they may properly be added here. The unrhymed lyrics introduced by my father into some of the opening chapters of this romance appear to have been suggested by some fragments of Mimnermus, and composed about the same time as "The Lost Tales of Miletus." Indeed, one of them has been already printed in that work. The following verses, however, which are rhymed, bear evidence of having been composed at a much earlier period. I know not whether it was my father's intention to discard them altogether, or to alter them materially, or to insert them without alteration in some later portion of the romance. But I print them here precisely as they are written.

L.

FOR PAUSANIAS.

Partially borrowed from Aristophanes' "Peace," v.

Away, away, with the helm and greaves,
    Away with the leeks and cheese![1]
I have conquer'd my passion for wounds and blows,
And the worst that I wish to the worst of my foes
      Is the glory and gain
      Of a year's campaign
    On a diet of leeks and cheese.

I love to drink by my own warm hearth,
Nourisht with logs from the pine-clad heights,
    Wh'ch were hewn in the blaze of the summer sun
To treasure his rays for the winter nights
    On the hearth where my grandam spun.

I love to drink of the grape I press,
    And to drink with a friend of yore;
Quick! bring me a bough from the myrtle tree
    Which is budding afresh by Nicander's door.
Tell Nicander himself he must sup with me,
And along with the bough from his myrtle tree
We will circle the lute, in a choral glee
    To the goddess of corn and peace.
For Nicander and I were fast friends at school.
Here he comes! We are boys once more.

When the grasshopper chaunts in the bells of thyme
I love to watch if the Lemnian grape[2]
Is donning the purple that decks its prime;
And, as I sit at my porch to see,
With my little one trying to scale my knee,
To join in the grasshopper's chaunt, and sing
To Apollo and Pan from the heart of Spring.[3]
      Listen, O list!

Hear ye not, neighbours, the voice of Peace?
"The swallow I hear in the household eaves."
      Io Ægien! Peace!
"And the skylark at poise o'er the bended sheaves,"
      Io Ægien! Peace!
Here and there, everywhere, hear we Peace,
Hear her, and see her, and clasp her—Peace!
The grasshopper chaunts in the bells of thyme,
And the halcyon is back to her nest in Greece!

---

[1] Τυροῦ τε καὶ κρομμύων. Cheese and onions, the rations furnished to soldiers in campaign.
[2] It ripened earlier than the others. The words of the Chorus are, τὰς Λημνίας ἀμπέλους εἰ πεπαίνουσιν ἤδη.
[3] Variation—
    "What a blessing is life in a noon of Spring."

IN PRAISE OF THE ATHENIAN KNIGHTS.

Imitated from the "Knights" of Aristophanes, v. 565, etc.

Chaunt the fame of the Knights, or in war or in peace,
Chaunt the darlings of Athens,[1] the bulwarks of Greece,
Pressing foremost to glory, on wave and on shore,
Where the steed has no footing they win with the oar.[2]

On their bosoms the battle splits, wasting its shock.
If they charge like the whirlwind, they stand like the rock.
Ha! they count not the numbers, they scan not the ground,
When a foe comes in sight on his lances they bound.

Fails a foot in its speed? heed it not. One and all[3]
Spurn the earth that they spring from, and own not a fall.
O the darlings of Athens, the bulwarks of Greece,
Wherefore envy the lovelocks they perfume in peace!

Wherefore scowl if they fondle a quail or a dove,
Or inscribe on a myrtle the names that they love?
Does Alcides not teach us how valour is mild?
Lo, at rest from his labours he plays with a child.

When the slayer of Python has put down his bow,
By his lute and his lovelocks Apollo we know.
Fear'd, O rowers, those gallants their beauty to spoil
When they sat on your benches, and shared in your toil!

When with laughter they row'd to your cry "Hippopai,"
"On, ye coursers of wood, for the palm wreath, away!"
Did those dainty youths ask you to store in your holds
Or a cask from their crypt or a lamb from their folds?

No, they cried, "We are here both to fight and to fast,
Place us first in the fight, at the board serve us last!
Wheresoever is peril, we knights lead the way,
Wheresoever is hardship, we claim it as pay.

"Call us proud, O Athenians, we know it full well,
And we give you the life we're too haughty to sell."
Hail the stoutest in war, hail the mildest in peace,
Hail the darlings of Athens, the bulwarks of Greece!

[1] Variation—
"The adorners of Athens, the bulwarks of Greece."
[2] Variation—
"Keenest racers to glory, on wave or on shore,
By the rush of the steed or the stroke of the oar!"
[3] Variation—
"Falls there one? never help him! Our knights one and all."

THE END.

RICHARD CLAY AND SONS, LIMITED, LONDON AND BUNGAY.

www.ingramcontent.com/pod-product-compliance
Lightning Source LLC
Chambersburg PA
CBHW022143300426
44115CB00006B/321